Monday 3:30PM 74/75 lot Starbucks

Karen = B/C Dialogue
Addictive thinking · Twerski

great quote for book p. 226.
quote B CO-Oscar Wilde p 225.

148-149 "Emmaus nar"
p 155, ?

. Dec 8, 9, 10, 11

JESUS

Shrr w p 33 Mack vs Crossan
        social agenda vs aimless, clever
                teacher

p 34 how does Jesus launch a
    social vision from platform as
    a peasant?

p 39 Jesus as spiritual innovator like
    Buddha.

p 58 use in PS 233
    alternate approaches to psycho-biography
    — psychoanalytic
    — developmental
    — adult development (Levinson)
weighing adult experiences (NOLS, AA)
avoiding unilateralism /
        complex interaction p 55-58
great man fallacy p 58

Also by Donald Capps,
published by Chalice Press:

Social Phobia: Alleviating Anxiety in an Age of Self-Promotion

Edited by Donald Capps,
published by Chalice Press:

Re-Calling Ministry, by James E. Dittes

JESUS

A PSYCHOLOGICAL BIOGRAPHY

DONALD CAPPS

Chalice Press®
St. Louis, Missouri

Art Director: Michael Domínguez
Cover art: Christ at the Pillory by Antonella da Messina, Erich Lessing Fine Art
    Collection
Cover design: Scott Tjaden
Interior design: Elizabeth Wright

This book is printed on acid-free, recycled paper.

Visit Chalice Press on the World Wide Web at
www.chalicepress.com

10 9 8 7 6 5 4 3 2 1   00 01 02 03 04

Library of Congress Cataloging–in–Publication Data

Pending

Printed in the United States of America

If a wise man should appear
in our village, he would
create in those who conversed with
him a new consciousness of wealth,
by opening their eyes to unob-
served advantages; he would
establish a sense of immoveable
equality, calm us with assurances
that we could not be cheated, as
every one would discern the checks
and guaranties of condition. The
rich would see their mistakes and
poverty; the poor, their escapes
and their resources.

RALPH WALDO EMERSON

Contents

Preface

Three decades ago, biblical scholars began turning to the social sciences (especially sociology and cultural anthropology) to inform New Testament studies. This turn to the social sciences has been enormously illuminating, shedding new light on the social world of early Christianity. It has also, however, produced new disagreements among biblical scholars. One is that increased appreciation for the social complexity of first-century Palestine has led to quite different "portraits" of Jesus, depending on whether one emphasizes the larger sociocultural milieu—with its Hellenistic influences—or whether one focuses on the more circumscribed social milieu of traditional Judaism. Was Jesus more heavily influenced by the larger Hellenistic culture, or was he more embedded in traditional Jewish culture?

A second, related area of disagreement concerns the social roles that were available to Jesus and his adoption of—or self-identification with—one or more of these roles. Recognizing that Jesus was more than the sum of the activities ascribed to him by the gospel writers, scholars have turned to various sociocultural types of religious authority (e.g., holy man, sage, magician, messiah, itinerant Cynic) in an effort to define his sociocultural identity. In some cases, a scholar will consider one of these identities central and will view his activities as the expression of this identity. In other cases, a scholar will show that Jesus integrated two or more of these sociocultural types. In virtually all cases, scholars have contended that Jesus put his individual stamp on a preexisting sociocultural type, making it distinctively his own. Conversely, if he is not seen to have modified or transformed a sociocultural type, this is virtually tantamount to saying that it was not central to his identity. Each of these types has its proponents, and the very plurality of such sociocultural types—and the plausibility of their applicability to Jesus—has created considerable disagreement as to what Jesus understood his mission to be about and who he understood himself to be.

I do not claim that more explicit use of psychological theories and concepts will resolve all of the issues resulting from the introduction of the social sciences into Jesus studies. I do contend, however, that a psychological point of view may be very helpful precisely at those points where scholars find themselves at an impasse. When Jesus studies turned to the social sciences, they embarked on a journey that leads to psychology, for the questions that are now being posed about Jesus cannot be answered adequately in terms of sociological theories and categories alone. Many of the unsolved problems in contemporary Jesus studies center around the issue of Jesus' identity. This is an issue that proved to be irresolvable on theological grounds and thus figured significantly in the turn to the social sciences. It is not, however, an issue that can be settled on sociological grounds alone, since it also has a psychological dimension. The questions "Who was Jesus?" and "What did Jesus understand himself to be about?" are ones that take us inevitably into the psychological realm. Yet, except for a few notable exceptions, biblical scholars have been reluctant to allow psychological theories and concepts to inform their studies of Jesus. In contrast to their increasingly adept use of theories drawn from the social sciences, they have not made significant or sustained use of the personality sciences. Since they are attempting to understand an individual–Jesus–their failure to employ psychological theories of the person or self is both odd and arbitrary. While I do not expect that readers will agree with everything I have to say about Jesus in this book, I hope that I will at least make a convincing case for the usefulness of psychological theories and concepts in the study of the historical Jesus.

This book is divided into three parts. The first part focuses on the current state of historical Jesus studies by considering the "portraits" of Jesus developed by four major contemporary scholars: E. P. Sanders, John P. Meier, John Dominic Crossan, and Marcus Borg. While these four do not comprise the whole range of contemporary portraits of Jesus, they are representative figures who, when viewed together, give us a good, clear sense of the current "state of the art." By focusing on these four scholars, I will take a few initial steps toward formulating my own psychological portrait of Jesus, indicating both where an approach to the historical Jesus informed by psychological theories and concepts would be in fundamental agreement with a given portraitist, and where it would necessarily find itself in disagreement. As will become clear, I believe that anyone engaged in the task of formulating a psychological portrait of Jesus must build on the work of the scholars in the field. Otherwise, the resulting portrait will be highly idiosyncratic and not very credible. I also believe, however, that the psychologist needs to go beyond stating agreements and disagreements with the established scholars in the field and take a risk, similar to theirs, by constructing a full-scale portrait of Jesus. I am, of course, aware that the portrait I contrive here will be no less subject to criticism. I hope, however, that the criticisms are not ones that challenge the right of a psychologist to develop a portrait of Jesus–as though the very enterprise of a psychological portrait of Jesus is illegitimate–but are, instead, addressed to specific interpretations, claims, and proposals, as this is precisely the level on which I have made my own critiques of the portraits of recognized scholars in the field.

The second part of the book focuses on methodological considerations. Its first two chapters concern the methods of psychobiography of individuals and psychohistory of groups. I address the more salient arguments that have been used to challenge the psychological study of historical individuals and provide illustrations of what I consider to be effective uses of psychological theories and concepts in the study of such individuals. I also focus on the psychohistorical study of social groups, illustrating this approach with previous studies in this historical genre. I contend that the psychobiography of individuals and psychohistory of groups can be done responsibly if one attends to these issues of methodology, and I make the claim that, for the psychological study of Jesus, it is vitally important that the psychobiographical enterprise be located within the larger context of the psychohistorical one. This section of the book concludes with a chapter on the social world in Jesus' day. Here, I attempt to provide a relatively brief but accurate picture of what those scholars who have introduced the social sciences into the study of Jesus are able to say with some confidence about the social world in which Jesus lived. This chapter considers a variety of sociocultural features of this social world, focusing on those that will have the greatest relevance for the portrait of Jesus presented in the third section of the book.

Parts 1 and 2 comprise the first five chapters of this eight-chapter book. While it may seem odd that half of the book is taken up with what may appear to be preliminary matters, with the actual portrait of Jesus relegated to the last half, readers who know John Dominic Crossan's *The Historical Jesus* (1991) will not find this altogether odd or surprising, as Crossan does not embark on his own portrait of Jesus until the eleventh chapter of his fifteen-chapter book. Because I am as much concerned with making a case for the validity of this enterprise as with contending for my own portrait of Jesus, these preliminary matters are actually central to the book and essential to this portrait. While some of the illustrative material in the chapters on psychobiography and psychohistory may seem unrelated to the study of Jesus in his first-century Palestinian world, my hope is that the reader will recognize their significance to the project as a whole. This material not only lays the methodological foundations for part 3, but also prefigures much of its content as well.

Part 3, then, consists of three chapters on Jesus. The first focuses on the social world of his family of origin and formulates a picture of Jesus' personal location within this family. It thereby intends to shed light on what one biblical scholar calls the "hidden years" of Jesus, that is, the years before he became a public figure. Through the use of psychological theory combined with textual analysis, a general profile of Jesus' childhood and early adulthood can, in my view, be constructed. The second chapter centers on his social role as a healer and gives particular attention to how his personal location in his family of origin prepared him for the adoption of this role. It also explores how his disposition to assume the role of healer converged with the need for such a healer in the peasant culture with which he was most familiar. I focus specifically on the influence of familial and village interpersonal conflicts in creating a susceptibility to the diseases and disorders that Jesus treated. While this focus on Jesus' role as healer is perhaps what the reader would expect of an author who is trained in the psychological disciplines, my goal here is to show that the healer role was in fact central to Jesus' personal identity and to his being accorded prominence among his own contemporaries. The final chapter takes a step back from this focus on his role as healer and seeks to show how Jesus expanded this role into a larger religious perspective, one that I attribute to what I call his "utopian-melancholic personality." This chapter is intended to take the full measure of the man Jesus, and to make the case that he was neither an "apocalypticist" nor a "social reformer"–the two visions of him that are frequently posed against one another–but "something else." This "something else" is what I seek to identify, using psychological theories in support of an effort to see Jesus "whole." In this chapter, I focus on the disturbance in the temple as the event that integrates his location in his family of origin, his role as healer, and his utopian-melancholic personality. This event is the culminating action toward which his personal location in his family and his social role as healer converged. By giving central importance to this event, we are able to have a coherent image of Jesus, to see him as having a coherent self-identity.

In the brief epilogue, I discuss possible implications of this psychological portrait of Jesus for a contemporary response.

Acknowledgments

I am especially indebted to Jon Berquist for suggesting that I write a book on Jesus and for his astute advice and unflagging support as the writing progressed. The whole Chalice Press staff has been wonderfully supportive. Mark Allan Powell graciously provided me a manuscript copy of his book *Jesus as a Figure in History*, subsequently published. I owe a longstanding debt to David Bakan, Professor of Psychology at the University of Chicago when I was a graduate student, who introduced me to psychoanalytic methods of biblical interpretation and opened my eyes to the distinctively Jewish context out of which Freud's own theories were formulated. Conversations or communications with Evelyn Brister, John Capps, Karen Capps, James Charlesworth, James Dittes, Marion Goldman, Scot McLean, and Harold Remus provided valuable insights and helped sharpen my interpretations; they do not, of course, bear responsibility for the views expressed here. Joan Blyth-Lovell typed the final manuscript; she is a model of quiet professionalism.

My favorite Bible verse in boyhood was John 14:6: "Jesus said to him, 'I am the way, and the truth, and the life. No one comes to the Father except by me.'" In the course of writing this book, I was mindful of the desire to keep faith with this boy and have done so, I believe, by striving to write a study of Jesus that was not afraid to ask questions in search of a more reliable truth. This book is dedicated to him.

Contemporary Portraits of Jesus

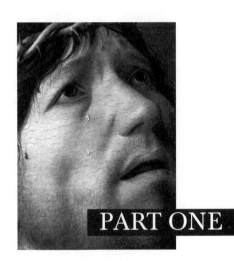

PART ONE

1

Portraits of Jesus: E. P. Sanders and John P. Meier

In the introduction to his book on portraiture, Richard Brilliant notes that he is drawn to portraits "because they give life to historical persons, freed from the bonds of mortality. Portraits stock the picture galleries of my memory with the vivid images of people, once known or previously unknown, now registered, preserved, and accessible through works of art that have become momentarily transparent. It is as if the art works do not exist in their own material substance but, in their place, real persons face me from the other side or deliberately avoid my glance" (Brilliant, 1991, 7).

In recent years, the word "portrait" has been used to describe the efforts of scholars to shed new light on biblical personages. We have, for example, Bruce J. Malina and Jerome H. Neyrey's *Portraits of Paul: An Archeology of Ancient Personality* (1996). In Jesus scholarship, the word "portrait" is used with some frequency. In *Jesus in Contemporary Scholarship*, Marcus J. Borg devotes a chapter to "portraits of Jesus" (1994, 18–43). In *Jesus as a Figure in History*, Mark Allan Powell uses the word portrait to describe the work of many of the most important contributors to contemporary Jesus scholarship (1998). In this and the following chapter, I focus on four representative portraits of Jesus by contemporary scholars, making substantial use of the efforts of Borg and Powell to describe the essential features of each portrait.

Before I embark on this discussion, I should perhaps acknowledge the objection that the word "portrait" applies to visual arts and is therefore being misused when applied to verbal discourse. In his study of biography and portrait painting in seventeenth- and eighteenth-century England, however, Richard Wendorf points out that there is nothing to preclude our seeing biography, for example, and portrait painting as analogous or parallel: "The parallel simply suggests that the functions of the two arts, the impulses that lie behind them, some of their methods (and many of their effects) are often strikingly similar, and that what the painter accomplishes with the brush and what the biographer achieves with the pen deserve the same kind of comparative analysis that has been devoted to poetry and painting" (1990, 6). He notes further that common to both biographies and painted portraits is the fact that they are not "merely historical, factual, documentary works of art; they often serve as *personal* documents, attempts to capture—on paper or on canvas—what is lost or certain to fade" (9–10). Another similarity is that both biography and portraiture involve a negotiation between "fidelity to nature"—thus balancing virtues and imperfections, beauties and blemishes—and an aesthetic tradition that encourages the painter and biographer "to ennoble nature without entirely deserting it (the portraitist may 'shadow the more imperfect side')" (11).

There are also differences. Wendorf notes, for example, that biography adds a temporal sequence that must be sufficiently extensive to allow the emergence of the contours of the life. In contrast, the portrait painter must "take full advantage of the 'pregnant moment'—the sublime, single blow. The artist may wish to capture a distinct and significant moment in a subject's life, similar to the 'break-through' stage that is associated with crucial episodes in biography and autobiography, or choose to suspend time by creating an idealized portrait in which the subject is released from temporal contingencies" (16–17). Brilliant notes that this desire to capture the subject's noncontingency leads portrait artists to "eschew the representation of strong expressions of feeling because traditionally they are thought to reflect transitory states of being and are therefore an obstacle to the artist who seeks to capture the essential stability of the self, existing beneath the flux of emotions" (112). A question that will concern us here is whether contemporary portraits of Jesus do, in fact, reflect to some extent the values and preferences of portrait painters and whether or not this is a good thing.

Marcus J. Borg's book, published in 1994, considers six portraits of Jesus, those by E. P. Sanders, Burton L. Mack, Elisabeth Schüssler Fiorenza, Richard A. Horsley, John Dominic Crossan, and his own. His chapter on portraits of Jesus is based on an earlier essay that did not include Crossan, but the subsequent publication of Crossan's *The Historical Jesus* (1991) and *Jesus: A Revolutionary Biography* (1994) led him to include an addendum on Crossan. His portraits focus on authors whose contributions to Jesus research were published between 1983 (Schüssler Fiorenza) and 1994 (Crossan). Mark Allen Powell's book, published in 1998, includes a chapter on "snapshots" of Jesus and five chapters on "portraits" of Jesus. The authors included in the "snapshots" chapter include Horsley, Geza Vermes, Morton Smith, Ben Witherington III, and F. Gerald Downing. Their contributions to Jesus studies range from Vermes' first book (1973) to Witherington's third book (1994). The "portrait" chapters focus on Crossan, Borg, Sanders, John P. Meier, and N. T. Wright. The contributions Powell considers in these chapters range from Sanders (1985) to Wright (1996).

We should be concerned if Borg's and Powell's lists do not substantially overlap, as this would suggest that there is not much consensus about who are the significant voices in historical Jesus studies today. But this is not the case. Sanders, Borg, and Crossan appear on both "portrait" lists, while Horsley appears on Borg's list and in Powell's "snapshots" chapter. Missing from Powell's lists altogether but present in Borg's "portrait" list are Schüssler Fiorenza and Mack. Schüssler Fiorenza's omission from Powell's list is most likely due to the fact that, as Borg notes, her text, *In Memory of Her*, is not a "book-length study of the historical Jesus," though it does contain "a comprehensive sketch" (1994a, 23). Mack is noted by Powell in his discussion of Downing but not featured in either his "snapshots" or "portraits" chapters. The two scholars who are included in Powell's "portraits" but not in Borg's—Meier and Wright—had not written their major works on Jesus at the time Borg republished his original essay. For our purposes here, it is not terribly important that we ask why Horsley is a "portrait" figure for Borg and a "snapshot" figure for Powell. Nor need we raise the question why Vermes, Smith, and Witherington, all on Powell's "snapshots" list, are not included in Borg's "portraits." The important point is that their lists overlap to a considerable degree, suggesting that there is a cadre of scholars who comprise the first rank in historical Jesus studies today.

Borg and Powell discuss twelve separate authors altogether. Seeing the need to pare this list down, I have decided to focus on their presentations of the following authors: Sanders, Meier, Crossan, and Borg. By selecting these four, I have deleted two authors (Schüssler Fiorenza and Mack) from Borg's six portraitists and one (Wright) from Powell's five portraitists. I have included one author (Meier) who appears on Powell's list but not on Borg's. Borg notes in a footnote, however, that only the first volume of Meier's projected three volumes had been published at the time he added his discussion of Crossan's work and that this volume "takes the reader only up to the beginning of Jesus' ministry" (43). He implies that Meier would have been included in his survey of North American portraits had an additional volume been available.

Before I take up Sanders and Meier in this chapter, I should indicate briefly how Borg and Powell introduce their discussions of the various portraitists. Borg's concern was to use the selected portraits to "demonstrate the strength of the current resurgence in Jesus scholarship and disclose the central questions dominating the current discussion" (18). These portraits indicate that, after decades of "relative lack of interest, a 'third quest' for the historical Jesus is underway. Each portrait or *Gestalt* is interesting in its own right as a construal of the traditions about Jesus and as an exercise in historical reconstruction. Taken together, they illustrate the range of options in contemporary Jesus scholarship and point to the likely focal points of Jesus research in the 1990s" (18).

He further suggests that these portraits reflect two important traits of the renaissance in Jesus research. One is that the question of Jesus and eschatology has again risen in North American scholarship. In his view, the consensus that dominated Jesus research through much of the twentieth century, based on the view of Jesus as "an eschatological prophet [who] sought to understand his mission and message within the framework of imminent eschatology," has undergone serious erosion (18–19). His own informal poll of North American scholars engaged in Jesus research revealed that the majority no longer think that Jesus expected the imminent end of the world in his generation: "Though the old consensus has not yet been replaced by a new one, non-eschatological understandings of Jesus are emerging, as are nonobjective and this-worldly understandings of eschatology" (19).

The second important trait is that the 1980s produced a great increase in understanding of the social world of first-century Palestine. This was due, to some extent, to the discovery, publication, and analysis of new archeological and manuscript materials. It was also due to a greater extent, however, "to the accelerating use of methods and models from other disciplines, especially the social sciences, cultural anthropology, and the history of religions. These models and methods enable us to see existing material in new (and typically more interrelated) ways. We thus not only know more 'facts' about first-century Palestine, but we also understand the dynamics of that social world better" (19). These two characteristics of the renaissance in Jesus research provide the framework for Borg's consideration of the portraits: "What role does eschatology play in each image or construal of Jesus? Is it central, denied, or integrated into another overarching image of Jesus?" And "How is Jesus seen in relationship to his social world? Is his social world of little or no consequence to him, or is it central to understanding his activity, message, and aim?" (19).

Because he intends to be more comprehensive, Powell's approach is not as focused as Borg's "two characteristics" investigation. He does, however, clarify what he intends by differentiating "snapshots" from "portraits." The subtitle of his "snapshots" chapter–"Contemporary Images of Jesus"–indicates that his concern in the chapter is to examine "a few of the images for Jesus that have been suggested by modern scholars. The studies discussed in this chapter are not intended to be comprehensive; the scholars who present them do not necessarily claim that the image they describe offers a complete picture of who Jesus was. In most cases, they are calling attention to an aspect that they find especially significant or one that they may feel has been neglected" (52). The images presented are those of social prophet (Horsley), charismatic Jew (Vermes), magician (Smith), Jewish sage (Witherington), and Cynic philosopher (Downing). The "portraits" attempt to offer a more complete picture of who Jesus was. Given the influential nature of the studies presented in the "snapshots" chapter, the scholars represented in the "portraits" chapters "have had to wrestle with the ideas presented in this [snapshots] chapter. They have either had to incorporate these aspects of Jesus into their overall portraits or explain why they think particular images are not fitting" (Powell, 52).

Thus, Powell's working assumption is that such images contribute to the task of determining "who Jesus was." A portraitist's decision whether or not to incorporate a given image is an important statement about who the portraitist understands Jesus to have been. A related, underlying assumption is that Jesus' identity was complex, that it is unlikely that he was a unidimensional figure. The more of such images an author incorporates into his "overall portrait," the more complex the portrait becomes, especially if one or more of these images appears not only to complement another image, but stands in some sense or degree in conflict with it. Thus, the portraitist, prodded by the work of the "image" makers, confronts much the same problems and difficulties as the portrait painter. As Brilliant points out, the portraitist is under considerable internal (as well as external) pressure to "give coherence and meaning" to the subject's life (129). This becomes a more difficult achievement when, as in the case of Jesus, numerous "snapshot" images of him are deemed to be true, if partial, reflections of who he really was. The very fact that several portraits of Jesus have been put forward in recent years indicates the complexity of the problem. By focusing on four such portraits here, we will gain an appreciation for the difficulty of capturing what Powell calls "the figure of Jesus." We will also, however, discover the value of multiple portraits.

Jesus as Reasonable Visionary

Formerly a biblical professor at Oxford University and in Canada, and now a professor at Duke University, E. P. Sanders is the author of two books on Jesus, *Jesus and Judaism* (1985) and *The Historical Figure of Jesus* (1993). Powell indicates that the first book was regarded as a monumental contribution to Jesus studies at the time of its publication, receiving several major book awards, while the second offers a more popular account of Sanders' key ideas, updated somewhat as a result of further reflection and dialogue. Borg notes that Sanders' *Jesus and Judaism* is probably the best known of the books by the five portraitists discussed in his original article, though he now believes that Crossan's *The Historical Jesus* will prove to be of even greater importance.

As Powell notes, the uniqueness of Sanders' method is that he does not begin with an analysis of Jesus' sayings, but with a list of virtually indisputable facts about Jesus. These facts, as presented in *Jesus and Judaism*, are that Jesus (1) was baptized by John the Baptist; (2) called disciples and spoke of there being twelve; (3) confined his activity to Israel; (4) was a Galilean who preached and healed; and (5) was crucified outside Jerusalem by the Roman authorities. Also, after his death, some of his followers continued as an identifiable movement, and at least some Jews persecuted at least parts of the new movement.

In the second book, Sanders expanded his list of almost indisputable facts. Here, Jesus (1) was born in 4 B.C.E. near the time of the death of Herod the Great; (2) spent his childhood and early adult years in Nazareth, a Galilean village; (3) was baptized by John the Baptist; (4) called disciples; (5) taught in the towns, villages, and countryside of Galilee (apparently not in the cities); (6) preached "the kingdom of God"; (7) went to Jerusalem for Passover about the year 30 C.E.; (8) created a disturbance in the temple area; (9) had a final meal with the disciples; (10) was arrested and interrogated by Jewish authorities, specifically the high priest; and (11) was executed on the orders of the Roman prefect, Pontius Pilate. After his execution, his disciples at first fled; then they saw him (in what sense is uncertain) after his death. As a consequence, they believed that he would return to found the kingdom and formed a community to await his return while seeking to win others to faith in him as God's Messiah. While the list in his second book is significantly expanded over the list in his first book, missing from the second is that Jesus' ministry included healings, that he spoke of twelve disciples, that his ministry was restricted to Israel, and that some Jews persecuted some parts of the movement. This does not mean, however, that he no longer believes these to be true, only that he presents them more cautiously, but with supporting evidence.

According to Sanders, the key to understanding Jesus is interpreting the facts about his life in light of what is known about his social world. By social world, he means the world of first-century Palestinian Judaism. Because Christians have viewed Jesus over against Judaism, Sanders contends that they have caricatured the Jewish religion that Jesus himself espoused and, as a result, have created a caricature of Jesus himself. Sanders' portrait locates Jesus in the restoration eschatology prevalent in first-century Judaism. Jesus' disturbance in the temple area and his selection of twelve disciples correspond to key components of restoration eschatology, namely, the renewal of the temple and the reconstitution of the twelve tribes of Israel. While Powell discusses Sanders' views on both points, I will focus, in the interests of brevity, on Jesus' action in the temple.

All four canonical gospels contain accounts of the disruption in the temple, and most Jesus scholars believe not only that such an incident actually occurred, but that it was also the immediate cause of his death. It is assumed that Jesus did not enter the temple itself, but created a disturbance in the temple area. Given the massive size of this area, his action seems to have been limited in scope. Powell notes, "He did not surround the temple complex with an army and order all business transactions to stop. Apparently, he just turned over a few tables in one section of the area surrounding the temple—an area specifically designed for the sort of commerce that was being conducted there" (118). The question is why he did this. "If it was not a determined attempt to shut down the entire enterprise or (as no scholar would suggest) simply a spontaneous tantrum on his part, then what did he expect to accomplish?" If it was "staged as a symbolic demonstration," what was it supposed to symbolize? (118).

In Sanders' view, it was not an effort to reform—or "cleanse"—the temple, but to destroy it symbolically, thus questioning its continued existence. The point of this destruction was not to suggest divine punishment of the Jewish people. Rather, it signified that God was going to replace the old temple with a new one, an event that would usher in the restoration of Israel: "Whether Jesus thought the new temple would be on earth or in heaven cannot be determined and is somewhat inconsequential. What is more important is that a new temple meant a new age; God was about to inaugurate the long-awaited kingdom, in which all covenant promises would be fulfilled" (119). Thus, according to Sanders, "Jesus looked for the imminent direct intervention of God in history, the elimination of evil and evildoers, the building of the new and glorious temple, and the reassembly of Israel with himself and his disciples as leading figures in it" (120). In this sense, he viewed himself as a prophet of Israel, and the symbolic action at the temple was comparable to symbolic actions associated with those of earlier prophets (e.g., Isaiah going naked for three years, Jeremiah wearing a yoke around his neck). Such symbolic actions not only "stage" a future event, but also indicate that it is imminent.

Powell concludes that, for Sanders, identifying Jesus as an eschatological prophet achieves two things. It allows for a reasonable explanation of both Jesus' own self-consciousness and of the identity attributed to him by the early church. "The clearest and possibly the most important point that can be made about Jesus' view of himself," says Sanders, is that "he regarded himself as having full authority to speak and act on behalf of God" (121). This does not imply that he saw himself as the Messiah or spoke of himself as the Son of God; even if he did refer to himself as the "Son of man," we can no longer determine in what sense he meant this. Rather, he presented himself as "a charismatic and autonomous prophet" whose authority "was not mediated by any human organization, not even by scripture" (121).

If Jesus did not claim to be anything more than a prophet, why was he brought before the Jewish authorities (specifically, the high priest)? If the incident in the temple was not an armed assault, which would surely have resulted in his capture and execution and the hunting down of his supporters (which did not happen), why was he executed? Why wasn't the action considered comparable to Jeremiah's wearing of a yoke, an embarrassment to the authorities but surely no grounds for execution? Sanders doubts that Jesus was considered either by Caiaphas the high priest or Pilate the Roman appointed governor as posing any serious political threat. More likely:

> Caiaphas had Jesus arrested because of his responsibility to put down trouble-makers, especially during festivals. Jesus had alarmed some people by his attack on the Temple and his statement about its destruction, because they feared that he might actually influence God. It is highly probable, however, that Caiaphas was primarily concerned with the possibility that Jesus would incite a riot. He sent armed guards to arrest Jesus, he gave him a hearing, and he recommended execution to Pilate, who promptly complied. (124)

In Sanders' view, Jesus did not intend his disturbance as an act of martyrdom. Instead, he believed that God's intervention in Israel's troubles was imminent. As Powell states Sanders' view, Jesus "thought this when he entered Jerusalem, and he appears to have continued to think this even after the temple incident when he may have realized that his own days were now numbered" (125). The saying attributed to Jesus at the meal with his disciples—"I will never again drink of the fruit of the vine until that day when I drink it new in the kingdom of God" (Mk. 14:25)–indicates that Jesus believed God would intervene and bring in the kingdom before he was arrested and executed. Because his expectations were not realized, his cry from the cross—"My God, my God, why have you forsaken me?" a reminiscence of Psalm 22–is also viewed by Sanders as an authentic saying of Jesus, not merely one attributed to him by early Christians. Were it not for the appearances (in some form) to his disciples, they too would have despaired. Instead, these appearances caused them to believe that he would return to bring God's kingdom about.

Despite the fact that Sanders' portrait has been extremely influential, it has also been sharply attacked. The major points of contention concern: (1) his emphasis on Jesus' location within the social world of Palestinian Judaism and corresponding de-emphasis of the influence of the Hellenistic world of the Roman empire; (2) his assumption that Jesus expected God to inaugurate a new age through some direct disjuncture in history; and (3) his corresponding de-emphasis of Jesus' role as a social reformer. Concerning the latter two issues, Powell notes that several of Sanders' critics consider there to be authentic material in the Jesus tradition that *does* point toward social and economic reform. Richard A. Horsley, for example, sees Jesus as wanting to foment a social revolution; he was executed because Roman authorities perceived–correctly–that he was stirring the people toward a *social* ("bottom up") rather than a *political* ("top down") revolution (Powell, 53). Sanders responds to this criticism, "It is a question of emphasis," adding that "Jesus doubtless had views about the social, political, and economic conditions of his people, but his mission was to prepare them to receive the coming kingdom of God" (Powell, 127–28).

Regarding Jesus' location within the social world of Palestinian Judaism, critics contend that contrary to Sanders' claims, Jesus *did* come into significant conflict with his contemporaries over matters of law (e.g., sabbath rules and other purity codes). If Jesus was a prophet as Sanders claims, he would surely have been involved in disputes with his own Jewish community. Others criticize Sanders' view that there is insufficient evidence to support the claim that Jesus required repentance of sinners. He surmises that Jesus may have omitted this feature of restoration eschatology because John the Baptist had taken care of that part of the overall task and notes a "paradoxical tension," wherein Jesus apparently required high standards for his followers, such as prohibiting divorce among them, and yet "the overall tenor of Jesus' teaching is compassion toward human frailty" (128). Thus, Sanders' reply to his critics that "it is a question of emphasis" seems to apply here as well. As noted, his portrait of Jesus is intended as a corrective to Christian caricatures of Judaism (where divine grace is presumed to be nonexistent).

Borg's construction of Sanders' portrait of Jesus is similar to Powell's, though much less detailed. Thus, only Borg's criticisms of Sanders will concern us here, and these are essentially the three that Powell has identified. He contends that,

> although Sanders seeks to place Jesus firmly within a Jewish social world, Jesus ends up having very little to do with it. Jesus' relationship to it remains abstract, almost ideological. Sanders relates him to the world of ideas: the ideas of Jewish restoration theology and the Jewish law understood as "covenant nomism." With both of these, according to Sanders, Jesus fits nicely. But precisely because Jesus differs so little from his social world, he seems remarkably unconcerned with it. He is not very interested in the historical direction of his people or about the shape of Jewish life. Rather, it is Jesus' ideas about eschatology, and his acting out his convictions about a new temple that get him in trouble. Indeed, Jesus is so unconcerned about his social world that he is curiously other-worldly, or perhaps better, next-worldly. (Borg, 1994b, 21)

As Sanders himself puts it, "It is almost inconceivable that Jesus himself did not expect the imminent end or transformation of the present order" (Powell, 216).

Where there does not seem to be any serious dispute, however, is Sanders' view that Jesus' action at the temple was a symbolic destruction, not a "cleansing" of its allegedly dishonest business practices. Even Crossan, who is virtually at opposite poles to Sanders in his emphasis on the influence of the Hellenistic social world on Jesus, agrees with Sanders on this point (Crossan, 1994, 130–33). Nor is there any serious dispute over Sanders' claim that this incident was the immediate cause of Jesus' death. Also, few take exception to his claim that, had Jesus not appeared to his disciples (in some form), they would not have been inspired to galvanize around the belief that he would return to bring the kingdom into being. Rather, the main disputes center around his view that Jesus did not differ significantly from the Judaism of his day and that he anticipated that God would intervene in human affairs in such a dramatic manner that healings and social reforms at best foreshadowed the coming reign of God.

I will return to Sanders' (and other Jesus scholars') interpretation of Jesus' disturbance at the temple in chapter 8. For the moment, I would simply note that if Sanders' portrait of Jesus were visual, it would present Jesus in the temple, thus taking "full advantage of the 'pregnant moment'–the sublime, single blow" (Wendorf, 15). This would be the "break-through" moment in Jesus' career, when he would experience release from "temporal contingencies" (16). This portrait would be diminished if it were to present Jesus as acting under the influence of "strong expressions of feeling" or "the flux of emotions" (Brilliant, 112). Thus, we should not be surprised that Sanders responds to the question of whether Jesus intended to die and thus deliberately provoked the authorities in the temple disruption: "It is not historically impossible that Jesus was weird," but "other things that we know about him make him a *reasonable* first-century visionary"(Powell, 125, his emphasis). Nor should we be surprised by Powell's supporting comment that no scholar would suggest that Jesus' temple disruption was "simply a spontaneous tantrum" (118).

While Borg worries that Sanders has insufficiently emphasized Jesus' social investments, my concern is that he downplays the emotional side of Jesus. Of course, his action in the temple was not a "spontaneous tantrum," as though he were behaving like an ill-tempered, petulant child intent on forcing God's hand. But this does not mean that we cannot endorse the following comment by Erik H. Erikson regarding the actions of any public figure: "Every adult, whether he is a follower or a leader, a member of a mass or of an elite, was once a child. He was once small. A sense of smallness forms a substratum in his mind, ineradicably. His triumphs will be measured against this smallness, his defeats will substantiate it" (1963, 404). This "pregnant moment" in Jesus' career was more complex–emotionally speaking–than Sanders allows. Does his expectation of the imminent kingdom of God fully account for this symbolic act? Were there other psychological factors or influences involved? Might the symbolism itself point to underlying psychological motivations? In chapter 8 I will explore these very questions in considerable detail.

Jesus as an Atypical Jew

A priest educated in Rome, John P. Meier is currently professor of New Testament at the Catholic University of America in Washington, D.C. As Powell notes, Meier's study of Jesus began as a simple prelude to a commentary on Matthew's gospel. As he kept encountering questions that had not been adequately resolved, however, Meier began to consider a major study of Jesus. As of Powell's (and my own) writing, two of a projected three (or more) volumes have appeared. Published under the general title *A Marginal Jew: Rethinking the Historical Jesus*, the first volume is subtitled *The Roots of the Problem and the Person* (1991). The second is subtitled *Mentor, Message, and Miracles* (1994).

As Powell indicates, Meier sees Jesus as "marginal" in two senses. One is that Jesus in his own times was "at most a blip on the radar screen of the Greco-Roman world." The other is that while Meier, like Sanders, views Jesus within his Jewish world, Meier wants to recognize what made him distinctive. Jesus was Jewish but was atypical in several key respects: "Jesus appears to have remained celibate. He left his home and family to pursue an itinerant ministry. He eschewed fasting and prohibited divorce. His teaching evinced a style and content that did not jibe with the views and practices of the major Jewish religious groups of his day" (Powell, 132). His eventual fate resulted from these departures from typical Judaism. As Meier notes: "By the time he died [Jesus] had managed to make himself appear obnoxious, dangerous, or suspicious to everyone, from pious Pharisees through political high priests to an ever vigilant Pilate. One reason Jesus met a swift and brutal end is simple: he alienated so many individuals and groups in Palestine that, when the final clash came in Jerusalem in 30 A.D., he had very few people, especially people of influence, on his side" (132–33). The political marginality of this "poor layman from the Galilean countryside with disturbing doctrines and claims" was because he was "dangerously anti-establishment" and lacked a "power base in the capital" (Powell, 133).

Powell begins his review of Meier with commentary on his methodology, noting his concern with following the principles of strict historical science: "For Meier, historical science demands strict attention to clearly-defined criteria and detailed public presentation of evidence to account for even the smallest point of each argument. This, he claims, is why his work is so long" (Powell, 134). As Meier puts it: "Time and again while writing this [his first] volume, I have been constrained to reverse my views because of the weight of the data and the force of the criteria. My own experience has convinced me that, while methodology and criteria may be tiresome topics, they are vital in keeping the critic from seeing in the data whatever he or she already has decided to see. The rules of the road are never exciting, but they keep us moving in the right direction" (Powell, 135).

In addition to the criteria that Meier employs in making judgments in matters of authenticity (including multiple attestation, coherence, embarrassment to the early Christian community, and the criterion of Jesus' rejection and execution), Powell makes particular note of his distinction between the "real" and the "historical" Jesus. He cites Meier's view that the historical task is "necessarily reductionist. The object of historical inquiry is not ultimately the 'real Jesus' but only those aspects or facets of him that are amenable to academic study" (Powell, 133). Meier notes: "In contrast to the 'real Jesus,' the 'historical Jesus' is that Jesus whom we can recover or reconstruct by using the scientific tools of modern historical research. The 'historical Jesus' is thus a scientific construct, a theoretical abstraction of modern scholars that coincides only partially with the real Jesus of Nazareth, the Jew who actually lived and worked in Palestine" (Powell, 133). Powell notes that "Meier has affirmed elsewhere that he personally does believe in the virgin birth, the miracles, and the resurrection of Jesus. These matters would belong to the large portrait of what he regards as 'the real Jesus,' but they do not necessarily belong to the smaller portrait of what he regards as 'the historical Jesus'" (133). Powell indicates, however, that Meier's work has not in fact been faulted on the grounds that his Catholicism might compromise his "professional neutrality." Indeed, "the implications of his conclusions are at least as challenging to the Catholic faith" as they are to other perspectives. Meier's historical research leads, for example, to the conclusion that the gospel writers considered the brothers and sisters of Jesus to be "blood" siblings, not cousins; he attributes the cousins hypothesis to later ecclesiastical developments relating to Mary's perpetual virginity. Thus, while Meier does not "deny" various tenets of the Catholic faith, he "prescinds" from them on the grounds that he is engaged in exclusively historical research.

Meier's portrait of Jesus begins with his early years. He admits that not much can be known with certainty about Jesus' origins, "though the few facts that can be affirmed put him ahead of most historical figures from the ancient world" (Powell, 135). There is multiple textual attestation that Jesus was born during the reign of Herod the Great, and therefore before 4 B.C.E., the year of Herod's death. The most likely birthplace was Nazareth, since Jesus is widely attested to have been from there. The tradition that he was born in Bethlehem cannot be ruled out but probably reflects later theological interests rather than historical fact. For Meier, the claim that Jesus' mother was a virgin at the time of his birth has multiple attestations (Matthew and Luke) but was not open to verification even in Jesus' own lifetime, much less today (Powell, 135).

Meier notes that Jesus was Jewish and was raised as the firstborn son of Joseph and Mary in a family that included at least four brothers (James, Joses, Jude, and Simon) and at least two (unnamed) sisters. The names of family members, including Jesus' own name (identical to the Hebrew *Joshua*), "recall significant figures from Israel's past, suggesting that the family may have nurtured the pious hopes for the restoration of Israel that were common in this environment. Joseph may even have claimed to be of the lineage of David, a fact that would later help to fuel messianic expectations with regard to Jesus" (Powell, 135). Jesus' mother, brothers, and sisters apparently outlived Jesus, but Joseph probably died before Jesus began his ministry. Meier considers reliable the New Testament reports "that there was tension between Jesus and his family during his life but that later some of his siblings were prominent leaders in the movement that continued in his name" (Powell, 135).

Meier also makes a special point of Jesus' celibacy. As Powell observes, despite a significant amount of information about family members, "all sources are completely silent with regard to Jesus having a wife or children. Meier notes that it would have been highly unusual for a man in Jesus' social position to choose a life of celibacy but decides that this nevertheless appears to have been the case. Thus, Jesus would have been marked among his peers as exceptional or odd at an early point" (135–36). Meier also assumes that Jesus, "like his father," was a carpenter, a trade that involved building parts of houses in addition to the fashioning of furniture. As such, he would have been poor, "but not one of the 'poorest of the poor.' He did not know 'the grinding poverty of the dispossessed farmer, the city beggar, the rural day laborer, or the rural slave.' He had a trade that involved a fair level of technical skill and—Meier adds incidentally—one that marks him as healthy if not muscular" (Powell, 136). While Powell here refers to Joseph as Jesus' "father," Meier prefers to call him Jesus' "putative father." This is not because he sees any merit in theories of Jesus' illegitimacy, but because the virginal conception of Jesus has multiple attestation. As for Jesus' literacy and general level of education, Meier believes that "Jesus would have spoken Aramaic, some Greek, and perhaps some Hebrew [the traditional language of Jews]. While there is no indication that he received education outside of his home, Meier is inclined to think that he was literate" (136).

Powell concludes his account of Meier's reconstruction of Jesus' early life with Meier's "own theory as to why the Bible is silent" about "the hidden years" of Jesus' adolescence and early adulthood: "'Nothing much happened.'

Apart from remaining single, Jesus appears to have been 'insufferably ordinary.' He did nothing that could earn him religious credentials or gain him a power base" (136). This all changed, however, when he "was about thirty-three years old." He left home "for reasons unknown and traveled to the Judean countryside to be baptized by a man named John." In a section titled "Mentor," Powell summarizes Meier's two-hundred-plus pages on John the Baptist with the notation that he considers John "to be 'the one person who had the single greatest influence on Jesus' ministry'" (136).

I will not discuss this summary at length. I want, however, to take note of two selected issues. The first concerns the meaning of Jesus' baptism by John. Powell writes:

> Since John offered his baptism for forgiveness of sins and protection against judgment, we must assume that accepting this baptism was for Jesus an act of confession and repentance. Meier warns, however, against construing such repentance in terms of "the introspective conscience of the West" [a term coined by biblical scholar Krister Stendahl in his studies on Paul]. Rather than focusing on individual sins or personal peccadillos, Jesus' repentance would have involved humble admission that he was a member of a sinful people (the rebellious and ungrateful nation of Israel), accompanied by a resolve to be different. (137)

A second issue is the fact that "accepting John's baptism also implied recognition on Jesus' part that he was now, in some sense, a disciple of the Baptist." On the other hand, Jesus "at some point [left] John's circle and began his own ministry." His break from John "was a moderate one." Thus, Meier disagrees with some scholars who view this break as an apostasy from John and also dismisses the view "that Jesus continued throughout his ministry to see John and not himself as the final eschatological figure who would bring in the kingdom of God" (Powell, 137). He rejects these "simplistic scenarios" and instead "attempts to delineate the distinctive aspects of Jesus' ministry without obscuring the enduring influence that the Baptist had on him. Jesus was no 'carbon copy' of John, but 'a firm substratum of the Baptist's life and message' remained with Jesus throughout his ministry" (Powell, 137).

In Meier's view, a major continuity between Jesus and John was that while Jesus differed from John in "accent and style," he was united with him in his effort "to prepare unrepentant Israel for a coming crisis involving salvation and judgment." In this respect, Meier differs with Sanders, who does not believe that Jesus linked the collective repentance of his people to his anticipation of the deliverance. In contrast, Meier contends that while his preaching "moved in emphasis from God's imminent fiery judgment to God's offer of mercy and forgiveness," Jesus "never abandoned John's message of judgment. This eschatological, even apocalyptic notion that the day of divine reckoning was at hand remained one element of Jesus' own preaching. Also, like

John, Jesus chose to remain celibate, gathered disciples, and conducted a ministry to Israel. Jesus even imitated John's practice of baptizing disciples, and probably continued to baptize disciples throughout his ministry" (Powell, 137–38). In fact, the practice of baptism "flowed like water from John through Jesus into the early church, with the ritual taking on different meanings at each stage of the process" (138).

On the other hand, Meier believes that Jesus' employment of the "kingdom of God" symbol was not derived from John. Instead, it reflected a "conscious, personal choice." For this reason, the study of this symbol offers a privileged access into Jesus' message. One meaning of the phrase (perhaps the dominant one) involved expectations regarding the imminent future, and his exorcisms were proof that the kingdom of God is already present in some sense. Against those (especially Crossan and Borg) who consider the "present sayings" authentic but reject the idea that the kingdom in Jesus' view was "yet to come," Meier believes that the "already/not yet" tension is not inherently contradictory. Furthermore, such concern for logical consistency, he notes, "may be beside the point when dealing with an itinerant Jewish preacher and miracle worker of first century Palestine" (Powell, 140). This also implies, however, that his miracles played a central role in his eschatological framework. As Powell indicates, "Meier accepts as a historical fact that Jesus did perform extraordinary deeds that were deemed by himself, his supporters, and his enemies to be miracles" (140). For Meier, "The miracle tradition has better historical support than many facts that are commonly accepted, such as that Jesus was a carpenter or that he used the word *Abba* in his prayers. The rejection of this tradition can only be viewed as an imposition of a philosophical concept on objective research" (140). But Powell adds: "This is not to say that [for Meier] Jesus actually did work miracles, an affirmation that would also impose a philosophical concept on the evidence. What we can affirm is the attribution of miracles to Jesus *during his own lifetime...*The early church did not simply invent this tradition and make up the miracle stories at some point after Jesus' death. At least, it did not make up all of them" (140, his emphasis). Meier concludes that if the tradition that Jesus worked miracles is to be rejected as unhistorical, then "so should every other Gospel tradition about him" (Powell, 140).

Meier's five hundred–page analysis of the miracles stories in the canonical gospels leads to his judgment that the reports of miracles that are most likely to go back to the historical Jesus include the exorcisms of the possessed boy and of Mary Magdalene, two healings of paralytics (the one of the man at the pool of Bethesda, the other of the man let down through the roof) and of three blind persons, the healing of the official's boy, and the raising of Jairus' daughter from the dead. The exorcism of the Gerasene demoniac, the raising of the widow's son at Nain, the raising of Lazarus, and the feeding of the multitudes may also have a "historical core." Those that reflect the theological interests of the early church are exorcisms of non-Jews and most of the nature miracles (walking on water, changing water into wine, stilling storms, and cursing the fig tree). A key text for Meier is the statement (in Q) where Jesus describes his ministry in these terms: "The blind receive their sight, the lame walk, the lepers are cleansed, the deaf hear, the dead are raised, the poor have good news brought to them" (Lk. 7:22). In Meier's view, "Miracle working probably contributed the most to [Jesus'] prominence and popularity on the public scene–as well as to the enmity he stirred up in high places" (Powell, 140).

Meier's third volume was still in preparation as Powell's book went to press, but Powell indicates that early reviews suggest that it will emphasize Jesus' mission "as involving some sort of restoration of the nation of Israel," a view based, much as it is for Sanders, on the claim that Jesus' reference to his inner circle as "the twelve" is historically authentic. Meier also intends to discuss Jesus' relation to the Mosaic law and to advance the view (against Sanders) that "Jesus did assume the right to rescind or change parts of the law," basing his authority to do so on "his own ability to know directly and intuitively what was God's will for his people" (142). As Powell indicates, this leads naturally to the question, "Who did this man think he was?" Meier's intention is to address this question of Jesus' own perceived identity by exploring "the eschatological or messianic designations that existed in Judaism at the time of Jesus. He has said that he thinks 'at least some of Jesus' followers believed him to be descended from King David, and that they therefore took him to be the Davidic Messiah'" (Powell, 142).

As for why Jesus was crucified, Meier's plan is to delineate the variety of factors causing him to be viewed as dangerous: He announced the coming of a future kingdom that would soon put an end to the present state of affairs; he claimed to be able to teach the will of God authoritatively, sometimes in ways that ran counter to scripture and tradition; he performed miracles that attracted a large following; and he exhibited a "freewheeling personal conduct" through open fellowship with recognized sinners. If some Jews also took him to be the Davidic Messiah, this would make an already volatile mix "positively explosive." The staged entry into Jerusalem and the demonstration in the temple would then be "the match set to the barrel of gasoline" (Powell, 142).

Powell concludes that Meier's portrait of Jesus closely resembles that of Sanders, especially in that he sees Jesus "as an eschatological Jewish prophet who was primarily concerned with announcing and, in some sense, enacting the divine restoration of Israel." Unlike Sanders, however, "Meier thinks Jesus did engage his contemporaries in conflicts over the law and he affirms that Jesus did regard the coming kingdom as already present in some definitive and significant way" (143). Also, unlike Sanders, who insists that "no aspect of Jesus can truly be regarded as unique," Meier contends that the "atypical configuration of Jesus' characteristics" makes him unique.

Concerning criticism of Meier's portrait, Powell suggests that the sort of detailed critiques leveled at other portraitists have not yet been made of Meier's work. This is partly because his work is "recent and incomplete," but may also be due to others not wanting to tangle with Meier on his turf. That is, there are those who believe that he begins with a conception of Jesus and that this influences his decisions about the historical evidence: "Skeptics find his Jesus to be conveniently amenable to Christianity, even to Catholicism. Some question whether it is possible for anyone to begin with no conception of Jesus and then blandly accumulate information regarding him until they are able to construct a disinterested portrait" (145). In fact, Meier would apparently not disagree with them on this point, as he says that there is no "neutral Switzerland of the mind." To him, the solution to this problem of subjective distortion

> is to admit honestly one's own standpoint, to try to exclude its influence in making scholarly judgments by adhering to certain commonly held criteria, and to invite the correction of other scholars when one's vigilance inevitably slips. In my own case, I must candidly confess that I work out of a Catholic context. My greatest temptation, therefore, will be to read back anachronistically the expanded universe of later Catholic teaching into the "big bang" moment of Jesus' earthly ministry. In what follows I will try my best to bracket what I hold by faith and examine only what can be shown to be certain or probable by historical research and logical argumentation. I hope non-Catholic scholars in particular will point out where I may fail to observe my own rules by reading Catholic theology into the quest. At the same time, Catholic readers of this book should not be upset by my holding to a strict distinction between what I know about Jesus by research and reason and what I hold by faith. (Meier, 1991, 6)

These introductory comments recall his distinction between the "real" and the "historical" Jesus. This, in the skeptics' view, is a deceptive distinction. It is one thing to say that the "real" are those "facts" and "aspects" of Jesus that are inaccessible because there is no historical evidence about them. It is quite another to say that the "real" Jesus is the "historical" Jesus plus the Jesus who is known to us through the eyes of faith. Meier wants to claim the latter as well, for his historical portrait is designed, albeit in a "reduced" size, as one that is congruent in its essential characteristics with the larger portrait of the Jesus of the expanded universe of later church teachings. Is it merely coincidental, then, that his portrait of the historical Jesus bears a striking resemblance to the portrait of the Jesus of Christian faith and practice?

That Meier manages to offer a portrait of the historical Jesus that is not at odds with the Jesus of Christian faith may therefore illustrate Richard Brilliant's view that portraitists have a tendency "to avoid 'unpleasant' expressions because of their negative connotations" (Brilliant, 112) and to impose "conformist attitudes on the presentation of the subject," allowing "the successful portraitist to encase his subjects within the masks of convention"

(112). Similarly, the "historical" Jesus that Meier has reconstructed should prove, by and large, compatible with the "real" Jesus of Christian faith:

Such a distinction [between "what I know about Jesus by research and reason and what I know by faith"] is firmly within the Catholic tradition; for example, Thomas Aquinas distinguishes carefully between what we know by reason and what we affirm by faith. This book remains in the prior realm, while of course not denying the relevance of investigations into the historical Jesus for faith and theology. It is simply a matter of asking one question at a time. I would be delighted if systematic theologians would pick up where the book leaves off and pursue the line of thought further. (6)

He assumes—for good reason—that systematic theologians would have little difficulty building on his accomplishments. It is little wonder, therefore, that skeptics contend his portrait of the historical Jesus is not achieved on historical grounds alone, but is already framed by the Jesus of subsequent faith affirmations.

The more specific concerns that his portrait raise for me, however, relate to instances where he makes implicit psychological judgments. For example, he asserts that we know little about the "hidden years" of Jesus' childhood and early adulthood because he was "insufferably ordinary." The one exception to his ordinariness was that he was probably celibate. His view that Jesus' early years were ordinary and unexceptional, however, requires him to explain how such an ordinary person could become extraordinary later on. His explanation appears to be that Jesus' association with John the Baptist changed him and altered the course of his life. As Powell puts it: "Then, when [Jesus] was about thirty-three years old, he left home for reasons unknown and traveled to the Judean countryside to be baptized by a man named John" (Powell, 136).

This explanation is not, however, without its problems. Of course, it is possible that Jesus lived a very ordinary life until an experience or set of experiences occurred that utterly changed the whole course and direction of his life. We cannot rule out this possibility. This, however, is the reconstruction to which we should resort only after other efforts to account for Jesus' "atypicality" had failed. Such efforts might begin with why Jesus remained unmarried, or "celibate." His desire to devote himself fully to his mission may explain this, but then we would expect that his sense of having a special mission would have preceded or occurred simultaneously with his decision to remain celibate. In Meier's reconstruction, Jesus' celibate life course was determined years before his encounter with John the Baptist. Meier offers no explanation for why Jesus was not married prior to this encounter.

Meier's observation that Jesus "left home for reasons unknown" and went out to be baptized by John might be viewed as admirable restraint, a refusal to assign reasons or motives where the historical evidence is silent. On the other hand, Meier subscribes to the widely held view that there were tensions between Jesus and his family. It is not, therefore, far-fetched to suggest that there may have been a connection between these tensions and his decision to go out into the desert for an extended period of time. Nor is it inappropriate to wonder what caused these tensions and when they began to emerge. Did they begin after he began his public ministry? Or did they begin much earlier? If earlier, might there be a connection between these tensions and his probable unmarried status? If there was such a connection, Meier's claim that Jesus' early life was "insufferably ordinary" begins to look less secure. One might then ask whether the "hidden years" were hidden not because they were ones of common ordinariness, but because they were, in their own way, as atypical as his adult years proved to be. I will return to these important and complex issues in chapter 6.

Meier's resort to conventional explanations on these matters may be due, in part, to their personal relevance, that is, his own celibate status. His emphasis on Jesus' "celibacy" is reminiscent of Erik Erikson's comment that Luther's interpreters seemed to want to "take literal and unashamed possession of him, of the great man's charisma" (Erikson, 1958, 30). If so, this suggests that one may make every effort to "bracket" what one "holds by faith" and still be vulnerable to another comment by Erikson, that "the artist withdraws behind his art even while offering an image of himself in his work" (Erikson, 1987, 46). If this is true of Meier, it does not by any means mark him as atypical, for there is some degree of self-portraiture in all portraiture. Brilliant cites an extreme example of this in the work of twentieth-century artist Francis Bacon, whose "portraits of popes, friends, patrons, of himself, all seem to look alike, as if he were seeking to express himself through their contorted images. To the degree in which they can be distinguished from one another, each portrait retains its own integrity; to the degree that they resemble one another, they implicate the artist in each image as if he mirrored his own anxious appearance in their faces" (Brilliant, 156). Neither Sanders nor Meier has made such an egregious self-intrusion into his portrait of Jesus, but Sanders' view of Jesus as a "*reasonable* visionary" and Meier's view of him as "insufferably ordinary" despite his celibacy may be instances of the portraitist offering an image of himself in his work. Whether this image fits the "facts" about Jesus is the question that will concern us throughout this study.

While there is much in these two portraits of Jesus that I have no reason to question, those aspects that *are* questionable are those where they make implicit psychological judgments. Sanders does so when he presents Jesus as having acted "reasonably" in the temple incident, despite the fact that he also believes Jesus acted as he did because he expected the imminent end of the world. These claims are not easy to reconcile. Meier does so when he depicts Jesus' early years as "insufferably ordinary," yet acknowledges that his celibacy would have impressed his own contemporaries as "exceptional" or "odd," that there were tensions between Jesus and his family, and that the adult Jesus was an "atypical" Jew. In order to make his case for the ordinariness of Jesus' early years, Meier has had to place great emphasis on Jesus' relationship to John the Baptist as a turning point in his life, as though it were a kind of conversion experience. I believe a more persuasive case can be made for the psychological continuity between his early and adult years, for the childhood of Jesus was not "ordinary," even by first-century standards. As indicated, I will present this argument in chapter 6.

2

Portraits of Jesus: John Dominic Crossan and Marcus J. Borg

John Dominic Crossan and Marcus J. Borg are often discussed in tandem because their portraits of Jesus share common assumptions about how Jesus scholarship needs to be carried out. Their books on Jesus have also enjoyed a wide readership, and they are undoubtedly the best known contemporary Jesus scholars outside the academic guild. There are significant differences between their portraits of Jesus, however, and the fact that they share much in common makes these differences the more noteworthy. Our discussion begins with Crossan.

Jesus as Religious Bandit

As previously noted, Borg added Crossan, professor emeritus at DePaul University in Chicago, to his earlier essay on portraits of Jesus following the publication of Crossan's *The Historical Jesus: The Life of a Mediterranean Jewish Peasant.* Borg heaps effusive praise on this book: "It could be the most important book on the historical Jesus since Albert Schweitzer's *Quest of the Historical Jesus* at the beginning of this century, both because of its brilliance, elegance, and freshness, and because of its likely effect on the discipline" (Borg, 1994b, 33). He notes that Crossan has subsequently written a more popular version, *Jesus: A Revolutionary Biography,* "which he affectionately refers to as his 'baby Jesus' book." He adds: "With these two books, Crossan has established himself as the premier Jesus scholar in North America" (33). Little wonder that his work has also been subjected to more intense criticism than any other contemporary Jesus scholar.

Borg's discussion of Crossan's method is relatively brief. The method involves a combination of a stratification of the Jesus tradition into four "layers" (30–60 C.E., 60–80 C.E., 80–120 C.E., and 120–150 C.E.) and a quantification of the number of independent attestations of material that he arranges into complexes (e.g., all sayings referring to "kingdom and children" or "trees and hearts"). Thus, a complex that occurs in the first stratum and receives four independent attestations (e.g., the "kingdom and children" complex) has considerable claim to being a saying that is "something like something Jesus said." This is a "tightened and refined version" of the criterion of multiple attestation. A second part of Crossan's method is his interpretation of material found in the earliest layer by means of models and insights drawn from cultural and social anthropology, medical anthropology, the sociology of colonial protest movements, and several other disciplines. In Borg's view, this part of Crossan's method shifts the discipline itself from a simply "historical" to a "multi-disciplinary approach" (34).

Borg asks: "What picture of Jesus emerges in Crossan's book?" In a sentence, "Jesus was a Jewish Cynic peasant with an alternative social vision" (34). As a peasant himself, Jesus considered peasants his primary audience. While "peasant" implies a specific social class, it also has two immediate implications for Crossan. One is that Jesus was not of the "scribal class" and did not have "scribal skills or scribal awareness" (34). Most likely, he did not know the scriptures as texts and neither read nor quoted from them. His message and activity needed to be accessible to peasants, so it was not theoretical but concrete: "Jesus' message must not have been as 'talky, preachy, speechy' as much of the scholarship has presented it" (34–35).

He was also a "Jewish Cynic," meaning that he was both like and unlike the Hellenistic Cynic teachers. He was like them in that he taught and enacted a shattering of convention that involved practice, not just theory, reflected in a way of looking and dressing, eating, living, and relating. What differentiated him from Hellenistic Cynic sages is that they were urban, active in the marketplace, and individualistic, while Jesus addressed rural peasants and had a social vision. This social vision was embodied in his two most characteristic activities, which together disclosed his "corporate plan" and alternative "social vision." The first was his role as a healer. To characterize this role, Crossan uses the term "magician," partly because it is provocative, but also because it is descriptively accurate. By definition, the magician is "a healer operating outside of recognised religious authority, and therefore outside of the system." Magic is thus "religious banditry" and is to religion what social banditry is to politics. It is "subversive, unofficial, unapproved, and often lower-class religion" (Borg, 35). Crossan assigns great importance to Jesus as a healer: "No recent scholar, at least not in North America, has made Jesus' healing activity so centrally important" (Borg, 35).

The second characteristic activity of Jesus centers around the meal, specifically, Jesus' endorsement and practice of "open commensality" (or eating at the same table). This activity was tightly linked to Jesus' healing role, for in exchange for free healing, he and his companions would be given a meal by peasants:

It was not *payment* for healing (though it tended to become that as the tradition developed, when local hospitality came to be understood as the "wages" of the wandering charismatics). Rather, for Jesus and his earliest followers, open commensality embodied an alternative social vision. To eat with others without regard for social boundaries...subverted the deepest boundaries society draws: between honor and shame, patron and client, female and male, slave and free, rich and poor, pure and impure. (Borg, 35)

Thus, for Crossan, "magic and meal together, free healing and common eating, 'embodied a religious and economic egalitarianism that negated the hierarchical and patronal normalcies of Jewish religion and Roman power'" (Borg, 35).

Borg indicates that Crossan's portrait of Jesus is noneschatological in the sense that he denies an "apocalyptic eschatology to Jesus," parting company with John the Baptist in this regard: "Jesus did not understand the kingdom of God as an apocalyptic event in the near future, but as a mode of life in the immediate present" (36). Thus, Crossan's portrait "departs from the previously dominant eschatological consensus, and offers a social vision that shattered the taken-for-granted conventions of his day" (36).

While generally laudatory, Borg, in a footnote, makes a brief critical comment about Crossan's treatment of the issue of Jesus' healings, noting its "ambiguity." His criticism is addressed to Crossan's use of a distinction made by medical anthropologists between disease and illness. This distinction says that disease is the physical condition, while illness consists of the social meanings attributed to the physical condition. The question is whether Jesus healed one or both. Crossan believes that Jesus cured illnesses, but not diseases. Borg asks: "But can 'healing illness' without 'curing disease' make much sense in a peasant society? Are peasants (or anybody else, for that matter) likely to be impressed with the statement 'your illness is healed' while the physical condition of disease remains?" (43).

If Borg's discussion of Crossan's portrait begins on a laudatory note, so does Powell's, but with a significant caveat. He notes: "No other scholar of the historical Jesus is more admired by his or her opponents. 'Crossan is one of the most brilliant, engaging, learned and quick-witted New Testament scholars alive today,' opines N. T. Wright, before going on to conclude that the Irish savant's views about Jesus are nevertheless 'almost entirely wrong'" (84). As Wright is English, there is perhaps a note of nationalism in this assessment. In any event, Powell goes on to note that Crossan "has earned the praise through years of devotion to far-ranging scholarship. Archeology, anthropology, sociology, source criticism, literary criticism—if a field has any usefulness for contemporary study of the New Testament, Crossan, it seems, has been there and left his mark...His knowledge of the ancient world appears to be encyclopedic" (84).

Unlike scholars who conceive of Jesus research in terms of a "search" or "quest," and consider the current renaissance in Jesus studies to be the "third" of such quests since the early nineteenth century, Crossan's preferred term for what he does is *reconstruction*. In his own words, it is "something that must be done over and over again in different times and different places, by different groups and different communities, and by every generation again and again and again" (84). Like Borg, Powell discusses Crossan's method in some detail, noting his stratification of sources and his heavy reliance on the criterion of multiple attestation. He points out, however, that Crossan's dating of early sources has been strongly criticized. For example, "Crossan places a good deal of apocryphal material in the earliest layer, including most of the Gospel of Thomas and a 'Cross Gospel' that he has reconstructed from the passion narrative of the Gospel of Peter. The main material from the New Testament to fall into this earliest layer is the Q source and a group of miracle stories found in both Mark and John" (86). According to N. T. Wright, "All but a few within the world of New Testament scholarship would find this list extremely shaky, and all except Crossan himself would have at least some quite serious points of disagreement with it" (Powell, 86).

A second level of operation involves historical reconstruction of the place and time in which Jesus lived. Drawing on a wide variety of sources, Crossan focuses on the political realities, but he also takes account of how business was conducted, how houses were built, how medicine was practiced, and so forth. According to Powell, "The goal at this level of investigation is to establish a context for understanding who Jesus was and what his words and deeds would have meant" (86). Especially important for his reconstruction of Jesus' social world are the general situation of peasant unrest and the specific phenomenon of Cynic philosophers. He describes Palestine at the time of Jesus as being in a period of *turmoil,* the first of three stages (followed by *conspiracy* and *open unrest*) leading to the disastrous war with Rome in 66–70 C.E. Powell notes:

> The principal causes of this turmoil were oppressive taxation and social policies that continued to worsen from year to year. Within this context, Crossan describes various types of peasant resistance that could be found; tales of protesters, prophets, bandits, and messiahs are all recounted by the Roman historian Josephus. All this will serve as background to his presentation of Jesus as a somewhat different type of subversive, one that he thinks is best described by the term *magician.* (87)

The phenomenon of Cynic philosophers, which Powell explores in his "snapshot" of F. Gerald Downing and Borg discusses in his portrait of Burton L. Mack, is also important to Crossan's portrait. The Cynics, whose presence in Palestine was due to its Hellenization, viewed life as a struggle of "nature against culture," and their allegiance was clearly with the former. They advocated an abandonment of the cultural world, which in their view was irredeemable, and took a sceptical view of programs for social reform. Crossan views Jesus as "a peasant Jewish Cynic," thus suggesting that he was both similar to, and different from, the Greek and Roman Cynics of his day. Powell notes that, in principle, this level of Crossan's methodology is the least controversial one. What *is* debated, however, is the relevance of particular information about Cynics for understanding Jesus. Crossan "is sometimes thought to cast his methodological net too far and wide, bringing into play information about Greco-Roman society that may not have had much bearing on life in the villages of Palestine. At issue is the extent of the Hellenization of Galilee" (87). On this point, scholars are sharply divided.

Crossan's third level of operation involves analysis of Jesus' movement from the perspectives of social and cultural anthropology. Here he draws on a range of studies "regarding pre-industrial peasant societies, colonial protest movements, and so forth, illuminating the value such a culture would place on honor and shame and describing the tensions that would evolve from a system of patron-client relationships" (Powell, 87). For Crossan, an especially important feature of Mediterranean society was its system of brokerage. About ten percent of the population was composed of aristocrats and their retainers, with the rest being artisans, peasants, and others (i.e., beggars, bandits, and other "expendables"). In lieu of a middle class that would serve as a buffer between the upper and lower classes, there were brokers or clients of wealthy patrons who would then become patrons to others. Crossan portrays Jesus as advocating a "brokerless kingdom," calling on people "to rely on God alone," and thus issuing a fundamental challenge to the very fabric of his social world. While this aspect of Crossan's work has received general acceptance, Powell notes that some have raised criticisms, such as that Crossan confuses the social categories of "peasant" and "artisan" (Jesus being a member of the latter group) and that he adopts uncritically Richard A. Horsley's view that Jesus' affront to the traditional system of brokerage amounted to a form of banditry (bandits being those who both exploited and subverted the system). Powell concludes that "Crossan's method ultimately consists of an attempt to bring these three levels of operation together. He seeks to interpret the source material that he considers most likely to be historically authentic in light of what his historical reconstruction and interdisciplinary analysis reveals about Jesus' historical and social context" (88).

Powell next moves to Crossan's portrait of Jesus, and like Borg, he emphasizes Jesus' two most characteristic activities, *magic* and *meal.* He notes Crossan's view that magic, "the term religious leaders use to denigrate miracles done by the wrong sort of people," has social implications. As Jesus "hints in one story, those who are healed without going through the appropriate channels may conclude that they are forgiven as well (Mk. 2:1–12)." Thus, what need do they have for official religious brokers (i.e., the priests and scribes)? The exorcism stories may also be viewed in light of the larger political situation in Palestine, for cultural anthropology provides evidence that "widespread belief in demon possession is most typical for societies in which there is an occupying colonial power" (Powell, 90). Thus, following the earlier work of Paul W. Hollenbach (1981), Crossan notes that demons are named "legion" in the story of the Gerasene demoniac, a term used to designate a contingency of Roman troops. As Powell notes, "When the demons enter a herd of swine and rush into the sea, one can easily catch an image of Palestinian hope, an image of Roman soldiers–demons–pigs running back into the sea from whence they apparently came" (90). Employing Mary Douglas' proposal that the physical body is a microcosm of the social body, Crossan suggests that exorcisms are a form of "individuated symbolic revolution" (90).

Such examples of Jesus' magical powers support Crossan's view that the historical Jesus cured people of illness, "the social meaning attributed to their condition, essentially by liberating them from their internalization of the social system." Powell puts it this way: "Through Jesus' actions, for instance, lepers were deemed clean and reintegrated into society. To ask whether their lesions actually closed would impose a modern notion of healing that misses the point. The lesions remained, but as far as people in the first century were concerned, Jesus was able to heal the sick" (89). As for the exorcisms, Crossan believes that Jesus did perform them, that "he and his observers believed a literal spiritual being that had invaded a person's body was forcibly ejected. But Crossan does not himself believe such spirit-beings exist; he assumes Jesus was delivering people from some sort of psychosomatic trauma similar to what might be diagnosed today as multiple personality disorder" (89).

Because Jesus opposed the brokerage system that characterized all of society, including medical treatment, Crossan emphasizes that he healed people *gratis*. We recall in this regard the gospel accounts (Mk. 5:25–34; Lk. 8:43–48) of the woman who had been suffering from hemorrhages for twelve years and "had endured much under many physicians, and had spent all she had." Thus, instead of payment, Jesus received a meal in exchange for the healings, which meant that he did not elevate himself above the peasant class. In turn, the form of "table fellowship" that he advocated, and which symbolized his understanding of the kingdom of God, was a totally open one. As Powell notes:

> In Jesus' social setting, meals were governed by rules of conduct that went well beyond modern concern for etiquette. Strict guidelines determined who was allowed to eat with whom and where the participants were expected to sit…Meals, even more than an individual's body, were viewed as microcosms of society, and so were fraught with symbolic meaning. Mere participation in a communal meal implied a general endorsement of the other diners, and acceptance of one's specific place at the table implied recognition of one's social standing relative to that of the others. (90)

In the face of such conventions, Jesus "made a point of indiscriminately eating with anyone, including those who were regarded as outcasts." Thus, "meals themselves were integral to the mission" as "Jesus' generosity with spiritual aid would inspire villagers to generosity with physical sustenance." Because health care and food are basic needs of life, his demonstration that people can receive these things directly from God and from each other struck at the very heart of the prevailing brokerage system. If people were actually to begin sharing with each other, "they would have little need for patrons, much less brokers" (Powell, 90). Crossan explains why the enterprise Jesus initiated could be called a "movement": "This mission we are talking about is not, like Paul's, a dramatic thrust along major trade routes to urban centers hundreds of miles apart. Yet it concerns the longest journey in the Greco-Roman world…the step across the threshold of a peasant stranger's home" (Crossan, 1991, 341).

Thus, in Crossan's portrait, Jesus was a social and political reformer who had "a strategy for building or rebuilding peasant community on radically different principles than those of honor and shame, patronage and clientage" (Powell, 91). The corollary of this view is that, unlike John the Baptist, Jesus did not think in apocalyptic terms. His was an "ethical eschatology," one that favored nonviolent resistance to systemic evil, and one that does not wait for God to judge the world, but assumes that God is waiting for us to act nonviolently to redeem it. The danger was that he would become the new broker of God's privileges. To prevent this, he remained itinerant and required itinerancy of his followers, thus avoiding the threat that his headquarters would become a new locus of brokerage where pilgrims would come to receive healings in exchange for monetary contributions to defray maintenance expenses. Furthermore, he showed reluctance to identify a group of individuals as his "disciples." Instead, he had "companions," and his relationship to them was not "one of mediation but of empowerment. 'The kingdom is not his monopoly… He does not initiate its existence. He does not control its access'" (Powell, 91).

Crossan's portrait also includes considerable attention to Jesus' death. He hypothesizes that Jesus visited Jerusalem (which, in his view, was not Jesus' customary practice), "where the act that had played so well in rural Galilee was met with swift and brutal resistance. His message of spiritual and economic egalitarianism created a disturbance at the temple…and this time soldiers were on hand who were well-trained at dealing with such disturbances. Jesus was hauled outside the city and crucified. He died. The soldiers then either left his body on the cross or threw it on the ground and covered it with dirt" (Powell, 91). What happened to it? Crossan explains:

> What exactly made crucifixion so terrible? The supreme Roman penalties were the cross, fire, and the beasts. What made them supreme was not just their inhuman cruelty or their public dishonor, but the fact that *there might be nothing left to bury at the end.* That bodily

destruction was involved in being cast into the fire or thrown to the beasts is obvious enough. But what we often forget about crucifixion is the carrion crow and scavenger dog who respectively croak above and growl below the dead or dying body...I want to emphasize that Roman crucifixion was state terrorism; that its function was to deter resistance or revolt, especially among the lower classes; and that the body was usually left on the cross to be consumed eventually by the wild beasts. No wonder we have found only one body from all those thousands around Jerusalem in that single century. Remember those dogs. And if you seek the heart of darkness, follow the dogs. (Crossan, 1994, 126–27, his emphasis)

Crossan admits that this is guesswork. As Powell notes, however, this is precisely his point. After the disturbance in the temple and Jesus' arrest, his disciples fled, and no one knows what happened next. While the fact of his crucifixion is established by Roman and Jewish sources in addition to Christian ones (multiple attestation!), Crossan considers the passion-resurrection narratives fiction, an amalgamation of a male exegetical tradition based on Jewish scriptures dealing with suffering and vindication and a female tradition of lament and ritual mourning, the latter explaining why much of the burial and resurrection story is told from the perspective of women. Thus, where Sanders simply views as factual that Jesus appeared to his followers after his death (though in what form is uncertain), Crossan emphasizes the existence of traditions—scribal and ritual—to account for the passion-resurrection narratives. The burial tradition itself can be seen to have evolved "from burial by enemies to burial by friends, from inadequate and hurried burial to full, complete, and even regal embalming." As Powell puts it, Crossan believes the burial tradition underscores "the intolerable nature of the truth. By Easter morning, no one who cared knew where the body of Jesus was. But everyone knew about the dogs" (Powell, 93).

While Crossan's reconstruction of the events in Jerusalem disconcerts some readers, Powell contends that his desire is not to offend Christian sensibilities: "His demeanor is decidedly different from those scholars who delight in scandalizing the pious" (94). Crossan noted, for example, that his chapter in *The Historical Jesus* on the passion narratives was the hardest to write, not merely because of the lack of sources, but also because (in his words), "It is hard not only for those who have faith in Jesus, but also for those who have faith in humanity, to look closely at the terror of crucifixion in the ancient world...But since that world did in thousands what our century has done in millions, it is necessary to look with cold, hard eyes at what exactly such a death entailed" (94).

Powell's discussion of Crossan continues with a section on early Christian developments, based on Crossan's *The Birth of Christianity* (1998), where he seeks to show what happened in the first two decades after the execution of Jesus and prior to developments evident in Paul's writings. If, as Meier says, Jesus' childhood through early adulthood were the "hidden years," these two decades were the "lost years." While they have bearing on the historical Jesus, being the period when traditions about him were developed, I will leave this discussion to one side and conclude with Powell's summary of the major critiques that have been leveled at Crossan's work.

Most of these have centered on what critics consider his "unwarranted skepticism" in his approach to sources, "ignoring the basic biographical interest implied by the literary genre of the canonical Gospels, and assuming that Jesus' disciples would be quick to invent sayings for their teacher" (Powell, 95). Critics also contend that the passion narratives assumed a fairly fixed form earlier than Crossan assumes and are, therefore, a more reliable account of the events of the last week of Jesus' life than he recognizes. Sanders, for example, locates the final supper *after* the disturbance in the temple, when Jesus was aware that he was being sought by the authorities, whereas for Crossan the disturbance precipitated his immediate arrest and execution. No last supper, no trial, and, as we have seen, no burial. What disturbs his critics is that he sets aside his own criteria of first strata and multiple attestation (as they pertain to the last supper story) when it is convenient for him to do so, or when they do not suit conclusions he has reached on other grounds.

This also means that acceptance of his portrait of Jesus is likely to hinge on how he carries out his other two levels of analysis (historical and social/cultural). Most debated in this regard is the analogy he draws between Jesus and Cynic philosophers, though Powell indicates that in his most recent work he has de-emphasized a direct influence of Cynicism on Jesus, acknowledging that there is no way to know for certain whether Jesus even knew about the Cynics. Thus, "For Crossan, the point of invoking the Cynics is not to determine the derivation of Jesus' ideas or to identify a conscious model for his ministry and life style. The point, rather, seems to be to find a roughly contemporary historical analogy, to discuss a similar movement about which we know a good deal in order to help us form hypotheses about how Jesus' movement would have been perceived" (Powell, 97). This response mollifies some of his critics but causes others to ask why he persists in referring to Jesus as a Cynic at all.

Related to his use of a Hellenistic model–Cynicism–to gain an understanding of Jesus, Crossan is also faulted for underplaying Jesus' Jewish roots, such as his failure to compare Jesus' teachings, instead, to those of the Jewish sages. His response to such criticisms is that the Judaism of Jesus' time was itself Hellenistic, "and the most significant distinction between its various types was whether they embraced an inclusive or exclusive perspective toward Hellenism" (Powell, 97). Thus, Jesus was thoroughly Jewish, "but a representative of inclusive Hellenistic Judaism rather than of some sort of conservative, rabbinical variety. Jesus was more interested in adapting the customs of Israel than preserving them" (97).

As indicated, another criticism centers on his view of Jesus as a magician. Need one call Jesus a magician merely to make the point that he healed independently of the religious establishment? Why not simply call him a miracle worker and thus avoid what many view as a rather pejorative and unnecessarily inflammatory term? Powell indicates that, in his more recent work, Crossan seems to have bowed to the pressure of his colleagues and to have set aside the miracle worker/magician distinction. No doubt, those who regret that Crossan may be trimming his sails in this case are in the minority, but it should be noted that his original contention for the "magician" label was intended to focus discussion on the fact that illness is as much a social as a physiological phenomenon. Therefore, it matters a great deal who is considered to have authority to declare an individual ill and whole again. As Crossan explains this fundamental point: "In all of this the point is not really Galilee against Jerusalem but the far more fundamental dichotomy of magician as personal and individual power against priest or rabbi as communal and ritual power. Before the Second Temple destruction, it was magician against Temple, thereafter magician against Rabbi...If a magician's power can bring rain, for what do you need the power of temple priesthood or rabbinical academy?" (Crossan, 1991, 157–58). Because Jesus predated the development of the rabbinical academy, his quarrel would have been with the temple priesthood. By minimizing his role as magician and bowing to pressure to view him as a miracle worker, one could say that Crossan risks obscuring the fundamental connection between Jesus' role as healer and his opposition to the temple system. (I will develop this point further in chapter 7.)

Powell identifies other criticisms of Crossan, such as his nonapocalyptic portrait of Jesus. Meier, for example, contends that "future transcendent salvation was an essential part of Jesus' proclamation of the kingdom" (Powell, 98). Powell himself suggests that Crossan sets up false alternatives, and needlessly so, between the "this-worldly" ethical eschatology that he ascribes to Jesus and the apocalyptic eschatology ascribed to John the Baptist. Powell notes the dynamic tension between "the already and the not yet" prominent in all three synoptic gospels. For him, Crossan's portrait of Jesus as concerned with this-worldly affairs would not suffer from recognition of this dynamic in the life and mission of Jesus himself.

Other critics fault Crossan for his emphasis on the marked difference between the Jesus of history and the Christ of Christianity. On this point, he exhibits little interest in accommodating his critics. This is because he believes—and thinks his critics are unwilling to consider—that Christianity "lost its soul" in its efforts to convert the Roman Empire. As Powell describes Crossan's position: "This began, innocently enough, with a theological move that interpreted Christ as a mediator between God and humanity. In itself, and properly understood, such a move did not have to be devastating" (99). But, unfortunately, this understanding of Jesus "as a broker (mediator) may have facilitated a later move away from inclusive service toward the accouterments of power. The effects of such a move became evident by the time of Constantine, when Christianity became the official religion of the empire and the church's leaders (male bishops) now expected to be served by others" (99). Crossan's *Jesus: A Revolutionary Biography* concludes on this note: "As one ponders that progress from open commensality with Jesus to episcopal banquet with Constantine, is it unfair to regret a progress that happened so fast and moved so swiftly, that was accepted so readily and criticized so lightly? Is it time now, or is it already too late, to conduct, religiously and theologically, ethically and morally, some basic cost accounting with Constantine?" (201).

Most criticisms of Crossan come from those who consider his views extreme, for example, his "unwarranted skepticism" regarding sources. Few criticize him for not being radical enough. Powell does note, however, that his view of Jesus as a Cynic is "more tempered" than that of F. Gerald Downing, "especially as it comes to expression in his later work" (Powell, 96). Such "tempering," also indicated in his later tendency to "downplay" his earlier distinction between magician and miracle worker, has been resisted by a minority of Jesus scholars. Burton L. Mack, for example, believes that Jesus was similar to the Cynics in that he had no strategy for social change whatsoever. As Borg describes Mack's position: "Though Jesus' Cynic-style teaching contained a social critique, it was a genial, clever, and often playful ridiculing of the preoccupations that animate and imprison people. There was no engagement with specifically Jewish concerns or institutions. Jesus had no mission vis-a-vis Judaism." Indeed, he had "no sense of mission or purpose; in an important sense, he was aimless" (Borg, 1994a, 23). In Mack's portrait, Jesus was "a striking teacher, a gadfly or mocker, who dined in private homes with small groups of people. His clever teaching caught the imagination of some, enough so that they continued the practice of eating together after his death; from this emerged the various Jesus groups" (22–23). Thus, Mack thinks Jesus was closer to Greco-Roman Cynics, who had no social programs, while Crossan thinks that a *Jewish* Cynic would necessarily have a social, not an individualistic, perspective, and this would translate social critique into social reform. His magic/meals association is central to his argument. For Mack, however, "Only a core of wisdom teaching, stripped of any world-ending or world-building elements, is authentic to Jesus" (23).

I will return to Crossan's work in subsequent chapters, and the degree to which I will do so indicates my endorsement of Borg's view that Crossan's work has great importance for Jesus studies. It also reflects my own view that his work is especially important for the psychological study of Jesus. This is rather ironic, because Crossan makes little if any use of the psychological sciences in his work. As we have seen, Powell observes that "if a field has any usefulness for contemporary study of the New Testament, Crossan, it seems, has been there and left his mark" (23). Since Crossan does not make use of psychology in any explicit way (no psychological texts appear in his references), we might conclude from this that biblical scholars do not consider psychology to have "any usefulness for contemporary study of the New Testament." In Crossan's case, however, I believe that his non-use of psychology reflects an inherently cautious attitude toward a psychological reading of the early source material. Such caution is reflected, for example, in the following comment in *Jesus: A Revolutionary Biography*: "Jesus is not necessarily the first-born child of Joseph and Mary. He could just as easily be their youngest, for all we know" (23). Such caution, however, leaves him somewhat vulnerable to the charge of "unwarranted skepticism," as well as to the criticism that if he has been willing to exhibit considerable boldness in his reconstruction of Jesus as a social figure, why is such boldness missing from his psychological portrait of Jesus?

A second concern relates to Crossan's use of medical anthropology's views to inquire into just what it was that Jesus healed when he engaged in the role of magician. While I would endorse his use of the distinction between illness and disease, I share Borg's concern that this creates an ambiguity as to what Jesus did and did not cure. While this ambiguity may be inevitable, given the fact that illness (as socially defined) and physical disease are interactive, I believe that much of this ambiguity is resolvable by taking a closer look at the specific nature of the illnesses that Jesus was said to have cured. It can be shown, I believe, that most were psychosomatic, the result of the somatizing of socially induced anxieties. If so, curing the illness (i.e., anxiety) may also cure the disease. I discuss this further in chapter 7.

A third concern relates to Crossan's view that Jesus identified with the peasant class *and* that he had a social vision that he evidently sought to actualize. As we have seen, his emphasis on Jesus' social vision, with its connection of magic and open commensality, counteract the "talky, preachy, speechy" view of Jesus so endemic to Jesus scholarship. This reflects a shift in emphasis in his own work, as his earlier writings focused to a considerable degree on Jesus' parables and sayings (Crossan, 1973, 1980, 1983). In *The Historical Jesus* and *Jesus: A Revolutionary Biography*, he constructs a more active, less teaching-oriented Jesus. A similar emphasis on the activities of Jesus occurs in the recent work of Robert W. Funk and The Jesus Seminar titled *The Acts of Jesus: The Search for the Authentic Deeds of Jesus* (Funk et al., 1998). While this shift from a "talky, preachy, speechy" Jesus to a Jesus whose acts are thoroughly consistent with the Hellenistic emphasis on being "a man of deeds" and not of words only (see Weintraub, 1978), Crossan's picture of Jesus as having a social vision that might be instantiated in the real world is complicated, even subverted, by the claim that Jesus was a member of the peasant class.

Crossan's own discussion in *The Historical Jesus* of what it was like to be a member of the peasant class in first-century Palestine indicates that peasant cultures are ones in which talk often substitutes for actions, typically because actions are either presumed to be impossible (one's power is limited) or too risky (one could lose what one already has). Decisive actions may therefore be few and far between, and those that *are* undertaken are often impulsive, not a part of any discernible strategy for real social change. Crossan notes in this regard the accusations "tossed at peasants by their literate describers and aristocratic oppressors throughout the centuries. Peasants, we read, are dull, dumb, and dishonest; they are slow, stupid, lazy, and indifferent" (Crossan, 1991, 29). Against this simplistic view, however, he cites the argument by James Scott, based on field work among Malaysian peasants, that peasants' higher class detractors "accurately describe but inaccurately recognize what are actually the 'weapons of the weak...the tenacity of self-preservation–in ridicule, in truculence, in irony, in petty acts of noncompliance...in resistant mutuality, in the disbelief in elite homilies, in the steady grinding efforts to hold one's own against overwhelming odds–a spirit and practice that prevents the worst and promises something better'" (29). Crossan follows Scott's observations of Malaysian peasants with the following Irish tale. "Lost English huntsmen to Irish peasant in late nineteenth century Donegal: 'Did the gentry pass this way, my good man?' 'They did that, your honor.' 'How long ago?' 'About three hundred years ago, your honor'" (29–30).

Thus, peasant cultures rely on talk as a means of self-regulation and self-preservation as well as for containing impulsive violence. For those who have little money to spend on entertainment, talk is also cheap and in virtually endless supply. It is a welcome refuge from overwhelming boredom. If Crossan's portrait of Jesus as a Jewish peasant is correct, then his picture of Jesus as seeking to instantiate a new social order may be vastly overdrawn. The fact that the peasant revolts cited in his *The Historical Jesus* were mass demonstrations, and that Jesus' own actions in Jerusalem were symbolic, is consistent with peasant class tendencies *not* to envision social reform as such, but to engage in reactive and symbolic demonstrations against threats to tradition and the status quo. Such acts of resistance, fraught with symbolic meaning, are born of a sense that there is little to lose by so acting, but (paradoxically, perhaps) there is also little to gain.

A related point is that Crossan's emphasis on the exchange of healings for food may underemphasize the intrinsic value of conversation in peasant society, especially conversation that counters despair by means of deprecating humor and irony (its victims being those who occupy higher social positions) and dreams of utopia (which are not actually acted upon). While Crossan does not mean to suggest that Jesus was offered food only on the provision that he perform a miracle (this tit-for-tat would violate the intrinsic generosity involved), it seems likely that Jesus and his traveling companions were offered meals in exchange for stimulating conversation and interesting gossip from the villages they had recently visited in their perambulations. Also, if his group was, at least superficially, indistinguishable from the bandit groups that roamed the countryside preying on the weak and vulnerable, villagers may have offered the group food and lodging from fear of the consequences of refusal of hospitality. It should also be noted that some healings would have been performed on social isolates–crazed young men living in (banished to?) the hills–making the magic/open commensality relationship seem rather forced. I will return to the issues I have raised concerning Crossan's portrait of Jesus in chapters 7 and 8.

Jesus as Spirit Person

According to Powell, Marcus J. Borg, professor of religion and culture at Oregon State University, "prefers not to talk about 'the historical Jesus' as a figure of the past who can be studied apart from religious or spiritual concerns" (Powell, 102). Instead of talking about "the Jesus of history" and "the Christ of faith," Borg advocates speaking of "the pre-Easter Jesus" and "the post-Easter Jesus": "Both are historical realities, subject to study and critique, and both are significant for theology and faith" (102). Borg describes his own portrait of Jesus as one that consists of four major images. Jesus was a social prophet, an initiator of a movement whose purpose was the revitalization of Israel, a charismatic healer or "holy person," and a subversive sage (Borg, 1994b, 26). The first two are the subject of *Conflict, Holiness and Politics in the Teachings of Jesus* (1984), while the latter two are emphasized in *Jesus: A New Vision* (1987).

In *Conflict, Holiness and Politics*, Borg argues that the dominant ethos of the Jewish social world in first-century Roman Palestine, "its cultural paradigm" or "core value," was holiness, understood as purity: "Holiness generated a social world ordered as a purity system, with sharp boundaries not only between places, things and times, but also between persons and social groups" (1994, 26). The ethos of holiness had become embodied in a politics of holiness. Conflicts about holiness and purity were therefore political, with the historical shape and direction of Israel at stake. From careful examination of the synoptic traditions' reports of conflict over holiness issues–table fellowship, Sabbath conflicts, purity texts, and temple controversy–Borg concludes that Jesus radically criticized holiness as the paradigm structuring his social world and advocated compassion as the alternative paradigm for the transformation of Israel's life. In effect, he replaced "Be holy as God is holy" with "Be compassionate as God is compassionate." Compassion, like holiness, was firmly grounded in Jewish tradition, so the conflict between Jesus and his Jewish opponents was an intra-Jewish one, with Jesus opposing the religious elite who represented the dominant "holiness" ethos.

Unlike Sanders and Meier, but like Crossan, Borg argues that immediate eschatology was not a part of Jesus' message. To some extent, this is corollary to his emphasis on Jesus' involvement in the revitalization of Israel: "As a prophet, Jesus was much more concerned about Israel's historical direction and shape than about a kingdom beyond the eschaton" (27). He bases this view on the grounds that the "coming Son of man" sayings are not considered by most biblical scholars to be authentic Jesus sayings. (Crossan shares this view, though he suggests that Jesus may have used "Son of man" language, not in reference to himself, however, but as a way of talking about the generic individual, much as the word "one" functions in English [Crossan, 1991, 242].)

In his later book, Borg adds the other two features of his portrait of Jesus, those of "holy person" and of a sage or wisdom teacher. The "holy person" theme is derived from his use of "a cross-cultural and interdisciplinary typology of religious personality types [to] help order the traditions about Jesus" (Borg, 1994b, 27). His understanding of the holy person is derived from the history of religions, cultural anthropology, and psychology of religion and designates "a person experientially in touch with the holy who also becomes a conductor of the holy." These holy persons are usually viewed as agents of the holy, "often as healers, but also as prophets, lawgivers, clairvoyants, diviners, oracles, rainmakers, and gamefinders" (40). Borg notes that the holy person was central in the Jewish tradition, "from Moses and Elijah through the prophets to charismatic healers near the time of Jesus," and credits Geza Vermes with having introduced this element into the current discussion of Jesus (Vermes, 1973). Like other holy persons, Jesus "had an experiential relationship to the spirit...and this realization is central to his historical identity: a charismatic healer with a vivid sense of the reality of God. Indeed, it is tempting to see him as a Jewish mystic" (Borg, 1994b, 27).

Jesus was also a sage, a teacher of "a world-subverting wisdom that has emerged in the parables and aphorisms scholarship of the last twenty years" (27–28). When placed in the context of a cross-cultural understanding of conventional wisdom, this scholarship reveals that "Jesus' wisdom both subverted conventional wisdom (the broad way) and invited his hearers to an alternative path (the narrow way)" (28). Borg concludes:

> With the images of holy person and sage added to prophet and movement founder, a fairly full portrait of Jesus results, an image that integrates much of the Jesus tradition. He was a charismatic healer who also felt called to a public mission that included radical criticism of the dominant ethics of his social world and affirmation of another way. He spoke as both a subversive sage and a prophet and initiated a movement whose purpose was the revitalization of Israel. (28)

In his discussion of Borg's portrait of Jesus, Powell notes that he is "less explicit about methodological considerations" than other scholars. In general, though, he tends to "go with the flow" of mainstream historical criticism, "accepting what most scholars would regard as reliable without proposing novel theories regarding sources or criteria of authenticity" (Powell, 103). He relies most heavily on material in the three synoptic gospels and gives minimal attention to the apocryphal writings. Nor does he privilege the Q source to the extent that many other scholars do. This acceptance of mainstream scholarship fits his basic agenda, which is to discern what "kind of person" Jesus was, rather than concern himself with whether Jesus said or did particular things that are attributed to him. Thus, Borg writes: "Though we cannot ever be certain that we have direct and exact quotation from Jesus, we can be relatively sure of the *kinds* of things he said, and of the main theses and thrusts of his teaching. We can also be relatively sure of the kinds of things he did: healings, association with outcasts, the deliberate calling of twelve disciples, a mission directed to Israel, a final purposeful journey to Jerusalem" (Powell,

103). By noting the types of sayings and deeds attributed to Jesus, Borg believes that "we can sketch a fairly full and historically defensible portrait of Jesus...We can in fact know as much about Jesus as we can about any figure in the ancient world" (103). As Powell notes, once the task is defined as determining what kind of person Jesus was, Borg's method flows from this: "He uses an interdisciplinary approach to interpret the general tendencies of the Jesus tradition from a perspective informed by sociology, anthropology, and a study of the history of religions" (103). Specifically, this involves comparing the images of Jesus presented by the tradition with "classic 'religious personality types'" that are known to appear cross-culturally and within the history of Israel. Comparative studies of other religious and social figures offer analogues for understanding how Jesus related to his social world.

Powell notes that the four images Borg ascribes to Jesus—healer, sage, movement-initiator, and social prophet—are related to two focal points: social world and spirit. The social world was "the center of [Jesus'] concern (not just the background for his activity) and the Spirit was the source of his sense of mission and of the perspectives from which he spoke." Thus, "a spirit person" is "the umbrella designation under which the other four descriptions will fit, the glue that holds them all together" (104). In Jesus' world, the existence of a world of spirit, "a level of reality in addition to the visible world of our ordinary experience," was taken for granted. This other world was a reality to be experienced, but since it lay beyond sensory perception it could only be known through mediation. Because some individuals were viewed as experiencing communion with this spirit world more frequently or more vividly than most, others would turn to them for help in experiencing it and gaining access to its efficacies (104).

Jesus' baptism by John was an event that clearly identified Jesus as a spirit person. On this occasion, he is said to have seen a vision of the heavens opening and the Spirit of God descending on him "like a dove" (Mk. 1:10). Thus, like Ezekiel some centuries before, Jesus saw the heavens opened, momentarily seeing into the other world, as if through a door or "tear" in the fabric of the heavens. Borg acknowledges that there is some historical uncertainty about the "heavenly voice" that declared Jesus' identity to him: "Thou art my beloved Son; with thee I am well pleased" are words that "perfectly express the post-Easter perception of Jesus' identity...and this calls their authenticity into question." If this statement, however, is not taken to mean the unique Son of God, but is "given the meaning which similar expressions have in stories of other Jewish charismatic holy men, then it is historically possible to imagine this as part of the experience of Jesus. For they too had experiences in which a 'heavenly voice' declared them to be God's 'son'. If read in this way, the words not only become historically credible but are a further link to charismatic Judaism" (Borg, 1987, 41). Other accounts of Jesus' identity as a "spirit-filled person" are the transfiguration and the awe—or sense of the numinous—that people felt in his presence (46).

If one was uniquely "spirit-filled," it was assumed that such a person would have special spiritual powers. As Powell states: "Borg regards the assertion that Jesus was a healer and an exorcist as 'virtually indisputable' on historical grounds. He cites multiple attestation of accounts in the earliest sources and points out that 'despite the difficulty which miracles pose for the modern mind,' healings and exorcisms were 'relatively common in the world around Jesus'" (105). Borg notes that the gospels freely grant that some of Jesus' opponents—the Pharisees—were able to cast out demons, and that the Jewish leaders who opposed the early Christians late in the first century did not claim that Jesus' healings were false or misrepresented. Instead, they accepted them as authentic but attributed them to power derived from an evil spirit. Thus, "The healing ministry of Jesus loses its uniqueness in the light of historical study, but for that very reason gains in credibility" (106). Borg avoids trying to explain how modern medical science might understand these healings, noting that "a psychosomatic explanation that stretches but does not break the limits of our modern worldview" misses the point, which is that the healings were experienced as an incursion of otherworldly power:

> Historically, we must acknowledge that Jesus presented himself as a person through whom such power could and did operate, and that those around him experienced him as a channel for such power. The fact that the power was said to operate for healing is also significant, for it indicates what sort of spirit person Jesus was. The world knew, for instance, of spirit-empowered warriors or of prophets who could curse their opponents in ways that would bring affliction upon them. Such stories are not found in reliable sources for Jesus. (Powell, 106)

While the image of Jesus as sage has been a popular one in contemporary Jesus studies (see also Witherington, 1994), Borg's view that it is only one of several facets of "the kind of person Jesus was" is noteworthy. As Powell points out, for Borg, "it is but one expression of Jesus as a charismatic spirit person" (106). In addition, unlike Crossan and Mack, Borg does not appeal to the Cynics as an influence or analogy, but he does appeal to Buddha and Lao Tzu, seeing Jesus as similar to them "in that he proclaimed a way of transformation based on insight into how things truly are" (106). Of course, such appeals would not be based on historical influence, but on the characteristics of religion, viewed cross-culturally. This "way of transformation" involved questioning the conventional wisdom (or "what everybody knows") in the culture of his time. (Crossan, in *In Fragments* [1983], makes a similar argument, showing that Jesus' aphorisms challenge the proverbial wisdom of conventional belief.) If the conventional wisdom viewed reality as organized on the basis of rewards and punishment—life going well for those who do "right" and poorly for those who do "wrong"—Jesus, in Borg's view, challenged such conventional wisdom by pointing to a spiritual world of cosmic generosity: God feeds birds who do not labor and provides sun and rain for the crops of good and bad people alike. Borg concludes: "What distinguished [Jesus] from most of his contemporaries as well as from us, from their conventional wisdom as well as from ours, was his vivid sense that reality was ultimately gracious and compassionate" (106). This way of teaching was neither doctrinal nor ethical, but perceptual. Jesus invited his hearers to see differently and to live in accord with his vision.

From this vision, social and political change would be anticipated. Thus, the third feature of Borg's portrait of Jesus—the movement initiator—focuses on the implications of Jesus' alternative vision for the renewal and transformation of Israel. Because he views Jesus' calling of the twelve as "one of the most certain facts of Jesus' ministry" (sharing Sanders' position in this regard), and because he interprets this as a symbolic reconstruction of the twelve tribes of Israel, Borg sees Jesus as having had a specific commitment to Israel, one that sought to overcome the purity system of Jewish convention by challenging its penchant for strict boundaries and categorization. The distinctions that undergirded Jewish society—Jew and Gentile, man and woman, oldest son and younger siblings, and so forth—were inevitably hierarchical, "leading to a rigid mindset concerning what roles were appropriate for whom and what status should be assigned to people occupying those roles. Undergirding the whole system was the fundamental notion that holiness must be protected by *separation*" (107–8). By violating these boundaries and categories, the movement he initiated challenged the traditional social structure: "They demonstrated concern for the poor that went well beyond almsgiving to suggest commitment to radical redistribution of resources. They also spoke and acted in ways that counseled peaceful nonresistance to the Roman oppressors. They did all these things in a spirit of joyful celebration, claiming that true purity was internal" (108). The social implication of Jesus' teaching was that Israel should be an inclusive people, an egalitarian community.

The fourth feature of Borg's portrait of Jesus, the social prophet, is developed through analysis of the stories that depict Jesus in conflict with the various leaders of Israel. In these stories, Jesus speaks and acts in ways similar to the classical prophets of Israel. Like them, he perceived that Israel was confronted with a threat that presented an indictment of those responsible, and he summoned people to repentance. The threat was not the imminent end of the world, but the political destruction of Jerusalem and the temple. The only way such a catastrophe could be averted was if a new politics of compassion would replace the politics of holiness. Jesus' critique of the purity system was primarily aimed at ruling elites who were the beneficiaries of the holiness code. These included the wealthy landowners and the leaders of the temple cult. The question for Borg is the extent to which the peasants whom Jesus addressed also accepted this ideology. "Would peasants, for example, have viewed an untouchable as an untouchable?" Was this their conventional wisdom as well, and, if it was, would they have been as resistant to Jesus' prophetic vision as the ruling elites? Borg admits that this question is virtually impossible to answer with any certainty. As Powell puts it: "We cannot be sure whether Jesus the social prophet merely spoke aloud what many thought privately or whether he put into words a viewpoint most had never considered. Either way, he found an audience" (109).

Borg believes that Jesus' prophetic role caused his death. It involved two symbolic acts: The first was riding into Jerusalem on a donkey's colt, thus demonstrating that the society he envisioned was one of peace, not war. The second was overturning the money changers in the temple to protest "the sacred order of separation" that the sacrificial system of the temple cult represented. As a symbolic act, the disruption in the temple was "limited in area, intent, and duration, done for the sake of the message it conveyed" (109). What happened next is difficult to reconstruct, but Borg theorizes that some of the Jewish authorities in charge of the temple interrogated Jesus and then handed him over to Pilate, alleging that he was a political claimant. He was then charged with treason and executed as an insurrectionist. As an advocate of nonviolence, he did not pose a direct political threat, but he did present a threat to the social order, as the temple leaders and Pilate perhaps rightly discerned.

While Borg rejects the idea that Jesus prophesied an imminent end to the world, he did speak about "the kingdom of God," using this as a "tensive symbol," that is, "one with a number of nuances of meaning" (110). It may refer to the unseen world of spirit that coexists with the seen world, and Jesus may thus have believed in a final consummation, when the two worlds would be reunited at the end as they were unified at the creation of the world. But this does not mean that he believed in an imminent end to the world. Rather, he viewed Jerusalem and the temple as in danger of destruction. As far as the resurrection of Jesus is concerned, Borg affirms that the post-Easter Jesus is real, and not merely an article of belief. As Powell puts it: "The notion of resurrection implies that Jesus entered into another mode of being, that he is no longer limited by space and time, but is able to be present—as a living, experiential reality—with his followers in a new way" (110). This view does not require an empty tomb: "Borg admits that the empty tomb stories are relatively late and confused, but dismisses their significance for accepting the truth of the resurrection" (110).

Borg's portrait of Jesus has received positive response by many scholars because it has points in common with those of other scholars whose views have seemed irreconcilable. Powell notes: "The combined images of Jesus as healer and sage are similar to those that play heavily into Crossan's portrait, while the image of movement initiator parallels the work of Schüssler Fiorenza and that of social prophet echoes concerns important to Horsley. Even the characterization of Jesus as a charismatic spirit person resonates with contributions offered by Geza Vermes," who views Jesus as a Jewish holy man (Powell, 110). Thus, Borg's portrait is a bridge between those who emphasize the Hellenistic matrix for Jesus and downplay his eschatological teaching and those who emphasize the Jewish matrix and his eschatological views. Because he views Jesus as both very Jewish and noneschatological, however, Borg is subject to critique by those who consider these emphases irreconcilable.

Another criticism is that Borg tends to polarize holiness and compassion and thus ignores the source material, such as sayings on divorce and adultery, that indicates Jesus was concerned about maintaining purity in a moral sense. Along similar lines, others contend that the purity codes were not as oppressive as Borg makes them out to be, since they were considered voluntary. Only a small minority of Jews chose to maintain themselves in the relatively high state of purity expected of priests. Thus, his portrait is subject to criticism by those (Sanders, for example) who argue that the "politics of holiness" ascribed to first-century Palestinian Jews are Christian misrepresentations of Judaism. Because Sanders attributes such misrepresentations to the Lutheran theological tradition, the fact that Borg was Lutheran (although he is now Episcopal) might be used to account for his emphasis on the marked differences between the politics of holiness (law) and the vision of compassion (grace).

Other criticisms are that if Borg is willing to ascribe other Jewish religious types to Jesus, why not that of Messiah as well? Also, since he affirms that Jesus called God "Abba" (a personal form of "Father"), why does he deny that Jesus "identified himself as the Son of God in some specialized sense or that his teaching might have included reflection on the intimacy of his own (unique?) relationship to God?" (Powell, 112). Finally, if Jesus was unable to effect a change in society's core value from holiness to compassion, why would people have continued to care about him after his death? Would they not have viewed him as a failed movement initiator? Powell believes that Borg would respond to the latter criticism by appealing to the experience of Jesus after Easter. His followers would have understood that they were advancing his work by advocating and representing compassion in the world, both as an individual virtue and as the core value of his alternative wisdom, and his alternative social vision. They would also constitute themselves as a "community of memory that celebrates, nourishes, and embodies the new way of living that we see in Jesus" (Powell, 112).

On two of the issues that Borg's critics raise, I am inclined to agree, but for different reasons. The first is his tendency to set holiness and compassion against one another and thus to downplay the theme of holiness in Jesus' message. Given the evidence that Jesus manifested a concern for maintaining purity (at least in some respects), we might view the purity/compassion theme as reflecting a tension within Jesus himself, one that was coming to resolution at the time of his death. If he underwent baptism by John, this in itself would be indicative of a personal concern for holiness (or purity). Also, it appears that his disagreements with John, which may have been fundamental to his break with him, centered on how holiness was to be understood (i.e., as an external form such as fasting or as a reflection of one's underlying intentions).

Compassion, then, would be expressed toward those who could not claim to be pure or holy for social or legal reasons, who could not, in effect, clear their name no matter what they did. In my view, we should explore this issue as a matter of possible personal import for Jesus himself. Could it be that he viewed *himself* as one for whom the claim of holiness depended upon a compassionate God who would set aside the customary social and legal criteria for holiness? If so, holiness is not so much set aside as acquired outside the official religion.

I take a similar position regarding Jesus' identification of himself as Son of God. While I am persuaded by arguments (made by both Borg and Crossan) that the association of Jesus with "Son of man" sayings is not one that Jesus himself made, this does not rule out the possibility that he viewed himself as being God's son in some "specialized sense" (as Powell puts it) and that there was, therefore, a special sense of intimacy in his relationship to the Father. This view of his relationship to God—as an unusually personal one—may then have been the basis for later applications of "Son of man" sayings to him. This view would be consistent with the tendency of the scribal tradition (as noted by Crossan) to find scriptural conventions for things Jesus was remembered to have said and done. Crossan's view that Jesus was not schooled in these scriptural conventions, however, prompts me to ascribe these allusions to his sonship to more immediate, personal concerns. I explore these in chapter 6.

This leads to my own criticism of Borg's portrait. On the one hand, the most attractive feature of this portrait for the psychologist is his emphasis on the issue of personality, that is, his focus on the question of what kind of person Jesus was. In one sense, this enables him to build a bridge between biblical and psychological studies, for the study of personality is one of the more important subdisciplines of psychology. As Powell notes, however, Borg's understanding of personality is primarily informed by typologies of the religious personality as formulated by historians of religion, cultural anthropology, and psychology of religion. Such typologies can be found in Wach (1944), Weber (1963), Schoeps (1968), and various others. Each typology differs from the others, but common types include mystic, seer, shaman, magician, saint, martyr, sage, prophet, priest, and reformer. Such typologies are also found in psychology of religion, for example, William James's (1982) distinction between the saint and the mystic.

On the other hand, while Borg shows that Jesus fits several of these religious personality types, this does not necessarily mean that he thereby sheds light on Jesus' personality, psychologically understood. Erik H. Erikson, for example, views Luther and Gandhi as "*homo religiosus*" (Erikson, 1958, 261–63; 1969, 395–409) and ascribes to each the role of reformer, but this does not mean that such identifications of Luther and Gandhi as "reformer types" reveals much about their unique individuality. In a sense, the psychologist's work begins precisely where the historian of religion's work ends. Regarding Borg's portrait of Jesus, therefore, one would want to ask why Jesus came to identify with not one or two, but *four* religious personality types. If this is so, what does it tell us about him? While the integration of two religious personality types (e.g., mystic and sage) is not uncommon, that he seems to have embraced four types is certainly remarkable. This being so, one may attempt to explain it in terms of his own self-understanding, attribute it to the traditioning that occurred after his death, or some combination of the two. Given the role of traditioning in the case of other religious personalities— where they are conformed by their followers to preexisting religious types— we need to ask whether this has occurred in the case of Jesus as well. If so, one should not be surprised that Jesus can be shown to have "represented" so many of these types, in spite of the fact that his ministry was apparently of rather brief duration. In turn, this may mean that Borg's portrait of Jesus is based on something of a tautology. That is, he sees what the synoptic gospels want one to see, namely, that Jesus was a "complete" or "highly nuanced" religious leader, one who managed to balance, perhaps even reconcile, various contradictory elements in a society that, while Jewish, was also Hellenistic. Thus, in Borg's portrait, the question of the real identity of the historical Jesus is not so much answered as creatively avoided.

Sir Joshua Reynolds, the eighteenth-century painter, viewed historical painting as a higher artistic form than portraiture because the latter cannot aspire to "the ideal," since it depends on likeness to a particular individual. As Paul Barlow notes, for Reynolds,

> "An History-painter paints man in general; a Portrait-painter, a particular man, and consequently a defective model." If individuality is a "defect," portraiture can only elevate sitters by omitting some of the peculiarities of their appearance. "If a portrait painter is desirous to raise and improve his subject, he has no other means than by approaching it to a general idea." For Reynolds, then, the problem of portraiture lies in the *difference* between individual appearance and a "general idea." (Barlow, 1997, 224)

The "general idea" in Borg's case is the religious personality typology. By this means, he appears to have shown that Jesus overcame certain contradictions within Judaism itself (e.g., reconciling two religious types, such as sage and prophet, that are not easily reconcilable), and that he resolved certain conflicts within himself (i.e., by dealing with the problem of his own religious identity by adopting all the identities that were attractive to him). I acknowledge that a spirit-filled person may manifest many "gifts of the spirit." Nonetheless, I think that Borg is under some obligation to explain how Jesus managed to integrate within himself four identifiably different religious personality types, especially given the relative brevity of his public life.

Finally, it is noteworthy that Borg has a favorable view of psychology of religion and is especially appreciative of James's *The Varieties of Religious Experience.* As his discussion of James in *Jesus: A New Vision* indicates, he notes that James "finds the origin of belief in an 'unseen' world in the experience of 'religious geniuses' who experience *firsthand* the realities of which religion speaks, and carefully distinguishes this primal experience from what he calls 'secondhand' religion, the beliefs that people acquire through tradition" (Borg, 1987, 35, his emphasis). In *Meeting Jesus Again for the First Time* (1994b), he cites James's observation that we are only separated from this other reality "by filmy screens of consciousness. When these screens of consciousness momentarily drop away, the experience of Spirit occurs" (34). Borg's use of James is commendable, especially in light of the fact that biblical scholars generally hold psychologists and their theories at arm's length. It should be said, however, that James was not the kind of psychologist who sought to discern the personal issues, problems, or motivating factors that influence an individual to believe in an "unseen" world or prompt one to experience the "unseen world" in a particular manner or form. I suggest that the psychoanalytic tradition is in a better position to penetrate the conventional images that quickly grew up around Jesus and complicated the task of discerning his individuality, what Erik H. Erikson called his "sense of 'I'" (1981). As we will see in the following chapter, however, the psychoanalytic approach to historical figures has provoked considerable criticism.

Methodological
Considerations

PART TWO

3

The Case for Psychobiography

One of the striking features of Jesus research—and daunting for the non-expert—is the attention it gives to methodological matters. As our discussion of the four portraits in the previous chapters makes clear, methodological issues have had an extremely important influence on scholarly conclusions regarding Jesus. This concern for methodology distinguishes the genuine Jesus scholar from those who invoke Jesus in support of their own ideological viewpoints or who write novels about him. While no portrait of Jesus is based on methodological considerations alone, many of the debates and controversies within the field of Jesus research center on the judgments of individual scholars regarding methodological considerations. These include dating of sources, criteria for judging materials to be authentic, the use of comparative historical materials or analogues, the role that other disciplines are allowed to play in reconstructing the life of Jesus, and so forth.

One would like to claim that a comparable methodological sophistication has prevailed in the psychological study of historical figures, but this has not generally been the case. The field of psychobiography has lacked the methodological rigor characteristic of historical studies generally and, for this reason, has evoked a great deal of censure (Barzun, 1974; Stannard, 1980). A concern for improved methodology has emerged in recent years, however, and several important texts address this problem directly. William McKinley Runyan's work has been especially important (1984, 1988). This chapter reviews some of the methodological discussions in the field of psychobiography, thus demonstrating that many scholars presently engaged in psychobiography are aware of its methodological pitfalls and of ways in which these pitfalls may be minimized. I will especially consider those developments in psychobiographical theory and practice that have bearing on the psychological study of Jesus.

What, precisely, is psychobiography? In *Life Histories and Psychobiography: Explorations in Theory and Method* (1984), Runyan writes: "As a preliminary distinction, psychohistory can be divided into two main branches, that of psychobiography, dealing with the study of individuals, and group psychohistory, dealing with the psychological characteristics or formative experiences of groups such as the Nazi youth cohort, American slaves, or Hiroshima survivors" (200). Thus, psychobiography is a subdiscipline of psychohistory, which, broadly defined, is "the application of psychology to history" (200). Runyan notes, however, that a more precise definition of psychobiography is necessary. For example, Erik H. Erikson and others have argued that every biography includes the use of an implicit psychology, which raises the question whether all biography is therefore psychobiography. Runyan does not think so and therefore proposes that psychobiography is "the *explicit* use of formal or systematic psychology in biography" (201, my emphasis).

While psychobiography is usually traced, historically, to Sigmund Freud's *Leonardo da Vinci and a Memory of His Childhood* (1910/1957; see also Collins, 1997), Runyan emphasizes that it is not necessarily psychoanalytic. Rather, "works which employ psychoanalytic theory may be described as psychoanalytic psychobiography, which is a subdivision of psychobiography, along with behavioral psychobiography, or phenomenological psychobiography" (201). The view that it necessarily employs an "explicit personality theory" is also too restrictive, as this would exclude biographical studies that make use of social psychology, developmental psychology, and other branches of psychology. Moreover, it would exclude studies that make use of conceptual frameworks, typologies, or methods (such as content analysis, graphology, or personality assessment procedures) that do not make use of *theory* per se. Hence, Runyan's preference is for a broad definition of psychobiography as the "explicit use of formal or systematic psychology in biography."

Criticisms of Psychobiography

Runyan also notes that the "field of psychobiography is marked by considerable controversy over its methods, abuses, and accomplishments" (202). To explore the methodological status of the field, he focuses on a number of issues that have evoked the greatest controversy between psychobiography and its critics, and within the ranks of psychobiographers themselves.

The Problem of Inadequate Evidence

The first is the question of *inadequate evidence.* Runyan quotes T. Anderson's observation that "the historian's most serious objection to psychohistory is that sweeping declarations about actions or personalities are based on sparse evidence." He cites a review of a psychobiographical study of Adolf Hitler that alleges that some of its most important conclusions "are based on non-existent, unreliable, or misinterpreted evidence." A frequent charge against psychoanalytic psychobiography is that "you can't put the person on the couch," or, as historian Jacques Barzun puts it, everything that the psychobiographer "uses–his 'tools,' his 'method,' his 'data'–is indirect and necessarily scant: the patient is absent, and the clues he may have left to his once living psyche are the product of chance. Diaries, letters, literary work form a random record, in which expressions of mood are more frequent than evidence of actions...Compared to the volume of data elicited under therapy and consciously directed at relevance and completeness by the analyst, this trickle from written remains seems almost negligible" (Barzun, 1974, 46). Relatedly, there is the criticism that if childhood experience is especially influential, this is the very life period for which the psychobiographer is least likely to have adequate information. As one critic puts it: "Freudian psychology has not been of much use to the historian, who is usually unable to penetrate the bedroom, the bathroom, or the nursery. If Freud is right, and if these are the places where the action is, there is not much the historian can do about it" (Runyan, 1988, 203).

Runyan acknowledges that such allegations of insufficient evidence, evidence of the wrong kind, and not enough evidence from the most critical period (from the point of view of the theory itself) "need to be taken more seriously than they have been." He notes that "both Freud in his study of Leonardo, and Erikson in his analysis of Luther have been severely criticized for developing psychological interpretations from inadequate data about early experience" (1984, 203–4). Instead of abandoning the enterprise, however, he advises that attention is "best devoted to historical figures about whom there is sufficient evidence to develop and test psychological explanations," and, "in the absence of evidence about childhood experience, some types of early developmental explanations are best avoided, as psychological theory is often not sufficiently determinate to permit accurate retrodictions or reconstructions" (204). This, however, "in no way impairs the possibility of developing psychological interpretations of the many aspects of behavior and experience of historical individuals for which there is adequate evidence" (204).

Runyan also notes that the psychobiographer enjoys certain evidential advantages over the psychotherapist. One is that patients in psychotherapy may not have lived through important life experiences. Consequently, reactions to these experiences that may be revealing of personality are not available for interpretation. By contrast, in psychobiography the development and mid-stages of the subject's life are available for inspection, as are its ultimate unfolding and final resolution. A second is that the psychobiographer is not limited to information derived from the subject alone, but is able to draw on outside sources. Thus, one is "able to learn how a variety of other informants perceived the situations the subject was in, and their reactions to the individual's personality" (205). A third is that, if the subject is a literary or creative person, one has a wealth of creative material that often expresses inner psychological states and conflicts. These may, with caution, be drawn upon in interpretation of the subject's personality. Many creative individuals have been more articulately expressive of their inner states and experiences than the typical therapy patient. A fourth advantage is that there are sometimes substitutes for a person's dreams or free associations. Runyan cites a study that analyzes Theodore Roosevelt's drawings and caricatures in adolescence, which portray himself and family members turning into animals. Freud originated this approach, as he made use of Da Vinci's notebook sketches and paintings in the analysis of his conflicts relating to his illegitimate birth, his separation from his birth mother due to his father's marriage to another woman, and the fact that he was the only one of his father's eleven sons to be excluded from his father's will. A fifth advantage is that the evidence used in psychobiography is available to others, so that original interpretations may be critically examined and alternatives proposed and tested. This contrasts with psychotherapy, where the data are typically unavailable to the public, making it less likely that such a corrective process will take place.

Of course, these advantages need to be weighed against the advantages that accrue from personal, face-to-face involvement with the patient, a model that Erikson adapted to his second major psychobiographical study, *Gandhi's Truth* (1969), by talking directly with Gandhi's adversaries in order to gain personal impressions of what Gandhi was up against and what sorts of reactions he would have elicited from these others. These are not, however, insignificant advantages. At the very least, they enable the psychobiographer to counter the argument that psychobiography is automatically precluded because one is unable to put the subject on the couch. As Alexander and Juliette George point out in their study of Woodrow Wilson (1964), psychoanalysis is a long process because the objective is therapeutic change. Most often, diagnoses are formulated in the first two or three sessions. The psychobiographer usually has far more material from which to make such a diagnosis than is gathered in these initial sessions. Thus, the fact that one cannot put the subject on the couch is a rather weak objection to psychobiography.

The Problem of Reconstruction

A second controversial issue concerns reconstruction. While all historical work involves reconstruction, the special problem that concerns Runyan is the use of psychoanalytic theory to reconstruct or postdict what must have happened in childhood. He cites psychoanalyst Phyllis Greenacre's comment, in her study of Jonathan Swift and Lewis Carroll, that childhood experiences can be "reconstructed from known characteristics, problems, and repetitive actions supported by memory traces," and that "the experienced psychoanalyst knows just as definitely as the internist observing later sequelae of tuberculosis…that the deformity is the result of specific acts upon the growing organism" (206). Such reconstructions, however, have not gone uncriticized, "even when executed with considerable sophistication." Runyan cites criticisms of Erikson for reconstructing Luther's relationship to his mother on the basis of adult behavior. As one critic put it: "In his study of the young Luther, Erikson literally invents little Martin's relationship to his mother, using as a basis (as a 'document') the behavior of Luther the man…Erikson does not interpret a repetitive behavior on young Luther's part in terms of an unconscious dynamic; he jumps from a presumed characteristic of the Reformer to the inferential reconstruction of essential data about the latter's family environment" (206). As Erikson's reconstruction of Luther's relationship to his mother has bearing on my own interpretation of Jesus, I will return to this criticism later in this chapter.

Runyan notes, somewhat wryly, that psychobiographers have not gone to the exteme of hagiographers, who have sometimes reconstructed entire lives on the basis of nonexistent information. He cites the case of Bishop Agnellos of Ravenna in the ninth century, who wrote a series of lives of his predecessors. Agnellos confessed that in some instances, "in order that there might not be a break in the series, I have composed the life myself, with the help of God and the prayers of the brethren" (206). Still, Runyan is troubled by those psychobiographers who retrodict an earlier event and then, assuming that it is firmly established, use it as basis for inferences about other matters. He decries such abuses of retrodiction. On the other hand, he cites the argument of J. Cody, author of a psychobiographical study of Emily Dickinson, that a paleontologist reconstructs the scattered bones of a fossil skeleton according to the laws of comparative anatomy, and the engineer assembles the shattered metal of an aircraft that has exploded in flight according to its known dimensions: "In either example, what provides the gestalt and guides the interpretation placed on each discrete particle is a body of general knowledge—the laws of bone structure in the one case, the structure or blueprints in the other" (207). He argues, therefore, that "psychoanalytic theory has discovered conflicts and motives believed to be operative to some degree in all lives, and that when many pieces of evidence are available the theory can sometimes be used to perceive the relationships among the authentic bits of evidence, and to make inferences about the rough structure of missing pieces of evidence. This is equivalent to making plaster bones in reconstructing a fossil skeleton" (207). In his own study of Dickinson, Cody assumes that Emily experienced a cruel rejection by her mother early in life, because "many of her statements, her choice of certain recurring metaphors and symbols, and the entire course of her life, viewed psychoanalytically, argue for the truth of this assumption" (207–8). Of course, the crucial qualifier in this case is that "many pieces of evidence are available." The issue for any use of such retrodiction in the case of Jesus is whether there is enough evidence to justify or warrant any use of this procedure. If few bones remain, the use of a single plaster bone may change—and distort—the entire configuration.

In short, Runyan issues a strong cautionary note regarding the procedure of retrodiction, emphasizing that it is risky and in some cases unjustifiable. In light of the uncertainties of developmental theory, the lack of empirical support for psychoanalytic genetic theory, and the multiple possible processes leading to any given outcome, the case for excluding such retrodictions altogether is a very strong one. If retrodiction is to be practiced, however, the reconstructions should at least be clearly labeled as such and distinguished from events for which there is documentary evidence (208).

The Problem of Reductionism

A third charge frequently leveled against psychobiography is that of reductionism. One form of this critique is that psychological factors are overemphasized at the expense of external social and historical factors. Another is that psychobiography focuses excessively on psychopathological processes and gives insufficient attention to normality and creativity. In the early history of psychobiography, such works were sometimes called "pathographies," thus emphasizing their concern with abnormal psychology and betraying a personal or ideological bias against the subject who had the dubious distinction of being selected for study. A third type of reductionism is to explain adult character and behavior exclusively in terms of early childhood experience while neglecting later formative processes and influences. As one critic observes, "What is chiefly wrong with the conventional psychoanalytic biography is its crude unilateralism. It suggests a one-to-one relationship, arguing that the protagonist did this or that because of some painful experience in childhood" (209). Runyan notes that Erikson identified this form of reductionism as "originology," or "the habitual effort to find the 'causes' of a person's whole development in his or her childhood conflicts" (209). Two other reductive fallacies are "the critical period fallacy," which attempts to build a study of a person's life around a certain "key" period of development, and "eventism," or discerning in some important episode in the subject's life the prototype of all subsequent behavior and/or *the* turning point in life from which all subsequent events derive. These oversimplifications impose an unnatural order, shape, and direction on the often amorphous and fitful course of a human life, even one that exhibits considerable purposefulness and intentionality.

Runyan does not dispute the claim that too many psychobiographies have suffered from one or more of these flaws, but he also notes that a number of contemporary psychobiographers have been aware of such dangers and are avoiding them by integrating the psychological with the social and historical by analyzing not just pathology, but also strengths and adaptive capacities, and by studying formative influences not just in childhood but throughout the life span. It may also be noted that many standard biographies are also prone to similar reductionistic fallacies. These are not unique to psychobiography.

The Relationship of Childhood Experience and Adult Behavior

We have already addressed the relationship of childhood experience to adult behavior in our discussion of reconstruction and reductionism. Additional criticisms have been issued from within the field of psychology, however, such as by those who represent more recent developments in psychoanalytic theory that provide more complex ways of analyzing childhood experience. Others argue that the effects of early deprivation may be substantially modified by later experience and therefore contend that early experience, of whatever nature or form, rarely has a direct impact on adult personality. Rather, early experience shapes early personality, which influences the kinds of later environments one is likely to encounter, which in turn influence later experience, which affects personality, and so on in a complex interactive cycle.

Furthermore, the causal structure of the life course is such that there are usually a variety of alternative paths or processes leading to a given outcome (212). Runyan cites Erikson's work on the life cycle as influential in this regard:

> The study of formative influences throughout the life cycle makes analysis more complicated, but it also has certain advantages for psychobiography in that early childhood experience, for which evidence is frequently unavailable, is no longer so predominantly important... One of the advantages of Eriksonian theory, in which character and identity are importantly shaped at later ages, is that the psychobiographer is more likely to have usable evidence in this period of the subject's life. (213)

An important feature of Erikson's theory of development and growth is that the individual is not only in a reactive position, responding to past experiences, but is also making decisions in anticipation of the future and is therefore being "drawn" by the future, by events and experiences that are yet to emerge.

In support of this more interactive and less unicausal and unilateral approach, F. Crosby and T. L. Crosby applied a quantitative rating system to seventy-nine books and articles in political psychobiography and, in light of their criteria (adequacy of evidence, consideration of plausible rival hypotheses, reference to relevant theoretical and empirical literature, etc.), they found that studies focusing on "coherent whole" or "pattern explanations" of adult behavior met these criteria better than those relying on causal explanations via childhood experiences.

Trans-Historical and Cross-Cultural Generality in Psychological Theory

Psychobiographers are often criticized for applying a parochial psychological theory to individuals of other cultures and historical periods. This criticism was voiced by historian Lucien Febvre in 1938: "How can we as historians make use of psychology which is the product of observation carried out on twentieth-century man, in order to interpret the actions of the man of the past?" (Runyan, 1984, 215). As a recent critic of psychohistory has argued: "The psychohistorian employs theoretical models and cognitive assumptions created from the material of the present—and then imposes them on the past. In so doing, he or she must assume that in most fundamental ways all people, at all places, at all times, have viewed themselves and the world about them in substantially the same fashion." Thus, paradoxically, psychohistory is ahistorical: "Perhaps the single most important achievement of modern historical thinking has been the growing recognition that life in the past was marked by a fundamental social and cognitive differentness from that prevailing in our own time" (215–16).

What is the validity of such criticisms? Runyan acknowledges that psychobiographers have at times been unaware of such cultural and historical differences. He contends, however, that this is a problem for all biographical writing and is not, at least in principle, insurmountable. He proposes several steps that the psychobiographer may take to moderate the problem. First, the psychobiographer must learn enough about the subject's social and historical context to have an adequate frame of reference for interpreting the meaning of specific actions, statements, and practices. Second, the study of relevant comparison groups and of local contexts within the subject's social and historical world may help in developing understandings of the individual. Such study assists the psychobiographer in differentiating the subject from others in the same social and historical context (216). Runyan recommends abandoning the attempt to discover the "uniqueness" of the subject in the strict sense of "different from all others," focusing on that which is "particular or specific to the individual (which may or may not be shared with others)" (174). In this way, one avoids the problem of having to identify characteristics or experiences that are "very rare or uncommon." Instead, the psychobiographer is content with a more flexible definition of individuality and thus with identifying aspects of the subject's personality, situation, and experience that are "relatively rare or relatively uncommon, and, on occasion, perhaps even unique" (174–75).

In support, Runyan introduces a formula by sociologist Clyde Kluckhohn and psychologist Henry Murray that says that persons are like *all* others in some ways, like *some* others in other ways, and like *no* others in still other ways. This suggests that at least some psychological conceptualizations or theories will hold universally. On the other hand, one cannot afford to ignore the context-boundedness of many psychological theories, and one needs, as a psychobiographer, to examine closely what aspects of one's psychological conceptualizations and theories are applicable to the culture or historical era to which the subject belongs:

> In short, errors have sometimes been made in naively assuming that psychoanalytic or other psychological theory could automatically be applied to individuals in any cultural or historical setting, but this does not at all mean that psychohistory does not work or cannot work. Rather, psychobiographical interpretation is a complex three-tiered intellectual enterprise which needs to draw not just on those theories which hold universally, but also on group and context-specific generalizations and on idiographic studies [that is, ones that seek to identify the individuality or sui generis qualities] of the particular individual. (217)

The Place of Psychoanalytic Theory in Psychobiography

As noted earlier, psychoanalytic theory has been of preeminent importance in psychobiography. The early psychobiographers were psychoanalysts who viewed this field as applied psychoanalysis. As a consequence, "the psychobiographical enterprise is still predominantly psychodynamic" (Runyan, 1984, 217). Even though psychobiography is now often defined more broadly to recognize the contributions and validity of other psychological theories and approaches, many believe that psychoanalysis remains the theory of choice. As Peter Loewenberg argues, psychoanalysis is preferred because it is a historical theory of development and "is also concerned with the complexity of emotions and motivations while behavioral psychology is not, making psychoanalysis applicable to a wider range of complex historical phenomena than any other theory" (Runyan, 1988, 218). What troubles Runyan about psychoanalysis as the primary methodology for psychobiography, however, is that its advocates tend "to compare psychobiographical methodology to psychoanalytic treatment, with the implication that the latter is to be approached as closely as possible" (218). He argues, instead, that "rather than taking the therapeutic situation as a methodological ideal…the clinical encounter needs to be placed into a larger epistemological context and to be seen as one among many research methods, each with its own strengths and weaknesses" (219).

On the other hand, there must be a reason why psychoanalysis continues to be the most widely employed approach in psychobiography. Given the criticisms that have been launched against it, one has to wonder why it continues to be the theory of choice. One possible reason, in Runyan's view, is that psychoanalytic theory has a special relevance to the kinds of explanatory and interpretive problems encountered in psychobiography. This is because it seems effective in explaining just those kinds of "odd or unconventional patterns of behavior that the psychobiographer feels are most in need of explanation" (1984, 220). Another is that psychoanalysis provides a set of conceptual tools that are flexible enough to be used to construct interpretations of a wide range of particular patterns of individual behavior: "This characteristic of the theoretical system may be a liability for some theory-testing purposes, but a virtue for interpretive purposes" (221). Still another is that psychoanalytic theory satisfies a need to find pattern or meaning, though sometimes such patterns can be found in biographical material even where none actually exist, or at least not the ones suggested by the theory. Finally, it may be that "psychodynamic theory is profoundly true in some ways, not necessarily all of it, but at least parts of it. Perhaps working intensely with biographical data leads writers to find that psychoanalytic theory repeatedly proves itself more illuminating or more useful than any other body of psychological theory" (221).

Runyan concludes that psychoanalytic theory needs to be used selectively, avoiding those aspects that accumulating evidence suggests are incorrect, and considering its implications in a self-critical manner. One way to develop such a self-critical stance is to become knowledgeable about other theories and approaches that may have an equally strong heuristic claim on the discipline. With this in mind, he identifies other approaches to psychobiography that have demonstrated particular promise. One is behavioral theory, which has been used by P. T. Mountjoy and M. L. Sundberg to argue that Benjamin Franklin's efforts to arrive at moral perfection may be viewed as an early example of behavioral self-management. Another is the use of trait-factor and psychometric methods, as in Kenneth Craik's application of standard personality assessment procedures such as the adjective check list, trait-rating scales, and Q-sort personality descriptions to Adolf Hitler and to Woodrow Wilson and other U.S. Presidents. Social psychology, especially the use of theories of social perception and cognition, has proven valuable in the study of political leaders. Perhaps the most promising of all alternative approaches, however, is developmental psychology, "which is concerned with the description and explanation of changes in behavior and psychological structures" (226).

To be sure, Erikson's work in psychobiography indicates that there is often a considerable overlap between psychoanalytic and developmental approaches. Runyan notes, however, the use of Piagetian concepts in H. E. Gruber's study of intellectual growth and change in the career of Charles Darwin. Another theoretical framework that appears potentially promising for psychobiographical purposes is Daniel Levinson's theory of adult development (1978). While this theory has various psychoanalytic elements, it is quite eclectic, employing, for example, C. G. Jung's theory of individuation to provide theoretical support for the "midlife transition." Employing Levinson's concept of the mentor, B. Kellerman examined two important mentoring relationships in the career of Willy Brandt before he became Chancellor of West Germany (Runyan, 1984, 227). This aspect of Levinson's theory, however, may have been derived from Erikson's *Young Man Luther*, which explicitly identifies Dr. Von Staupitz as "Martin's spiritual mentor" (1958, 17).

While nonpsychoanalytic psychobiography exists, Runyan concludes that it is scattered and disorganized, appearing in discrete bits and pieces, and has not developed anything like the cumulative tradition of psychoanalytic psychobiography. At present, there appears to be no serious contender on the horizon to threaten the position of psychoanalysis as the dominant theoretical orientation in the field (1984, 230).

A Three-Tiered Intellectual Enterprise

Finally, Runyan proposes that psychobiographical interpretation is a complex, three-tiered intellectual enterprise that needs to draw not only on those theories that appear to hold universally, but also on group and context-specific generalization, and on the specific features of the biographical subject. As this proposal occurs within his discussion of "trans-historical and cross-cultural generality in psychological theory," the implication is that psychoanalytic psychobiography gives inadequate attention to the middle tier, the issue of the subject's likeness to *some* others.

This charge is often expressed as the "great man fallacy," where the subject is represented to be utterly unlike those with whom he could, in fact, be reliably compared. Another version of the charge is that the psychobiographer tends to neglect the various social-cultural groups and processes that have had impact on the subject's life. The division of the discipline of psychohistory into psychobiography and the psychological study of groups has contributed to this problem. While this division has served certain definitional purposes, helping to clarify methodological differences between psychobiography on the one hand and the psychology of groups on the other, it makes the branch of psychobiography especially vulnerable to the criticism that its practitioners have seemed unaware of cultural and historical differences. In his discussion of the case study method, Runyan points out, following the work of D. B. Bromley, that "the person must be seen in an 'ecological context'; that is to say, a full account must be given of the objects, persons and events in his physical, social and symbolic environment," and that the "proper focus of a case-study is not so much a 'person' as a 'person in a situation'" (1984, 162). In effect, this "person in a situation" focus creates a bridge between psychobiography and psychohistory (the subject of chapter 4).

When Is Retrodiction Warranted?

Several issues that Runyan raises in his survey of criticisms of psychobiography have particular relevance to the psychobiographical study of Jesus. Two that I want to explore in more depth are retrodiction and the use of childhood experiences to interpret adult behavior. I will illustrate these two issues with Erikson's study of Luther and Richard Bushman's study of Benjamin Franklin. As we have seen, retrodiction is the positing of childhood events or relationships on the basis of what is known about an individual as an adult. As noted earlier, Erikson was criticized for his retrodictive construction of Luther's early "relationship" to his mother. I would like to examine this example in some detail, as this will provide certain guidelines—or criteria—for its use. My purpose is not to make a case for regular or indiscriminate use of retrodiction, but rather to indicate defensible grounds for its selective use. My point will be that Erikson feels justified in doing so because he views Luther as being like *some* other persons (Kluckhohn and Murray's category "b").

The paragraphs in question occur in Erikson's chapter in *Young Man Luther* titled "Obedience—To Whom?" in a section in which he provides a description of Luther's family of origin. He mentions Luther's later story, recorded in *Table Talk*, about how Luther's mother whipped him for stealing a nut—"until the blood came"—and Luther's wry observation that such discipline "drove him into monkery," an action that was "against the wishes of my father, of my mother, of God, and of the Devil" (Erikson, 1958, 71). Apart from this single reference to Luther's interactions with his mother as a child, Erikson notes that biographical texts report that "of Luther's mother we know little." There is Luther's "mention that some of her children 'cried themselves to death,' which may have been one of his after-dinner exaggerations; and at any rate, what he was talking about then was only that his mother had considered these children to have been bewitched by a neighbor woman" (72). There is also an indication that, whereas Luther's father was "suspicious toward the universe," his mother

> was more interested in the imaginative aspects of superstition. It may well be, then, that from his mother Luther received a more pleasurable and more sensual attitude toward nature, and a more simply integrated kind of mysticism, such as he later found described by certain mystics. It has been surmised that the mother suffered under the father's personality, and gradually became embittered; and there is also a suggestion that a certain sad isolation which characterized young Luther was to be found also in his mother, who is said to have sung to him a ditty: "For me and you nobody cares. That is our common fault." (72)

These quotations from *Young Man Luther* are filled with qualified, even ambiguous language—"may have been," "sources suggest," "it may well be," "it has been surmised," "there is a suggestion." Thus, it is not surprising that Erikson begins the next paragraph, which still concerns Luther's mother, with the comment: "A big gap exists here, which only conjecture could fill." He continues:

> But instead of conjecturing half-heartedly, I will state, as a clinician's judgment, that nobody could speak and sing of heaven as Luther later did if his mother's voice had not sung to him of some heaven; that nobody could be as torn between his masculine and his feminine sides, nor have such a range of both, who did not at some time feel that he was like his mother; but also, that nobody would discuss women and marriage in the way he often did who had not been deeply disappointed by his mother—and had become loath to succumb the way she did to the father, to fate. (72–73)

Thus far, Erikson has centered on interpersonal and intrapersonal matters quite familiar to a "clinician." In this sense he is drawing on his professional expertise (much like the paleontologist reconstructing a skeleton). But he continues: "And if the soul is man's most bisexual part, then we will be prepared to find in Luther both some horror of mystic succumbing and some spiritual search for it, and to recognize in this alternative some emotional and spritual derivatives of little Martin's 'pre-historic' relation to his mother" (73). In this statement, Erikson clearly goes beyond his areas of clinical expertise and makes inferences that we would expect from an expert in religious studies. Even so, one doubts that such an expert would associate Luther's "horror of mystic succumbing" and "spiritual search for it" with "little Martin's 'pre-historic' relation to his mother."

When faced with such a glaring case of retrodiction, based on the flimsiest of empirical evidence, Erikson's own psychoanalytic colleagues may well be inclined to accuse him of projection, that is, of having created Luther's relationship to his mother out of Erikson's understanding of *his* relationship to *his* mother. On the basis of what is known about Erikson's early relationship to his mother (Erikson, 1975, 26–28; see also Friedman, 1999), one may indeed argue that these statements, attributed to his "clinical judgment," derive from his own childhood experience. In itself, however, this does not constitute a decisive argument for or against this use of retrodiction. As I see it, Erikson offers three arguments in support of its use. The first is that he has seen other men in the clinical setting and is drawing on their recollections of their early childhood relationships with their mothers in support of his clinical judgment about Luther. One problem with this argument, however, is that the reader is not told anything about these other men (clinical materials are not publicly available), so we do not know how valid such comparisons to Luther might be. Did Erikson have other patients whose experience would not support this view of Luther and his mother? On what grounds, then, does he draw on his experience of some patients and not others in the absence of "data" or "facts" about Luther's early childhood? In my view, this is Erikson's weakest argument for engaging in this retrodiction. At the very least, it takes inadequate account of the criticism that psychoanalytic biography claims a trans-historical perspective.

The second argument draws on what is known about the adult Luther (his musicality, his denunciations of women and marriage, etc.) and retrospectively applies these to his relationship to his mother. This is the form of retrodiction that Runyan addresses in his discussion of the problem. It is expressed in the charge that Erikson "jumps from a presumed characteristic of the Reformer to the inferential reconstruction of essential data about the Luthers' family environment." In effect, this is an implied criticism of psychoanalytic theory itself, for psychoanalysis is a theory that assumes that "traces" of an individual's childhood may be discerned in subsequent adult characteristics. Because it calls the very essence of psychoanalysis into question, this criticism, as stated, is difficult to counter. A better way to state it, however, would be to say that Erikson has not provided sufficient evidence to support his association of Luther's adult characteristics and his construction of Luther's relationship to his mother in early childhood. Yet, later in the book, he provides more evidence. This occurs in his discussion of Luther's objections to "the Madonna's mediation in the popular scheme of religion" (121). He suggests that Luther's attitude toward Mary, especially his doubts that she is able to save him, relates to his struggle for life in early childhood and conveys an implicit blaming of his own mother for the deaths of his siblings (and corresponding rejection of his mother's defense that the children were bewitched by a neighbor woman). Of course, Erikson could be mistaken in his view that Luther associates Mary with his own mother, but this association counts for him as supporting evidence for his retrodictive construction of Luther's relationship to his mother in early childhood. Historian Roland Bainton challenges this association; but then, he also rejects Erikson's portrayal of Luther's mother (1971, 454–60).

Erikson's third argument in support of this retrodiction is implied in the second one but is not actually articulated until the epilogue to *Young Man Luther*. It occurs in a discussion of the "integrity crisis," which comes "last in the lives of ordinary men" but is "a life-long and chronic crisis in a *homo religiosus*" (Erikson, 1958, 261), for existential concerns are the very core of such a one's identity. He devotes several paragraphs to a description of *homo religiosus*, noting, for example, that

> he is always older, or in early years suddenly becomes older, than his playmates or even his parents and teachers, and focuses in a precocious way on what it takes others a lifetime to gain a mere inkling of: the questions of how to escape corruption in living and how in death to give meaning to life. Because he experiences a breakthrough to the last problems so early in his life maybe such a man had better become a martyr and seal his message with an early death; or else become a hermit in a solitude which anticipates the Beyond. We know little of Jesus of Nazareth as a young man, but we certainly cannot even begin to imagine him as middle-aged. (261)

Thus, "No wonder that [*homo religiousus*] is something of an old man (a *philosophus*, and a sad one) when his age-mates are young, or that he remains something of a child when they age with finality" (261–62). Thus, the theme of sadness, which first appeared in Erikson's association of Luther's "sad isolation" with a corresponding sadness in his mother, reappears in his description of *homo religiosus*. His reconstruction of Luther's relationship to his mother in early childhood is based, therefore, on his judgment that Luther belonged (with others for whom existential concerns are self-defining) in a group of individuals known as *homo religiosus*. Central to this retrodiction is the belief that those who belong in this group shared a similar "pre-historic" relation with *their* mothers. If this reasoning sounds circular, it is. It is also, however, a testable hypothesis, and one that I will explore later in my own discussion of Jesus.

Significantly, Erikson's use of retrodiction has also enabled him to address, implicitly, a form of the charge of reductionism that theologians often raise, that is, that psychologists "reduce" the religious (or spiritual) to psychodynamic processes. This criticism seems to have informed Roland Bainton's contention that "Luther's theological development might have been just the same if he had been left an orphan in infancy" (1959, 410). Erikson disagrees, for he believes that he has identified a common link between those who have become *homo religiosus* in their adult lives, namely, a "pre-historic" relation to their mothers similar to the one he attributes to "little Martin" Luther. Thus, if his retrodiction is based on Luther's similarity to *some* others, this is not other men seen in therapy, but other men who are also *homo religiosus*. My question is whether Jesus, also a *homo religiosus*, had a similarly vexed childhood relationship to his mother. Is such a supposition consistent with what is known about the adult Jesus? Because the mother in this case *is* Mary, our task is somewhat simplified, as it is unnecessary to make the psychodynamic association that Erikson needs to make between Luther's adult views of Mary and his childhood experience of his own mother.

Childhood Experience and Adult Behavior

As Runyan notes, one of the most complex and difficult issues in psychobiography is that of assessing the influence of childhood experience on adult character and behavior. A seismic shift has occurred in recent years from a simple, unicausal model to a "growing belief that the effects of early deprivation can be substantially modified by later experience and that behavior and personality are shaped and changed throughout the life course" (1984, 211). Thus, "the argument is not that early childhood experiences have no effects, but rather that the effects of such experiences are mediated by intervening experiences and contingencies" (211–12). Runyan's use of "early deprivation" to illustrate the point is noteworthy, having relevance to the preceding discussion of Erikson's *Luther* and to Richard L. Bushman's psychobiographical study of "conflict and conciliation" in the life of Benjamin Franklin (1966). Bushman's is a sophisticated exploration into the relationship of childhood experience and adult character and behavior, one that avoids the criticism that psychobiographers make unwarranted, simplistic connections between childhood and adulthood. This study illustrates Runyan's point that "if evidence on early experience is available, the effects of such experience ought not be applied directly to adult personality, but rather traced through a sequence of intervening stages and processes" (212).

A specialist in colonial American history, Bushman acknowledges that many historians manifest "considerable reluctance about embracing psychology or even accepting work where psychological considerations are evident. Few are prepared to assimilate psychology in the way that many anthropologists accepted psychoanalysis in the 1930s" (Bushman, 225). He cites several of the same problems that Runyan summarizes. What he finds promising, however, is the fact that Erik Erikson "has argued that early crises shape susceptibilities which develop into fixed patterns of widely differing form depending on the quality of life" (227). While this viewpoint forces the historian to relinquish hopes "for a handbook of single, simple causes of human conduct," it offers a more promising prospect:

> While less helpful in offering crisp diagnoses, psychology may be more helpful than expected in discovering a person's—or a group's—characteristic patterns of acting. Sometimes the historian himself notices the pattern before consulting the psychology book, but often he cannot; finding the pattern may be the most difficult part and the place where personality theory can be of greatest aid. Psychology sensitizes the researcher to new connections and draws into a pattern data normally regarded as insignificant. This may be its most important contribution, and one that is verifiable by historical criteria. (227)

Bushman notes that psychological theory raises a number of questions one might not normally think to ask. For example, how does the subject characteristically respond to authority? Does the subject perceive it as helpful and friendly, as cruel and domineering, or as distant and uninterested? Does the subject react to control by submitting, rebelling, reasoning, or pandering to authority? Such questions may also be asked about relations with equals or with persons over whom the subject exercises authority. They may be asked about the subject's perception and reactions to intimacy or to a whole range of emotions. He notes: "Merely pursuing the questions will often disclose patterns; knowledge of certain observed psychological syndromes will suggest others...The patterns may be very simple, or they may be more complex; but they can be verified and made relevant to historical concerns" (228). On the other hand, this search for patterns is not unique to psychobiography, for "every biographer looks for patterns that help explain his subject's life. Familiarity instills a more or less vague sense of a characteristic style. The problem is to crystallize these feelings into clear propositions which illuminate a large number of specific events" (229).

Bushman recommends beginning with an episode that appears representative, noting that it may be necessary to try several episodes before the outlines of a pattern begin to appear. For his brief psychobiographical study of Benjamin Franklin, he chooses an episode recounted in Franklin's *Autobiography*. Sixteen-year-old Franklin was apprenticed at the time to his brother. His brother, although married, did not keep house, but boarded himself and his apprentices with another family. The episode in question began when Franklin happened onto a book that recommended a vegetable diet. He decided to try it out. His refusal to eat meat, however, created an inconvenience in the household where he was staying and provoked comments about his "singularity." In response, he learned how to cook vegetarian meals, and then proposed to his brother that if he would give Franklin half the money he paid for his board, Franklin would board himself, a proposal to which his brother immediately agreed. Franklin found that he could save half of what his brother gave him for food, which provided additional funds for books. Another advantage of the arrangement was that he could remain at the printing house when his brother and the other apprentices went to their meals, and he could eat a light meal that, together with the quietude, gave him a "clearness of head" for study. As Bushman notes, in addition to the other advantages this arrangement afforded, Franklin gained "a modest triumph over his brother," since he was also learning while his brother and the others spent time eating. The pattern revealed by this episode may be summarized as follows:

1. Franklin had a dispute over his singular ways of eating.
2. He withdrew from the situation of dispute and made himself independent by developing a skill and striking a mutually advantageous bargain.
3. He thereby obtained compensation in various forms and gained an implicit sense of triumph over the person with whom he had struck the mutually advantageous bargain.

Does the formulation of the pattern need to include the specific fact that the dispute concerned Franklin's "singular ways of eating"? Couldn't one simply note that he "had a dispute"? Bushman says no. The details are important because "Franklin had an incredible memory for what he was fed, so diet may turn out to be important. Its singularity remains for the same reason. Franklin often operated as a lone wolf standing against the common opinion" (231). Throughout his autobiography, he emphasizes the skills he developed independently and their relationship to his ability to make mutually advantageous bargains.

While this construction of a pattern in Franklin's way of relating to others seems rather straightforward, Bushman notes that "psychological notions have already influenced the analysis." How so? "The idea of a compensating skill is psychoanalytic, and the notion of withdrawal was suggested by Erik Erikson's conception of personality vectors" (231). Still, the pattern requires fuller development, and this means relating it to the more general structure of which it is one particular. For this, Bushman turns to "psychoanalytic conceptions about the formation of character in childhood," and, more specifically, to a stage of development that contains "emotional meanings" similar to those reflected in the reported episode. Drawing on Erikson's discussion in *Childhood and Society* (1963) of the mother-infant relationship, he writes:

> In the early months of life, a baby derives the most blissful satisfaction from nursing at its mother's breast. The combination of warmth, love, food, and pleasant sucking sensations impart a sense of perfect peace and union with its universe. The eruption of teeth disturbs this bliss, causing pain in the very place where pleasure previously centered. Teeth also disrupt the peaceful relation with the mother, for in biting to relieve its pain, the infant hurts the mother and causes her withdrawal. Erikson reports that clinical experience shows this situation to be the origin of a dilemma: the yearning to bite conflicts with the yearning for nourishment and for the continuation of blissful well-being. The child must restrain the urge to bite and learn to obtain food without hurting. Its feelings are overshadowed by the anxiety of being responsible for the destruction of the happy union with the mother. (232)

All of this is forgotten, but "for those especially affected by this crisis the problem of getting without hurting continues into adult life. The meaning of food expands to include all sustenance for the ego, praise or approval or love, which makes a person feel pleased with himself and accepted in the world" (232). The question, how to get these ego supplies without hurting, becomes a continuing one: "Time after time he construes experience in terms of this body language and worries about his own responsibility for cutting off the source of supply" (232).

Bushman notes that one cannot rely on a single element in the episode for reconstructing Franklin's adult personality, for "any given fact can have various interpretations in a psychoanalytic system" (233). A vegetarian diet, for example, could signify fear of "being polluted by corrupt substances" rather than fear of hurting another (233). Therefore, "the appropriate analytical structure must correspond to a whole pattern of responses. In this instance, the concern about food, the discomfiture of the provider, and the effort to obtain compensatory rewards without hurting one another all seemed to fit. Throughout [the autobiography], giving and getting are prominent moral issues" (233).

This introduction of the psychoanalytic structure leads to a reformulation of the pattern as follows:

1. Franklin was concerned about how to get supplies. His point in the vegetarian episode and in virtually all that follows was that his methods of seeking gratification invariably brought rewards. Throughout his autobiography, this quest is assumed to be basic.

2. He feared that he would hurt others in the process of getting supplies and therefore avoided hostilities. Psychoanalytic theory says that a person may unconsciously enjoy the sadistic pleasure of hurting and may also seek revenge on the provider who fails him, but Franklin combats these dangerous urges by consciously or unconsciously avoiding hurtful actions. Thus, rather than fight for his rights, he would withdraw from hostilities. While sharp words may well have passed across the dinner table, in his recounting of the episode he presents himself as placid and utterly noncombative, as preferring to withdraw rather than inconvenience anyone. Nor does he make much of a point of the fact that it was his actions that created the conflict in the first place.

3. He looked for ways to obtain supplies without hurting. In the vegetarian episode, the development of a skill and a mutually advantageous bargain are the chosen means, and the money and books are the supplies to be obtained. The skill permitted him to get food on his own, without relying on another provider. Later, deploying his skills and devising clever bargains became standard methods of "earning gratification without relying on anyone's fickle affection" (233).

4. He needed to justify his actions when involved in a hostility, or at least to determine how much blame to accept for it. According to psychoanalytic theory, the child wonders if he destroyed the "unity with the maternal matrix" and tries to reassure himself that he was not guilty. In the vegetarian episode, Franklin admits that he "occasioned an inconvenience," but describes himself as innocent of any malice aforethought. His adoption of the new diet was a lighthearted experiment, not a willful dogmatism designed to disturb the boardinghouse table. In the two occasions in his autobiography where he acknowledges taking unfair advantage of another (once involving his brother, another when he propositioned a woman), he uses the printer's term *erratum*, which tends to minimize the degree of hurtfulness inflicted on the other and implies that such mistakes are correctable.

As thus formulated, Bushman views this pattern as a hypothesis, one that helps to make sense of various episodes recounted in the autobiography. It is not dependent on the supposition that Franklin's childhood manifested considerable tension with his mother. The latter is a false quest, because

> it misinterprets the meaning of the psychoanalytic construction. The description of the infantile conflict was not primarily intended as an account of events, though there are grounds for believing they occurred, but as a symbolic representation of emotional structures present in the adult Franklin. Childhood traumas created a lasting vocabulary of analogs by which Franklin construed experience. Evidence of this vocabulary in action is the proof we seek. The infantile crisis is recounted because it is the simplest and most coherent way of highlighting patterns which continue into adulthood. (234)

While Bushman does not mention this, Franklin was the twelfth of thirteen children. Unlike the "tensions with his mother" assumption, this fact offers objective grounds in support of the theory, in that one would assume that supplies would not have been plentiful in the Franklin household, that his position in the birth order would require him to develop skills in supply acquisition, and that it would be prudent, given the greater physical strength of his older brothers, that he acquire supplies by ostensibly peaceful means. Thus, birth order theory would support Bushman's analysis (Sulloway, 1996).

The remaining pages of Bushman's study focus on episodes in Franklin's adult life, especially his role as a skillful negotiator in behalf of colonial interests. His ability to maintain amicable relationships with his counterparts in Britain and France worried his American colleagues. As Bushman points out, however, "In reality Franklin never betrayed his constituents' interests. He simply preferred cordial relations, whether with friends or enemies, to any form of open hostility" (238). We need not consider these episodes here, for our concern has been to use Bushman's study to illustrate how a psychobiographer may relate childhood experiences and adult personality without resorting to a simplistic, unicausal model. Instead, the psychoanalytic psychobiographer looks for patterns and uses psychoanalytic theory to discover them. In this sense, the infantile conflict is "a symbolic representation of emotional structures present in the adult Franklin" (238).

I have acknowledged in this chapter the liabilities involved in psychobiography. On the other hand, I have also presented the case for its countervailing strengths, which argue for its potential value for reconstructing the adult personality of Jesus. Thus far, however, the case for its use has been largely methodological. Carrying out the reconstructive task, I will make specific use of psychoanalytic theories and concepts, including its theories of ambivalence and image-splitting, of anxiety as symptomatic of the avoidance of both external and internal dangers, and of the role of unconscious motivation in human action. Ultimately, the value of a psychoanalytically oriented portrait of Jesus will depend on the cogency of these theories and concepts when applied to Jesus. It has been necessary to address methodological issues, however, in order to make the case that such an enterprise is not inherently illegitimate.

4

The Psychohistory of Groups

"If unstable meanings surface in the portraits it is because the contradictions are within the cultural matrix."

KATHLEEN NICHOLSON (1997, 58)

In the previous chapter, I noted the distinction between two branches of psychohistory: psychobiography, or the study of individuals; and group psychohistory, dealing with the psychological characteristics or formative experiences of groups. I also noted that case study methodology requires that the individual be seen in an "ecological context," which is to say that a full account must be given of the objects, persons, and events in an individual's physical, social, and symbolic environment; and that the proper focus of a case study is not so much a "person" as a "person in a situation." Since this "ecological context" or "situation" normally involves group affiliations, I noted that the distinction between psychobiography of individuals and group psychohistory is a rather arbitrary one. A psychobiography is unthinkable without some significant attention being paid to the subject's group affiliations.

Another useful distinction, however, is that between the psychohistory of the groups and the psychological study of the emotional attitudes and standards of a society, or group within this society, and thus with how social groups enforce norms of emotional expression among their members. Especially noteworthy in this regard is a society's view of what constitutes appropriate intrafamilial as opposed to interfamilial (or neighborhood) emotional expression. Through its focus on groups, psychohistory is able to concern itself with the "emotional climate" within which individuals and groups live their lives, work out their conflicts, and so forth. The larger emotional climate is an important part of the "ecological context" of the individual and of the group. In this chapter, I will focus on the psychohistory of groups and will

69

take particular note of the ways in which groups become the locus of emotions, both in their expression and their control.

Given our interest in Jesus, the groups that will concern us in this chapter are the family and the village. These social entities have received significant attention from psychohistorians and have great relevance for the psychobiographical study of Jesus. While the illustration from colonial America that I will be presenting here is not a perfect analog for the study of first-century Galilee, I have chosen it because there are important similarities between them. Among these are the ways in which conflicts within and between families are adjudicated in village life, how persons who deviate from village social norms are treated and controlled, the role of sexual misconduct in village conflict, and the effort to find explanations and remedies for diseases and illnesses. While father-son conflicts were also prevalent in both societies—especially in adolescence and young adulthood—there were also subtle tensions between mothers and sons, and these were traceable to the earlier, more formative childhood years. Displacement of both conflictual situations onto nonfamilial village personages was very common. Both societies had a heightened sense of the presence of evil in their midst, and both had supernatural explanations for this. While assignment of guilt was an important matter in official religious and legal systems, shame played a more fundamental role in everyday interpersonal and intravillage interactions. In addition, both societies were fear and anxiety prone and felt themselves beset by dangers, both external and internal.

Family Conflict in Plymouth Colony

The psychological study of the family is now an established field within psychohistory. This was not always the case. In a 1971 essay titled "What is Psycho-history?" historian Bruce Mazlish acknowledged that Erik H. Erikson's life histories are characteristically weak in their exploration of collective acts or mass settings. He proposed addressing this problem by giving the family a central importance in psychohistory:

> The family, potentially, is where psychological and sociological theories can best intersect. It can serve as a mid-point between life-history and group-history. In doing a life-history, we can analyze relations in an individual family, e.g., Hitler's family. In working towards group history, we can analyze "the German family" as an ideal type or model family. Obviously, the individual family, e.g., Hitler's, its typicality and uniqueness, can only be understood in terms of our understanding of the model family, e.g., the German; and vice-versa. (Mazlish, 87–88)

The special contribution of psychohistory to family history is its use of psychoanalytic theories that "call our attention to certain recurrent and universal features of *all* familial situations" (88). Mazlish is quick to add, however, that psychohistory must balance this attention to universal features of family life with sociological investigations that address the influence of social and economic class on family practices. Thus, "in the psychohistoric understanding of the family, sociology is as important as psychology" (89).

By "universal features" of all familial situations, Mazlish has in mind such aspects as infantile sexuality, parent-child relations, parental disciplining practices, attitudes toward what is clean and dirty, and so forth. These and many other aspects of family life are universal, but they are "historically affected." Parent-child relations for example, are strongly influenced by the particular family structure, and this is "laid down by history, whereby a South Italian family differs from a North American one," its very elements being affected by historical forces (89). Whether these qualifications should have prompted Mazlish to abandon any notion of "universality" is open to question. Certainly, one would not want to propose that psychology deals only with universals, while sociology allows one to explore concrete cases. On the other hand, his view that psychological and sociological theories complement one another is vitally important.

John Demos' psychohistorical studies of family life in colonial America are especially valuable for our purposes here because of his emphasis on the interrelationships between family and village life. In *A Little Commonwealth: Family Life in Plymouth Colony* (1970), he notes that

> the family was joined to other institutions and other purposes in an intricate web of interconnections. It did not stand out in any special way from adjacent parts of the social backdrop; it acquired no distinctive aura of emotional or ideological significance. Its importance, while impossible to doubt, was more assumed than understood—was, indeed, so basic and so automatic as to be almost invisible. Family and community, private and public life, formed part of the same moral equation. The one supported the other, and they became in a sense indistinguishable. (186)

In contrast, the family today "stands quite apart from most other aspects of life," and we assume that when a family member "goes out into the world," he or she is crossing a very critical boundary. Thus, it requires considerable imagination for us to appreciate and understand the "invisible web" that characterized social life in early American settlements (186). In the following discussion, I will be especially interested in what Demos has to say about the interactions between family and village life, particularly in the area of emotional conflict.

Demos begins *A Little Commonwealth* with the observation that historians have generally been concerned with the larger units of social action—region, class, party, and ethnic or religious group. It has been left to the behavioral sciences—anthropology, sociology, psychology—to demonstrate the fundamental importance "of the smallest and most intimate of all group environments, the family" (viii). Where family studies do occur, there is little agreement about research procedures, source materials, and terminology. In the face of such disagreements, one response has been to descend to the level of local, almost personal history. Demos views his research on Plymouth Colony as such a study in local history. He argues, however, that there were broad similarities between family life in Plymouth and other American colonies. Moreover, the family in general "often provides a kind of common denominator, or baseline, for a whole culture whose various parts may differ substantially in other respects" (ix).

As for available source material, he notes that most investigations of family life are bedeviled by one fundamental circumstance, that is, the subject is something that the people of the time took so much for granted that it seemed to require little formal comment. The situation of Plymouth, however, affords three types of sources, including physical artifacts (furniture, books, utensils, clothing, etc.), a large assortment of wills and inventories, and the official records of the colony and of individual towns within the colony. Literary materials—books and essays, speeches, letters, journals, and so on—which often bulk largest in historical research, are usually in short supply in regard to family questions, and this is especially so in the case of Plymouth. Only one source, the works of John Robinson, the original Pilgrim pastor, has proven consistently helpful. In a sense, Pastor Robinson is to Plymouth Colony what Josephus is to the study of first-century Palestine.

The features of Demos' study of Plymouth Colony that are most relevant for our purposes are the relationships between parents and children and between husbands and wives, especially in terms of interpersonal conflict. Relatedly, we are interested in ways in which conflicts that were not resolved by family members themselves were handled or adjudicated by the village (i.e., issues of social control over family deviance). Various aspects of Demos' work may be considered psychohistorical because he makes explicit use of psychoanalytic theories. For example, in his exploration of themes of individual development, he uses Erikson's life cycle theory, justifying this choice on the grounds that Erikson's theory "recognizes quite explicitly the historical process." Thus, it invites historians' contributions to further development and modifications of the theory by testing it against the record of earlier periods and societies (129).

In his discussion of childrearing practices, Demos makes particular use of Erikson's second life cycle stage—autonomy versus shame and doubt—to analyze a feature of Plymouth family life that resonated throughout adult life and was at the heart of the social contradictions of village life. Noting that siblings were born roughly two years apart, which was consistent with the practice of breast-feeding an infant for about twelve months, he suggests that "for the first year or so a baby had a relatively comfortable and tranquil time. Often he must have been set close to the fireside for warmth. His clothing was light and not especially restrictive, yet the covers laid over him heightened his sense of protection. And most important, he had regular access to his mother's breast—with all that this implies in the way of emotional reassurance" (134). True, the death rate for infants under one year due to illness was substantially higher than for any later age, but "this fact may well have encouraged an attitude of particular concern and tenderness toward infants" (134).

Beginning in the second year, however, this emotional climate was abruptly changed. Parents were now expected to discipline the child and to do so with unusual determination and zeal. Demos cites Pastor Robinson's rationale for a no-nonsense approach to parental discipline. Robinson writes:

> And surely there is in all children a stubbornness, and stoutness of mind arising from natural pride, which must, in the first place, be broken and beaten down; that so the foundation of their education being laid in humility and tractableness, other virtues may, in their time, be built upon. Children should not know, if it could be kept from them, that they have a will of their own, but are in their parents' keeping; neither should these words be heard from them, save by way of consent, "I will" or "I will not." (135)

Demos views this as a "blanket indictment of the child's strivings toward self-assertion, and particularly of any impulses of direct aggression. The terms 'break' and 'beat down' ('destroy' is also used further on) seem to admit of no qualification" (135). Moreover, Robinson urged that this disciplinary program begin very early, as it was to be accorded "the first place" in a whole sequence of socialization. Demos concludes that the second year of life, bounded at either end by experiences of loss (weaning near the beginning, the arrival of a sibling near the end), was greatly exacerbated by "the crushing of the child's assertive and aggressive drives" (136).

While this pattern is striking in itself, Demos notes that it gains added significance when set alongside an important theme in the adult life of the colonists, "the whole atmosphere of contention, of chronic and sometimes bitter enmity" (136). The most critical area of emotional conflict—both interpersonal and intrapersonal—was "a tight cluster of anxieties about aggression. To read the records of Plymouth, and also those of other New England settlements, is to sense a very special sort of preoccupation with any overt acts of this character. Here, it seems, was the one area of emotional and interpersonal life about which the Puritans were most concerned, confused, conflicted" (137). Robinson's essay "Of Anger" describes the "wrathful man" as "like a hideous monster," with "his eyes burning, his lips fumbling, his face pale, his teeth gnashing, his mouth foaming, and other parts of his body trembling, and shaking" (Demos, 137). He found nothing whatsoever to say in favor of anger, no circumstance that could ever justify its expression, for anger "hath always evil in it."

Demos suggests that the connections between harsh disciplining of children after a period of emotional closeness, and adult suppression of anger and anxieties relating to aggression may be understood in light of Erikson's developmental theory. Here again, the second stage of the life cycle, with the crisis of "autonomy versus shame and doubt" at its emotional core, is especially relevant. According to Erikson, this stage "becomes decisive for the ratio of love and hate, cooperation and willfulness, freedom of self-expression and its suppression" (Erikson, 1963, 254). If the child receives no support for his "wish to 'stand on his own feet'," he will be overcome by that sense of "having exposed himself prematurely and foolishly, which we call shame, or that secondary mistrust, that 'double-take,' which we call doubt" (Erikson, 1959, 68).

For Demos, the evidence from Puritan New England makes a strikingly good fit with this developmental theory, "for considerations of shame (and of 'face-saving'–its other side) loom very large in a number of areas of their culture. Such considerations are manifest, for example, throughout the legion of court cases that had to do with personal disputes and rivalries. Many of these cases involved suits for slander or defamation–where the issue of public exposure, the risk of shame, was absolutely central" (138–39). When convictions were obtained, defendants were usually required to withdraw their slanderous statements and to apologize for them in public. The threat of public ridicule was also implied in the common punishment of sitting in the stocks. Erikson's view that each developmental stage is related to an institutional aspect of collective social life also applies because the second stage relates to "the principle of *law and order*, which in daily life as well in the high courts of law apportions to each his privileges and his limitations, his obligations and his rights" (Erikson, 1959, 73). Demos comments, "Surely few people have shown as much concern for 'law and order' as the Puritans" (Demos, 139).

Once established in the manner outlined here, Demos claims that "the same style of parental discipline was probably maintained with little significant change for quite a number of years" (139). The biblical commandment to "honor thy father and mother" was fundamental in parent-child relationships, and the force of law stood behind it. The relevant statute directed that

> If an Childe or Children above sixteen years old, and of competent Understanding, shall Curse or Smite their natural Father or Mother; he or they shall be put to Death, unless it can be sufficiently testified that the Parents have been very Unchristianly negligent in the Education of such Children, or so provoked them by extreme and cruel Correction, that they have been forced thereunto, to preserve themselves from death or Maiming. (100)

Another statute prescribed the same punishment for behavior that was "stubborn or Rebellious," or for any sort of habitual disobedience. If a son acted in this manner, parents were required to bring "him before the Magistrates assembled in Court, and testifie unto them, that their Son is Stubborn and Rebellious, and will not obey their voice and chastisement" (101).

While extreme and cruel correction was prohibited, physical punishment was clearly allowed. When Robinson spoke of "beating down" the natural will of the child, his congregation would not have assumed that he was speaking metaphorically. More direct evidence that physical beating was considered an appropriate form of discipline, however, is that *adults* were publicly whipped for acts of fornication (Demos, 1982, 30).

In his exploration of later childhood, Demos focuses mainly on the issue of education, noting that it was not until 1670 that any formal education occurred in Plymouth Colony. This was when John Morton appeared before the town meeting and offered his services as a teacher. In 1673 funds were allocated for the building of a school. In the fifty years preceding, young boys would work with their fathers at planting and fence-mending, while girls would assist their mothers with cooking, spinning, and candlemaking. The society was at best partially literate, and Demos guesses that there was "a new intensity in the religious tutelage or 'catechizing' provided for children; and perhaps they began to learn the 'three R's'" (1970, 142). In any event, the most important "educative" institutions were the church, the community at large, and above all the family: "Here, in the context of the total household environment, values, manners, literacy, vocation were all transmitted from one generation to the next. The process was none the less real for being only partly conscious" (144).

In young adulthood, the major occasions for conflict between parents and their offspring centered around the selection of marriage partners and the division of the family property among the male offspring: "The desire of a young person to make his own choice of courtship partners *could* generate considerable conflict with his parents," and an early court order directed that "none be allowed to marry that are under the covert of parents but by their consent and approbation" (154). The court especially deplored the attempts of young men unfit for marriage, due to their "young years" and "weak estate," to "inveigle" the daughters and maidservants. To make sons "fit" for marriage, fathers were expected to turn over a portion of the property to them on the occasion of their marriages. Complicating the expectation that young men have sufficient "estate" in order to marry was the relatively high marriage age (average: 27 years for men, 22 years for women). This meant that illegitimacy was a continuing problem. As pregnancy was the most reliable evidence that fornication had occurred, punishment for fornication was severe—a fine of ten pounds or a public whipping—and applied equally to both parties. A girl who refused to reveal the man's identity became subject to a trying ordeal. When delivery of the child was actually in progress and her powers of resistance were presumed to be at their lowest ebb, the midwives were likely to charge her to tell whose baby the child was: "The authorities wished to discover the father in these cases in order to punish him and to make him financially responsible for his child's maintenance" (152–53). Often, however, the woman was fully prepared to name her partner due to feelings of jealousy or resentment of being abandoned. Numerous paternity cases appear in the court records, some quite complicated, as the men might contest the allegations, and it was the task of the court to determine who was telling the truth.

Young single men would often live in the home of another family, and young women, through arrangements by their fathers, would live as maidservants in the homes of other villagers, usually family relatives. This meant that young unmarried persons were not under constant parental surveillance. Thus, fornication was not as carefully controlled as we—with our views of Puritans as sexually repressed—may have assumed. Occasionally, a group of young single men might live in a house together, but this would be an anomalous situation, and strongly discouraged by the community.

Sexual intimacy between couples who were already officially "betrothed," while not officially condoned, received a relatively light penalty (about one-fourth the penalty for the same offense by those who were not betrothed). This very different scale of punishment may actually have encouraged premarital sexual relations among betrothed couples. On the other hand, newlyweds who produced a child in substantially less than nine months after marriage were subject to immediate punishment. Given the possibility of a premature birth, the opinions of midwives and other women at the delivery were usually decisive. Failure to fulfill the contract to marry would create the likelihood of legal action and a damage suit of considerable proportions. For example, a long, complicated court case spanning two years involved an initial decision in favor of the plaintiff, the man, against the woman for reneging on the contract. It was overturned, however, when she presented evidence of behavior by him that justified her refusal. As Demos notes, the laws against adultery were written so as to cover married and "betrothed" people in exactly equal manner. An especially troubling case of disputed paternity arose from a premature birth to a couple recently married. The husband contended that he could not have been the child's father and so persuaded the court. Suspicion pointed to the woman's own father, thereby raising the specter of incest. Among the evidence presented was the father's admission that after he became aware of his daughter's pregnant state, he failed to bring the couple together to enquire about it, or to bear witness against his daughter's wickedness (103–4).

Because young men were highly dependent on their fathers for an estate sufficient to their marriageability, fathers would ordinarily give their sons a portion of their property at marriage, and the sons would build a house on this portion. Married couples would not live with parents and were allowed to live with a married brother or sister for a very circumscribed period of time (for example, while their own house was under construction). Usually, the father's assignment of a portion of his property would be considered an informal gift, which would then be legalized through his will at the time of his death. This meant that fathers continued to hold considerable leverage over their sons. The following case illustrates how such nebulous arrangements could lead to considerable family tension and conflict. Samuel Ryder, the father, died, leaving two sons (Benjamin and John) as his chief heirs, while excluding a third (Joseph) altogether. Yet, some time previously Joseph had built a house on a piece of his father's land, with the expectation of receiving formal title to it in his father's will. Now, obviously distressed, he sought to break the will in an appeal to the court. Two depositions from a couple named Matthews described the specific events out of which the whole sequence of trouble had developed. Elizabeth Matthews deposed that Joseph's mother came into the house where Joseph was living (presumably the Matthews' home), and cried and wrung her hands, fearing that Joseph would go away. She assured Joseph that his father had said "you shall never be Molested." Samuel Matthews testified that the morning Joseph's house was raised, his father came out and marked the ground with a stick, and bid Joseph to set his house where it now stands. Matthews confirmed his wife's testimony that Joseph's mother feared that he would leave and added that if "hee went shee would Goe to" (166). This testimony suggests that Joseph was the focus of conflict between his father and mother, and that his father sought to punish him for his mother's emotional attachment to him by reneging on his earlier, favorable treatment of his son, which appears to have been involuntary.

Shaming as a Method of Forcing Social Compliance

These excerpts from Demos' *A Little Commonwealth* may give a more negative picture of family life in Plymouth Colony than he himself paints, in part because I have centered on areas of emotional conflict between parents and children in both early childhood and young adulthood. They show, how-ever, that as the children grew into adults, the emotional tenor of parent-child relationships did not change to any significant degree. As Demos notes, while children at about six or seven years old were dressed like little adults, they were treated as children well into adulthood. If beaten for disobedience or willfulness as small children, they were also beaten for fornication as young adults. There was no abrupt shift from childhood dependence to adult inde-pendence, for, until their fathers' deaths, they were not fully independent of parental legal and emotional control.

Demos emphasizes the role that shaming played in family and village life as a means to effect social compliance. We have been taught to view Western societies as "guilt cultures" (and Asian ones as "shame cultures"), so this em-phasis on the role of shaming in Puritan societies may come as something of a surprise. This distinction between a "shame" and "guilt" culture, however, is false and misleading when applied to a society like Plymouth Colony. As Erikson points out, "Shame is an emotion insufficiently studied, because in our civilization it is so early and easily absorbed by guilt" (1963, 252). His developmental theory reflects this observation, as the third stage, which fol-lows the "autonomy versus shame and doubt" stage, is "initiative versus guilt." Its corresponding social-institutional form is the *dramatic*. In Plymouth Colony the purest form of the dramatic was the sermon, which portrayed the cosmic battle between the forces of good and evil in emotionally charged imagery. The social institution that conflated these two stages, however, was the trial, whether conducted by the church in its excommunication proceedings or by the civil courts.

An especially interesting excommunication proceeding, preserved in the official documents of First Church of Boston, occurred in 1640–1641. The verbatim account is reproduced in Demos' *Remarkable Providences 1600–1760* (1972). Charges were brought against Ann Hibbens, wife of a wealthy Boston merchant, for slander and defamation of character. She had accused a local carpenter of having overcharged her for some furniture he had made for her. An out-of-court settlement was attempted through arbitration worked out by another local carpenter, to which her husband agreed. Mrs. Hibbens, however, contended that the carpenters had acted in collusion and refused to accept the terms. The second carpenter, a member of First Church, brought the charges against her.

In the first set of proceedings, she was censured for her statements against the carpenter and for failing to allow her husband to handle the dispute with the carpenters. Her defense that she was not acting out of self-interest but was protesting the high prices charged by the village craftsmen was rejected. As Rev. John Cotton put it, "All this you now relate is only to excuse yourself, and lessen your own fault, and lay blame on others" (228). The decision to censure rather than formally excommunicate was intended to give her opportunity to repent in the weeks ahead. Five months later, however, she was brought before the church because her subsequent behavior reflected an unrepentant spirit, the chief evidence of which was her public criticism of the church's handling of the earlier trial against her. This time, the elders had little disposition to hear her out, for she had in effect defamed *them*. Moreover, it was again noted that she had usurped her husband's authority. Mr. Hibbens testified that he had "some exercise of spirit with her" when she would not accept the negotiated settlement. He also noted that she had made a partial confession of guilt to the offended carpenter, "confessing her error with tears," but the elders were unimpressed. His testimony, meant to defend himself (and her) against the charge that she had made "a wisp of her husband," was the last straw. Members of the congregation immediately called for excommunication. After the pastor had delivered a lengthy and vitriolic condemnation, the proceedings concluded with Mr. Hibbens expressing his hope that his wife would someday be restored to the church fellowship. This was not to be. Two years after his death (in 1654), she was convicted in the courts on the charge of witchcraft and sentenced to death. Evidence presented in support of the witchcraft charge was her uncanny ability to hear what her neighbors were saying (about her?) outside normal hearing range. She was one of only five or six persons executed for witchcraft in New England prior to the Salem hysteria in 1692, thirty-six years later.

The most dramatic feature of the excommunication trial was its shift from the dynamics of guilt to those of shame as it progressed. Issues of sin, guilt, and repentance were prominent at the formal level of deliberation throughout the proceedings, but when it became obvious that Mrs. Hibbens would not throw herself on the mercy of the church elders, the underlying dynamics of shame began to surface. In the censureship proceedings, some parishioners expressed the desire to "help in the work of humiliation upon her heart." In his sermon prior to these proceedings, Rev. John Cotton preached on "hypocritical humiliation" and, in his opening statement, encouraged her to "take shame to your face" and "abase yourself." At the excommunication proceedings, however, the pastor and elders took upon themselves the task of shaming *her*. One parishioner compared her to Moses' sister Miriam, noting that "this Sister hath been diligently searched and viewed and upon the search she is found leprous and diverse spots are risen and do manifestly appear to the congregation, therefore, according to the law of God, I think she ought to be pronounced unclean and as a leprous person put out from amongst us" (235). He added, "And if our Sister should go home and God should strike her sick or lay any other judgment upon her or should take her away before the next Lord's Day, I know not how the church should answer it before God; but [I think] that the blood of her soul would be required at our hands for neglecting to apply that remedy which God hath appointed for the healing of her sin and [for the] recovering her of her disease" (235).

In his final excommunication statement, the Reverend Mr. Cotton pronounced her "to be a leprous and unclean person...You have scorned counsel and refused instruction and have like a filthy swine trampled those pearls under your feet...And so as an unclean beast and unfit for the society of God's people, I do from this time forward pronounce you an excommunicated person from God and His people" (238). Thus, leprosy served as a metaphor for her sinful, unclean condition, and to this metaphor was added the even more damning epithet of "filthy swine" and "unclean beast." He also noted that she had sown "discord and jealousies, not only between Brethren but between our church and others, our Elders and others" (238), indicating that the whole matter had become deeply embarrassing for the church in its relations in the wider community. Thus, the subtext of this formal investigation into Mrs. Hibbens' guilt, one conducted with considerable attention to legal process and protocol, was the deeper emotionality of shame, especially as reflected in Rev. Cotton's vitriolic judgment upon her spiritual state.

Four years earlier, in the heresy trial of Anne Hutchinson, who was banished to Rhode Island, Cotton had told her that her heresy–her figurative, spiritual adultery–would lead inevitably to literal adultery: "And though I have not herd, nayther do I thinke, you have bine unfaythfull to your Husband in his Marriage Covenant, yet that will follow upon it" (Kibbey, 1986, 111). When Hutchinson gave birth to a stillborn child during the controversy, an elder, Thomas Weld, described the fetus as "30 monstrous births, or thereabouts, some of one shape, some of another, none of all of them of human shape," for "as she had vented misshapen opinions, so she must bring forth deformed monsters." John Winthrop, governor of Massachusetts at the time, wanted to see for himself. He dug up the buried corpse and then summoned the midwife, "who at first confessed it was a monstrous birth, but concealed the horns and claws, and some other parts," until she was charged to tell the whole truth (113). Notice here that the midwife, as in cases of early pregnancy, was placed in the extremely difficult position of having to "confirm" the allegations of the authorities against other women. Also, as Demos notes in *Entertaining Satan* (1982), while scores of midwives were never themselves associated with witchcraft, this possibility was always there: "Perhaps, at bottom, there was a link of antipathy: the midwife *versus* the witch, lifegiving, and life-taking, opposite faces of the same coin" (80).

The excommunication trial of Ann Hibbens and the banishment of Anne Hutchinson illustrate the role that shaming played in effecting social compliance. Women (or men) who violated social norms were publicly censured, ridiculed, and shunned. In addition, associations were made between immoral behavior and disease, with "leprosy" in the case of Ann Hibbens serving as a metaphor for her spiritual state. Moreover, it was assumed that God may punish the miscreant by inflicting her with physical illness (or, as in Hutchinson's case, the discharge of a "deformed monster"). The church's judgment was therefore designed to forestall a more serious divine punishment. One senses a deep, repressed rage, traceable to early childhood experiences of severe discipline, in Ann Hibbens' defiant stand against the elders and refusal to engage in her own humiliation. This, in turn, enraged her accusers, whose vitriolic verbal abuse replicated the rage of parents whose children dared to defy them.

The Emotionology of Witchcraft

Having focused on the role of shaming in effecting social compliance, I now want to turn to the larger issue of which shaming is part, that of the emotional ethos of the village as reflected in John Demos' psychohistorical studies of American Puritan society. His discussion of witchcraft affords an excellent vantage point from which to view the emotionality of a village. In their anthology of readings in psychohistory, Cocks and Crosby (1987) include a section on "The Psychology of the Group in History." One of the essays in this section, by Peter N. Stearns and Carol Z. Stearns (284–309), is concerned with "emotionology," or the historical study of emotions. Peter N. Stearns subsequently published a book-length study of the evolution of the emotion of jealousy in American history (Stearns, 1989). The authors define emotion as "a complex set of interactions among subjective and objective factors, redirected through neural and/or hormonal systems, which gives rise to feelings (affective experiences as of pleasure or displeasure) and also general cognitive processes toward appraising the experience; emotions in this sense lead to physiological adjustments to the conditions that arouse response, and often to expressive and adaptive behavior" (Stearns and Stearns, 284). As historians, Stearns and Stearns are interested in "the attitudes or standards that a society, or a definable group within a society, maintains toward basic emotions and their appropriate expression," and in the "ways that institutions reflect and encourage these attitudes in human conduct, e.g., courtship practices as expressing the valuation of affect in marriage, or personnel workshops as reflecting the valuation of anger in job relationships" (284).

In *Problems of Historical Psychology* (1960), Zevedei Barbu suggests that there are two approaches to the history of human emotionality: "Firstly, one can regard an emotional climate as an effect of various social and cultural conditions specific to the historical development of a community. On the other hand, one can regard it as a dynamic factor, i.e., a source of historical events within a specific community" (66). In commenting on the second approach, he notes that "psychological phenomena have a lower degree of determinability, consequently, a higher degree of freedom than social phenomena, and historical events in general" (66). Thus, if the historian explains an economic phenomenon, such as a case of monetary inflation, as due to "a certain emotional state of 'panic' in a social group," he gains some knowledge of this specific case, but does so at some risk, that is, "the risk of falling into an area of low determinability" (67). There is, however, another side to this problem:

> When a historian describes, or explains in psychological terms, he may lose a certain degree of precision, but in quite a different way, he makes an important advance in his knowledge of historical events. His grasp in the determining field of these events goes deeper. The reason for this is that most mental phenomena, particularly those belonging to collective emotionality, play the part of "general factors" in the determining field of historical events; they determine more than one event. They determine the structure of events. (67)

Thus, the disadvantage resulting from the indeterminability of mental events is compensated by the advantage derived from their structural character. This can be illustrated by the case of the historian who considers "the feeling of collective insecurity" to be one of the determining causes of Hitler's access to power: "Provided that he is aware of the irrational character of such feeling, he has now in his hands a factor of a kind which can give him the clue to a series of other events of the period, such as the specific character of economy, of political institutions, of international relations, of ideological trends" (67). Demos takes precisely this approach in his analysis of witchcraft in early New England. Two witchcraft cases will enable us to see how the punishment scenario, where the punished child experiences a complex of emotions of fear, shame, and rage, and where the punishing adult experiences anger (and, later, fear, when sons are physically strong enough to strike back), is recapitulated on a larger scale in the witchcraft controversies.

The first involves Rachel Clinton, a resident of Ipswich, who was arrested, tried, convicted, and imprisoned for witchcraft, but released as part of the general reprieve of 1693. She died of natural causes two years later, at the age of 66. Various charges were brought against Clinton. One man testified that she "hunched" several women of "worth and quality" with her elbow at the meetinghouse, and that the offended women asked him to refer the matter to the town selectmen. He did as requested, but then, while riding home that same night, he encountered a strange animal that first appeared like a cat, then a small dog. Further along, he noticed a giant turtle that moved as fast as he rode. At this point he "thought of Rachel Clinton" and immediately the little creatures and the turtle vanished. He also testified that Clinton entered Mary Fuller's home to charge Fuller with having told lies about her. During the heated argument that followed, a girl in a neighboring house belonging to Fuller's brother was reported to have fallen down dead (a report later modified to indicate that for three hours she was unable to move or speak). Another deponent said that Clinton threw a stone at him. While it fell short by three or four yards, it continued rolling toward him, touching the toe of his foot, whereupon "my great toe was in a quiet rage, as if the nail were held up by a pair of pincers" (20).

By her mid-fifties, Rachel Clinton had gained a widespread and enduring reputation for witchcraft. Who was this Rachel Clinton, and how did she become so notorious? Drawing on a genealogical study of the Clinton family and many court cases, Demos provides a rich account of her troubled life. She was the daughter of a wealthy currier, Richard Haffield, who immigrated to New England in 1635 with his wife and five daughters. Rachel, the fourth, was six years old at the time. Her father had a son and two daughters by a former wife. Rachel's mother, of much lower status, was a maidservant when he married her. After her father's death when Rachel was ten, her mother was initially successful in conserving the family resources, but in time the family fortunes gradually declined. Unlike other wealthy widows who made attractive mates, she never remarried and was later declared insane. Rachel herself remained single for another twelve years, living with her mother in a little house near the milldam, which her mother had purchased from the town.

At the age of thirty-six, Rachel married Lawrence Clinton, a twenty-two-year-old man who was an indentured servant. Rachel paid Robert Cross, to whom Clinton owed an additional three-and-a-half years service, twenty-one pounds for his release from his contract. This led to a court case brought by Thomas White, Rachel's brother-in-law, who, after this unusual payment for the groom's freedom came to light, was given official powers of guardianship over the affairs of Rachel's mother. He alleged that Rachel did not have the right to use her mother's funds in this way, and also contended that Clinton and Cross had acted in collusion, with Rachel serving as a witless dupe. Rachel at first defended her husband, but as the case wore on, she changed her position, largely because she was now charging him for desertion and adultery. She also brought charges against a man named John Clarke for having "lain with her," which Clarke denied, leading the court to sentence her to a public whipping. While the court sentenced Clinton to prison for failure to support his wife, he continued to shirk his obligations, and she petitioned for divorce. Despite a court case charging him with fornication with a maidservant and ordering him to pay paternity damages, the court denied Rachel's petition and again ordered Clinton to meet his obligations to her. Meanwhile, she was pursuing extramarital interests of her own, and she and a man named John

Ford were charged on "suspicion of uncleanness and other evil practices." Eventually, the general court in Boston granted her request for a divorce. According to local tradition, Rachel lived the remainder of her life in a hut on Hay Island near Ipswich Harbor. She became a ward of the town, appearing several times in the town records under the name "Clinton," "Haffield," and sometimes just "Rachel." This familiar use of her given name suggests that she was a town fixture. The witchcraft charges all date from the final decade of her life, when she was dependent on public assistance. Demos guesses that her fellow townspeople begrudged her need for public support, while she felt that this support was insufficiently generous: "Significantly, in at least two instances her supposed witchcraft stemmed from unsuccessful attempts to beg food and/or drink from neighbors" (33). These incidents, however, were part of a life-history in which she went from a position of wealth to one of abject poverty. Demos believes that her jostling of the women of "worth and quality" at the meetinghouse was a none-too-subtle reminder to them that, years earlier, she would have joined these women near the front of the church. He also mentions that Rachel, being a single woman, was especially vulnerable to charges of witchcraft. As we have already seen, Ann Hibbens became vulnerable to such charges when she lost her husband's protection following his death. Demos concludes: "With Rachel, victim and victimizer were two halves of the same whole. Simply put: events combined against her, depriving her of wealth and dignity, and she responded out of a deep, angry despair. But was there *more* than mere 'response' on Rachel's part? Was there also some veiled complicity—such as one finds in habitual victims?" (35). Given the paucity of evidence, Demos considers the latter question unanswerable, but what is incontrovertible is that "women like Rachel were fitted to the role of 'witch' at least in part because they were so profoundly *vulnerable*" (35).

She was vulnerable, in part, because she struggled against the loss of her original social standing in the community. Rachel was one of those unfortunates who seemed difficult to classify, as she could be a "witless dupe" on some occasions and an importuning plaintiff on others. Moreover, her life was one in which shame played a predominant role, both as a chronic condition and as an episodic reality. The episode that seems most symbolic of her humiliation was the stone-throwing incident in which the missile fell several yards short of its intended target. Yet, even this hapless act of angry/fearful display added to the village lore of her uncanny power to injure. It may also be noted that, while her problems originated in her own family, the charges of witchcraft were brought by neighbors. This supports Demos' point that conflicts between family members were displaced into village relationships, thus enabling families to live in relative harmony while exacerbating conflict in the community.

If shame was a major dimension of Rachel Clinton's life, it was accompanied by a strong element of defiant shamelessness. There were the various charges of fornication with men, one lodged by Lawrence Clinton himself, who was one of the persons who found her in a compromising situation with John Ford. Erikson explains this shamelessness in terms of rage. If shame is "essentially rage turned against the self," and is expressed in the desire for invisibility,

> too much shaming does not lead to genuine propriety but to a secret determination to try to get away with things, unseen–if, indeed, it does not result in defiant shamelessness...There is a limit to a child's and an adult's endurance in the face of demands to consider himself, his body, and his wishes as evil and dirty, and to his belief in the infallibility of those who pass such judgment. He may be apt to turn things around, and to consider as evil only the fact that they exist: his chance will come when they are gone, or when he will go from them. (1963, 253)

Perceiving this desire to rid oneself of them–of their disapproving eyes–they may well believe that the person who has been shamed beyond endurance has the power to act on these desires. Hence, events that may admit of other, more prosaic explanations may be explained as due to a supernatural agency– an evil one–working in the shamed one's behalf.

The predominant social setting for conflict, antecedent to witchcraft charges, was the transfer of goods, services, and information. One party– usually the alleged witch–apprehends the other in order to obtain a specific resource. Typically, the approach is rebuffed. This, in turn, evokes a "threatening" or "cursing" response and leaves a residue of bitterness on both sides (294–95). In such encounters, the initiative belongs to the "witch," who requests a favor (e.g., breast milk), asks the other to sell a limited resource (e.g., eggs or hay), seeks opportunities for employment (e.g., to plow, keep the cows), or asks for privileged information, especially about court proceedings. If the request is refused (e.g., because one needs the limited resource for one's own family), this refusal is typically met with angry words on both sides. Psychodynamically, this mutual resentment over being importuned and refused may recapitulate the conflict between parent and child in early childhood. We can appreciate, therefore, Benjamin Franklin's pragmatic solution of looking for ways in which both parties gain something from the interchange.

As Demos points out, however, such exchanges between neighbors revealed a deep contradiction within Puritan society between the expectation of neighborliness and family individualism. Those more fortunate were likely to resent a neighbor's appeal for help, because they were uncomfortable refusing. The resulting guilt was fertile grounds for witchcraft accusations, in that subsequent misfortune could be attributed to retaliation by the witch. For example, a woman who refused her neighbor's request for a pound of cotton suffered a stabbing back pain as soon as the other woman departed. While nineteenth-century American psychiatrists would attribute these physical effects to unconscious guilt, this woman had no other explanatory system than that she was the victim of her neighbor's revenge. The frequent use of cursing language added cogency to this explanation.

The second case study illustrates how the alleged witch might exploit the fear he evoked in his neighbors. In the long roster of early New Englanders accused of witchcraft, John Godfrey stands out because he was single and male. Other men were accused at various times, and four or five were executed, but most were husbands of accused women and thus guilty by association. Godfrey, bound in service to a gentleman from the region of his birth in England, came to New England in his mid-teens. He settled in Newbury. Several years later, he sued two different men for slander and won both cases. In the same decade, he was a defendant three times for "suborning a witness" and for "lying." During the next decade he made no court appearances, but scattered references to land deeds indicate that he had moved from Newbury, and lived briefly in Rowley, Haverkill, and Andover. From 1658 until his death in 1675 he was in court at least once a year, and in some years, many times. Most disputes dealt with property—land, money, bonds, wheat, corn, rye, oxen, sheep, cloth—and most involved relatively small values: "Taken as a whole, the records depict a man continually at odds with his peers, over a host of quite specific, personal, and mundane affairs" (38).

When Godfrey was about forty, he lodged several suits for debts owed to him by various residents of Haverkill. While his position was fully supported by the verdicts, the issue of witchcraft was almost immediately raised and presented to the court by petition of eleven persons. Each alleged that events having no "natural cause" had followed "upon differences betwixt themselves and one John Godfrey, resident of Andover or elsewhere at his pleasure" (39). Godfrey countersued on the grounds of slander, and while the local jury sustained his complaint, it added that "notwithstanding [we] do conceive that by the testimonies he is rendered suspicious."

According to witness testimony, Godfrey would offer to keep the cows that belonged to a resident or to the county, and when his offer was not accepted, he would express his "displeasure" and soon thereafter cattle from the herds would vanish. On one occasion, he went one evening to the home of a townsperson and was given food and lodging for the night. The next morning, he accosted the daughter of his host, claiming that her husband owed him "more than he was worth" and that her clothes, therefore, belonged to Godfrey. When her father disagreed with Godfrey, saying that *he* had provided her the clothes, Godfrey "rose up in a great rage and knocked his head against the manteltree and threatened my father and I that we should get nothing by it before that summer passed. Then presently upon it I went and gave my father's three swine some meat, and the swine was taken with foaming and reeling and turned around and did die" (40). Later, Godfrey demanded money from her husband for witnessing before the court, but her husband said to come for the money another time and he would pay him. He also rebuffed Godfrey's offer to keep his oxen. With this refusal, Godfrey declared that one of the oxen would never come home alive again. Shortly thereafter one of the oxen was found dead. Demos concludes: "Indebtedness, threats, angry accusations, and 'losses' of property or health: such were the central ingredients of an oft-repeated sequence" (41).

Besides his frequent resort to threatening statements, Godfrey would also say things that startled, confused, or annoyed his listeners. According to an Andover resident, an odd-looking bird flew through their door as Godfrey entered. Efforts to catch it proved unsuccessful, but the bird "vanished" quite suddenly. When the man of the house asked "wherefore it came," Godfrey answered, "It came to suck your wife." He also flaunted religious conventions, trying, for example, to collect debts on the Sabbath, and "never allowed himself those moments of ritual self-abasement so familiar to the Puritans" (52). A witness alleged seeing a devil's teat under his mouth when he yawned in church; while the teat was no doubt her own fantasy, the yawn most likely was not. Another witness reported that Godfrey had come to a place where some cattle were bewitched and said, "I will unwitch them," and soon they were calm. As Demos notes, "Here, then, was a truly remarkable, even supernatural talent, and yet it could not be trusted. *Un*witching and *be*witching were too closely related—in cow-keeping, as in any other activity. When joined in a man of bad temperament, such powers assumed a highly menacing aspect" (42). On one occasion, a boy on horseback was startled by what looked like a crow, and suddenly the horse fell to one side with the boy's leg underneath. According to the boy, Godfrey called at the house two days later to inquire how he was doing. In the course of conversation Godfrey said, "Every cock-eating boy must ride. I unhorsed one boy the other day, and I will unhorse thee, too, if thee rides." Then he added that the boy would have died if he had been a man, to which the boy's mother responded, "How can thee tell that? There is none but God can tell that, and except thee be more than an ordinary man, thee cannot tell that." But Godfrey bade her hold her tongue, and said he knew better than she and repeated what he had said. Weeks later, the boy's father testified that his son was very ill, with swelling in the body every night. Demos concludes that Godfrey managed to arouse fear and apprehension in virtually every encounter with neighbors (47). Godfrey became so notorious that his name was involved even in court cases where he had no direct involvement. For example, a defendant was alleged to have slandered a county magistrate by asserting that "he was as bad as Godfrey in usury." Another defendant said the plaintiff in the case had so mistreated him that he would have gotten better treatment "from Godfrey himself."

Demos summarizes Godrey's life and career in terms of six attributes: (1) he was single; (2) he had no settled habitation; (3) he was extremely mobile; (4) he was rough, provocative, and unpredictable; (5) he was extremely demanding; and (6) conflict was the normal condition of his life. For all his deviance, he was not, however, an "outsider," a common sociological view of accused witches. As Demos notes: "He was, after all, a familiar participant in a variety of everyday situations. At one time or another he had his bed and board from many of his neighbors, he worked alongside (and for) other men...indeed, it might well be argued that he was a special sort of *insider,* so deeply did he penetrate the thoughts and feelings of his peers" (55). In fact, Demos suggests that Godfrey's fellow New Englanders saw *themselves* in him, for as aggressive, angry, and grasping as he was, so were they, though to a much less exaggerated degree: "Petty disputes among neighbors, and 'heart-burning contentions' within whole towns or religious congregations, were endemic to the history of early New England" (55). The John Godfrey problem would not go away, no matter what the court decided in a particular dispute, for, in a real sense, "This was a problem deeply rooted in the collective life of the community, and in the individual lives of its various members. It is not too much to say...that there was a little of Godfrey in many of the Essex County settlers; so his future and their's remained deeply intertwined" (56).

If the Ann Hibbens and Rachel Clinton cases reveal the role of shame—and shamelessness—in New England witchcraft controversies, the Godfrey case draws our attention to the corresponding role of fear. Emotions of shame and fear underlay the anger and aggression that were such an evident part of the villagers' interactions, and Godfrey was especially adept at exploiting his opponents' fears. If Clinton and Hibbens responded to the high value placed on "taking shame on one's face" by displaying a defiant shamelessness (Clinton through sexual profligacy, Hibbens through refusal to accept the elders' condemnation), Godfrey displayed a fearlessness that was the envy—if largely unconscious—of other villagers. He was charged with suborning witnesses and evidently gave false testimony for payment in trials not his own; he broke the sabbath conventions, and he spoke openly about "the power of witches," suggesting that if they were not "kindly entertained," the devil would come and see that they were avenged (41). If he was accused of being a witch, he had done much to invite this accusation, daring his neighbors to bring such accusations into a court of law. This suggests a defiant fearlessness akin to Ann Hibbens' and Rachel Clinton's defiant shamelessness. If so, as a single man without a home or regular occupation, he could afford such defiance because, in a real sense, he had nothing to fear. Imprisonment—which happened on occasion—afforded a place to stay. Unlike other villagers, he had nothing to protect, no property that he feared losing, no family member who was dependent on him, no social standing of which he could be deprived. As a herdsman, he was already at the very bottom of the social ladder.

He was also able to use the courts to rule in his favor for lack of evidence of witchcraft, then turn around and sue his accusers for slander. Unlike the destruction of a neighbor's property, the charge of witchcraft was unprovable. Little wonder, then, that he fanned the flames of witchcraft against himself, for this gave his behavior a curious kind of cover, a protection from the full force of the law. Oddly enough, the "devil" *was* his protector, and was perhaps more effective in the conflicts of everyday life than the God his neighbors worshiped.

Demos notes that fear in the new settlement "was an elemental part of life." As a long-term resident remarked, "many and great was the terrors" of native Americans. He recalls that "several families which did live back a ways from the river was either murdered or captivated in my boyhood, and we all did live in constant fear of the like" (344). Then, there were the wolves: "The noise of their barkings was enough to curdle the blood of the stoutest, and I have never seen the man that did not shiver at the sound of a pack of 'em… We do not hear 'em now so much, but when I do I feel again the young hatred rising in my blood, and it is not a sin because God made 'em to be hated" (344).

In addition to these external predators, there were fears of a more psychological nature, and these, Demos suggests, were even more menacing. He explores these psychological fears in his effort to explain why the majority of those accused of being witches were women between forty-five and fifty-five years of age, and the majority of the accusers were men in young adulthood. (Adolescent girls were the third leading group "afflicted" by the phenomenon.) Demos discusses at length why middle-aged women were most likely to be accused, but I will concentrate on his psychoanalytic explanation for why these women's accusers were disproportionately young adult males. While he recognizes that young men in New England had difficulty achieving economic independence from their fathers, a deeper issue for Demos is the problem all young men face, namely, the break from an "emotional matrix" in which they have been sustained and guided through their early years:

> Expressed in formal terms, this means the relinquishment—or at least the dramatic realignment—of underlying "infantile" ties. And among such ties none is more powerful, and ultimately compromising, than the one which pulls (back) toward mother. The danger is of double-barreled "regression," to infantile dependence and infantile sexuality. (Our highly pejorative term "mother's boy" captures both elements. Such a person continues too long and too much to rely on the support and approval of his mother, while also retaining her as his primary "love object." As a result, he does not—inwardly—grow up.) The opportunity, on the other hand, is to act by and for oneself, to move ahead toward new (age-appropriate and "non-incestuous") loves. Therein lies the route to maturity. (156–57)

Recall Joseph Ryder in this regard. While he had gained a certain independence from his mother by living in the Matthews' home, her fear that he would move away from the village prompted her to plead with him to build his house on his father's property. If he did not, she promised or threatened to leave her husband and her other sons and go with him. Joseph acceded to her lamentations and, apparently against his better judgment (because he knew his father harbored ill will against him), built his house on his father's land. It is remarkable that in a new world, where land was plentiful and cheap, so many sons built homes on their fathers' land, thus condemning themselves to decades of dependency and (as in Joseph's case) the uncertainty that the sons would be able to hold on to what they had. Given the fathers' rather grudging, and mistrustful, division of their land among the sons, one suspects that the mothers were the parents most determined to keep their sons at home. But what does this have to do with witchcraft? Demos explains:

Young men supplied a far larger number of victims than any other category. Moreover, their sense of liability to attack can be interpreted as expressing several convergent strands of inner concern with women of their mothers' generation. In the first place, the witch commands extraordinary power over them and their possessions. (They continue to feel the strength of the "maternal object.") At the same time, they strike postures of resistance and repudiation—refusing the witch's requests for cooperation in routine aspects of everyday experience, and leading the charge against her in the courts of law. (They wish, however they can, to break the "incestuous" tie.) For this the witch grows angry with them, and punishes them severely. (They feel guilty, and deserving of punishment, for what they are about.) But when the witch attacks them, she does so indirectly, i.e., through familiars, or by striking down their cattle. (Distance is still maintained; in fantasy, as in social reality, the "maternal object" must not come too close.) The entire situation is complex and keenly felt—and *vulnerability* is right at the heart of it. (157)

We may ask, however, why these young men perceive the witch to be so punitive, especially when they are seeking to *break* the "incestuous" tie? In my view, the explanation lies in the punishment scenario of early childhood, when the mother, after a year of tender indulgence of her infant son's desires, suddenly turns against him, becoming, as it were, witchlike. Her face clouds over, there is anger in her voice, and she beats him. I would further suggest that this beating scenario is an emotionally charged one, for the beating—while painful—is also sexually stimulating for the boy (perhaps for the mother as well). Thus, the guilt he feels for the willfulness that prompted the beating is insignificant in comparison to the guilt he experiences as a consequence of the beating itself, which has stimulated illicit sexual fantasies. This highly charged emotional scenario is displaced in the fantasy of the witch who attacks his wife, children, or livestock, all extensions of himself. The witch does not strike him personally, but he experiences these as punishments for which he is directly to blame, punishments due to repressed—and, therefore, emotionally potent—incestuous desires toward his mother.

As Demos notes, the mother's early, almost exclusive involvement in her son's life contributed to his sense of her "magically formidable" qualities. This term, derived from Dorothy Dinnerstein, "would serve nicely to describe witches, as perceived by their victims and accusers" (204). Not surprisingly, therefore, belief in the magical powers of witches declined in America when the idea of "breaking the child's will" gave way to more "enlightened" views of children born with a clean slate. With these changes, the mother also became less sexually stimulating to her male child, less the object of incestuous fantasies stimulated by her physical attacks on her very impressionable boy.

This takes us back to John Godfrey. What distinguished him from these other young men was that he was completely unattached and had none of the emotional entanglements that other young men experienced with their mothers. As he put it, he could "kindly entertain" the witches so that they would not be "grieved or vexed with anybody." He had decided upon a course that other young men were not free to follow, of giving the witches the "beer and victuals" they wanted (41). One suspects that the source of his uncanny hold on the men who both testified against him and allowed him into their homes was that he "submitted" to the witches, thus symbolically enacting the incestuous scenario between son and mother from which other men recoiled. In effect, he acted out their repressed fantasies. In the process, he also made a mockery of the fathers with their arcane rules of "law and order" (by suborning witnesses, witnessing for pay, etc.).

Thus, by "entertaining" the witches, he was ensuring that the devil would *not* wreak his destruction on the village by avenging the inhospitality of the villagers toward the witches. Better the death of a single cow than the destruction of the whole herd, the frightful illness of one child than the deaths of all. As the settlers well knew, the devil could–and sometimes did–send in the natives to set fire to their homes, forcing them either to burn to death in their homes or be slaughtered when they ran out into the open. We may think of Godfrey's strategy as an insurance policy; the price for protection was the son's agreement to "entertain" the witches, to regress to infantile dependence and sexuality. Given the high degree of symbolic awareness among the early settlers, Godfrey's comment that he would give the witches the "beer and victuals" they requested could surely have an implied sexual connotation, one where the roles of nurturer and receiver of nurturance are reversed, where the witch indulges her own oral dependency needs through the agency of her obliging son, a reenactment of the earliest scenario of sexual pleasure.

Back to Rachel and Lawrence Clinton: Rachel's troubles began when she bought Lawrence's freedom in exchange for his marriage to her, a woman fourteen years older. Her brother-in-law contended that she had been the "witless dupe" of Clinton and Cross. But this is to take a nonpsychoanalytic view of the matter. For the sum of twenty-one pounds that, in any case, belonged to her mother, Rachel gained a power over Clinton not unlike that of a mother over a young adult son. Like Godfrey, Lawrence Clinton was unattached (no family members in America) and was therefore the perfect "victim" for Rachel's "bewitchments." He tried to escape–by living in neighboring communities and taking up with other women–but Rachel countered by gaining a court order requiring him to provide regular maintenance. In addition, she took up with other men, and it was Clinton himself who discovered her with John Ford in "unlawful familiarity" (31). Like the men who would take Godfrey to court while entertaining him in their homes, Lawrence Clinton sought to escape from Rachel but was unable to leave her for good. Perhaps it was Rachel's and John Godfrey's seemingly uncanny emotional hold over their victims that made them appear to be witches or in league with witches. If so, this uncanny hold was dynamically rooted in the mother-son relationship, especially as experienced in the whippings the mother inflicted on her boy in early childhood, where fear of punishment and the shame of sexual provocation and response were so entangled as to be virtually indistinguishable. As Godfrey perceived, its lesson was that the son should "give" his mother what she "wanted" lest she be "grieved or vexed." If he didn't comply, he risked the devil's own intervention. Better, then, to keep the matter between mother and son. These things must be kept in the dark, maintaining the appearances of "law and order."

Given his psychohistorical interests, Demos notes that one cannot rely on the writings of New England clergymen to gain a true picture of the phenomenon of witchcraft in their communities: "Among the clergy there was great interest in the literally diabolical elements—the Devil himself, and a vast satanic conspiracy against organized religion (in which witches played subordinate parts). Yet among ordinary villagers and tradesmen these priorities were reversed, with witchcraft and its immediate manifestations constituting the main interest" (173). Perhaps this explains why Godfrey was given to yawning during church services, implying that the clergy were out of touch with their people. So, too, were judges and magistrates, with their application of standard rules of evidence to a phenomenon—like the emotional power of the punishment scenario—that was invisible. Demos' psychoanalytic interpretation reveals what they were missing. The evidence that mattered in a court of law was not the kind of evidence that would bring to light the underlying dynamics, especially those involving mothers and sons. We should therefore exercise a healthy suspicion of the literary tradition (as represented by Pastor Robinson's writings) and also be careful about taking the court records at face value. Neither gives a true picture of the emotionology involved. Psychoanalysis is a necessary, not an optional, reconstructive method, if we want to know why the witches exercised an uncanny power over the confused, frustrated, and angry young men of early New England.

Fear, Anxiety, and Panic

In this discussion of the emotional dimensions of family and village life in early New England, I have mostly centered on structural matters (i.e., the family and village as interrelated organizations of collective life). Now I would like to look briefly at matters of group process, especially the ways in which a given society may experience an escalation of emotionality leading eventually to widespread group panic. Zevedei Barbu contends that there are variable degrees of emotionality in collective life, that some societies are more reflective of "emotional ambivalence" than others (Barbu, 57). This is because reason and emotionality are antithetical, and "reason is a balancing structure," its main function being "to establish a certain degree of gradualness, continuity and consistency in human behavior" (57). On the whole, emotionality works in the opposite direction:

> It has often been said that the "logic" of emotional life is that of black and white, of the "all-or-none" principle. There is no neutral ground between extreme tendencies. Love borders on hatred, courage on fear, arrogance on servility, piety on impulsiveness and violence. This

implies that individuals whose minds are dominated by emotional factors are liable to inner contradictions in their behavior; they swing in their emotional behavior from one extreme to another, from the extreme of love to that of hatred, from aggression and arrogance to servility, from piety to violence. (58)

To illustrate this phenomenon of emotional ambivalence, Barbu cites Tacitus' famous history of Rome under Tiberius, which describes in some detail the sycophantic habits of the people, and of the senators in particular, with their exaggerated need "to protect their position by subservience." In Tacitus' view, "they were men fit to be slaves," whose self-abasement gradually turned into persecution. Barbu observes:

> By this remark he seems to grasp the very essence of the case, i.e., the ambivalent attitudes created in a group of people by fear and insecurity. The only superfluous word in his formulation is "gradually." This is because attitudes of servility and flattery existed in the people described by him side by side with suspicion and aggression; so did love and hatred. The people's attitudes toward the strong were ambivalent: admiration and love were mixed with denigration and hatred. The same people showed servile submission towards the powerful, and aggressive domination leading to persecution of the weak. Hence the swing in their behavior between lack of self-respect and a morbid need for self-assertion and power. (58)

In a similar analysis of group emotionality, Erikson concludes *Childhood and Society* (1963) by tracing the role that fears from early childhood continue to play in the lives of adults, especially in their susceptibility to personal anxieties and collective panic. Demos provides an excellent bridge to Erikson's topic in a brief comment on the role that anxiety played in New England village life:

> Stated bluntly: Some victims of witchcraft were made ill, at least in part, by their own anxiety. Anthropologists have long remarked on this phenomenon in studies of premodern cultures all around the world. A man (or woman) who believes himself (or herself) to be the target of witches may sicken—may even die—under circumstances that defy medical explanation. There is no disease entity, and no ingestion of poisonous substance. Of course, the culture's explanation—witchcraft—then seems all the more plausible. But, in fact, biological science does support an alternative view. Intense affect—especially "great fear" and "great rage"—is frequently associated with profound physiological disturbances, widespread through the organism. Adrenal production, the activity of the musculature, the nervous system, heart rate, and blood circulation are all significantly involved. These affects are functional in the short term (e.g., in mobilizing the system

to meet an immediate and extreme challenge), but profoundly *dys-functional when continued over a period of many hours or days*. The key factor is a gradual decline in blood pressure, with resultant damage to the nerve centers, the feet, and other vital organs. Unless the condition can be somehow reversed the entire organism is progressively weakened. The process retains in all phases its connection to affective stress–to melancholy foreboding, to anxiety, to outright terror. Indeed, in fatal cases death can be attributed to a "true state of shock." (193)

Erikson's discussion of the dynamic connections between personal fears and anxieties, on the one hand, and group panic, on the other, occurs within a larger discussion of the methodological issues involved in the reconciling of history and psychology. He takes historians to task for their naiveté regarding psychological matters and clinicians for being oblivious to the role of historical processes in the lives of the individuals they treat. His specific concern, however, is that a crucial clinical insight–"that the individual is apt to develop an amnesia concerning his most formative experiences in childhood"–has not been incorporated into the interpretations of history. While historians and philosophers may recognize a "female principle" in the world, they pay little attention to "the fact that man is born and reared by women…Mechanistic man and rationalizing man continues to identify himself with abstractions of himself, but refuses to see how he becomes what he really is and how, as an emotional and political being, he undergoes with infantile compulsions and impulsions what his thought has invented and what his hands have built" (1963, 404). Why this contradictory behavior? It has a "psychological basis– namely, the individual's unconscious determination never to meet his childhood anxiety face to face again, and his superstitious apprehension lest a glance at the infantile origins of his thoughts and schemes may destroy his single-minded stamina. He therefore prefers enlightenment, away from himself; which is why the best minds have often been least aware of themselves" (404).

Every society consists of individuals in the process of developing from children into parents. To ensure continuity of tradition, a society needs to prepare its children for parenthood, and "it must take care of the unavoidable remnants of infantility in its adults" (405). Such infantility has many features, but especially noteworthy are fears that endanger not from without but within, and are manifest in one's "angry drives," "sense of smallness," and "split inner world." Given these, the adult "is always irrationally ready to fear invasion by vast and vague forces which are other than himself; strangling encirclement by everything that is not safely clarified as allied; and devastating loss of face before all-surrounding, mocking audiences, and this in world affairs as well as in personal affairs" (406).

While closely related, fears and anxieties may be differentiated in this way: "Fears are states of apprehension which focus on isolated and recognizable dangers so that they may be judiciously appraised and realistically countered.

Anxieties are diffuse states of tension (caused by a loss of mutual regulation and a consequent upset in libidinal and aggressive controls) which magnify and even cause the illusion of an outer danger, without pointing to appropriate avenues of defense or mastery" (406–7). They often occur together: "If, in an economic depression, a man is afraid that he may lose his money, his fear may be justified. But if the idea of having to live on an income only ten times instead of twenty times as large as his average fellow citizens causes him to lose his nerve and to commit suicide," then the fear of losing his money has become "associated with the anxiety aroused by the idea of having to live a role not characterized by unlimited resources" (407). Thus, "we have nothing to fear but anxiety," for it is not fear of a danger–which we may be able to meet with judicious action–but of the associated state of aimless anxiety "which drives us into irrational *action*, irrational *flight*–or, indeed, irrational *denial* of danger. When threatened with such anxiety, we either magnify a danger which we have no reason to fear excessively–or we ignore a danger which we have every reason to fear" (407). The fears that provoke anxieties in children "reach into adult life" and may take the form of "neurotic anxiety, which, after all, is recognizable as such, kept in bounds by most, and can be cured in some." They may also, however, reappear in the more terrifying form of "collective panics and in afflictions of the collective mind" (413).

To Erikson, the major weapon an individual or society has against such anxieties and panics is judiciousness, "a frame of mind which is tolerant of differences, cautious and methodical in evolution, just in judgment, circumspect in action, and–in spite of all this apparent relativism–capable of faith and indignation" (416). But there is a price for this judicious frame of mind, that is, that one must "forfeit the mechanism of projection," of casting "everything that feels alien within one's own heart onto some vague enemy outside." Such forfeiture "endangers the unbalanced and neurotic individual who, in choosing to pursue the judicious outlook, is now confronted with the dangers within, of 'introspection' and 'introjection,' and over-concern with the evil in himself" (417). As early New England residents tell us, there is a limit to how much introspection and introjection an individual can tolerate, especially when others no less blameworthy are able to avoid such painful introspection because they belong to the dominant class. In his discussion of shame, Erikson alludes to "an impressive American ballad in which a murderer to be hanged on the gallows before the eyes of the community, instead of feeling duly chastened, begins to berate the onlookers, ending every salvo of defiance with the words, 'God damn your eyes'" (253). In a society that reflected more the appearance than the reality of judiciousness, precisely among the dominant class, it is little wonder that the mechanism of projection was so ubiquitous, as was the anxiety that both fueled and was fueled by it.

I have focused in this chapter on family and village life, especially highlighting the powerful emotions triggered by social conflict at the familial and village level, because this is the level of analysis that seems least in evidence in contemporary portraits of Jesus. In spite of scholars' interest in Jesus' social world (the subject of the following chapter), surprisingly little attention has been paid to intrafamilial and interfamilial conflict at the village level. This is due, in part, to the paucity of data, making it difficult to come to firm judgments about the nature of family and village life in first-century Palestine. There is general acceptance, however, of the method of drawing on sociological and anthropological studies of analogous societies when done with sufficient caution and reserve. Thus, one is somewhat surprised that the portraitists discussed in the first two chapters do not give greater attention than they do to the microlevel situtation in which Jesus lived out the days and years of his life.

With its preoccupations with legal claims, its sensitivity to evil influences in the community—especially with regard to illness and personal misfortune—and its concern to identify some of its members as social deviants requiring severe punishment and ostracism, early New England community life sheds important light on the emotional ethos of first-century Palestinian family and village life. Of course, there are significant differences as well. This chapter, however, alerts readers to the issues that will concern us in our formulation of a psychological portrait of Jesus that is sensitive to the social environment in which he lived.

1) legal pre-occupation

2) sensitivity to evil influence

3) concern to identify some as social deviants

→ protection

5

The Social World of Jesus' Day

The preceding chapters suggest that Jesus studies and psychological biography are on convergent paths. As we saw in chapter 1, an important characteristic of contemporary Jesus research is its interest in the social world of first-century Palestine. As we saw in the chapters on psychobiography and psychohistory of groups, there is increasing awareness in psychohistorical studies of the need to progress beyond the trans-historical and cross-cultural generality of earlier psychohistorical efforts and to view the person "in a situation." This means locating the psychobiographical subject in the "ecological context," which includes "the objects, persons and events in his physical, social and symbolic environment." This does not preclude an attentiveness to possible indications of trans-historical factors, as occurs in Marcus J. Borg's and Erik H. Erikson's efforts to identify characteristics of *homo religiosus.* The quest for such more universalizing features, however, cannot be at the price of removing the subject from his situatedness.

As pointed out by Malina and Neyrey (1996), another important consideration is that our own emphasis on individuality was relatively unknown in first-century Palestine. Whereas we focus on what makes a person unique, the social milieu in which Jesus lived considered a person's social affiliations to be self-defining. Persons were defined, for example, by their connection to a village, an ethnic group, or an occupation. Thus, while we tend to describe individuals in terms of their individual characteristics or traits, the individual in Jesus' time would be identified by sociocultural stereotypes. This creates a certain irony in the case of Jesus, and for two reasons. One is that *our* emphasis on individuality is partly due to the influence of Christianity itself (cf. Weintraub, 1978). The other is that Jesus research has been driven to a great degree by its desire to identify what made Jesus unique (like *no* one else). The portraits of Jesus that we reviewed in chapters 1 and 2 may be viewed as efforts to identify the individual uniqueness of Jesus—his "atypicality," as Meier puts it. Each portrait offers its own view of what made Jesus unique, such as Crossan's contention that Jesus linked magic and meal together in a new creative synthesis, or Borg's view that Jesus integrated several types of religious authority in one message and mission. Critics take Sanders to task for, in their view, failing sufficiently to account for Jesus' uniqueness within the Judaism of his day, as if to say that he would not have attracted followers if there was nothing unique about him.

On the other hand, Jesus scholars recognize that to identify his uniqueness one must first place him "in a situation." For this, I will adopt a zoom-lens approach to his social world, beginning with Mediterranean societies in general, then certain social and political matters relating to the Galilee region in Jesus' day, and, finally, kinship practices in first-century Judaism.

The Honor-Shame Ideology in Mediterranean Societies

Crossan's *The Historical Jesus* is especially valuable for the picture it provides of the deeper social, political, and cultural conflicts of the first half of the century in Palestine in general and the Galilee in particular. His considerations begin with the fact that Palestine is located on the Mediterranean Sea. What the nations clustered around the Mediterranean share in common is an ecology composed of rugged topography with fertile river basins. He quotes David Gilmore:

> "It is this intra-national contrast between remote, inaccessible mountain peaks and rich agricultural valleys that lies at the heart of Mediterranean ecosystems. Throughout the region, one finds independent, egalitarian communities of peasants, tribesmen, or pastoralists in the marginal hills, and in the adjacent plains something vastly different—the latifundium, the great estate, the commercial farm, heir to the Roman villa...often worked by day laborers under harsh conditions." (Crossan, 1991, 5)

Presuming ecological constants over the centuries, Gilmore also cites these sociocultural ones:

> "A strong urban orientation; a corresponding disdain for the peasant way of life and for manual labor; sharp social, geographic, and economic stratification; political instability and a history of weak states; 'atomistic' community life; rigid sexual segregation; a tendency towards reliance on the smallest possible kinship units (nuclear families and shadow lineages); strong emphasis on shifting ego-centered, noncorporate coalitions; [and] an honor-and-shame syndrome which defines both sexuality and personal reputation." (Crossan, 7)

Continuing, Gilmore notes that "most villagers share an intense parochialism," "intervillage rivalries are common," there is "a general gregariousness and interdependence of daily life characteristic of small, densely populated neighborhoods," and "institutionalized hostile nicknaming" (7). An "evil eye belief is widespread" and is "probably one of the few true Mediterranean universals. It is also one of the oldest continuous religious constructs in the Mediterranean area" (7). There are also religious, marital, and political constants: "Religion plays an important institutionalized role in both north and south, as do priests, saints, and holy men...Dotal marriage (dowry) is practiced in only 4 percent of the world's cultures, and is limited geographically to eastern Eurasia and the Mediterranean basin." At the micropolitical level, "emphasis on informal personal power rather than formal institutions is reflected in the reliance on patronage" (7).

While cautioning against the assumption that these sociocultural "constants" apply uniformly to Mediterranean societies from ancient to modern times, Crossan draws extensively on Gilmore's list throughout his interpretation of the Galilee at the time of Jesus. In the pages that immediately follow this citation from Gilmore, however, he especially focuses on the "honor-and-shame syndrome which defines both sexuality and personal reputation." While he chooses this theme mainly to illustrate how one may take a proposed Mediterranean constant and study it "both across present space and past time and from fieldwork to biblical text" (8), the topic itself is of considerable interest for anyone who takes seriously the task of locating Jesus in his sociocultural context.

To show its relevance, Crossan draws on John Davis' work on the anthropology of Mediterranean sexuality. Davis argues that "the limits of endogamy [marrying only within one's own tribe or social group] and exogamy [marrying only outside the tribe] are debated throughout the length of Genesis," so its stories ask repeatedly but implicitly, "How closely related must you be in order to be one people and how other must you be in order to be a spouse? Other sex? Other family? Other lineage? Other tribe? Other nation?" One answer is given in the nomadic period, when the patriarchs are willing to give their wives (as "sisters") to power brokers in exchange for pasture, a form of "sexual hospitality" (8). A very different answer is given in the later sedentary situation of political independence, where not only are wives no longer given in sexual hospitality to outsiders, but neither are daughters to be given to them in marriage. The guardians of this new system are the women's mothers, not their fathers. This system may, however, be contravened in situations of dominance, where, for example, a victorious army murders the men and takes their wives as their own. Davis' analysis of the Genesis stories reveals the historical roots of the constant of the "shame-and-honor" syndrome. While this example focuses specifically on sexual matters, it relates to personal reputation as well, for in situations in which sisters are threatened, the personal reputation of her brothers is also at stake. While the brother's ability to protect his sister usually applies to extrafamilial threats, the story of the rape of Tamar (2 Sam. 13:1–22) portrays one brother (Absalom) avenging another's (Amnon) incestuous act.

With the Davis study serving as a kind of baseline, Crossan discusses the "honor-and-shame syndrome" in Mediterranean societies and groups in greater detail. What do these terms mean in the Mediterranean context? He quotes Pierre Bourdieu's statement that

> the point of honor is the basis of the moral code of an individual who sees himself always through the eyes of others, who has need of others for his existence, because the image he has of himself is indistinguishable from that presented to him by other people...Respectability, the reverse of shame, is the characteristic of a person who needs other people in order to grasp his own identity and whose conscience is a kind of interiorization of others, since these fulfill for him the role of witness and judge...He who has lost his honor no longer exists. He ceases to exist for people, and at the same time he ceases to exist for himself. (9)

While the bases for honor and shame differ across gender lines, these understandings of honor and shame apply to both genders alike.

Crossan next quotes John G. Peristiany, who emphasizes that "honor-and-shame are the constant preoccupation of individuals in small scale, exclusive societies where face to face personal, as opposed to anonymous, relations are of paramount importance and where the social personality of the actor is as significant as his office" (10). Thus, within the exclusive group, honor-and-shame relationships are well-defined, non-overlapping, and non-competitive. Outside the group, however, honor-shame rankings are insecure and unstable: "In this insecure, individualist world where nothing is accepted on credit, the individual is constantly forced to prove and assert himself. Whether as the protagonist of his group or as a self-seeking individualist, he is constantly 'on show,' he is forever courting the public opinion of his 'equals' so that they may pronounce him worthy" (10). This security within the family and insecurity outside the family is true for all levels of society. A member of the lower classes is not, for example, exempt from this requirement to prove himself worthy.

Because this honor-and-shame dynamic brings to mind a range of comparisons—from medieval chivalry to contemporary North American street gangs—Crossan asks whether the honor-shame dynamic, seemingly so universal, is no longer a useful, distinguishing Mediterranean characteristic? The answer, he suggests, lies in David Gilmore's comment that Mediterranean honor is a "libidinized" social reputation. It is this "eroticized aspect of honor—albeit unconscious or implicit—that seems to make the Mediterranean variant distinctive" (10). Thus, what distinguishes Mediterranean societies from others is that the primordial values of honor and shame "are deeply tied up with sexuality and power, with masculine and gender relations" (10). The honor-and-shame moral system is thus "gender-based." Gilmore concludes, "It is this pervasive sexuality that is particularly characteristic of Mediterranean value systems, of Mediterranean codes of honor and shame. In this, the codes may be distinguished from parallel moral systems elsewhere" (11), from Japan, for example.

Crossan next introduces the issue of social stratification in order to explore the complexities of honor in Mediterranean societies. According to John Davis, there are three main forms of stratification: bureaucracy, class, and honor; and each is related, more or less directly, to the distribution of wealth (11). If class and bureaucracy are objective forms of stratification and relatively easy to identify as such, honor is highly subjective and thus both variable and volatile. Stratification by bureaucracy is clear, for example, when a villager has to approach a government civil servant. The villager fully expects that the government official will assert his administrative dignity and that the interaction will be highly impersonal. The villager will not confuse the encounter with his own hierarchy of honor and shame. A similar clarity exists when members of different social classes have dealings with one another. A lower-class individual expects to be treated officiously, even as a higher-class person expects to be treated deferentially. As long as such expectations are met, the issue of honor and shame does not arise. Such encounters are not, for example, inherently shaming for the person of a lower class.

Why, then, is there an honor-shame stratification at all? And to what situations does it, in fact, apply? Davis notes that, among the authors he surveyed on this issue, only Jane Schneider has asked and attempted to answer the fundamental questions: Why does honor exist? Why is it seemingly so essential to Mediterranean social life? Schneider's answer focuses on the problem of resource competition between pastoralists and agriculturists. Unlike pastoralism in Central Asia, pastoralism in the Mediterranean was challenged by the continuous expansion of agriculture. Because sea transport was easy, technologies for the production of agricultural surpluses were developed for lands that might otherwise have remained pastoral (being dry and mountainous). Landlords devoted vast regions to the production of wheat for export, so that in much of the Mediterranean, Schneider notes,

> pastoralism and agriculture coexisted, competing for the same resources in a way that fragmented the social organization of each type of community and blurred the boundary between them. In the absence of the state, pastoral and agricultural communities in their midst developed their own means of social control—the codes of honor and shame—which were adapted to the intense conflict that external pressures had created within them, and between them. (Crossan, 12)

Pastoral societies, whether nomadic and moving over an extended territory or moving back and forth between one established area and another, became vulnerable and pressured by the agricultural community. Under such pressure, "its basic economic units became smaller and more independent of one another. To survive, pastoralists must become selfish" and "make selfishness a virtue" (quoted in Crossan, 12). The more difficult it became to find large extensions of suitable grazing land, regular access to adequate water supplies, and a predictable route of migration, the smaller the basic economic unit became. Thus, large extended families or clans were a handicap in the management of herds. To survive, families needed to become nuclear. In effect, pastoralists also became "little more than specialists within agricultural communities" (quoted in Crossan, 13).

What is the bearing of honor-shame on this pastoralist versus agriculturalist social structure? While one may imagine a single nuclear family being quite self-sufficient in its ability to maintain its flocks and herds and to obtain and control access to needed pasture and water, it would need to turn outside itself for wives and husbands. Or, as Crossan puts it: "If, for example, there were only two nuclear families in the world, they could compete with each other to their heart's content for everything else desirable, but they would have to cooperate with each other for mates" (14). Thus, scarcest of all scarce resources are marriage partners, because these by definition cannot come from within the nuclear family. Because incest is precluded, a family that is otherwise self-sufficient needs to suspend selfishness as a virtue and cooperate with another family for mates. In this one instance, family survival depends on cooperation, not self-sufficiency.

In Schneider's view, this brings honor and shame into the picture. Why? Because concern for honor "grows when contested resources are subject to redivision along changing lines, when there is no stable relationship between units of power and precisely delineated patrimonies, i.e., when the determination of boundary lines is subject to continual human intervention" (quoted in Crossan, 13). The insularity of the nuclear family is violated, its boundedness made porous, when it reaches beyond itself for marriage partners. Concern for honor also arises "when the definition of the group is problematical; when the social boundaries are difficult to maintain, and internal loyalties are questionable. Shame, the reciprocal of honor, is especially important when one of the contested resources is women, and women's comportment defines the honor of social groups" (13–14).

An especially important issue in this regard is the family's ability to certify to the other family the "quality" of the women involved in the transaction. Even if women are viewed as similar to other contested resources, they are, after all, "a very special and even unique resource among such resources. The future of the family depends on the individuality of the new life in a way it hardly does on the individuality of sheep, or pasture, or well" (14). This explains the "almost mythological importance of virginity in Mediterranean codes of honor and shame." It was essential that the family be able to assure the receiving family of the sexual purity of their sister or daughter, which meant that fathers and brothers were expected to restrain themselves, and to protect their women from outsiders as well. Honor thus becomes of crucial importance where a family's marriageable women are concerned. The family may have conflictual relations with other families in other respects, but in this one area, such conflicts need to be set aside. Crossan quotes Julian Pitt-Rivers:

> "When it is said that 'we fight with those with whom we intermarry'
> or vice-versa…[it means] that we, as individuals, give our daughters
> to members of the groups with whom we, as a collectivity, have

relations of conflict. The two types of relationship, collective hostility and affinity through marriage, are the opposed aspects of an ambivalence and it is the second which qualifies the first and sets limits to it, bringing it under control of the longer-term interests represented by the descendants who result from intermarriage." (Crossan, 14)

In his comments on the role that virginal purity plays in the honor-shame dynamics of Mediterranean society, Crossan alludes to Mary, "the Virgin-Mother." If "virginity is the living symbol and incarnate emblem of the [family] group's closed-off combativeness," it is then "easy to understand the importance of Mary, as Virgin-Mother, in such circumstances. She is exactly what one wishes for but can never obtain: maternity without the loss of virginity, progeny without the necessity of sex, and, therefore, competition for resources without the need to cooperate for the most important one" (14). In effect, she represents the myth that the family can reproduce itself from within and do so in a manner that does not violate laws of purity.

Thus, at one extreme there is the myth of the virgin-mother (the most honored woman of all, and alone of her sex), and at the other, the victim of incest (the most degraded, shameful woman of all). Between these extremes are the women who are certifiably pure. Special cases are those already encountered in our discussion of the New England Puritans, that is, women who have had consensual or nonconsensual sex with nonfamily members, and women who have had premarital sex with the men to whom they are betrothed. Especially problematic in the latter case are situations where the male fails to fulfill the marriage contract. Given this range of real-life possibilities, and the ambiguities as to the facts in specific cases, we can appreciate the instabilities and ambiguities associated with the honor-shame dynamic in Mediterranean societies. It is also understandable that Schneider would refer to honor-shame not as a structural element (thus analogous to bureaucracy and class) but as an ideology, one that, like all ideologies, complements "institutional arrangements for the distribution of power and the creation of order in society" (14). More surprising is the implication that to the degree there is any real "individuality" in ancient Mediterranean society, it inheres in the marriageable woman. In contrast to her, the brothers are not a unique or special resource. Of course, for this very reason, she may become the victim of special exploitation and abuse.

A Patronal Society

As Gilmore notes, another sociocultural constant of Mediterranean society is the fluidity of its systems of power and influence. This is reflected in its "shifting ego-centered, noncorporate coalitions" and its emphasis, at the micropolitical level, "on informal personal power rather than formal institutions," especially as reflected in its "reliance on patronage" (7). To understand the role of patronage in Mediterranean society, Crossan considers the social strata in agrarian societies, citing Gerhard Lenski's work. In Lenski's view, agrarian societies are characterized by marked social inequality, with "pronounced differences in power, privilege, and honor" (Crossan, 45). He identifies nine social classes with a huge gulf separating the five upper from the four lower classes. The upper five are the ruler (a separate class), followed by the governing, retainer, merchant, and priestly classes. On the other side of the great divide are the peasant class (the vast majority of the population), followed by the artisan, unclean and degraded, and expendable classes. The expendable classes, comprising about 5–10 percent of the population in normal times, include a variety of types, such as petty criminals, outlaws, beggars, and underemployed itinerant workers, all forced to live solely by their wits or by charity. Despite high rates of infant mortality, the occasional practice of infanticide, the more frequent practice of celibacy, and adult mortality due to war, famine, and disease, agrarian societies usually produced more people than the dominant classes found it profitable to employ. Furthermore, while upward mobility occurred (e.g., the merchant class usually evolved upward from the lower classes), so that lower members of a higher class might be well below the higher members of a lower class in terms of power and privilege, the greatest mobility in the long run was downward, and this was especially true among the lower classes.

Given the importance of the honor-and-shame ideology in Mediterranean societies, patron-client relationships were a principal means, along with kinship, by which this ideology was institutionalized. In important ways, this informal system was more important than social stratification. Crossan quotes Thomas Carney, who describes antiquity as "a society based on patronage, not class stratification," and which therefore resembled

> a mass of little pyramids of influence, each headed by a major family– or one giant pyramid headed by an autocrat...The client of a power wielder thus becomes a powerful man and himself in turn attracts clients. Even those marginal hangers-on to power attract others, more disadvantageously placed, as their clients. So arise the distinctive pyramids of power–patron, the first order clients, then second and third order clients and so on–associated with patronage society. (Crossan, 59)

Crossan notes that the patronage system was not only pervasive but corruptive, for promotion and privileges were the direct result of favors to friends, and friends of friends. Whole towns might benefit by favors obtained through one of their citizens from the emperor or other influential persons. It was customary for municipalities to adopt distinguished men, sometimes by the dozen, as patrons. Brokerage was thus the means by which power and influence were disseminated through the system, as "the broker is one who sustains a double dyadic alliance, one as client to a patron and another as patron to a client" (60).

Crossan cites several recent works on the patronage system that note its informality, its inherently exploitative nature, and the fact that it insinuates itself into virtually every aspect of the social system. One analyst noted that "patronage is unsymmetrical, involving inequality of power; it tends to form an extended system; to be long-term, or at least not restricted to a single isolated transaction; to possess a distinctive ethos; and, whilst not always illegal or immoral, to stand outside the officially proclaimed formal morality of the society in question" (66). Another team of analysts notes its "peculiar combination of inequality and asymmetry in power with seeming mutual solidarity expressed in terms of personal identity and interpersonal sentiments and obligations" (66). Another notes that the patronal system is based on "general acceptance by the rural mass of the prevailing socio-economic system and value structure which allowed them to be exploited; as long as the system of patronage provided them with a living they returned their loyalty to the master" (67). Still another notes that the patronage system in Mediterranean societies exploited—and sustained—a "sharp social stratification" with "relative and absolute scarcity of natural resources" and little upward social mobility: "Power is highly concentrated in a few hands, and the bureaucratic functions of the state are poorly developed. These conditions are of course ideal for the development of patron-client ties and a dependency ideology" (67).

While patronage and clientage are modes of social relationship and political organization, they may also have religious significance. Crossan quotes Anthony Hall's definition of the patron as "a person of power, status, authority and influence...an employer, a ceremonial sponsor or even a protecting saint" who is "only relevant in relation to a less powerful person or 'client' whom he can help or protect" (68). In a discussion of "religious clientelism," James Scott notes that "the relationship between a 'saint,' prophet, or religious teacher and his followers may often be viewed as a patron-client relationship," and that "networks of religious patronage may constitute a 'shadow' social structure in potential conflict with secular forms of authority" (68). Christianity came to reflect this patronal system. As G. E. M. de Ste. Croix notes, "Just as the terrestrial patron is asked to use his influence with the emperor, so the celestial patron, the saint, is asked to use his influence with the Almighty" (69). Crossan later argues in *The Historical Jesus* that Jesus was a vigorous opponent of the patronal system, and that his policy of reciprocity (meals for magical healing) and itinerancy were key to this opposition. As noted earlier, for Crossan, Jesus envisioned a "brokerless kingdom" (225).

In *Palestine in the Time of Jesus* (1998), K. C. Hanson and Douglas E. Oakman point out that a key structural feature of the patronage system was its inequality between patron and client: "Patrons are elite persons (male or female) who can provide benefits to others on a personal basis, due to a combination of superior power, influence, reputation, position, and wealth. In return for these benefits, patrons...could expect to receive honor, information, and political support from clients. Clients, on the other hand, are persons of lesser status who are obligated and loyal to a patron over a period of time" (71). Most often, this was an informal arrangement, but there were expectations of enduring loyalty. The authors summarize the major elements of the patron/client relationship, noting that it (1) is usually particularistic (exclusive) and diffuse (covering a wide range of issues); (2) involves the exchange of a whole range of social interactions (power, influence, inducement, commitment); (3) entails a "package deal," so that power, influence, and so on, cannot be given separately (useful goods, for example, must accompany loyalty and commitment); (4) entails unconditionality and long-range social credit (i.e., benefits and obligations are usually not exchanged simultaneously, and, hence, a binding relationship based on a sense of "unfinished business" is maintained); (5) involves a strong element of interpersonal obligation, even if relations are often ambivalent ones; (6) entails relations that are strongly binding, but informal and unofficial, and often opposed to official laws of the country; (7) is proclaimed to be lifelong and long-range, but may in fact be abandoned voluntarily; (8) is vertical (hierarchical) and dyadic (between individuals or networks of individuals), and thus undermining of horizontal group organization and solidarity of other patron-client relationships; (9) is based on a strong element of inequality and difference between patron and client (social stratification), where patrons monopolize certain positions of crucial importance to clients, especially access to means of production, major markets, and centers of society; (10) is nonexclusive (i.e., a client may have more than one patron, usually for different purposes); and (11) occurs on the same sliding scale as friendship, with increased likelihood that it will be perceived as friendship as the social inequality of patron and client decreases (72).

Given our interest in the emotionology of a society, the degree to which the patron-client relationship is structurally resistant to rationalization is worth noting. It operates outside of the legal system (with its binding contracts) and is therefore dependent on informal—hence emotional—expectations of honor, loyalty, commitment, and so forth. As Hanson and Oakman indicate, it is inherently ambivalent, binding and yet not absolutely binding, and demanding of loyalty but not absolute loyalty (as both parties might have several patron-client relationships, some of which might be inherently competitive). Thus, it is not unlike the relationship of a father to several sons, where differential treatment is the norm, not the exception. It should also be noted that, through the patron-client relationship, the social system manifests considerable—if masked and informal—individualism. To be sure, it is vertical and dyadic, but it is entered into and dissolved by individuals and thus operates outside the official lines of the society, undermining the social system based on recognized social groupings (including class, kinship, etc.).

As indicated, the honor-shame ideology is central to the patron-client relationship. In exchange for influence and inducements, the patron expects to receive honor. As Hanson and Oakman point out: "What patrons had to offer clients was a wide variety of 'services'" (physical protection against enemies, legal support, food, money, citizenship, work, appointment to an official post, freedom from taxes). Conversely, "What clients had to offer patrons was first and foremost honor, the primary 'commodity' and value in the Mediterranean...By praising the benefits of one's patrons in the community, his or her honor and reputation increased, which might have the residual effect of their increased influence" (73). Clients also "honored" patrons by giving them their loyalty and support, "which might be expressed in performing tasks, collecting information, spreading rumors, backing the patron in a factional fight, or attending funerals" (73). Because such honor in exchange for services would be public–one does not honor another in secret–a client who was well-treated and thus also especially indebted would, predictably, become the object of envy and jealousy. Mistrust was another emotional element, as a patron might have grounds for doubting the loyalty of a client who was known to have another patron. While, as Hanson and Oakman point out, a client might have more than one patron for "different purposes," these purposes could be separated only in principle. In reality, the client with two or more patrons would need to be constantly on guard that he was not perceived to be disloyal owing to the overlapping interests of patrons.

In short, the patron-client relationship introduced a high level of anxiety into social relationships. No one was secure in this type of social relationship, yet it was integral to how things were done in Mediterranean society. If one wanted to be an integral part of the society, one could not remain aloof from the patron-client system. While it was informal and unofficial and entered into voluntarily, this does not mean that it was structurally marginal or, for an individual, optional. If one chose not to participate in this informal social relationship, or was excluded from it, one experienced a kind of social nonbeing. And this applied to members of lower as well as higher classes.

The Peasant Class

Crossan devotes a full chapter to the peasant class, not only because it was numerically the largest but also because, in his view, Jesus would have belonged to it. In the epigraph to his chapter "Peasant and Protester," he quotes Richard A. Horsley's point that

> "as participation in determining the shape of their own lives is denied to a colonized people, they may retreat further into their own cultural or religious traditions. Their religious traditions and rites take on increased importance as the only dimension of their life that remains under their own control. As a way of preserving some semblance of dignity, colonized people had to focus all the more on their distinctive religious traditions, rites, and rituals as symbols of their former freedom and self-determination. This tends to make them all the more sensitive about violation of these symbols." (124)

In the body of this chapter, Crossan cites Horsley's contention that the Jewish peasantry was "the original source of historical change and its ramifications" in mid–first-century C.E. Jewish Palestine (124). While this contention may seem inconsistent with Horsley's earlier statement that colonized people "retreat further into their own cultural or religious traditions," this is not the case, for, at least on occasion, the peasant class made trouble for the elite through protests and resistance (in the form of passive withdrawal through strikes and demonstrations, banditry, and terrorism) and outright revolt (when protest and resistance is met with a repressive response, ranging from intimidation through harassment to imprisonment, torture, and death). Thus, while the peasant class is inherently conservative, it may, under certain historical conditions, mobilize against the ruling classes. As Crossan shows later in the chapter, this is exactly what occurred in mid–first-century Palestine. He cites several instances of successful nonviolent protest.

We should also consider, however, that the everyday existence of peasants involves silent protest. Crossan notes that the term "peasant" means something structural and relational, not only occupational (e.g., farmer) or geographical (rural). That is, the peasant classes, while certainly agricultural and rural, live in relation to market towns and are therefore part of a larger population. Thus, the primary criterion for defining peasant society is structural–the relationship between the village and the city. The central common denominator in the social, economic, religious, juristic, historical, and emotional aspects of this relationship is that peasants have very little control over the conditions that govern their lives. Also, because they are rural cultivators whose surpluses (over and above what they need for their own subsistence) are transferred to the governing classes to underwrite their own standard of living, peasants are continually vulnerable to exploitation. As the governing classes' standard of living increases, the peasants' share of what is produced decreases.

The peasant class–unlike the governing classes–therefore has little vested interest in increased productivity, as it knows it will not be the beneficiary of greater surpluses. Instead, its allotment will remain constant, meaning that its percentage of the yield decreases. Thus, to the extent that the accusations commonly hurled at peasants are true–that they are passive-aggressive, stubbornly refuse to adapt to new, more efficient technologies resulting in greater production, are untrusting and suspicious–the reasons for this are systemic. Since they have no direct way to increase their own share of available supplies, their own best interest is to maintain the status quo, however unsatisfactory this may be. Given its size (the largest social class in first-century Palestine), a communally organized traditional peasantry, reinforced by a functionally useful slowness, imperviousness, and stupidity–apparent or real–can be a formidable force (127). Crossan quotes James Scott in this regard: "Most subordinate classes throughout most of history have rarely been afforded the luxury of open, organized, political activity. Or, better stated, such activity was dangerous, if not suicidal…For all their importance when they do occur, peasant rebellions–let alone revolutions–are few and far between. The vast majority are crushed unceremoniously" (127). For this very reason, however, it is especially important "to understand what we may call *everyday* forms of peasant resistance–the prosaic but constant struggle between the peasantry and those who seek to extract labor, food, taxes, rents, and interest from them. Most forms of this struggle stop well short of outright collective defiance." Instead, they take the form of "the ordinary weapons of relatively powerless groups: foot dragging, dissimulation, desertion, false compliance, pilfering, feigned ignorance, slander, arson, sabotage, and so on." These are forms of class struggle that "require little or no coordination or planning; they make use of implicit understandings and informal networks; they often represent a form of individual self-help; they typically avoid any direct, symbolic confrontation with authority…When such strategies are abandoned in favor of more quixotic action, it is usually a sign of great desperation" (128). In effect, the peasantry are "more radical at the level of ideology than at the level of behavior, where they are more effectively constrained by the daily exercise of power" (128).

Later, in his chapter on "John and Jesus," Crossan returns to Scott's views on the ideologies of peasant societies. Scott notes that these are usually constructed as alternative symbolic universes, ones that make

> the social world in which peasants live less than completely inevitable. Much of this radical symbolism can only be explained as a cultural reaction to the situation of the peasantry *as a class*. In fact, this symbolic opposition represents the closest thing to class consciousness in pre-industrial agrarian societies. It is as if those who find themselves at the bottom of the social heap develop cultural forms which promise them dignity, respect, and economic comfort which they lack in the world as it is. A real pattern of exploitation dialectically produces its own symbolic mirror image within folk culture. (263)

At the risk of some overgeneralization, Scott suggests there are some common features of this reflexive symbolism:

> It nearly always implies a society of brotherhood in which there will be no rich and poor, in which no distinctions of rank and status (save those between believers and unbelievers) will exist. Where religious institutions are experienced as justifying inequities, the abolition of rank and status may well include the elimination of religious hierarchy in favor of communities of equal believers. Property is typically, though not always, to be held in common and shared. All unjust claims to taxes, rents, and tributes are to be nullified. The envisioned utopia may also include a self-yielding and abundant nature as well as a radically transformed human nature in which greed, envy, and hatred will disappear. While the earthly utopia is thus an anticipation of the future, it often harks back to a mythic Eden from which mankind has fallen away. (264)

Crossan concludes his chapter with this quotation and does not comment on it. I suggest, however, that we make careful note of Scott's two uses of the term *utopia*–"envisioned utopia" and "earthly utopia"–to characterize this alternative symbolic universe. I will suggest in chapter 8 that Jesus scholars have been so much under the thrall of "eschatology" that they have failed to recognize that Jesus–befitting his peasant roots–had utopianist proclivities, though in somewhat different form than as represented by Scott.

The Galilee in the Time of Jesus

While other characteristics of Mediterranean societies would merit exploration, these discussions of the pervasiveness of honor-shame dynamics, the importance of the patronal system, and the situation of the peasant class provide a broad overview of the societal features that are especially relevent to a psychological study of Jesus in his situatedness. I now want to turn to the Galilee region, where Jesus–with the exception of one or more visits to Jerusalem–spent his entire life.

In their chapter of *The Historical Jesus: A Comprehensive Guide* (1996) on the geographical and social framework of the life of Jesus, Gerd Theissen and Annette Merz point out that Galilee can be divided into three districts: Upper Galilee (with mountains between 600 and 1200 meters high); Lower Galilee (with heights between 100 and 600 meters); and the land around the Sea of Galilee. Generally regarded as Jesus' hometown (and his likely birthplace), Nazareth is in Lower Galilee. In the first century C.E., it was a Jewish settlement remote from the trade centers, and therefore of little political and economic importance to the region. At the time of Jesus, the inhabitants (estimated at between 50 and 2,000 persons, but most likely at the upper end of this range) were predominantly engaged in agriculture and lived in caves that were partly natural and partly dug in the chalk; some of the homes were extended by a roofed structure at the front. Nazareth is only about 6 kilometers (roughly four miles) from Sepphoris, a flourishing city with a Hellenistic Jewish stamp, which served as the capital of the Galilee until Herod Antipas founded Tiberias as the capital of the Galilee around 19 C.E. Howard Clark Kee (1992) notes that Nazareth overlooked the main route that led south and west from Sepphoris to Caesarea. Because the cities and trade routes of the Galilee, and especially the Via Maris near where Jesus grew up, were among the busiest in ancient Palestine, it may be assumed that Nazareth was strongly influenced by the dominant cultural atmosphere–Greco-Roman–of the region (15). Also, because Jesus' trade as a *tekton* means "builder and could well have included masonry, this opens the possibility that he was involved in the building of Sepphoris" (15).

The center of Jesus' public activity was Capernaum, which was located on the north shore of the Sea of Galilee, and is estimated to have had a population of 12,000–15,000 persons. The discovery of quantities of fishhooks among the ruins of Capernaum and the remains of an ancient harbor support New Testament reports that persons who made their living fishing were prominent among Jesus' companions (16). Capernaum was a frontier city from 4 to 39 C.E., thus having a detachment of Roman troops and toll station for a time, though it probably lost its political status when it lost its position on the frontier. Theissen and Merz note: "Now and then it is conjectured that this frontier situation was welcome to Jesus because he could escape politically explosive situations so rapidly by moving to another territory" (167). In any event, while Jesus was itinerant, and the actual places where he was active and the routes by which he traveled can no longer be reconstructed, his activity seems to have centered around the Sea of Galilee and its environs. Nazareth and Cana, which lie in lower Galilee, are the major exceptions. It is likely that his visits to these towns were prompted by the fact that Nazareth was his hometown.

Conspicuous by their absence in the synoptic tradition are the cities of Sepphoris and Tiberias (the latter being only 16 kilometers, or about eleven miles, from Capernaum). As these were the most Hellenized centers in Galilee, the fact that they are not mentioned as part of Jesus' itinerary seems to reflect his own sympathies with the country population, which was in tension with the Hellenized culture and the wealth concentrated in these cities. Theissen and Merz, however, cite one scholar's opinion that the absence of mention of these two cities was due to the failure of Jesus' ministry there, and the view of another that he avoided these cities not for religious reasons (e.g., their impurity) but to evade direct confrontation with Herodian power, a decision possibly based on the fate of John the Baptist. They conclude that the social milieu in which Jesus was active was therefore "the Jewish population in and around Galilee—above all where the influence of urban Hellenistic culture put Jewish identity in question. Here Jesus found openness to his preaching" (171).

In addition to social tensions between city and rural populations, there were tensions between rich and poor. Land was the primary source of employment, and social stratification was closely connected with land ownership. In the Galilee of Jesus' time, large and small estates coexisted, with many of the large landowners living in the cities and leasing their lands to tenants. There is circumstantial evidence to suggest that there may have been smallholders in Jesus' family (based on a report that the grandsons of Jude, Jesus' brother, were smallholders and supported themselves by working the land). It was common for families to be engaged in agriculture even if, for example, the family was involved in the building trade. Concerning agriculture, at least four groups can be identified: absentee landowners, leaseholders, free smallholders, and hired laborers. Conflicts between these four groups were common. Leaseholders resented having to hand over a large percentage of their produce to the landowner, hired laborers resented the treatment they received from leaseholders and smallholders, and smallholders were always threatened with debt if a weak harvest was insufficient to pay taxes, support the family, and provide seed for the next year's planting. The danger of falling to the next lower level or even further was a constant threat. Smallholders could fall to the level of leaseholder, and both groups could drop to the rank of hired laborers, beggars, and thieves at the bottom of the social hierarchy (173).

There were also social and political tensions between rulers and ruled. Herodian client princes reigned in the Galilee in the first century. The Romans employed this indirect form of rule where they felt they could not entrust a region to semiautonomous city republics. After the death of Herod I (called "the Great"), Palestine was divided between his three sons with Herod Antipas ruling from 4 B.C.E. to 39 C.E. over Galilee and Peraea. Philip, who reigned from 4 B.C.E. to 34 C.E., received a predominantly non-Jewish territory in northeast Palestine, and Archelaus was given the southern territory of Judea and Samaria. He was deposed after ten years, and Roman prefects, including Pontius Pilate, ruled the territory in the years that concern us here. While Herod Antipas' long reign in Galilee might suggest a stable political situation there, this was not the case. There were several revolts against him during his rule, and his transfer of the capital from Sepphoris to Tiberias in 19 C.E. was an attempt to settle a population there that was loyal to him. Most likely, the armed force for which he was later denounced to the Romans, causing the loss of his kingdom, was located in Tiberias. It is improbable that he needed the weapons only as a protection against external enemies (175).

Theissen and Merz also consider the religious character of Galilee. It was a Jewish enclave within non-Jewish territory and geographically separated from the religious center in Jerusalem. It is difficult, however, "to produce an adequate picture of the religious mentality in Galilee," not least because the rabbinic literature about Galilee was composed by Judean scholars who were forced to settle in Galilee. Thus, this literature "expresses the frustration of the rabbinic movement, which was emerging with an increasing claim to absoluteness, in the face of the resistance of the Galilean population to assimilation with it" (176). The few sources that allow insight into the religious self-understanding of the Jews of Galilee suggest a marked temple piety and loyalty to the temple in Jerusalem in times of crisis, a traditional belief that God alone is the owner of the land, and that God wants the Jews to protect the land from alien peoples. Their daily life would be based on the Torah, which they probably adapted to the requirements of agricultural life, just as the Pharisaic halakah corresponded to a more urban milieu. While Galilean sages were accused of laxity over laws relating to purity, the fact that the country people destroyed pictures of animals in Herod's palace and that John the Baptist's protests against the liberal manipulations of the marriage laws by the Herodians received a positive popular response indicates "a great concern to observe the Torah" (178).

As our earlier discussion of the peasant class suggests, urban-rural relations in first-century Galilee were of both cultural and political importance. In his discussion of these relationships, Sean Freyne (1992) emphasizes the cultural role of the cities, which were the main agents of social change. Employing a distinction formulated by R. Redfield and M. Singer, he suggests that cities may have two essentially contradictory cultural roles. One is orthogenetic, or "the carrying forward into systematic and reflective dimensions of an old culture," and the other is heterogenetic, or "the creating of original modes of thought that have authority beyond or in conflict with old cultures and civilizations" (76). The dominant social types in orthogenetic cities are scribes, who create a common legal system, and priests, kings, and chiefs, while those of heterogenetic cities are businessmen, bureaucrats (mostly foreigners), officials, military personnel, and tax collectors. Both types of cities have relationships with the villages in the surrounding countryside. In the case of orthogenetic cities this relationship is based on common loyalty to a shared worldview and acceptance of the past and its myths, whereas in heterogenetic cities the relationship is pragmatic, based on mutuality of interests despite mistrust at the cultural level and attempted myth-making for the future so as to cloak cultural differences. In terms of economic patterns, the relations between the orthogenetic city and its surrounding communities reflect a basic inequality, which is cloaked as social necessity or divine arrangement, while those of the heterogenetic city and its environs are openly exploitative, giving rise to resentment. Social unity is achieved by consensus in the case of orthogenetic cities, and dissent is perceived as disloyalty. Social unity is achieved by coercion in the case of heterogenetic cities, and dissent is perceived as rebellion.

Freyne argues that Jerusalem, an orthogenetic city, was the most influential urban center in the cultural life of the Galileans, having greater cultural influence over the majority of the population than the more Hellenized cities (Sepphoris and Tiberias), which were located in the Galilee itself. While the relationship between the cities of Galilee and surrounding villages were not uniformly hostile, "there can be no doubt that the rural animosities toward [these] cities were deep-seated and permanent." Furthermore, the primary basis for these animosities was not that these cities were centers of Greek culture, but was due "to the orthogenetic role of Jerusalem vis-a-vis Jewish culture in the Galilee. The prophetic lament for Jerusalem by the Jesus movement, stemming from the Q source and therefore dating to pre-70, suggests an emotional attachment to the holy city" (85). Also, according to accounts of the trial of Jesus, the high priests exploited the emotional attachment of the pilgrimage crowd to Jerusalem by suggesting that Jesus intended to destroy the Jerusalem temple. As Galilean peasant loyalties were firmly anchored in Jerusalem, the *literati* or scribes, protectors of the myths associated with the orthogenetic city,

> attempted to mould that loyalty along particular lines. They attributed the healing powers of the rural prophet, Jesus, to Beelzebub, the prince of demons, in an obvious attempt to denigrate any alternative myth among the ordinary populace. While this attempt appears to have had little impact in the Galilee, the charge about destroying the Temple had much more serious consequences and succeeded in removing the crowd's support in Jerusalem. (85)

While Freyne's reference to the trial indicates his assumption, unlike Crossan, that the trial narratives have a historical basis, the main point here is that Jerusalem held a strong emotional hold on the Galilean rural populace, and that the holy city was therefore a major factor in their resentment toward the Hellenized–heterogenetic–cities in their own region.

While Jesus' life was spent in Galilee, the locus of his death in Jerusalem is one of the most secure, rarely disputed facts about him. Theissen and Merz believe that Jesus went to Jerusalem by way of Peraea, thereby avoiding setting foot on non-Jewish soil by taking the more direct route through Samaria (178). Like the scholars discussed in chapters 1 and 2, they assume that he performed a symbolic action in the temple and suggest that the prophecy expressed or implied in this action and its consequences for Jesus are more understandable if we take account of the opposition between Jerusalem, the capital city, and Galilee. They note that prophesies against the temple were generally associated with prophets from the country (Micah, Uriah, Jeremiah, and several prophets in the first century C.E.). Jesus' prophecy occurred during a pilgrimage festival while the city of Jerusalem was full of country people. In this situation there were often tensions between the residents of Jerusalem and the country population, and the symbolic action that preceded the temple incident (entering the city on a donkey's colt) was most certainly celebrated by pilgrims, not city residents. In light of Freyne's analysis of Jerusalem's importance for rural Galileans, there is a certain irony in this tension between the citizens of Jerusalem and pilgrims from the region of Galilee. The Galileans, however, most likely had an idealized image of Jerusalem that conflicted with the reality to which its residents had become accustomed. A pilgrimage to Jerusalem may thus have been a rather disillusioning experience. In any event, because Jerusalem residents' economic well-being was connected with the temple, any criticism of the temple would be viewed as an attack on the very foundations of their lives. The temple aristocracy would have had little difficulty, therefore, in stirring the ordinary citizenry of Jerusalem against Jesus (179).

The Roman prefect probably resided in Herod's palace, which was located at a higher level than the temple, allowing members of his entourage to check on activities there. It is assumed that the place of Jesus' execution was Golgotha, which was probably located outside the city walls and was most likely the remains of an abandoned quarry. Thus, if his life began in a natural or dugout cave in the lower hills of Galilee, it ended in a quarry in Jerusalem. If Jesus, an artisan (or *tekton*), worked in stone as well as wood, death in an abandoned quarry has a certain tragic irony.

In his discussion of peasant revolts in mid-first-century Palestine, Crossan (1991) notes that the Jewish peasantry engaged in several effective general strikes. On one occasion, the strike was in response to Pilate's introduction into the city of Jerusalem of embossed medallions of the emperor attached to military standards. Another occurred in reaction to his use of funds from the sacred treasury to construct an aqueduct. In both instances, he was confronted with "massive unarmed and nonviolent refusal to cooperate based on a declared willingness to die rather than give in" (132). While these nonviolent protests were provoked by Pilate's affronts to the religious traditions of the Jewish people, Crossan notes that "for the ordinary people, religious protest may well have been the only way that social, economic, or political oppression could be challenged" (135). There were, for example, economic overtones to these massive public displays of resistance, as the mobilization of whole families at sowing time carried the unmistakable message that if Pilate did not back down there might be no crops to harvest the following year. Thus, economic threat carried a political threat as well, for without a harvest, the requirement of tribute to the Emperor could not be met, and the lack of food would lead to increased banditry and other forms of criminality and terrorism by the peasantry. Of the seven known nonviolent protests by the peasant classes in mid–first-century Palestine, four achieved their objectives without loss of life. What impresses Crossan about these strikes is their high "degree of political consciousness, of strategic and tactical planning, and of sheer crowd control" (135). The peasant class was clearly capable of outmaneuvering the ruling classes on occasion. Especially daunting in this regard was the widespread belief that the peasants of Galilee would give up their lives if it came to that. As Josephus writes: "The Galileans are enured to war from their infancy, and have always been very numerous; nor hath the country been ever destitute of men of courage" (641).

If their economic situation had always been problematic, why did an escalation of peasant restiveness occur in mid-first century? Drawing on Theissen's work (1978), Douglas Edwards (1992) discusses the possible reasons for this. As Theissen argued, it is the perception that one's economic status will change rather than the extent of one's poverty that is likely to contribute to disaffection and revolt. Edwards cites circumstantial evidence of such changes in the condition of the peasants in the lower Galilee: "In the early years of Herod Antipas' rule conditions were favorable for growth in the economy, an unusual situation since, generally, economic growth was sporadic in the static Roman economic system. Several events, however, combined to cause the economy to 'heat up' in the lower Galilee" (62). First, there were Herod Antipas' building projects, which included the building (or rebuilding in the case of Sepphoris) of two cities. Such building projects provided long-term employment for a significant number of people, skilled and unskilled, and workers from surrounding villages needed shelter, food, and other support services, which certainly would have boosted the local economy. In addition, support personnel were needed when the public structures were completed, including persons to maintain and repair buildings, the water system, the marketplaces, and so on. Thus, the building projects, which continued at least through the early to mid-twenties, contributed to economic growth in the region (63). A second factor was population increases. Surveys of the

Galilee region confirm a sharp increase in the number of villages in the late Hellenistic and early Roman period. In fact, it has been argued that the lower Galilee "reached a population density in late antiquity largely unsurpassed until the twentieth century" (55). As Edwards notes, "More people create a demand for increased food production and other support services, at least in the short run. Increased food production provides larger tax revenues which, in turn, allow more building or the continued maintenance of institutions" (63). The third and perhaps most important condition for economic growth was the *pax Romana* and Herod Antipas' willing acceptance of his role within the Roman order. The civic peace that followed the internal fighting for primacy in the Roman government prior to the Augustan period favored economic recovery and a degree of expansion. The general stability of Herod Antipas' rule also enabled him to control a strong economy.

Several factors, however, indicate that this period of economic prosperity did not last. By the mid-twenties, Tiberias and Sepphoris had, for the most part, been completed. A continual supply of funds was needed to support the new administrative structures and buildings. In addition, Herod Antipas entered a period of political instability epitomized by the dissolution of his marriage to his Nabatean wife and resultant tensions between himself and the Nabatean ruler, Aretas IV. He lost in a brief skirmish to Aretas and in 39 C.E. was displaced by Agrippa I, whose reign lasted only to 44 C.E. Edwards suggests that the rural areas would have been deeply affected by the changed economic situation, for after the building program was completed, they would no longer be part of an economy where they were beneficiaries of jobs and extra money. In addition, increased taxation would have been required to maintain the added bureaucracy and building, which would have created an atmosphere of perceived if not real decline in the standard of living of both the elite and peasant classes, creating conditions of volatility and increased hostility both between the rural and urban classes, and between the urban poor and the urban rich.

Crossan's discussion of the "Augustan peace" supports Edwards' analysis. While superficially a time of relative peace throughout Palestine, with only sporadic incidents of Jewish revolt against Roman rule, this was a period best described as one of *turmoil* (1991, 101–2). How much political unrest there was in the Galilee, however, has been a matter of considerable debate. Some have argued, for example, that Galilee, "a hotbed of guerillas for over a century, was strongly anti-Roman" (E. M. Smallwood, cited in Rapaport, 1992, 95). But, as Uriel Rapaport (1992) points out:

> In the period between 37 B.C.E. [the beginning of the reign of Herod the Great] and 66 C.E. [the political division of the Galilee, with eastern Galilee ruled by Agrippa II and western Galilee part of the province of Judaea], more than one hundred years, only one incident of explicit anti-Roman activity is recorded–the assault on the royal palace at Sepphoris in 4 B.C.E. and the seizure of arms there by

Judas, son of Ezekias–the reason for this perhaps being little direct Roman rule over the inhabitants of the area and the lack of a military presence there. (97)

While it would be a mistake to see the Galilee as a relatively peaceful region in Jewish Palestine–"The flare-up resulting from the Samaritan disruption of a convoy of Galileans en route to Jerusalem during a festival, for instance, may be seen as an indication of the belligerent spirit of the Galileans"–this incident "does not point to an anti-Roman movement in the Galilee" (97–98). Rather, it points to "an aspect of Jewish-Samaritan relations and of the sensitivity over pilgrimage to the Temple" (98).

Rapaport also notes that "the focus on Jewish anti-Roman activity was in Judea, around and in Jerusalem, in which the Temple, the most sensitive organ of the Jewish national body, was central" (101). This atmosphere "did not prevail in the Galilee, and the local leadership generally was able to restrain political resentment. Any tension created by Herod Antipas' construction of Tiberias was contained, and resentment of his behavior could not be easily turned against Rome" (101). Rapaport argues that even during the Jewish revolt against Rome of 67–68 C.E., "the Galilee did not take serious steps toward armed resistance or revolt against Rome. All that existed in 67–68 were a few pockets of resistance by some groups of rebels." Thus, the Galilee had at most a secondary position in the outbreak and course of the Great Revolt, its contribution to the revolt consisting mainly of "the heroic resistance of Jotapata and Gamia, and the Galilean troop(s) participating in the defense of Jerusalem...Galileans involved in violent clashes were either in Jerusalem at the time of the occurrences or somehow connected to the holy city" (101).

One reason anti-Roman sentiment would not have been pronounced in Galilee in the time of Jesus is that the Roman presence was probably not very large. According to Zeev Safrai (1992), the Roman army in Judea was rather small prior to 66 C.E., consisting of 3–6 auxiliary units composed in part of local militia from Sebaste and Caesarea. This would be a force in the neighborhood of 2,500–5,000 soldiers (104). From 70–120 C.E. this size probably doubled. Safrai estimates that about half of these troops were stationed in the Galilee. A Roman army unit was stationed at Sepphoris before 120 C.E. (the official arrival of the Roman army in Galilee) and a Roman military fortress was located on the hill above Tiberias; based on a reconstruction of the city, this unit was the size of a cohort (or 500–1,000 men). When Josephus arrived in Galilee in mid-60 C.E., his mission being to inhibit an uprising against Rome, he turned the bandits in the area into mercenaries (Crossan, 1991, 191). This suggests that there were insufficient Roman troops to pacify the region.

If Rapaport's account is accurate, social unrest in the Galilee was not occasioned by newly aroused anti-Roman sentiment, but by a generally "belligerent spirit" (97) that had characterized Galileans for a very long time. While scholars agree that Josephus' accounts of his own involvement in the Galilee are quite misleading, his description of the Galileans as "enured to war from their infancy" is no doubt accurate. This description is supported by Rappaport's contention that tensions in the Galilee "were generally less anti-Roman and more local–ethnic and social–in nature. As we draw nearer to the Great Revolt and to Josephus' report, the overall picture changes somewhat, but not too much: there was not much warfare against the Romans in Galilee and some of the activity was a product of local circumstances and the dynamics of the situation" (98). Thus, except for Galileans' emotional investment in Jerusalem, their grievances–and grounds for engaging in "belligerent" behavior–were local. This does not mean, however, that such behavior was not deeply felt. On the contrary, because it *was* ethnic and social, it was more personal than actions against Roman rule would likely have been. As Rappaport notes: "Josephus was sent to the Galilee to prevent its involvement in an uprising against Rome, and he achieved this easily and successfully. His opponents in the Galilee held similar politics and opposed him only for personal, local, and perhaps tactical reasons" (100).

We may conclude that what Josephus encountered in the Galilee was a deeply rooted Galilean temperament, nicely captured in Rappaport's characterization of their "belligerent spirit." This would seem to explain the "flare-up" in Samaria between the Samaritans and Galilean pilgrims and the fact that the Galileans could become involved in violent clashes in Jerusalem largely because they happened to be there at the time. This argues against a view of Galileans as committed to well-planned military objectives. Instead, they were prone to sporadic, quixotic, spur-of-the-moment acts of violence. This would also be consistent with Crossan's characterization of the Galilean peasants (based on James Scott's analysis of contemporary Malaysian peasants) as adept in the use of the "ordinary weapons of relatively powerless groups: foot dragging, dissimulation, desertion, false compliance, pilfering, feigned ignorance, slander, arson, sabotage, and so on." These forms of class struggle "require little or no coordination or planning; they make use of implicit understandings and internal networks; they often represent a form of individual self-help" (127–28). Scott refers to this as a "shadow society–a pattern of structural, stylistic, and normative opposition to the politico-religious tradition of the ruling elites," and he notes that such groups "are more effectively constrained by the daily exercise of power" (128). This implies that the ruling elites could never let down their guard. If, at the macrolevel, the Augustan peace prevailed throughout Palestine in the time of Jesus, in Galilee the "turmoil" was chronic, systemic, and, for this reason, always volatile. In Erikson's terms, Galilee was in a general state of anxiety at all times, with the threat of a general panic always a distinct possibility (Erikson, 1963, 413). If Galileans were "enured to war from their infancy," this also indicates that they were especially prone to allow or even encourage "the whole arsenal of anxiety which is left in each individual from the mere fact of his childhood" to "reach into adult life, and this not only in the form of neurotic anxiety" but "more terrifyingly...in the form of collective panics and in afflictions of the collective mind" (413).

A major contributing factor to Galilean volatility was the phenomenon of social banditry. As Hanson and Oakman note, whereas the urban elites sought the backing of a series of imperial states because their patronage provided protection and inducement, the peasantry had little or nothing to gain from these alliances: "Their perspective was that the elites continually bartered with foreign powers at the peasants' expense" (87). Moreover, the peasants' lot was the same whether their grain and produce were extracted by Roman or by Seleucid clients. The authors cite Eric Hobsbawm's description of peasant rebellions as "pre-political," in that such rebellions do not attempt programs of political reform or focus on the larger political parties. Instead, they react against economic, military, or ideological pressures reflected in new or increased taxes, occupation by foreign troops, disruption of temple functions, or the imposition of new gods, temples, and priesthoods (87).

One form of peasant rebellion is social banditry. Social bandits are peasants who have been repressed and separated from their land and village, usually as a result of excessive taxes that force them to sell their land, or having had their land confiscated by elites, or having broken a law enforced by the elites. They express their grievances against the ruling elites by organizing into raiding bands that steal to survive. Hanson and Oakman provide a detailed description of the context, operation, organization, and outcomes of social banditry. Contexually, social banditry, a rural phenomenon, appears when the social equilibrium is upset due to ecological and political/economic factors and is difficult for the state administration to deal with effectively. Often, rule by a foreign power ("colonization") is at the root of the bandits' disaffection with the political elites. Operationally, the bandits are often supported by the local peasants, usually staying close to their home villages, and they often provide tangible goods to their villages (e.g., sharing their booty with family members and friends). Organizationally, they are held together by the prestige of the leader, are usually limited to fifteen to forty members, and are composed of young, unmarried males (though whole families may be included). As for outcomes, social banditry does not bring about significant political change because the groups are too small and isolated, but social bandits may accompany or be integrated into a full-scale peasant revolt. They may also, however, be utilized or coopted by local elites for their own purposes, as happened when Josephus made them his mercenaries. Bandit groups last less than two years because their leaders get caught or authorities lose interest in them, which suggests that collective stealing is not their sole reason for existence (89–90).

As Crossan (1991) indicates, if a banditry group survives for several years, as sometimes happens, it likely has the support of one or more members of the ruling elite. He notes Anton Blok's critique of Hobsbawm's work because it "over-emphasizes the element of social protest and obscures the links which bandits maintain with established power-holders...Rather than actual champions of the poor and the weak, bandits quite often terrorized those from whose ranks they managed to rise, and thus helped to suppress them" (169).

Because their first loyalty is *not* to the peasants, social bandits are not class-conscious peasants who rebel as part of a wider rural rebellion. Instead, they are "individual peasants" who "grasp for power, and that moves them into a no-man's-land between those who never had it and those who already possess it" (170). Crossan notes that Hobsbawm, in responding to Blok's criticism, insisted that he had always emphasized the *social ambivalence* involved in the economics and politics of banditry, for the bandit is an outsider and rebel, yet, unlike other peasants, he acquires wealth and exerts power: "He is 'one of us' who is constantly in the process of becoming associated with 'them'" (170).

Crossan considers their "social ambivalence" in accounting for the reason the Roman reaction to them was far more violent than to ordinary criminals. They did not receive the same considerations under the law and received the most brutal death penalties in order to set a public example. Yet their number was relatively small, and their presence in Roman colonies was systemic and ubiquitous. He argues that their threat to the empire lay in the fact that, as long as they operated outside the official political structures, the bandits challenged the empire's monopoly on violence and also undermined its claim that its exercise of violence was founded on moral principle and moral justification. Thus, in the words of Brent Shaw, rural banditry revealed a fundamental weakness in the archaic state, namely, its inability to define adequately "its self-defined mandate of authority" (Crossan, 1991, 173). How could the state define the difference between the soldier who was an ex-bandit and the bandit who was an ex-soldier unless it could show that the emperor and army had a monopoly on violence that was not simply quantitatively greater but theoretically and qualitatively right? Thus, the threat of social banditry to the empire is that it "holds up to agrarian empire its own unpainted face, its own unvarnished soul" (214).

As noted earlier, Josephus succeeded in his "pacification" of Galilee by creating a mercenary force of ex-bandits. Crossan estimates that this force was about 5,000 strong and could melt back into the peasantry at a moment's notice. This arrangement served the propertied classes' interests as it controlled the bandits against their own most natural enemies and victims. In fact, Josephus' achievement was an instance of brokerage, as he taxed the propertied classes to support his mercenary army of ex-bandits. In his discussion of Josephus' effective strategy for averting social revolution, Crossan's comments on the long-standing history of conflict between Galilean bandits and the empire also provide some important psychological data involving mothers and sons. He cites Josephus' account of an event that preceded Herod the Great's appointment as ruler of the Galilee in 48 B.C.E. It was a

> somewhat paradigmatic encounter between Herod the not yet Great and the bandit chief Ezekias. Herod was son of prime minister Antipater, prime minister under Hyrcanus II, the Hasmonean prince who was ruler of Palestine under the authority of Sextus Caesar, the Syrian legate. Herod's murder of Ezekias and his brigands led to

Herod's promotion by Sextus Caesar as governor of Coele Syria and Samaria. Of particular interest in Josephus' account of this event is his statement that Hyrcanus' anger was further kindled by the mothers of the men who had been murdered by Herod, for every day in the temple they kept begging the people to have Herod brought to judgment in the Sanhedrin for what he had done. (175)

Crossan uses this quotation to argue, following Freyne, that Ezekias was a member of the Hasmonian nobility and not acting in favor of the Galilean peasants, but in reprisal for the loss of his own possessions and those of other nobles. Hyrcanus' arrest of Herod but Herod's acquittal on orders of the Syrian legate support this conclusion. While Crossan suggests that the mothers may simply be Josephus' own invention in order "to heighten the human theatre of the trial," it is noteworthy that Josephus introduces *mothers* in order to create a sense of high drama, and that he represents Hyrcanus as angered by the begging mothers, yet responding by having Herod arrested. Thus, Josephus implies that the mothers' begging to have Herod brought to justice forced Hyrcanus to act. If the bandits are important for their social ambivalence, their mothers are complicit in this social ambivalence.

Family and Kinship in Galilee

I have already discussed the importance of marriageable women for the honor-shame dynamics of Mediterranean society and have commented on the tensions involved in the "transfer" of a marriageable woman from her family of origin to the family of her husband. I now want to locate this discussion within the specific context of family and kinship systems in Galilean society at the time of Jesus.

In their chapter on kinship, Hanson and Oakman note that kinship was still the primary social domain in first-century Mediterranean societies: "Virtually no social relationship, institution, or value-set was untouched by the family and its concerns" (20). Kinship, however, was no longer the only implicit domain. In advanced agrarian societies, "politics had also contributed an identifiably separate set of institutions, even though heavily affected by kinship structures and relationships" (20). They add that, as Bruce Malina argued (1986), while religion constituted a separate, largely symbolic domain, it was embedded in either political or kinship domains (20–21).

Kinship was affected by the political sphere in terms of law (e.g., incest, rape, marriage, divorce, paternity, and inheritance laws). Conversely, kinship affected politics, most notably in patron-client relationships and developing networks of friends. Kinship was affected by religion in terms of purity, regulating who could have sex with whom, and the ethnic and religious status of one's spouse. Conversely, kinship affected religion in terms of descent, especially in the importance placed on lineages of priests and their wives, but also by regulating membership in the "political religion" centered in the temple. Kinship was also interactive with the economic sphere in terms of occupations, dowry and inheritance, and land tenure (21).

To explore this relation between family structures and social systems, Hanson and Oakman draw on Emmanuel Todd's proposal (1985) that family forms involved the following polarized variables: *liberty/authority* (What is the basis for spouse choice: freedom of choice, oldest generation chooses, custom decides, or no rules?); *equality/inequality* (Is the inheritance divided among the surviving children, or does only one child inherit, and do the married children reside with the parents?); and *endogamy/exogamy* (Is the social ideal to marry a close relative, or is this excluded by incest rules?) (21). Because family *forms* are more constant over time than *ideologies* about family, there may be a conflict between these. Also, there are always families that deviate from the prescribed form.

The best description of "the peasant ideal" was family as the *endogamous community*. This means that the marriage strategy was closer to the endogamous than the exogamous idea. Bringing strangers into the family was especially threatening, and, conversely, forms of intermarriage within the family that might be considered by other societies to be incestuous might not be so regarded. The structure of the family was that of a *community*. It was multigenerational (with genealogies playing an important role in the family's acclaimed honor). Spousal choice was controlled by custom and parents; the marriage was arranged by family negotiation and publicly announced through a betrothal ceremony and involved formal acts of reciprocity between families (including dowry, indirect dowry, and brideswealth). The postmarital residence was patrilocal (i.e., married couples would live in the house or neighborhood of the groom's parents), and married sons and their parents might continue to cohabit. In consequence, geographical and social mobility, especially among the sons, was severely restricted. This meant that there were structural deterents to downward mobility from generation to generation, but severe limits placed on upward mobility. The idea that a son would leave home to seek his personal fortune elsewhere was virtually unimaginable. Where possible, each son in the family received an inheritance, but the eldest son received a double portion.

The bride's dowry was a payment (full or partial) of the daughter's share of the family inheritance. While administered by her husband, it belonged to her and was inherited by her children. Thus, women had personal property independent of the property of their husbands, and it could not pass from her husband to his family or his children by another marriage. Brideswealth, involving the transfer of goods and services from the groom's to the bride's family, was also commonly practiced. It could take the form of gifts of jewelry and clothing to the bride, the purchase of furniture and household goods for the married couple, or direct payments to the bride's family. Whatever their form, these gifts from the groom's family solidified the relationship between families, and brideswealth given directly to the bride's kin had the practical utility of securing future wives for the groom's brothers from among the unmarried sisters-in-law. Indirect dowry (gifts to the bride) might also balance the dowry, thus enabling one of the two contracting families to avoid becoming too indebted to the other (in effect, their clients).

As indicated, the marriage contract was formalized by the betrothal, the period when the man and woman were promised to each other by their respective families and the families negotiated the dowry, indirect dowry, and brideswealth arrangements. The betrothal might take place shortly before the wedding, but it might also occur months, even years before the children were ready for marriage. As the betrothal was a binding agreement, a formal divorce was necessary to break it. The male was considered to be marriageable at age eighteen, but there are no surviving legal traditions regulating the age of marriage. The marriageable age of women was twelve or older. The impediments to a legal marriage were descent (near relatives as defined in Leviticus 18 and 20) and purity. Purity laws precluded marriage to a Gentile, marriage of an adulteress to her partner in adultery, the male's remarriage to his former wife if she had remarried in the meantime, and marriage of a castrated man or insane individual. While the father played a central role in the arrangement of marriages, brothers assumed patriarchal power over their sisters when they were heads of the kin-group.

Hanson and Oakman note that assumptions about gender were inseparable from kinship practices. Palestine was patriarchal in its structures and ascriptions. The privileged status of the male stemmed from the assumption that his "seed" created a child. Gender division, however, was rooted in male fears of the female: "Ancient Israelites did not simply construe females as different, but potentially *dangerous*. A man can be overpowered by a woman simply by looking at her [and] a daughter's chastity is described as the weak link in the family's shame" (24). Thus, "males must guard the females within the family and continually be on guard against females from the outside" (25). This gender division is made clear in honor-shame dynamics, with males "expected to embody the family's honor in their virility, boldness, sexual aggression, and protection of the family" and females "expected to keep the family from shame by their modesty, restraint, sexual exclusivity, and submission to male authority" (26). Gender division was also reflected in religious roles, with men functioning as priests (presiding over the sacrificial system) and women as midwives (thus controlling the procreative process). Politically speaking, this arrangement favored males, but it also implicated them in the religious demand for sacrifice in behalf of values that transcended their own personal self-interest. Thus, power carried a certain price, and honor required that one be prepared to pay it. Conversely, because seed is not self-germinating, women of childbearing years were essential to a family's desire to reproduce itself, and special honor was reserved for women who had successfully given birth to one or more male child.

Hanson and Oakman discuss divorce, noting that it signified the severing of ties between the two families, calling for the return of goods and property transferred at the time of betrothal. Divorce was a matter of considerable dispute among first-century Palestinian Jews. The school of Rabbi Shannai restricted the husband's divorce of his wife to cases of her adultery, while the Hillel school, probably reflecting the dominant practice, allowed a man to divorce his wife for any displeasure with her (43). Wives could obtain divorces in several instances, including a husband's impotence, his physical impurity due to illness or vocation (e.g., tentmaking, as in the case of Paul, which involved the handling of animal skins), her own impurity or refusal to have intercourse, or with her husband's consent.

Descent played an important role in first-century Palestine, with the honor of kin-groups almost always based on patrilineal descent (i.e., through males). Matrilineal descent (i.e., through females) played no role, but patrilineal descent was sometimes augmented with cognatic descent, which allows for including an honored ancestress in the line of descent, thus increasing the ascribed honor to the paternal family. Another more pragmatic reason for including women in family genealogies, however, was to differentiate the wife or concubine through whom the line is being traced from other women (e.g., David's son Adonijah, whose mother was Haggith, and his son Solomon, whose mother was Bathsheba). Family genealogies were arranged by generation. Several generations might be omitted for lack of information, to achieve schematic design, or to emphasize the importance of particular members. A genealogy could also help to identify potential marriage partners within the family as well as the actual outsiders who were allowed to marry into the kingroup. As inheritance rights were based on order of birth, the birth mother, and gender considerations, a genealogy could help in asserting or adjudicating inheritance rights, including the right to hereditary offices (such as the priesthood). Social status, especially through inclusion of illustrious ancestors, was also a rationale for a genealogy. For example, a genealogy asserting Jesus' descent from David would counter indications of his family's current social class (peasantry). Hanson and Oakman discuss Jesus' family as presented in the gospels, focusing on genealogies and peasantry, but I will defer this discussion to chapter 6.

While Hanson and Oakman's kinship discussion centers on first-century Palestine in general, Lawrence H. Schiffman (1992) considers whether the Galilee had its own unique practices, and specifically, whether they were more or less stringent. He considers several issues—marriage customs, vows or promises, tithes, and festivals and fasts—and concludes that, in general, Galileans had a higher degree of stringency in these matters of observance than the Judeans. His consideration of marriage customs is especially relevant. He argues, for example, that Galileans went much further than Judeans to ensure that the marriage contract protecting the woman's financial interests in divorce or widowhood cases were honored. Another difference between the Galilee and Judea involved the husband's claim that his wife's virginity was compromised before marriage. The normal procedure in Jewish marriage in this period consisted of two steps. The first or betrothal step meant that all aspects of the marriage were effected except cohabitation. With the second step of marriage, usually a year later, the relationship was consummated. Schiffman cites a difference between Judean and Galilean practice in this regard. In Judea, at least among some Jews, the groom was allowed to move into the house of his father-in-law during the period of betrothal. This custom led to the ruling that the groom in this case forfeited the right to make a claim that his wife was a nonvirgin (i.e., had had sexual relations with someone else). In Galilee, such cohabitation was not practiced, and therefore, in Schiffman's view, "this problem [i.e., the forfeiture of the nonvirginity claim] did not exist in the Galilee" (146).

Another difference concerned widows, specifically the period of time required to elapse between the death of the spouse and subsequent betrothal of marriage. An anonymous *mishnah* rules that widows must wait three months "in order to establish the paternity of a child who might be born, and hence the responsibility of child support" (147). Rabbi Judah, however, took an opposing position, declaring that the anonymous ruling was excessively strict, since a betrothed widow would not become pregnant with her new husband during the betrothal period, and a woman who had been betrothed but not married and whose future husband died would not have become pregnant in the betrothal period. Thus, he reasoned, the question of paternity would simply not arise. He made an exception to this ruling, however, in the case of the betrothed couples in Judea (thus siding with the anonymous *mishnah*) because, as Schiffman puts it, in Judea "the standards were much laxer and the possibility existed that intimacy may have led to sexual relations and pregnancy." Schiffman concludes, "Once again, the Galilee maintained a stricter standard than their Judean counterparts" (147).

Schiffman cites additional evidence of differences in marriage custom between Judea and the Galilee, all involving customs relating to premarital intimacies between groom and bride in Judea and involving the use of witnesses (i.e., the groom's best man) to protect against false claims of nonvirginity or fraudulent defense against such a claim. Because the Galileans did not practice these precautions—that is, of using a witness—Schiffman concludes that the Galilean bride and groom "generally relied on each other's upstanding character and entered the marriage expecting no dishonest claims. This was not the case in Judea, where such claims seem to have been much more common and where there was greater suspicion of fabricated claims or defenses" (148). In sum,

> the evidence shows that stricter observance and honesty prevailed in the Galilee. Both Judea and the Galilee had the same laws regarding the obligation of virginity for the unmarried, and both adhered to the biblical injunction regarding claims of the bride's nonvirginity. Yet the Judeans, because of their laxer moral standards, had to employ additional precautions unnecessary for the Galileans. Again, there is no Galilean halakhah, just more stringent observance of the same set of laws. (148)

Schiffman's argument is based on the presumption that specific regulations necessary in Judea were unnecessary in the Galilee because the sexual behaviors that made these necessary in Judea were proscribed in Galilee. The opposite side of the coin, however, is that if violations of these prohibitions *did* occur in Galilee, prospective husbands and wives did not have the legal protections that were afforded their Judean counterparts. Husbands who claimed their wives were nonvirgins would have much greater difficulty getting such claims recognized, and wives who were falsely accused of nonvirginity would have greater difficulty defending themselves. Thus, Schiffman is right to assert that the groom and bride needed to rely on the "upstanding character" of the other with respect to (1) the sexual purity of the bride; (2) the groom *not* making a false claim of nonvirginity; and (3) the bride *not* countering his claim of nonvirginity with a fraudulent defense. But the fact that they needed to rely more heavily on each other's "upstanding character" and refusal to make "fabricated claims or defenses" does not necessarily prove that "stricter observance and honesty prevailed in the Galilee." All that it proves is that, where stricter observance and honesty did *not* prevail, Galileans had significantly lower expectations of protecting their honor against the impurity or dishonesty of the other party. A groom who suspected that his future wife was a nonvirgin would be more reluctant to make any charges against her—or her family—because he would have fewer legal protections against fraudulent defenses. In short, what Schiffman's argument requires is concrete, empirical evidence of stricter observance in the Galilee region. While greater strictness seemed to be the official norm—the ideology—he offers no evidence that this norm was not sometimes, even regularly, violated. The greatest ambiguity would be cases of incest, where the family would have a particular interest in making a fraudulent defense against the prospective husband's claims of nonvirginity. Evidence from the early Puritans would suggest that the midwife might be an especially useful informant (or disinformant) in virginity disputes.

Study of Jesus' social world has become an integral part of the methodology of contemporary Jesus studies. The major findings of these explorations into his social world are vitally important for a psychological biography of Jesus. As we saw in our chapter on psychobiography, the focus of such a biography is necessarily the "person in a situation." I have centered here on features of Jesus' social world having particular relevance for the biographical portrait to be developed in the following chapters. As will be seen, the issue of honor and shame, especially as libidinized or eroticized, has special importance. Peasantry class issues are also central. By the same token, issues such as kinship and gender, and regulations concerning cohabitation and divorce, help to illumine his special circumstances. The discussion here of the absence of a significant Roman military presence in lower Galilee also has bearing on my contention (noted in the preceding chapter) that the social conflict with which Jesus was most familiar took the form of family and neighborhood conflict.

A Psychological
Portrait of Jesus

PART THREE

6

The Hidden Years:
The Fatherhood Question

Having explored contemporary portraits of Jesus, addressed methodological issues in the psychobiography of individuals and psychohistory of groups, and provided a broad overview of Jesus' social world, we are now in a position to formulate our psychological portrait of Jesus. I fully recognize that any portrait of Jesus that differs radically from the representative portraits reviewed in chapters 1 and 2 is likely to be suspect. There should be, at least, a family resemblance between a psychological portrait of Jesus and those of biblical scholars. If there is not, the reader has every right to assume that the psychologist—not these other portraitists—has produced a caricature, or worse. On the other hand, there should be enough that is distinctive about the psychologist's portrait to justify the claim that an explicit introduction of psychology into Jesus studies makes an appreciable difference. Thus, one must walk a fine line between the construction of a portrait that is too unique to be considered an authentic rendition of the subject and one that is a pale, amateurish copy of the original work of recognized scholars.

Another important consideration is that a psychobiographical portrait of any subject needs to be both coherent and complex. One may effect a coherent picture of someone by reducing this individual to a mere caricature, a cartoon character, a cardboard cutout. To merit our attention, however, a psychobiographical portrait requires the realization of a coherent image while preserving the subject's complexity. While this means that it needs to take account of various facets of the subject's life, it does not mean that each and every detail of the life must be considered. In fact, an excessively detailed portrayal of a subject's life may be counterproductive. Even in cases where the data are relatively sparse, a biographer needs to be selective. The portrait that I offer here is framed by the concerns raised regarding the portraits discussed in the first two chapters, together with themes and issues explored in the following three. These set the context for my discussions in the three chapters on the "hidden years" of Jesus, his exorcist-healer role, and his utopian-melancholic personality.

In this chapter, I take up the question I raised in connection with Meier's portrait of Jesus: Is it likely or plausible that Jesus' life prior to his emergence as a public figure was "insufferably ordinary"? I have no intention of resurrecting the fantastic images of Jesus' childhood and adolescence in the apocryphal infancy gospels of the second century C.E. and later (see Barnstone, 1984). Against *these* images, Jesus' early life was certainly "ordinary." As noted in chapter 1, however, Meier's view that Jesus' childhood-through-young-adult years were unexceptional requires him to account on other grounds for the atypicality of Jesus as an adult. He does so by suggesting that Jesus' life underwent a major change through his relationship to John the Baptist. While I would not wish to deny the enormous impact of John the Baptist on Jesus' life, what Meier leaves unexplained is the fact that Jesus seems to have been oriented toward a "celibate" life prior to meeting John, that there was tension between Jesus and his family, and the reasons why Jesus was prompted to join John and his group in the desert. I believe that these three issues point to problematic experiences in Jesus' earlier life, and there is considerable continuity, therefore, between Jesus' adult "atypicality" and his earlier years.

To make this case, one necessarily needs to engage in retrodiction (as discussed in chapter 3). As acknowledged there, this practice is risky in any case, as the evidence for childhood experiences is rarely adequate for even the most well-documented subjects. It is especially risky, however, in the case of Jesus, where the evidence is not only scanty but also difficult to interpret. Meier is the only one of the four portraitists who has had the courage even to attempt a reconstruction of the early life of Jesus (though Crossan has made several suggestions along these lines in his various writings on Jesus). Meier's reconstruction, however, suffers from not being informed by a dynamic psychology, relying instead on conventional, ad hoc surmises that do not add up to a coherent picture of Jesus' hidden years.

For a more coherent reconstruction of the hidden years, I will present three other authors who have written relevant books or articles and will then offer my own conclusions. I begin with John W. Miller, whose psycho-biographical study of Jesus (1997) is essentially supportive of Meier's perspective on the early years. His portrait emphasizes the death of Joseph as an interpretive key for unlocking some of the mysteries surrounding Jesus' life and career.

Miller's Emphasis: The Death of the Father

In *Jesus at Thirty*, Miller offers much the same explanation as does Meier for why Jesus' early years were "hidden" ones. He asks: Why is so little known "about the greater part of the life of one whose followers soon revered him as the most important figure in human history"? (33). He is not persuaded by the argument that "men and women of that age did not share our interest in the everyday affairs of their great men," for "curiosity about Jesus' early life soon became an important factor in Christian piety, resulting in a growing fund of stories about his childhood activities, many of them fantastic" (33). For him, a better conclusion would be that "Jesus' early years were unexceptional. They flowed along within the banks of the ordinary—a conclusion that would give added plausibility to the astonishment of both family and neighbors at the turn of events that led to his public career" (33). Unlike Meier, however, Miller seeks to explain why Jesus did not follow in Joseph's footsteps, but embarked on a public career. He also uses insights from developmental psychology to formulate these explanations.

His discussion of Jesus' formative years begins with a list of what he terms "hard data" concerning Jesus' childhood, youth, and early adulthood (32):

Name: Yeshua (Aramaic), Joshua (Hebrew), Jesus (Greek)

Date of birth: toward the end of the reign of Herod the Great (4 or 5 B.C.E.; Mt. 2:1)

Home village: Nazareth of Galilee (Jn. 19:19; Lk. 1:26)

Father's name: Joseph (Lk. 3:23, 4:22; Mt. 1:16; Jn. 1:45, 6:42)

Mother's name: Mary (Hebrew: Miriam; Mk. 6:3; Mt. 13:55)

Siblings: James (Jacob), Joses (Joseph), Judas (Judah), Simon, several sisters (Mk. 6:3; Mt. 13:55)

Place in family: firstborn (Lk. 2:7)

Occupation: carpenter (Greek: *tekton*), like his father (Mk. 6:3; Mt. 13:55)

Religion: Judaism

Marital status: uncertain

Miller's notation that Jesus' marital status is "uncertain" alerts us to the fact that, while his list purports to be "hard data," there is little that may be taken for granted or is not subject to debate in this entire list. He also acknowledges the paucity of information about the formative years, but suggests that the skeletal data outlined may bring us closer "to a better understanding of Jesus' early years and his experiences of his father in particular" (33).

First, there is the assertion that he was the firstborn in the family of four younger brothers and several sisters. This meant that family expectations and hopes were centered on Jesus. Therefore, "It is reasonable to imagine he would have been made to feel an especially heavy weight of responsibility to and for his parents" (33). Miller cites the parable of the prodigal son in which it is the elder son who stays home and takes care of the farm while the younger brother leaves to sow wild oats. He asks: "Is this an accident?" He also notes that Jesus' name means "Yahweh is savior" and brings to mind one of the great "savior figures" in Israelite history—the Old Testament Joshua. This name may reflect his parents' expectations of him and witnesses to the piety that must have characterized his home, as the names of his parents and brothers all come from "the earliest and most important periods of biblical history" (34). He acknowledges that Jesus' marital status is puzzling, as "celibacy poses certain problems in Judaic tradition." He cites the Babylonian Talmud indicating that a Jewish father had five principal responsibilities toward his son: to circumcise him, redeem him, teach him Torah, teach him a trade, and find him a wife. Traditions suggest that the latter should occur when the son is between sixteen and twenty-four years of age. Miller asks: "Why then did Jesus' father not find him a wife?" In light of the total silence regarding Jesus' father in the gospel accounts where Jesus' family is mentioned, the likelihood is

> that Joseph had died prior to the time of Jesus' mission at thirty. If it is true that Jesus' father failed to find him a wife, perhaps he died quite early, before Jesus was old enough for a wife to be found for him. On the other hand, Joseph's death could not have happened when Jesus was still a small child, for there were four younger brothers and several sisters in the family. This would suggest a date for this traumatic event sometime during Jesus' early teenage years. In that case, as eldest son (in accordance with the traditions of his culture), the mantle of leadership in the family would have fallen on him. (35)

That Jesus was referred to as "son of Mary" (Mk. 6:3), not "son of Joseph," may reflect these circumstances (35). If Mary's firstborn son became the breadwinner and family head at an early age, "it is not difficult to imagine why his marriage was delayed" (36).

Acknowledging that despite the few facts we have about Jesus' early years there is "much that remains obscure," Miller's next move is to offer "supplementary data" from his late life, thus employing the retrodiction method of psychohistorians who "frequently work backward to childhood from analogous experiences in the life of the adult. This would mean that data relevant to the theme of 'Jesus and his father' is not confined to factual reports out of his childhood, but can be derived as well from statements and experiences of the adult Jesus in which 'fatherhood' or 'fathering' is a factor" (36). Miller suggests that Jesus' emotional experience of "father" is evident at four points: (1) in his unique use of "Abba" (father) as a way of invoking God; (2) in what he taught about the importance of father-child relations; (3) in the portraits of "fathers" in his parables; and (4) in explicit references to fathers in several of his more memorable sayings.

Regarding the first point, Miller draws on J. Jeremias' view that "the complete novelty and uniqueness of *'Abba* as an address to God in the prayers of Jesus shows that it expresses the heart of Jesus' relations to God." He adds:

> It is not surprising, therefore, that the reality to which the name Abba pointed (God's fatherly love) permeates his teaching. "Call no man your father on earth," he once said to his disciples, "for you have one Father who is in heaven" (Mt. 23:9). The meaning of this striking admonition is not, obviously, that Jesus objected to small children calling their own fathers Abba, but that his disciples should refrain from addressing honored teachers or other distinguished figures in that manner. (37)

Miller notes Jeremias' view that the "sonship" that broke in on Jesus on the occasion of his baptism was reflected in his "Abba" response. There were, however, "emotional 'echoes'" of this experience in earlier father-son experiences. Because "Abba" is first and foremost a child's word, its "primal home is the deep affectional bond fashioned between father and son early in life." Thus, "his love of the word Abba as a term for addressing God not only reflects his experience at the time of his baptism, but must hark back as well to his earliest experiences with his personal father in his family of origin" (38).

Miller also notes Jesus' relations with children, as in Mark 9:33–37, when he takes a boy in his arms in "a warm paternal gesture," and, on another occasion, when he touches the children who were brought to him (Mk. 10:13; Lk. 18:15; Mt. 19:13). The latter communicates Jesus' view that there is more than humility at stake in being like a child, for becoming a child again means to learn to say "Abba" again: "It is not only humility, then, but the whole trusting, relaxed, and uninhibited rapport of children with their fathers that seems to have been especially appealing to Jesus" (39). What he felt about the father-son relationship is also reflected in the parables. Citing several parables, Miller concludes that "the dominant figures in the great majority of Jesus' stories are fatherly types in positions of responsibility who are shown executing these responsibilities in forceful, competent, but often surprisingly gracious ways" (39). Of course, there is father-son conflict in the stories as well, suggesting that "long before Freud, Jesus took note of ambivalence toward fathers as a disturbing factor in human relations, but it seems his own attitudes in this respect were unusually positive" (40). He also cites several sayings in which Jesus gives instructions regarding fathers, including his rejection of *khorban*, "a practice among the rabbinical elite whereby a son could avoid financial obligations to his 'father or mother' by dedicating the support that he owed them to the temple (Mk. 7:9–13)" (40).

What of Jesus' statements, however, about the need to "hate" one's own family, father included? Miller interprets these as reflecting Jesus' "treasured, newfound experience of *God* as gracious father, devotion to whose will (as this was unfolding through his mission) takes priority over everything else. A major testimony to the depth of his faith in this regard is his beautifully off-hand statement about the greater goodness of God as father compared to the flawed goodness of human fathers" (Mt. 7:9–11; Lk. 11:11–13). He asks: "Could Jesus have spoken of fathers and the father-child relationship so often and in such utterly realistic yet positive terms, had he not had a deeply meaningful experience somewhere along the way with his own personal father? To me the answer seems obviously, 'No'!" (40–41).

In his chapter on Jesus and his mother, Miller suggests that Jesus' profound experience of God as Father, reminiscent of his experience of his father Joseph as a loving and caring father, occurred at his baptism by John the Baptist. He hypothesizes that if Joseph was dead by this time, Jesus had to cope with both the responsibilities of being the firstborn son and his mother's tendency to lean "more and more on this resourceful eldest son" following the death of her husband, "thereby intensifying sibling rivalries" (53). This may shed light on the tensions between Jesus and his mother:

> An adolescent son, even an emotionally healthy one, who suddenly finds himself thrust into a surrogate husband-father role will understandably experience an identity-crisis. And such a crisis...can only be resolved by an act that can brook no compromise. A clear and definite choice will have to be made between mother and "God." The network of pseudo-obligations in which his life to this point has been enmeshed will have to be broken. And when the break comes, it is understandable if the mother is mystified and might even think her son "beside himself." (Mk. 3:19b–21) (53)

While leaving home, marrying, and establishing a home of his own would be a way to resolve the crisis, it was the prophetic preaching of John the Baptist "that summoned Jesus out and away from his maternal home into the wider world" (54). Himself an "awesome paternal figure," John enabled Jesus to deal with the quandary in which he found himself, and the words "from heaven" immediately after the baptism, "You are my beloved son, with you I am well pleased," reached him at his depths: "Jesus had found God and his father again. Simultaneously he had found himself as well. The claim of his mother upon him had been broken by renewed contact with his 'Father in heaven'" (54). Here, Miller presupposes that Jesus' experience of God as father was congruent—not dissonant—with his experience of his natural father. In renewing contact with God, a contact weakened by the death of Joseph and his subsequent pseudo-obligations, he also reestablished his bond with Joseph.

Miller views the baptism of Jesus as a "second birth," and draws explicitly on William James's *The Varieties of Religious Experience* to explain its importance in Jesus' life. He alludes to James's "sick souls" for whom, in order to find peace with God, "A conversion-type experience was required, an emotional reorientation of such magnitude that it could be likened to a 'second birth.' Prior to this conversion, it was as though these persons had hardly begun to live. They were agitated, conflicted, despairing. During the conversion experience itself, they reported encountering God in personal, tangible ways. From it they emerged surrendered, full of joy and a compelling sense of mission" (28). Jesus fits this "conversionist" model, which means that he must "have lived through a period of inner conflict before this event, as is typical of those who undergo experiences of this type" (28). This conflict centered on his "groping (unconsciously perhaps) for a next step, a way out of the ultimately sterile, guilt-producing surrogate role in which he found himself" (54).

This view that Jesus underwent a conversion experience is shared by Marcus Borg, who also invokes James's *The Varieties*. As Borg writes:

> The conversion, of course, was not from paganism to Judaism, for he grew up Jewish. Rather, as James defines it, *conversion* need not refer to changing from one religion to another, or from being nonreligious

to being religious; it may also refer to a process, whether sudden or gradual, whereby religious impulses and energies become central to one's life. It is reasonable to suppose that Jesus experienced such an internal transformation, which led him to undertake the ministry that he did, and that this probably had something to do with John the Baptizer. (1994b, 27)

What Miller adds to Borg's suggestions is the theory that the death of Joseph was the major catalyst behind the conversion, as Jesus' loss of his father had led to his assumption of "pseudo-obligations," which could now be set aside in order to embark on his true mission in life. This hypothesis enables him to present Jesus as having lived a normal, emotionally healthy childhood, only to have this tranquility shattered in his middle adolescence by the trauma of his father's death. As the firstborn son, his life would be the most affected by his father's death. This hypothesis also enables him to explain Jesus' strained relations with his mother and other family members, as the definition of Jesus' true mission in life meant that he would no longer be carrying out the responsibilities of the eldest son. Thus, Miller addresses the issue to which Meier alludes, but does not explain, that Jesus broke with "his extended family and village, after so many years of an uneventful life in their midst" in "his concomitant attempt to define a new identity and social role for himself" (Meier, 1991, 317). To Meier's question why Jesus rejected "the imposed identity and social function that the family and village provided the individual in exchange for the communal security and defense the individual received from the family" (317), Miller's answer is that this imposed identity was stultifying, inhibiting him from his true mission in life. In addition, Jesus' attempt to act as his father's surrogate had actually violated a deeper relationship that he had with his father—something more deeply personal—and also cut him off from his previous childhood experience of God as a loving and gracious father.

In short, Miller has provided a coherent psychological picture of Jesus' early life, one based on Jesus' positive relationship to Joseph. He affirms that Joseph was Jesus' father or, put differently, that Jesus experienced Joseph as his real father. Unlike Meier, who uses the term "putative father" for Joseph lest he give the appearance of rejecting the Christian belief in the virginal conception, Miller affirms that Jesus knew and experienced Joseph as his father. Moreover, this father-son relationship was a positive one, and therefore provided an experiential basis for Jesus' experience of God as, likewise, a loving and caring father. Miller also assumes that Joseph died during Jesus' adolescence, basing this on the "fact" that Jesus had six or more siblings (thus precluding Joseph's death during Jesus' childhood) and on gospel accounts of Jesus' mother and brothers (perhaps also sisters) journeying to where he was and asking about him, possibly with the intention of persuading him to return home to Nazareth.

Given the absence of any reference to Joseph in these gospel accounts, together with the fact that life expectancy of first-century Palestine was much shorter than our own, many, perhaps most, scholars assume that Joseph was no longer alive. In itself, this is not an unreasonable assumption, though Crossan notes that the exclusion of the father from these texts "might be interpreted in many different ways: Joseph was busy that day, was already dead, or was omitted to protect either the virgin birth or God as Jesus' true Father" (1991, 299). On the other hand, in noting in *Jesus: A Revolutionary Biography* that "Joseph may well have been long dead" (1994, 24), Crossan raises some doubts that Jesus was the firstborn because this view is secure "only in combination with Jesus' virginal conception taken literally, factually, and historically" (24). He thinks James acts more like a firstborn son than Jesus does (23–24), though Miller might explain this as a consequence of Jesus' having relinquished this role to his next eldest brother. Like Miller, Crossan also assumes that Joseph was a carpenter, viewing differences between Mark and Matthew in this regard as insignificant "in a world where sons usually followed their father's professions in any case" (24).

Miller (like Borg) also affirms that Jesus' baptismal experience was similar to a conversion experience. Also, more specifically than Borg, but in general agreement with Meier, he suggests that this experience brought to a culmination and resolution some deeply rooted identity conflicts. While he does not hold to the later tradition that Jesus was "without sin" or even the consciousness of sin (26–27), his interpretation of the baptismal experience as the resolution of identity conflicts somewhat downplays the fact that baptism, in its original sociocultural and religious context, was a Jewish purification rite. On the other hand, this interpretation enables him to emphasize the baptismal theme of "the second birth" (27–29). Thus, equally important to his emphasis on the loving–deceased–father is his view that Jesus' struggle centered, interpersonally, around a mother-son conflict. In his view, Mary did not understand Jesus' deep psychological and spiritual need to exert his independence. Her rather limited understanding was also evident in her attribution of demon possession to Jesus merely because he was determined to secure his independence from her.

Why does Miller give so much emphasis to Jesus' desire to achieve independence from his mother in his transition to maturity? Perhaps the most important reason is his concern to challenge the notion that Jesus may have been homosexual (66–70). In his chapter on sexuality, he points out that "numerous studies have demonstrated that a significant contributing factor in many instances of male homosexuality appears to be a parent milieu characterized by a dominating, possessive, sexually prudish mother and a weak, absent, or aloof father" (69). He cites "the well-known author and outspoken homosexual" Andre Gide's retelling of the story of the prodigal son, in which the son admits that his mother was the real reason for his returning home. Thus, in Gide's hands, the story becomes "a tale of a son who is still paternally alienated and hostile returning home to his mother after a failed attempt at living apart from her." In contrast, "Jesus at thirty appears to have become a free man so far as his mother was concerned, and during his public ministry he emerged as a passionate advocate of paternal reconciliation" (70). Thus, Miller's desire to put forward the view that Jesus' apparent celibacy does not imply a homosexual orientation plays a major role in his emphasis on Jesus' struggle to free himself from a mother who "tries to cope with the loss of her husband by leaning more and more on this resourceful eldest son" (53).

Schaberg's Emphasis: Jesus Was Considered Illegitimate

I now want to turn to a very different psychological portrait of Jesus' early years, one that both Meier and Miller strenuously reject (Meier, 1991, 222–26, 245–49; Miller, 41–43, 131). This picture is based on the view that Jesus was of illegitimate birth (of unknown or at least obscure paternity), a view advanced by Jane Schaberg in *The Illegitimacy of Jesus* (1987; see also Lüdemann, 1998).

Schaberg argues that Mary's conception of Jesus was by a man other than Joseph (the man to whom she was betrothed). Therefore, by first-century Jewish standards, Jesus was considered illegitimate, a bastard. While her primary concerns in this book are the implications of this view for Mary and only secondarily for Jesus, her argument is important for our concern to reconstruct the "hidden years" of Jesus' own life. Her illegitimacy argument directly challenges the Meier-Miller position that Jesus' early life was "insufferably ordinary," for an illegitimate child in that sociocultural and religious context could not possibly experience childhood and adolescence as "ordinary." More indirectly, her argument offers a counterthesis for why these early years are "hidden," as it implies that the early Christian community had something to hide or, at the very least, over which to exercise considerable damage control.

In her introduction, Schaberg contends that the two gospel authors, Matthew and Luke, who provide infancy narratives of Jesus, took his illegitimacy for granted: "Neither evangelist intends to deny the tradition of Jesus' illegitimacy. If each were asked about it, he would reply, 'Yes, I do intend to hand down this tradition. Yes, but…Both want to focus the attention of their readers on this 'but,' on the distinctive meanings they find in and beyond the 'scandal'; this is their major intention" (17). Thus, what she sees herself doing is attending to their minor intention, that of handing down the tradition that they have received, making it explicit where they left it inexplicit. She "talks about it, where they are silent; recognizes evasiveness, obliqueness, suppression, and the tendency to mystify as literary strategies used to promote patriarchy, and sometimes used to communicate realities that are considered socially unacceptable" (18).

Schaberg views the "absence" of Jesus' biological father in these gospels as itself a significant datum, arguing that "silence about him, his absence, should not be used to mean his nonexistence" (18). Thus, against those who would argue that one cannot make much, if anything, out of silence (see Gaventa, 1995, 11), she argues precisely the opposite. The silence means something. Therefore, the question that needs to be answered is: What does the silence mean, and, conversely, what does it *not* mean? In discussing Schaberg's views, I will focus primarily on her discussion of Matthew's account of Jesus' conception.

This discussion begins with the genealogy in Matthew 1, and more specifically, with the references to Tamar, Rehab, Ruth, and Bathsheba ("the wife of Uriah"). Among the four women, Schaberg notes that Ruth alone "is free from a taint of immorality in the rabbinic tradition," which instead stresses the problem of her Moabite ancestry, their concern being that Deuteronomy 22:3 ("No Ammorite or Moabite shall enter the assembly of Yahweh, even to the tenth generation") could be applied to David through Ruth. Yet Ruth may not be an exception, for

> A glance at some of the material from the rabbinic literature, targums, and translations shows that there is intense concern that the threshing floor scene receive careful exegesis by various methods in various periods, lest the reader conclude from the sexual allusions in 3:4, 7–9, 12–13 that Ruth and Boaz had intercourse there. We can conclude that such strenuous efforts to remove any hint of indelicacy implicitly acknowledge that a different reading was possible and persistent, even popular. (28)

Rabbinic discussion about the problem of Ruth's Moabite ancestry, less inherently scandalous, might therefore divert attention from these sexual allusions. In any event, Schaberg notes that Ruth risked an accusation of harlotry, but is praised by Matthew for taking the risk, as she was the mother of Obed, who fathered Jesse, who fathered David. Also, her story bears special resemblance to Matthew's construction of the story of Joseph's marriage to Mary. As Schaberg points out, accusation of improper sexual conduct, while actually made in the case of Tamar and implicit in the case of Rahab, is "avoided in Ruth's case by the secrecy of Boaz" (33). (Since Matthew carries on the tradition of secrecy, one might say that he has constructed Joseph in Boaz's image. I will return to this point later.)

Schaberg next considers the fact that, when Matthew reaches the final names of his genealogy, he breaks the pattern of A begot B, B begot C, which had been used throughout the genealogy, and says, "Jacob begot Joseph the husband of Mary; of her was begotten Jesus, called the Christ" (35). In Schaberg's view, "What is not said is clearly important. It is not said that Joseph, the husband of Mary, begot Jesus" (35). Thus, "Matthew is apparently trying to prevent the conclusion that Joseph was the biological father of Jesus." She cites a text, possibly originating as early as 200 C.E., in which a Jew, contesting the virginal conception view, concluded from verse 16 that Joseph *was* the biological father of Jesus. Matthew's concern to prevent this conclusion (that Joseph "begot" Jesus) has traditionally been explained as required by Matthew's subsequent indication that Jesus was virginally conceived. This seems the most obvious explanation for his use of the passive voice—"of her was begotten Jesus"—and the exclusion of Joseph from the conception itself. This is the basis, for example, for Miller's view that Joseph was the father of Jesus.

Schaberg disagrees with this explanation, however, contending that it would occur only to a person who reads this verse through the lens of the traditional interpretation of verses 18–25, the story of the conception and birth of Jesus. Before she takes up these verses, though, she notes the curious fact that in verse 17, Matthew states that the generations from Abraham to David, from David to the deportation to Babylon, and from the deportation to Christ, were each fourteen in number. Yet in the third section (vv. 12–16), Joseph occupies the twelfth generation and Jesus is the thirteenth. Schaberg argues against proposals that Matthew was simply inaccurate, that Jesus is to be counted twice (as Jesus and as Christ), that Mary is to be counted, or that God (as father of Jesus) should be counted. Instead, she theorizes that the name of Jesus' biological father is "conspicuously and consciously omitted from the genealogy...He is never named, either because Matthew and his sources did not know the name, or because it was suppressed. He is erased, but not completely; absent but not completely. Jesus' genealogy, then, does involve two kinds of human fatherhood: legal (Joseph's) and physical (the biological father)" (39). She concludes that Matthew has created a genealogy "whose functions are (a) to admit or at least raise the possibility of illegitimacy; and (b) to insist, via someone other than the biological father, on the legitimacy of a social/legal type (here, via Joseph, in Jesus' Abrahamic and Davidic descent)" (39). Thus, Joseph's adoption of Jesus as his son, legalizing his fatherhood of Jesus, is the central claim of this genealogy. What is not directly claimed, but implied in this central claim, is that Jesus was illegitimately conceived, for "Joseph is clearly referred to in Matt. 1:16 as the husband of Mary, but he is not said to have begotten Jesus" (41).

Schaberg next takes up the issue of the legal situation in this period in Palestine, focusing on betrothal and marriage laws. We have already discussed these matters in chapter 5, so I will not repeat her discussions here, but I *do* want to draw attention to one of her points that, on the basis of our earlier discussion, seems somewhat questionable. She cites the same mishnaic material presented in Schiffman's article, noting that Judea allowed sexual relations after the betrothal and before the marriage and therefore had sexual laws relating to claims by the husband that his wife was not a virgin. Because interim sexual relations were not permitted in Galilee, it was possible, in her view, for the Galilean husband to "bring a charge of adultery against his wife in court soon after the marriage if he suspected that she had not been a virgin at the time of their marriage, and certainly also if she was found pregnant in the interim between betrothal and marriage" (43). She suggests that it would be far harder for the Judean man to bring such a charge. In my view, however, the existence of laws in Judea governing charges and defense against these charges made it more, not less, probable that a Judean male would take the matter to court, for if his claim was truthful he would have the law on his side. In the more ambiguous Galilean society, where there was greater reliance on the honor of the individuals involved (the betrothed and her kinsmen), the husband would be less likely to press charges, as it would be a matter of his word against hers (or theirs). Assuming roughly comparable illegitimacy rates in the two regions, the conclusion to be drawn is that in Galilee there were probably *more* husbands who had little choice but to proceed with the betrothal arrangements in spite of the fact that their wives were nonvirgins and carrying another man's child. One would therefore guess that there was intense anger, resentment, and sense of helplessness among these "legal" but not "biological" fathers. Acceptance of the view that Joseph was not the biological but the legal father of Jesus thus raises the question whether Matthew presents a rather idealized picture of Joseph, and thus, by implication, of the relationship between Joseph and Jesus. I will return to this point later.

Schaberg next discusses Matthew's narrative, focusing on his account of how Joseph, "a just man" (i.e., Torah-observant) was "unwilling to expose [Mary] to public disgrace" and so "resolved to divorce her quietly" (44). The logic here is that "Joseph understood the situation to obligate or at least allow him, legally and morally, to divorce Mary rather than complete the marriage with the home-taking." But his judgment was overruled by the angelic command to take her home, explaining that "what is begotten in her is through the holy Spirit" (45). These verses present Joseph as suspicious regarding Mary's pregnancy and in a quandary as to what to do about it. Schaberg suggests that "adultery or rape are two normal alternatives Joseph had for explaining the pregnancy with which he was confronted. And two alternative actions were considered by him: to expose Mary to public shame or to divorce her secretly—the action he chose" (45).

Determining whether a woman had committed adultery or had been raped was itself a complex problem. In first-century Jewish law, adultery included acts of seduction, where the man succeeded in persuading a betrothed woman to consent to sex for pleasure or money. Rape would be declared if the man met her alone somewhere and forced her to engage in the sexual act when no one could come to her assistance. Deciding between these two possibilities could be exceedingly difficult, for it would need to be determined (1) whether she cried out and resisted or cooperated willingly; (2) whether she even *could* cry out and resist, or was bound and gagged, or overcome by superior physical force; and (3) whether the man had accomplices. If a betrothed virgin was determined to have been raped, her betrothed could either divorce her or complete the marriage. If seduction occurred, she was regarded as an adulterous wife. In this case, a variety of punishments could be meted out, ranging from execution, to stripping and public exposure of her genitals, to a public beating, to divorce. While the death penalty was probably rare, the story of the woman caught in adultery in John 8:3–11 indicates "that it was still discussed and threatened" (53). In Schaberg's view, "divorce was most likely, if not strictly obligatory, for the convicted adulteress" (53).

Assuming cases in which the question whether the act was seduction or rape was indeterminable, the presumption was probably that the woman was an adulteress. In this case, the betrothed husband would prefer to break the union, not because he was commanded to do so, but due to his repugnance toward marrying a woman who had grossly broken the law and the fact she had had intercourse with another man. If he suspected rape, he might decide to divorce her anyway. This means that he might not try to establish her guilt, which might be difficult to prove, and might prefer the course of sparing himself (and her) the public disgrace of a defamatory process (54). Once divorced, whether or not she was charged and convicted of adultery, the woman could marry again, but the pool of prospective husbands would be severely limited.

But what if she was pregnant, the situation that Matthew describes in his narrative? Schaberg focuses here on the fate of the child and cites Sirach and Wisdom of Solomon to indicate that the children of adulterers would suffer punishment and disgrace for what the parent had done. The Wisdom of Solomon text indicates that "none of their illegitimate seedlings will strike a deep root or take a firm hold. For even if they put forth boughs for a while, standing insecurely they will be shaken by the wind, and by the violence of the winds they will be uprooted." Their fruit "will be useless, not ripe enough to eat, and good for nothing." Moreover, the children will be "witnesses of evil against their parents when God examines them" (56). Schaberg also discusses the term *mamzer*, which occurs in Deuteronomy 23:2: "No *mamzer* will enter the assembly of Yahweh even to the tenth generation." But to whom does this term apply? It seems to apply to children of mixed marriages, incest, and forbidden unions. (The RSV translates this word "bastard"; the NRSV reads "Those born of illicit union.") Schaberg cites J. Jeremias' view that the oldest rabbinical view is that a *mamzer* is a child conceived in adultery. *Mamzerim* could not hold public office, take part in court decisions, or marry into priestly families, Levites, or legitimate Israelite families. At the end of the first century C.E., their rights to inherit from their natural fathers were in dispute. Schaberg concludes: "The word *mamzer* was considered one of the worst insults to a man. *Mamzerin* were among those called the 'excrement of the community.' But whatever the terms used to speak of the child of the seduced, divorced woman, it is clear that both the mother and child would suffer as social misfits" (57).

As for the woman's fate, even in the case of rape no man following the stricter *halakah* would be allowed to marry her. A man following a less rigorous *halakah* could marry her after the hearing establishing her innocence, in which case "the child of the rape would somehow be part of the family unit; yet it is reasonable to suppose that the publicity surrounding the hearing of the case would negatively and seriously mark both mother and child" (57). The most humane possibility would be the completion of the marriage, without a hearing, between a betrothed, raped woman and a man following the less rigorous *halakah*. This would at least protect her (and him) from a public hearing and the notoriety attending it.

But could her husband—would he—treat her son as his own? The situation was quite clear in the case of a man accepting his own natural son (or sons) born out of wedlock. He could testify that the child was his son, even his first-born, as the case might be, and his testimony would be considered conclusive in a court of law. The situation was murkier in the case of sons fathered by another man. On this issue, there was evidently disagreement in the period that concerns us here. The same scholar (Tschernowitz, cited by Schaberg, 58) who asserts that the father's own sons born out of wedlock could be considered heirs believes that the woman's son, raised by his adoptive father, would not be covered by the same statute.

In Schaberg's view, Matthew's account of Joseph's decision to divorce Mary is designed to emphasize that Joseph gave serious–even agonizing– thought to the options that were before him, and that he ruled out the option of a public hearing to determine whether she had been seduced or raped. By rejecting this option, he was shielding her and himself from (1) the public shame and questioning involved in the hearing; (2) the possibility of an accusation and conviction on the charge of seduction/adultery, with its punishment of a degrading divorce, perhaps with attendant indignities and certainly a bleak future; and (3) the reasonable likelihood that rape could not be proved. Formally, the quiet divorce would involve the delivery of the writ of divorce before two witnesses, and the return of the dowry. Because Matthew says that Joseph, responding to the angelic message, decided to proceed with the marriage, Schaberg believes that he likely judged that she was not an adulteress but was the victim of rape. This implies that he followed the less strict *halakah*. Schaberg also notes that the angel told *Joseph* to name the child, which is equivalent "to a formula of adoption" (61). Matthew concludes with the remark that, when Joseph took Mary home, he did not have sexual relations with her before she gave birth to a son, thus "stressing once again that Joseph could not be this child's biological father" (62).

Schaberg considers the difficult issue of the virginal conception, focusing on Matthew's statements that Mary was pregnant "through the Holy Spirit" (1:18) and that "the child begotten in her is through the Holy Spirit" (1:20). She acknowledges that virtually all modern critics think that Matthew 1:18 and 20 refer to a virginal conception, that is, without a human father and in a non-sexual manner. She contends, however, that "since nothing in the context of Matthew 1 *requires* us to read Matt. 1:18, 20 in terms of a virginal conception, these verses should be read against and as part of the wider Jewish and Christian context," that is, as an instance of "the interpenetration of divine and human fatherhood" (67). She has in mind texts that stress that God "acts" in and through human parenting, indicating that the initial act of creation is reenacted at the birth of every human being, and texts that emphasize the special status that comes from being "begotten" by God (e.g., Israel is God's "begotten," as are those with exceptional destinies, such as patriarchs, kings, prophets, and the Messiah). If Matthew 1:18 and 20 are viewed against this background, they will be read, as intended, as "figurative or symbolic."

Schaberg believes that what happened in the post-New Testament period is that "the metaphor of the divine begetting of Jesus was rejected as metaphor. Literalism produced the notion of a biological virginal conception, all but rupturing the connection with its Jewish and early Christian source in the metaphor" (67). This metaphorical reading would be consistent with Jewish views that sexual and divine begetting are integrated. Thus, "Matt. 1:18, 20 can be read to mean that the Holy Spirit empowers this birth as all births are divinely empowered, that this child's human existence is willed by God, and that God is the ultimate power of life in this as in all conceptions" (67). Therefore, "this child's existence is not an unpremeditated accident, and it is not cursed. The pregnant Mary is not to be punished" (67).

The primary grounds for believing that Matthew ascribes a virginal conception to Mary's "begetting" of Jesus is his insertion of the verse from Isaiah 7:14: "Behold, the young girl [Hebrew: *ha'alma*], will conceive and will give birth to a son, and they will call his name Immanuel." (The *King James Version* translates this word "a virgin," but the RSV and NRSV translate it "young woman.") Schaberg notes that the Greek translation for young girl [*he parthenos*], a virgin, does not necessarily mean biological virgin. In Genesis 34:3, for example, Dinah is twice called *parthenos* after Shechem has raped her. Even if the young woman were understood as a biological virgin, however, the Isaiah verse "seems simply to have meant that one who is *now* a virgin will conceive by natural means" (70). Schaberg believes that when Matthew chose the Isaiah citation, he was not thinking of a virgin conceiving miraculously, but rather of the law in Deuteronomy 22:23–27 concerning the rape or seduction of a betrothed virgin (*parthenos*), the law he presupposes in his presentation of the dilemma of Joseph. Thus, "the virgin betrothed and seduced or raped is, in the great Matthean paradox, the virgin who conceives and bears the child they will call Emmanuel" (72–73).

As indicated, Schaberg believes that Matthew and Luke were working with a preexisting tradition concerning the illegitimacy of Jesus. She hypothesizes that this tradition stemmed from the family of Jesus, "probably from Mary or from the brothers or sisters of Jesus rather than from Joseph, who does not appear in any story of the ministry" (152). She also believes that women would have had a special interest in and understanding of the early tradition about Jesus' conception, and that the story was communicated orally through them. They were therefore "the anonymous shapers and framers of the Jesus story" (154). This posits a very different source—far more sympathetic—than the view that stories of Jesus' illegitimacy were the result of Jewish calumny inspired by a deliberate misreading of Matthew's infancy narrative:

> If the story of how and when Jesus was conceived was family tradition, it is unlikely it would have been communicated to many. Rather, it would naturally have been kept secret. But leakage and rumor were possible, especially in the hometown, and its spread can be easily imagined during the ministry and afterwards, especially on the lips of those who did not accept either the claims Jesus made or those his followers made for him. (155)

For brevity's sake, I will not discuss Schaberg's interpretation of texts (such as Mk. 6:3 and Jn. 8:41) that have been viewed by other scholars as having bearing on the question of Jesus' illegitimacy. I want, however, to raise one issue concerning the implications of her perspective for Jesus' "hidden years." This concerns her view that Joseph treated Mary in a humane and merciful way, both in his decision to marry her and to accept her offspring as his legal child. The question, however, is whether Matthew is portraying Joseph from the perspective of the Matthean community itself, a portrayal that may be at odds, at least in part, with Joseph's actual response. While Schaberg understands Matthew's Joseph to be Matthew's creation (noting, for example, that early texts such as Mark do not even name Joseph as Jesus' father), various indications throughout her text suggest that she considers Matthew's Joseph to be authentic in its broad outlines. For example, she does not question Matthew's claim that Joseph was Jesus' legal father. Also, she assumes that the story of how Jesus was conceived, being family tradition, was kept relatively secret. This assumption, however, depends largely on the authenticity of Matthew's claim that Joseph, in proceeding with his marriage to Mary, provided "cover" for Mary and her son. But should we take Matthew's portrayal at face value? Could this part of the narrative be Matthew's own invention, more reflective perhaps of Matthew's viewpoint—perhaps even his personality—than of Joseph's? As various scholars have noted, the tradition regarding Mary is much more secure than the Joseph tradition. An article by Anthony Saldarini (1992) on the Matthean community sheds some light on this question.

Saldarini emphasizes that the Matthean community was still Jewish but was a deviant group within the Jewish community. He notes: "Deviance processes, far from driving a group out of society, often keep them in. Paradoxically, social theory has established that non-conformity, resistance to social structures, and deviance are always part of any functioning society" (23). We should therefore look for a considerable overlap between the views of the Matthean community and the society of which it was part, but also evidence of minority views on some issues. He notes that numerous biblical Jewish laws and community norms are affirmed or accepted by Matthew: the commandments, alms, prayer and fasting, care for the poor, circumcision, and so on. Though the list of practices and symbols Matthew shared with his fellow Jews is very long, he modifies the interpretation of the law so that it conflicts with those of other groups. Changes in *core symbols* include raising Jesus' status "as central authority and symbol," though not divine in the way later Christian theologians and councils defined it; a reweighting of matters of the law to provide a more flexible use and adaptation fitting the needs of Matthew's changing, alienated community, especially reflecting an emphasis on justice, mercy, and faith; and an apocalyptic orientation consistent with a deviant community. Changes in *social boundaries* included the welcoming of marginalized groups (sinners, tax collectors, non-Jews), while changes in *social structure* involved a decisive move away from prevailing modes of leadership and social organization, including a severely qualified support for the temple and its legitimacy, and an emphasis on egalitarian relationships with little differentiation and specialization.

Of particular interest here were changes affecting the laws, customs, and outlooks of the larger Jewish community involving purity regulations. The Matthean community qualified their importance without rejecting them totally. For example, they rejected divorce except for *porneia* (a kind of immorality). Recent scholarship on this exception suggests that it does not apply generally to "any sexual interference in a marriage" (e.g., adultery, rape) but to "marriage within forbidden degrees of kinship" (29–30). Thus, Matthew's more restrictive position on allowable divorce rules out adultery and rape as legitimate grounds for dissolving the marriage. In effect, it views incest as the only defensible grounds for divorce.

If we apply Saldarini's conclusions about the Matthean community to the case of Joseph and Mary, the fact that Matthew lumps together adultery and rape and views incest separately indicates that we cannot conclude that his portrayal of Joseph's more merciful intentions provides evidence that Mary was *not* considered blameworthy; that is, we cannot rule out the possibility that Joseph, as portrayed by Matthew, viewed her as an adulteress, not the victim of forcible rape. It may also mean, however, that he does not consider Mary's pregnancy to have involved incest, which *would* have been grounds, according to the Matthean community, for divorcing Mary. Most importantly, the Joseph that Matthew presents in his infancy narrative is congruent with his deviant views on divorce (e.g., 5:31–32; 19:1–12), views that ran counter to first-century norms (30). Given this congruence, we have reason to believe that Matthew's portrayal of Joseph is anachronistic, that he has Joseph acting in the ideal manner that he—Matthew—was advocating. The similarity between his portrayal of Joseph and his own views on this issue cast significant doubt on the factualness of his portrayal, raising the question whether Joseph actually adopted Jesus or whether, instead, Jesus was always known as "Mary's son," and whether, therefore, Joseph's alleged death has any relevance in this regard. Conversely, the fact that Matthew's Joseph is congruent with the Matthean community's views on divorce gives credence to the view that Joseph's actions in the matter were not significantly different from those of the dominant society, especially in light of indications (e.g., the traditional names of Joseph's sons) that he was traditional himself.

Matthew wishes to make the point that a "God-fearing" man *may* take the more merciful route that he portrays Joseph taking, that "God-fearingness" and mercy are not incompatible. The historical Joseph, however, may not have viewed it this way. If he proceeded with marriage plans, he may have done so because he realized he was trapped, either because he could not prove that he was *not* the child's father or because he did not have the requisite social standing in the community to bring charges that would have been taken seriously (e.g., the *seducer* had a higher social standing or greater political influence than Joseph and was therefore invulnerable to Joseph's charges). Significantly, Matthew "solves" this problem of unprovable charges and ineffectual allegations by limiting divorce to only the most narrowly defined cases (those of incest). He apparently views the legal distinction between adultery and rape as unprovable. Moreover, he does not consider adultery sufficient grounds for refusing to marry one's betrothed. In effect, he makes a virtue of a necessity, giving Joseph's change of heart religious legitimation as a response to an angelic voice. Whether an angelic voice can put a helpless man's resentment and rage to rest, however, seems doubtful. Matthew's Joseph is thus highly idealized.

Concerning Joseph's inability to contest the matter due to the superior social standing of the natural father, Edward Shorter's article on illegitimacy in Europe among the peasant classes is quite relevant (1971). He distinguishes between two types of illegitimate births, stable and unstable, and identifies two forms of each, expressive and manipulative. Stable forms of illegitimacy are *true love* (expressive sexuality) and *peasant bundling* (manipulative sexuality), and the two unstable forms are *hit-and-run* (expressive sexuality) and *master-servant exploitation* (manipulative sexuality). Before the eighteenth century, peasant bundling was the most prevalent form of illegitimacy in Europe, and some 1 to 2 percent of all births were of this type. It normally resulted from engaged couples who had sexual relations before marriage, which was customary, but delayed the marriage too long. Social authorities would put enormous pressure on hesitant males to wed their fiancées, and such pressure was persuasive largely because "the seducer had been, and would continue to be, resident locally and dependent upon the good will of his social betters" (55).

Master-servant exploitation happened mostly within the context of lower-class life: "At that humble level, the authority of the oldest journeyman or the master tanner, for example, may have been minimal in absolute terms, yet to the girl who swept out the shop it must have appeared commanding" (56). Thus, peasant bundling and master-servant exploitation were more common to rural peasant life, with peasant bundling occurring between couples intending marriage and master-servant exploitation involving seduction and rape. Of course, there were many gray areas between these two types. True love and hit-and-run were more common in urban areas and became more prominent during periods of social change, when people were "stepping out of their old places en route to new ones" (57).

Given the rural setting of Nazareth, the seduction or rape of Mary might then have occurred in the context of *master-servant exploitation*. Joseph may therefore not have been in a position to protest it. As Shorter, in his discussion of various socioeconomic variables and their association with illegitimacy rates, points out: "The laborers and live-in hired hands who worked for improving farmers all over Europe were highly prone to illegitimacy...In Germany, the great farms of Mecklenburg and Niederbayern employed workers among whom illegitimacy flourished" (60–61). Moreover, "a glance at maps of illegitimacy in any of these countries shows that counties...with a high concentration of landownership in the hands of a few have, by and large, high levels of bastardy" (61).

Shorter also notes that high levels of out-of-wedlock births in cities does not mean that rural women necessarily behaved more morally than urban women. Rather, "All statistics point to the city as a place where conception out of wedlock meant abandonment by one's lover" (66). In other words, in rural areas, greater social pressures were placed on males to consummate marriages where the woman was found to be pregnant. Thus, to the extent that European peasant life is comparable to first-century Galilean peasant life, Joseph would have been under considerable pressure to marry his betrothed whether she was pregnant with his or another man's child. Perhaps large landownership and the patronage system have particular relevance precisely here. One may imagine a scenario where Mary was the victim of master-servant exploitation and Joseph, lacking the requisite patronage, had little choice but to proceed with the marriage. As for how Mary became pregnant, the story in Ruth of the threshing-room floor would be as plausible a guess as any.

And what about Jesus? If Joseph felt he had little choice but to marry his betrothed, what were his obligations to Mary's son? For Schaberg, Joseph's naming of the child indicates that he made Jesus his legally adopted son, and further implies that he felt a moral obligation to treat Jesus as his own child. But we have already raised the question whether Matthew's portrayal of Joseph reflects the values of the Matthean community and not necessarily Joseph's own views and behavior. The injunction in Matthew 18:10, "Take care that you do not despise one of these little ones," and the invitation in Matthew 19:14, "Let the little children come to me, and do not stop them," reflect the views of the Matthean community. Similar attitudes toward children are likely to have been held by Jesus himself (Crossan places the "Kingdom and Children" sayings in the first stratum with multiple independent attestation). But are we to assume that these were the views of the historical *Joseph*? Not necessarily. In my view, Matthew has created a wonderful portrait of Joseph that reflects Matthew's own ideal self. He has superimposed his own image on Joseph, and Joseph thus epitomizes the core values of the Matthean community. We should not, however, confuse Matthew's Joseph with the historical Joseph. This conclusion, and its possible implications, brings us to the third of the three authors whose depiction of the "hidden years" invites our attention.

Van Aarde's Emphasis: Jesus as Fatherless Son

In an earlier article on the "third quest" for the historical Jesus (1995), Andries G. van Aarde argued that Jesus grew up as a fatherless son and that this fact should be taken into account when one considers Jesus' self-identification, his a-patriarchal ethos, his behavior toward endangered women and children, and especially his trust in God as his "Abba." His more recent concern is "to bring into historical Jesus research the association of the historical-critically established 'fact' that Jesus underwent a baptismal initiation ritual by John the Baptist" and his earlier proposal that Jesus was "someone who was fatherless from infancy, through childhood, to adulthood" (1997, 453).

To avoid the suggestion that his "Jesus as fatherless" construct is based on what was common to all fatherless individuals in the first-century Galilean situation, Van Aarde proposes that the "Jesus was fatherless" formulation be viewed as a Weberian "ideal type," and thus as offering no more—but no less— than a "coherent image" of Jesus (453). The specific question that concerns him, however, is "why the historical Jesus linked up with John the Baptist and submitted to the 'baptism for the remission of sins' and also why, once his road deviated from the Baptist's, Jesus, so unconventionally for his time, became involved with the fate of social outcasts, especially women and children" (454). His construction of Jesus as the "fatherless son of God" provides a general response to this question, and his use of social-scientific theory, specifically the "status envy hypothesis," enables him to explore the question in greater detail. His "Jesus grew up as fatherless" thesis has several features. They include an assessment of the Joseph tradition, a consideration of rules governing who was (and who was not) allowed to participate in temple worship, and the relation of these rules to marriage strategy. He also discusses family structure in the Mediterranean world, and focuses on the issue of a family in which the father is absent.

First, Van Aarde notes that the figure of Joseph as Jesus' father does not occur in the early sources (Thomas, Q, Paul, and Mark). Rather, "The Joseph tradition within Christendom clearly develops as a trajectory impelled by the anti-Christian calumny against Mary" together with the "associated evolution of the idea of a 'pure' or sinless birth of Jesus," an idea that involved asserting that Mary remained a virgin after Jesus' birth and even that she was herself the fruit of a "divine birth." In his view, there is no trace of this idea of a pure birth in the New Testament. Rather, it developed in the second century in the Protoevangelium of James and was continued in Pseudo-Matthew. He does not comment on whether he believes there even was a historical Joseph, but he indicates that the Joseph tradition was defensive and reactive and was preceded by a deeper tradition in which Jesus was understood to have been "the son of Mary." In his view, this implies that Jesus did not have a father in the sense of a father who was not merely "a begetter," but "a provider and protector." He cites in this connection V. C. Matthews and D. C. Benjamin's study of the social world of ancient Israel, where they argue that "it was not a child's birth that made it part of a household, but the father's decision to adopt it into the household. This, rather than birth, was the beginning of life, and the father exercising the power of life and death over his offspring was a 'godlike being'" (459).

Van Aarde next considers rules regarding personal status vis-a-vis Israelite religion. He cites J. Jeremias' list in *Jerusalem in the Time of Jesus* (1969) of people who were (or were not) given permission to be present in the assembly of God's people for the reading of the scrolls. This list includes priests, Levites, True Israelites, illegal children of priests, converts from heathendom, converts from those who earlier had been slaves but subsequently freed, bastards (born as a result of incest or adultery), fatherless individuals (those who grew up without a father or an adopted father and were therefore not embedded within the structures of honor), foundlings, eunuchs from birth, those with sexual deformities, hermaphrodites, and heathens (non-Jews). He cites Bruce Malina's point (1993) that the principle of classification in this list is the "marriage strategy" in the Israelite community, which in turn was determined by purity rules. During the period that concerns us here (the Second Temple period), this strategy was defensive, meaning that "all foreigners were shunned and only fellow-Israelites fully within the covenant were regarded as acceptable marriage partners" (463). This defensive strategy constituted the "chief mode of perception for the discussions of marital and sexual behavior" in the world of Jesus, its focus being on offspring, or "holy seed." The term "bastard" (*mamzer*) is the symbolic opposite of holy seed.

Van Aarde adopts Malina's reduction of the above list to seven categories based on marriage strategy. Priests, Levites, and full-blooded Israelites account for three categories. Illegal children of priests (children of priests who married prohibited women) and the two types of proselytes comprise the fourth category. The fifth is made up of bastards, the fatherless, foundlings, and those made eunuchs by human agency. The sixth category consists of those incapable of sexual relations (who could not therefore procreate "holy seed") and includes eunuchs from birth, the sexually deformed, and hermaphrodites. The seventh category comprises non-Israelites who, being outside the covenant, were considered impure and thus excluded from any kind of social relationship.

Van Aarde is especially interested in the fifth category. They were considered of low status because they were "simply not whole and complete." They were "of doubtful parentage, perhaps even of disreputable descent, and therefore their membership in the true Israel was, at least, suspect. They were certainly not regarded as being capable of transmitting covenant status" (464). They could marry others like themselves and even marry converts, but "they were disqualified from marrying into the 'true Israel'—those associated with temple worship" (464). He believes that the historical Jesus belongs in category five: "The image of Jesus as the fatherless carpenter, the unmarried son of Mary, who lived in a strained relationship with his village kin in Nazareth, probably because of the stigma of being fatherless and, therefore, a sinner, fits the ideal type of the fifth category" (464). This also means that he "was denied the status of being God's child," without the "status of proper covenant membership," and therefore "not allowed to enter the congregation of the Lord in terms of the ideology of the temple and its systemic sin" (464). This, however, is precisely where John the Baptist becomes relevant, for Jesus "shared the vision of John the Baptist that remission of sin could be granted by God outside the structures of the temple" (464). Through John's baptism, performed at the Jordan River, Jesus could–and did–experience symbolically what he was deprived of literally, which was the status of "a son of Abraham, son of God." The baptismal declaration–"And a voice from heaven said, 'This is my son, with whom I am well pleased'" (Mt. 3:17)–affirms this very status of sonship. Van Aarde concludes that Jesus' trust in God as his "Abba" "is certainly subversive of the patriarchal values underlying the marriage strategy" of the period (464). In effect, Jesus makes a claim to the status of God's sonship that is deemed illegitimate in the eyes of the official ideology, but not so from the perspective of John's baptismal rite of purification.

Because Jesus belongs in category five, the "historical claim may therefore be made that in terms of the criteria of the period of the Second Temple, Jesus was regarded as being of illegitimate descent" (464). Thus, Van Aarde agrees with Schaberg's view of Jesus as illegitimate, specifically citing her work. He emphasizes, however, that the diverse membership of the fifth category indicates that this could have various connotations. Within the frame of reference of the defensive marriage strategy and its purity ideology, "illegitimate" (or "bastard") *could* refer to a birth as a result of immorality, rape, incest, or seduction, but the word "whore" could also apply to "a woman who was not so fortunate to be within the circle of protection of her husband (or his substitute)" (465). In fact, this expression often related to "mixed marriages," as when a son or daughter of Abraham married someone "outside the covenant." During the first century, there was an insistence on the strength of priestly purity codes that Israelite men should divorce such women. The result was "fatherlessness or illegitimacy" (465).

Van Aarde's point is that there is no solid textual basis for viewing the conception of Jesus as a consequence of rape or seduction. The earliest texts that respond to calumny against Mary make no reference to her having been the victim of rape or seduction: "No allusions to this effect occur in the documents up to Justin's second century explicit response to this accusation. The credibility of this evidence can therefore not be founded on the principle of multiple, independent evidence. It is based on the so-called 'Yeshua ben Pantera' traditions in the Talmud and the Medieval Toledot, which are independent of one another and are extremely tendentious" (466). (The "Jesus, son of Pantera" tradition makes Jesus the son of a Roman solider stationed in Galilee at the time; Meier discusses this tradition in footnote material in 1991, 247–48). Thus, the picture of Jesus as "fatherless" does not require that Mary was either raped or seduced, but only that Jesus grew up as "fatherless," especially as defined by purity codes. In contrast to Schaberg, Van Aarde is therefore more concerned about the fate of Jesus as "fatherless" than about Mary as possible victim of seduction and rape. As "illegitimate," Jesus would not be allowed to enter the temple or to marry a "full-blooded" Israelite woman (466).

He concludes that Jesus grew up as a boy who "did not know who his father was," as "someone without identity," and as lacking a father who would be able to give him credibility. He cites several texts in support of this conclusion. The first are sayings in the Gospel of Thomas that "may indicate that his 'sin' is related to the fact that someone who did not know who his father or mother was (in other words, someone who had no 'identity' because he was not a 'son of Abraham') would be called a 'son of a whore'" (466). The relevant sayings are the following: "They said to Jesus, 'Come, let us pray today and let us fast.' Jesus said, 'What is the sin that I have committed, or wherein have I been defeated? But when the bridegroom leaves the bridal chamber, then let them fast and pray'" (104). "Jesus said, 'He who knows the father and the mother will be called the son of a harlot'" (105). The second is the well-known Mark 6:3 text in which Jesus, against the background of his rejection by his family, is referred to by Nazarene villagers as "son of Mary," not "son of Joseph." The third is Matthew 27:63–64, which portrays the chief priests and Pharisees gathered before Pilate and saying, "Sir, we remember what the imposter said while he was still alive, 'After three days I will rise again.' Therefore, command the tomb to be made secure until the third day; otherwise his disciples may go and steal him away, and tell the people, 'He has been raised from the dead,' and the last deception would be worse than the first." Van Aarde reads this passage as a reference to the defamatory campaign by the opponents of Matthew's community. According to this defamatory campaign, the legend with regard to the resurrection of Jesus is the "last deception," which is worse than the "first deception." The "first deception" relates to Matthew's conviction that, "despite his 'fatherlessness,' Jesus was legitimized by God as a 'son of Abraham'/'son of God' by virtue of the Joseph tradition," which states that "Joseph was commanded by an angel in a dream to marry Mary, who was pregnant through the Spirit of God" (467). In other words, Matthew is seeking to preempt both calumnies, the one that Jesus was not resurrected and the one that Jesus, despite his fatherlessness, was not legitimized by God himself. The fourth text in behalf of Jesus' fatherlessness is John 19:9, involving Jesus' silence when Pilate asks about his origins. Van Aarde notes: "According to rabbinical literature…a person who does not know who his father is must remain silent when confronted with his origins" (467).

In Van Aarde's judgment, these are all texts where "the defamatory claims of the opponents of the Jesus movement with regard to Jesus' illegitimacy are disputed." He suggests that the "same kind of apologetic tendency is found in the New Testament references with regard to Jesus' 'baptism for the remission of sins' by John the Baptist" (Mt. 3:14–17), especially as it emerges in the "without sin" motif of the letter to the Hebrews (4:15). This motif "suggests an embarrassment with regard to the nature of Jesus' birth," an embarrassment "not shared by someone like Paul," who writes in Galatians 4:4: "But when the fullness of time had come, God sent his Son, born of a woman, born under the law, in order to redeem those who were under the law, so that we might receive adoption as children. And because you are children, God has sent the Spirit of his Son into our hearts, crying, 'Abba! Father!'" For Paul, it required a man who was illegitimate to redeem others who were also illegitimate. Through him, the fatherless could at last voice a cry for the father that would be heard and acknowledged.

As noted earlier, Van Aarde uses "status envy" theory to provide a social-scientific explanation for Jesus' adoption of God as his personal "Abba." Status envy theory, presented in a study of the absent father by R. V. Burton and J. W. M. Whiting (1961), suggests that the process of identification and the development of identity are achieved "by the imitation of a status role that is envied." This happens in fantasy or play, and its driving force is envy of the person who enjoys the privileged status to which one aspires. *Attributional identity* is the status assigned to a person by other members of society; *subjective identity* consists of the statuses one currently occupies; and *optative identity* consists of statuses one wishes to occupy but from which one is presently disbarred (456). The aim of socialization in any society is to produce an adult whose attributed, subjective, and optative identities are congruent or isomorphic: "I see myself as others see me, and I am what I want to be." Such isomorphism, however, requires a transition marked by *status disbarment,* which produces *status envy* and a reaching out from attributed to optative identity. When society permits an individual to occupy this optative identity, there is then agreement on what one wants to be, what society says one is, and what one sees oneself to be. Children are disbarred from various optative identities by virtue of their status as children (as Crossan suggests [1991, 269], they are "nobodies"). They can fantasize themselves occupying such statuses, however, and in the course of time if circumstances allow, may come to occupy them in fact.

Van Aarde concludes that Jesus' *attributed identity* involves his fatherless status, which is how his society perceived him. This position disbarred him from being "a son of Abraham" and "son of God." His *optative identity* was to be a son of Abraham, hence son of God, and this is the status bestowed upon him through baptism by John the Baptist. Through it, he could call himself and be called by others a "son of God." Of course, this was a direct challenge to the established system and those who benefited from it, a system with its own attributional categories, and on the basis of which Jesus was disbarred from legitimate sonship.

To explore Jesus' *subjective identity*, Van Aarde draws on Diane Jacobs-Malina's work (1993). She presents the thesis that Jesus' social role was similar to that of "the wife of the absent husband." For her, Jesus did not act "according to the expected role of the eldest son in a patriarchal family," but more like the wife in a family where the husband is absent from the family. As Van Aarde summarizes her position:

> In patriarchal societies the belief is commonly held that a male presence is necessary lest a woman bring shame on the family. So, if her husband was absent, a woman had to serve his interest by strictly conforming to his wishes or instructions. This resulted in close social

scrutiny. A husband's absence imposed on his unsupervised wife even more rigorous expectations of decorum than those that normally applied. Although he was absent, he remained present to his children in his wife as his authorized agent, who had the responsibility to ward off any challenge to her husband's prerogatives. (461)

In Jacobs-Malina's view, this is the role that Jesus fulfills in the gospels in his relationship to God, his followers, and outsiders. Thus, his *subjective identity*, or the status he saw himself occupying, is that of the authorized agent of "Abba" and thus "the protector of the honor of outcasts, like abandoned women and children, giving the homeless a fictive home" (Van Aarde, 469). The corollary to this view of Jesus as "wife of the absent husband" is that *being* a father was not his *optative identity.* Growing up fatherless, his desire was to *have,* not *be,* a father. This is consistent with Van Aarde's assumption that Jesus remained unmarried, and that he did not father children himself.

Van Aarde draws on research on father-absent households in the early life of boys supporting his status envy hypothesis. This research shows that "war-torn" boys from father-absent households *behaved like girls* in fantasy behavior and also *showed very little aggression.* Such behaviors derive from the boys' first or primary identification with the mother. Their secondary identification led to behavior, overtly and in fantasy, that produced *fatherlike performance* (460). Ordinarily, this secondary identification would be fostered by the father's return from military service. From these studies, together with studies of Mediterranean family structure, Van Aarde concludes that as far as his *subjective identity* was concerned, Jesus may well have had a "diffused identity." Drawing on John Pilch's work on child-rearing practices in the Mediterranean world (1991), he notes that both "the feminine quality of nurture and the male quality of assertion were emphasized." In early childhood, the boy learned nurturing qualities from his mother, but at puberty he passed from "the gentle world of women to the assertiveness of late childhood and adulthood associated with the harsh, authoritarian world of male values" (468). It was expected that the adolescent male would embrace the "rigors of manhood, subjecting himself in unquestioning obedience to the severity of the treatment that his father and other males might inflict on him" (468). For Van Aarde, however, Jesus' fatherless status meant that his "primary identification" with the mother was never "clarified" by a "secondary identification" with the father. Therefore, he "seemingly behaved in [a] 'mother-like' manner as an adult" (468). It might be noted that this provides a psychological explanation for the nonviolence that Borg and others attribute to Jesus.

Jesus: Longing for Adoption

Van Aarde covers considerable ground in his article, and, because he does so, some of his arguments are more suggestive than definitive. His basic argument that Jesus "grew up as a fatherless son," however, enables him to provide a coherent image of Jesus, one that accounts for Jesus' emphasis on

God as "Abba" and the importance of the baptismal rite of purification that he underwent as a disciple of John. He also provides a psychological explanation for Jesus' opposition to the official religion of the temple, and for his advocacy of an alternative religious structure that does not condemn those who, because of their attributed identity, have been relegated to permanent outsider status by the official structure. Deviance theory (cf. Saldarini, 1992) predicts that some such alternative religious structure would have developed for persons excluded from the official structure. Furthermore, there would be a need for a person—or persons—in every generation to create such alternative structures as long as the official structure existed. In Jesus' own experience, this someone was John the Baptist, who offered a rite of purification enabling those who were outside the official structure to claim insider status, as "sons of Abraham" and "sons of God." When Jacobs-Malina's views are incorporated into Van Aarde's core argument, further explanation is provided for why Jesus could be a strong advocate for family purity (reflecting the mother's "rigorous expectations of decorum" during the husband's absence) and, at the same time, be an advocate for those deemed to be sinners and outcasts (offering them, in effect, "a fictive home").

There are several issues, however, that I want to raise concerning Van Aarde's argument. These issues are not designed to challenge the fundamental core of his argument (i.e., the association of Jesus' fatherlessness and baptism by John and what it represented to Jesus), but to press for clarification of other aspects of his "image" of Jesus as fatherless, leading to certain modifications of it. The first issue concerns the effects of accepting Bruce Malina's proposal that "bastards" and "fatherless" persons be lumped together into a single category, and a related issue regarding the fact that the original classification of "fatherless" persons (identified by Jeremias) apparently distinguished between "those who grew up without a father" and those who did not have "an adoptive father." Acceptance of Malina's collapsing of several types of individuals into a single category serves Van Aarde's purpose of dealing with "an ideal type" ("fatherlessness") and enables him to avoid any implication that he is making empirical claims about Jesus' father that cannot be substantiated. On the other hand, as our earlier discussion of social stratification in first-century Palestine indicates, seemingly small differences in social class could have very significant implications in the lives of the community and of the individuals of that community. As Crossan points out in his comments about Jesus as a member of the artisan class, his status would be that of one living in "the dangerous space between Peasants and Degradeds or Expendables" (1994, 25). Thus, we miss subtle nuances when we fail to distinguish between members of adjoining social classes in first-century Palestine. A similar point needs to be made concerning the classifications established for religious inclusion and exclusion. Except for making the point that the classification served the "defensive marital strategy" that prevailed throughout the Second Temple period, the truncated system devised by Malina is not as useful as the one, derived from J. Jeremias' work, on which it is based. Given Van Aarde's desire to introduce the issue of status envy into the discussion, this truncated version is detrimental.

In *Group Psychology and the Analysis of the Ego* (1921/1955) and *Civilization and Its Discontents* (1930/1961), Freud discusses a social phenomenon he calls "the narcissism of minor differences." In the latter, he notes that "it is precisely communities with adjoining territories, and related to each other in other ways as well, who are engaged in constant feuds and the ridiculing of each other—like the Spaniards and Portuguese, for instance, the North Germans and South Germans, the English and Scotch, and so on" (61). In the former, he points out that the same phenomenon occurs in smaller social units, as when "two families become connected by a marriage" and "each of them thinks itself superior to or of better birth than the other" (42). In "The 'Uncanny'" (1919/1955) he notes that those who consider themselves better or superior to another often attribute envy to the other and suspect that the envious one may take action (such as stealing their material possessions) to eliminate the differences between them (240). Since Jeremias' classification consists of *fourteen* categories, we may assume that the "narcissism of minor differences" was nearly ubiquitous in first-century Palestine. Thus, while it is certainly true that bastards, those who grew up without a father, and those who did not have an adopted father are all "fatherless," one elides important considerations (e.g., of *subjective identity* and *status envy*) when these three, together with foundlings and eunuchs by human agency, are placed in a common category. One will take a very different view of Jesus' "hidden years" depending on how one decides the issue of paternity itself.

One possibility is for a male child to have been a "bastard" (that is, conceived as a result of incest, adultery, or rape) but to have grown up with an adoptive father and, therefore, as legally legitimated. This appears to be Schaberg's view. According to both Schaberg and Van Aarde, it is certainly the view that Matthew wants to promote. Another possibility, however, merits consideration, which is that (1) Jesus was conceived as a result of seduction or rape (which Schaberg affirms but on which Van Aarde, at the very least, reserves judgment); that (2) Mary's marriage to Joseph *did* take place (the view that Schaberg takes and the view, naturally enough, of scholars who believe that Joseph was the natural father); and (3) that Joseph did not adopt Jesus. This reconstruction would not challenge Van Aarde's argument that Jesus was "fatherless," nor would it technically challenge his view that Jesus "grew up without a father," but it would create a more complex picture of his childhood, one that visualizes Jesus living in Joseph's household but not accorded full membership in it. In this scenario, Jesus remained legally—and psychologically—illegitimate, since Joseph did not take the legal actions necessary to legitimate him. It may also mean that Joseph did not assume the responsibilities of fatherhood, including (as described by Miller) having Jesus circumcised, redeemed, taught the Torah, taught a trade, and secured a wife.

Also, Jesus would not be accorded firstborn status and would not receive any portion of the inheritance. Relevant to this conclusion is Gerhard Lenski's point that "in most agrarian societies, the artisan class was originally recruited from the ranks of the dispossessed peasantry and the non-inheriting sons and was continually replenished from these sources" (Crossan, 1991, 46). Since Matthew's ascription of the carpenter's trade to Joseph is an addition to Mark's assertion that Jesus was a carpenter, the "fact" that Joseph was a carpenter is by no means certain. Jesus could have become a carpenter–*tekton*–because he was a "non-inheriting son" and not taught any trade by Joseph, Mary's husband.

There is evidentiary support for this reconstruction. One is the "fact" that Jesus had siblings, indicating that Mary had other children, presumably by her husband, Joseph. There is also the probability, as indicated by Miller and Van Aarde, that Jesus did not marry. In the proposed reconstruction, the reason was not that Joseph died before he could secure Jesus a wife, but that it was never his intention to do so. There is also the "fact" that "bastards" were generally the firstborn offspring of girls who, as they reached puberty, were in the vulnerable position of not being fully protected by their family of origin (perhaps because they labored outside the home) and were not yet under the protection of their husbands (in houses belonging to their husbands). Yet, as Jacobs-Malina argues, Jesus did not act according to the expected role of the eldest son in a patriarchal family (an argument that Miller, for very different reasons, also makes). It may, in fact, be quite convincingly argued that James (who is listed first among his brothers in Mk. 6:3 and Mt. 13:55) held this position in Joseph's household, and that he, in effect, continued in this role as firstborn in his leadership in the Jerusalem community. As noted earlier, Crossan (1994) suggests this very possibility: "I wonder, in fact, if the emphasis given [by the early church] to James, who is known to both Paul and Josephus as Jesus' 'brother,' might indicate that James was the oldest in the family and that his prominence after the death of Jesus was due not just to his renowned piety but to his leadership position in a family whose father, Joseph, may well have been long dead" (23–24). James's "renowned piety" could also have been due to his having received from Joseph the training in the Torah that Jesus, due to his illegitimacy, did not receive. In other words, Jesus was chronologically the eldest, but the status of eldest son went to James, Joseph's firstborn.

Frank Sulloway's study of birth order (1996) provides some empirical support for the view that Jesus did not act like a firstborn, as he shows that later borns are *more* likely than firstborns to take risks, to have conflicts with parents, to be revolutionaries in whatever careers they choose, and *less* likely to be protective of their status. One could argue that the very list of socioreligious categories that provides the basis for Van Aarde's study (with priests at the top and heathens at the bottom) is the kind of classificatory exercise in which firstborns engage in order to protect their priority status.

An example of a firstborn who was not accorded firstborn status is Leonardo da Vinci. He was born in the little town of Vinci, near Florence, in 1452. He was the first son of Ser Piero, a notary by profession, descended from farmers and notaries, and a peasant woman whose family worked on the farm owned by Ser Piero's family. They were neither married nor betrothed. In fact, a year or so after Leonardo's birth, Ser Piero married another woman whose family was of higher social standing. Leonardo's name is mentioned in a Florentine land-register for purposes of taxation as a member of his father's household, but he was never officially legitimated as one of his father's sons. When his father died, Leonardo wrote that his father left ten sons and two daughters, thus excluding himself. He was not included in his father's will and never married. Two facts about Leonardo are of special note. One is Freud's view (1910/1957) that Leonardo's repudiation of authority and his intellectual boldness were legacies "of his fatherless infancy" (Collins, 1997, 17). Another is his painting *The Last Supper,* which portrays the betrayal announcement. This emphasis on the betrayal announcement, instead of either the institution of the eucharist or identification of Judas as betrayer, was completely unprecedented in Christian art (Collins, 128). We may surmise that the painting was, for Leonardo, a sort of family portrait, with his twelve siblings represented by the disciples, and the artist, in the role of Christ, proclaiming that he was the victim of his *father's* betrayal. Of course, Jesus was a first-century Palestinian Jew while Leonardo da Vinci was a fifteenth-century Italian. Both countries, however, were Mediterranean and thus reflected much the same honor-shame dynamics. The emotional distance between the villages of Nazareth and Vinci is not nearly as great as the temporal and physical distance. It is also noteworthy that even though Ser Piero was the natural father, he did not consider Leonardo his legitimate son. We can well imagine, therefore, the resistance to adopting another man's son and treating him as if he were one's own. Such resistance may explain why Paul, for example, so emphasized God's adoptive fatherhood.

The story of Abraham and Isaac suggests a similar conflict. As David Bakan points out (1966), "The way in which the biblical story of Sarah's conception of Isaac is told raises questions concerning the authenticity of the paternity of Isaac and throws some light on Abraham's temptation to kill him" (212). The possibility of Abraham's not being the biological father was enough on the mind of the distinguished commentator Rashi for him to deal with it and deny it: "The proof is, according to Rashi, that the text reads, 'And these are the generations of Isaac, Abraham's son; Abraham begot Isaac.' Why does the biblical text deviate from its usual pattern here? If these are the 'generations of Isaac,' why does the biblical writer go backward to mention Abraham? And why is it necessary to say it twice?" Rashi explains: "Since the text wrote, Isaac, the son of Abraham, it became necessary to state, 'Abraham begot Isaac'; for the scorners of the generation were saying, From Abimelech did Sarah conceive, since for many years she tarried with Abraham and did not conceive from him. What did the Holy One Blessed Be He do? He formed the features of Isaac's face similar to Abraham, and there attested everyone, Abraham begot Isaac" (Bakan, 213). As Bakan interprets the binding of Isaac story, it involves Abraham's struggle to decide what to do about his doubts concerning his paternity of Isaac. Bakan notes the general ambivalence expressed in biblical texts regarding the firstborn son (i.e., cases where the issue of paternity is most likely in doubt; see also Levenson, 1993). We should not, therefore, take Joseph's adoption of Jesus for granted. Legal pressures to do so were not nearly as strong as pressures (as explained earlier) for proceeding with his marriage to Mary. In fact, because early Christianity affirmed adoption and was a deviant religious movement, the ascription of adoptive fatherhood to Joseph by the Christian community was integral to its deviant social position.

The tensions between Jesus and the other members of his family may also be attributed to Joseph's failure to legitimate him appropriately. As Van Aarde points out: "The father of a household was not only a begetter, but also a provider and protector. So it was not a child's birth that made it part of a household, but the father's decision to adopt it into the household" (459). Tensions between Jesus and his family could have been alleviated had Joseph adopted Jesus as his own, thus bringing Jesus under his own paternal protection in conflictual situations between Jesus and his siblings. Failure to adopt him would leave him vulnerable to household shaming. The story in Mark 6:1–6 concerning Nazareth villagers' response to Jesus' teaching in the synagogue may be viewed against the backdrop of Joseph's failure to teach Jesus the Torah, hence, their amazement and skepticism over Jesus' temerity, prompting these questions: "Where did this man get all this? What is the wisdom that has been given to him?" (6:2). Given their "unbelief" (v. 5), we may conclude that they were suspicious of precisely where or how he "got all this." If not from instruction in the Torah (which his legitimate brothers *did* receive), then from whom? Perhaps Beelzebul himself?

This reconstruction of the "hidden years" of Jesus does not fundamentally challenge Van Aarde's view that Jesus was "fatherless," but it pulls together several related "facts" about Jesus (e.g., that he had siblings) into a reasonably coherent psychological picture of his early years. If the early Christian communities in Palestine offered an alternative religious structure, one that emphasized the adoptive fatherhood of God, such emphasis on adoption may well reflect an empirical reality in first-century Palestine, and Galilee in particular. If Shorter's evidence from early modern Europe is applicable to first-century Palestine, we may conjecture that a consequence of the transition to large landownership in Galilee increased the illegitimacy rate as girls became vulnerable to master-servant exploitation, thus adding new complexities to the perennial problems relating to peasant bundling (i.e., the hesitant male phenomenon).

Neither does this reconstruction of Jesus' childhood and youth call into question Van Aarde's view that, subjectively speaking, Jesus had a "diffused identity" owing to his "fatherlessness." As noted, Van Aarde draws on John Pilch's work, showing that a male in Mediterranean society passed at puberty into "the harsh authoritarian world of male values," which entailed the "embracing of the rigors of manhood, subjecting himself in unquestioning obedience to the severity of the treatment that his father and other males might inflict on him" (468). As the author of the letter of Hebrews suggests, an illegitimate son was not considered worthy enough to receive the discipline that was routinely accorded a man's legitimate heirs. He alludes to Proverbs 3:11–12: "My child, do not despise the LORD's discipline or be weary of his reproof, for the LORD reproves the one he loves, as a Father the son in whom he delights," then adds: "Endure trials for the sake of discipline. God is treating you as children; for what child is there whom a parent does not discipline? If you do not have that discipline in which all children share, then you are illegitimate and not his children" (Heb. 12:7–8).

The implication is that illegitimate boys did not receive the discipline that was a sign of a father's love, and therefore did not become "sons" but remained "children." If we recall Crossan's view that children were considered "nobodies," and that Jesus is presented in various sources as an advocate of children (Gos. Thom. 22:1–2; Mk. 10:13–16; Mt. 19:13–15, etc.), then it would follow that Jesus may not have been referring to children in general, but to those adults who lacked the attributed identity of legitimate sons and heirs. If, as Van Aarde suggests, Jesus was not initiated into the world of sons by subjecting himself to the severity of the treatment that his father might inflict on him, this need not be because there was no male at the head of the household, but because Joseph did not view Jesus as worthy of a father's discipline. Thus, Van Aarde's argument that Jesus had a "diffused identity," one that was weakened by an insecurely grounded secondary identification (i.e., with the father), receives support from the reconstruction proposed here.

This, however, raises a further question: What was it that Jesus sought in a father and believed that he found in "Abba"? It does not necessarily follow from the reconstruction that I am offering here that Jesus sought a "kind" and "nurturant" father. On the contrary, a more plausible hypothesis would be that he would seek in "Abba" a father who demonstrated his love for Jesus by subjecting him to the same discipline that human fathers bestowed on their legitimate sons. We may assume that Jesus shared first-century Palestinian views of the father-son relationship, including the belief that a father demonstrates his love through his chastisements. In this regard, the author of the letter of Hebrews may well reflect, rather than distort, Jesus' own views regarding "Abba." Thus, the baptismal rite of purification is not necessarily, as Van Aarde indicates, an attack on "conventional patriarchal values." It *is*, however, subversive of the established, official religion from which Jesus, and many other young men, were systematically excluded. There may be far more aggressiveness, even militancy, in Jesus' invocation of "Abba" than Jacobs-Malina's thesis of "the wife of the absent husband" recognizes. In fact, his invocation of "Abba" may have an element of *anti*maternalism if it plays a role similar to the role the father plays in the life of the legitimate son, namely, to validate the rejection of "the comfort of childhood and the warmth of feminine values" (468). In fact, Van Aarde seems to have this very possibility in mind when he says that Jesus had a "diffused identity" (i.e., not a simply "maternal" one). He notes, for example, that "since Jesus called God his Abba, the followers of Jesus interpreted his suffering as a filial act of obedient submissiveness to God, his Heavenly Father" (468).

Jesus' desire for a father who could make him a man like other men may also have been a strong motivating factor in his decision to go out into the desert, where he would be tested for physical and moral courage. After all, young men living under colonial rule were precluded from official military service. Yet Josephus (1987) notes that Galileans were "enured to war from their infancy" (perhaps suggesting that their mothers were not as warm and nurturant as Pilch and Van Aarde assume) and neither "hath the country been ever destitute of men of courage, or wanted a numerous set of them" (641). In becoming a disciple of John, Jesus could become "a son of Abraham" and "son of God." He could also become a man like other men who had been initiated into manhood by their fathers.

Mark C. Carnes (1989) helps us understand John's appeal to young men like Jesus. He explores the rise of fraternal orders in America in the post–Civil War era and emphasizes the emotional power that their secret rituals held over young men: "There was something special about certain rituals that 'attracted,' 'charmed,' or 'lured' members, and many men were somehow predisposed to 'crave' or 'desire them'" (11). His chapter "Manna in the Desert" provides an account of the secret ritual of the Odd Fellows. He notes: "The proceedings commenced in so grave a manner that even the sceptical and inattentive initiates became quiet; never did they attempt humor. Some, especially the better-educated, were 'so wrought upon and their feelings so excited that they shed tears'" (34). During the ritual, the hall was cast into darkness and initiates were blindfolded: "This enhanced the impression of secrecy, but it also caused a reorientation in sensory perceptions. For many candidates the peculiar sound of the first initiation was its most memorable aspect, particularly the flat, low tones of male voices chanting, singing hymns, or reciting lines in the echoing expanses of the lodge" (36). Carnes notes that when membership dropped off, lodges would immediately reexamine their rituals, judging this and not peripheral issues—like the social benefits of belonging to a lodge—as the reason for disaffection. Perhaps there is a deep need among young men, transcending historical and cultural boundaries, for a fraternal order such as that provided by John the Baptist, one that also involved "a reorientation in sensory perceptions," making hallucinations of a heavenly father a not-unlikely occurrence for one who did not know who his real father was. Deprived of a father who treated him with severe love, such a one might find this void best filled by a man who was no less severe, dressed in "camel's hair, and a leather belt around his waist," whose "food was locusts and wild honey" (Mt. 3:4).

The Rules Governing Secrets

If one accepts Miller's view that Jesus was the son of Joseph, one is likely to agree with Meier that the "hidden years" of Jesus, at least up to his adolescent years, were very ordinary. Miller's view that Jesus suffered the loss of his father in his adolescent years, however, entails some modification of Meier's views for Jesus' late adolescence and early young adulthood. In Miller's reconstruction, Jesus was under considerable pressure as the firstborn with family responsibilities, exacerbated by the need of a young man to achieve autonomy from his mother. Eventually, Jesus relinquished the firstborn role, its responsibilities and prerogatives, and, through the baptism that occurred in the desert, had a "conversion-type" experience, one that could be likened to a "second-birth" (28).

If, however, one accepts Schaberg's and Van Aarde's view that Jesus was not the natural son of Joseph, that he was illegitimate (however this is understood in light of first-century Palestine's definitions), it becomes well-nigh impossible to agree with Meier that the hidden years of Jesus were insufferably ordinary. At the least, one would have to add the exceedingly large qualifier, "ordinary for a boy and young man viewed as illegitimate." While adoption of Jesus by Mary's husband would ameliorate some of the social effects of his illegitimacy, even this would not cancel the fundamental social stigma associated with illegitimacy and the religious judgments attached to it (as suggested, for example, by the Wisdom of Solomon). Also, if societal reactions to fornication in early New England and first-century Palestine village life were comparable, we may be certain that there would be strong community sanctions against a woman who had a child out of wedlock, and that these sanctions would redound on her child, causing his own social ostracism. The honor of his legitimate brothers and sisters may have been adversely affected as well.

If Jesus was viewed as illegitimate by villagers, and was therefore the victim of considerable social ostracism, this would have affected his marriageability, his occupational prospects, his chances for an education, and, of course, for participating in the religious life of the community. In that case, we would not be surprised if what most scholars believe happened did in fact happen, that is, that he left Nazareth to make his "home" in Capernaum; that he probably did not marry and father children of his own; that, like other dispossessed sons, he became a *tekton*; and that he exhibited at least *some* personality characteristics comparable to those of wandering Cynics. Nor would we be surprised that he went out into the desert, attracted by John the Baptist's alternative means—through baptism in the River Jordan—to experience legitimation as a son of Abraham/son of God. In other words, much that is "known" about the adult Jesus is consistent with the hypothesis that Jesus was illegitimate, and there is little that would contradict it. In addition, I have argued that the case is equally strong for the hypothesis that Joseph did not adopt Jesus as his legal son. While this reconstruction of Jesus' "hidden years" is based on unprovable "fact," such is also the case with Miller's reconstruction based on the death of Joseph. Neither Miller nor Crossan considers the possibility that Joseph is omitted from the story in Mark 3:31–35 (also Gos. Thom. 99) about members of Jesus' family asking for him because Joseph did not accept Jesus as his son. It remained for "Abba" to so accept him.

There is another observation to be made, however, about the reconstruction offered here, one similar to Mark Allan Powell's comment about Crossan's reconstruction of the events following the disturbance in the temple: "Most of this, Crossan admits, is guesswork—but that is his main point!" If one necessarily engages in guesswork regarding what happened to Jesus at the end of his life, it is no less appropriate that we engage in guesswork regarding what happened at the beginning. Thus, I am not convinced that we should avoid the kind of guesswork that Miller, Schaberg, Van Aarde, and I have engaged in merely because one's reconstruction will involve an argument from silence (Gaventa, 1995, 11). A relevant defense of such undertakings is formulated by David Bakan in his article on the retention and revelation of secrets (1967). He makes twelve propositions regarding secrets, four of which are especially relevant to our present discussion: (1) A secret is a secret by virtue of the anticipation of negative reactions from other people; (2) a secret is kept in order to maintain some given perception of one's self in others; (3) persons who associate with one another in the context of a larger group, who have a secret from that larger group, will create a metaphorical or otherwise cryptographical language in which to discuss the secret; and (4) to conceal a secret, one may tend to reveal a fabricated "secret," or a less-secret secret, in order to generate the impression that one is being open and frank (105).

These propositions demonstrate that there are "rules" associated with secrets governing their retention and revelation. While propositions 1, 2, and 4 especially apply to early Christians' defensive posture vis-a-vis opponents and detractors, proposition 3 has particular significance for texts, such as Matthew's gospel, intended for members of the community. The very fact that conditions are such that proposition 1 (i.e., anticipation of negative reactions from other people) obtains, makes proposition 3 (i.e., the creation of a metaphorical or otherwise cryptographical language for internal discussion of the secret) the more likely and necessary. As Schaberg shows, Matthew 1 does precisely this.

Thus, it is not necessarily the case that there is nothing to be made out of silence. As Freud notes in "The 'Uncanny'," (1919/1955), the "uncanny" (or *unheimlichkeit*) is "the name for that which ought to have remained hidden and secret, and yet comes to light" (225). Relating this to the psychoanalytic notion of repression, he suggests that the uncanny is nothing new or foreign, but "something which is familiar and old-established in the mind which has become alienated from it only through the process of repression" (241). Because there were matters in every village that "ought" to remain hidden,

European Jewish communities relied on the marriage-broker's knowledge of the village's "secrets," as well as her own discretion, to ensure that incest rules were not inadvertently broken. The scholar who works against the "virginal conception" of Jesus idea is, of course, engaging in an act of indiscretion. One's motive is not to scandalize, however, but to seek to overcome the estrangements that result from the process of repression.

7

Disabling Anxiety:
The Role of Village Healer

Our discussion of contemporary portraits of Jesus (chapters 1 and 2) indicates a resurgence of interest in Jesus as one who performed miracles. This resurgence is reflected in the fact that Meier devotes 500 pages of the second volume of *A Marginal Jew* to miracles, and that Crossan views Jesus' role as magician (or miracle worker) as integral to his social vision. While Borg and Sanders give proportionately less emphasis to the miracles in their respective portraits, Sanders has a chapter on miracles in *The Historical Figure of Jesus* (1993, 132–68), and Borg discusses the miracles in his chapter "The Power of the Spirit: The Mighty Deeds of Jesus" in *Jesus: A New Vision* (1987, 57–75).

In their discussions they typically divide the miracles into three types: healings, exorcisms, and nature miracles. Scholars tend to believe that the nature miracles were created by the early church, but at least some of the accounts of exorcisms and healings are authentic. While the modern difficulty with miracle claims is acknowledged, the following quotation from Cicero (106–43 B.C.E.) indicates that there were individuals in ancient society who were no less troubled by miracle claims: "For nothing can happen without cause; nothing happens that cannot happen, and when what was capable of happening has happened, it may not be interpreted as a miracle. Consequently there are no miracles" (Sanders, 1993, 143). Sanders adds:

> The view espoused by Cicero has become dominant in the modern world, and I fully share it. Some reports of "miracles" are fanciful and exaggerated; the "miracles" that actually happen are things that we cannot yet explain, because of ignorance of the range of natural causes. In Cicero's own day, however, very few accepted this strident rationalization. The vast majority of people believed in spiritual forces, and they thought that specially selected humans could contest

their power, control them or manipulate them. Jesus himself held this view. (143)

Sanders considers it "perfectly reasonable for us to explain ancient events in our own terms" and "plausible to explain as exorcism a psychosomatic cure" (159). The more important task, however, "is to make clear how Jesus' contemporaries and non-contemporaries viewed miracles. We also wish to know more particularly what Jesus' followers thought of his miracles, and as much about what he himself thought as is possible" (159).

Meier (1994) states his approach somewhat differently. His question is "whether there are reasons for thinking that at least the core of some of these [miracle] stories goes back to the time and ministry of Jesus itself. In other words, did the historical Jesus actually perform certain startling, extraordinary deeds (e.g., supposed healings or exorcisms) that were considered by himself and his audience to be miracles?" (617). As noted in chapter 1, he considers a significant number of these narratives authentic, that is, as going back to the time and ministry of Jesus. The theological question of authenticity—Are these deeds of Jesus "direct acts of God accomplishing what no ordinary human being could accomplish"?—is one he feels a historian should not try to answer. Neither should he seek a psychological explanation. In his exorcisms chapter, Meier notes that moderate or liberal Christians would probably join agnostics in seeing most—perhaps all—instances of "possession" as types of mental or psychosomatic illnesses. But "psychiatry is difficult enough to practice when the patient is next to the doctor on the couch. When the patient is some 20 centuries away, diagnosis is nigh impossible" (661). (In chapter 3, I responded to this very criticism of psychobiography—that is, that one cannot put a person from another historical era on the couch—and will not repeat the counterargument here.)

Borg takes the view that "despite the difficulty which miracles pose for the modern mind, on historical grounds it is virtually indisputable that Jesus was a healer and exorcist" (1987, 61). He bases this conclusion on three grounds: (1) multiple attestation in the earliest sources; (2) that healings and exorcisms were relatively common in the world around Jesus, both within Judaism and in the Hellenistic world; and (3) that even Jesus' opponents did not challenge the claim that powers of healing flowed through him; their claim was that his powers came from the lord of the evil spirit (i.e., Beelzebul) (61). The condition of "possessed" individuals who were the subjects of Jesus' exorcisms may be viewed as a psychopathological one, "which includes among its symptoms the delusion of believing one's self to be possessed" (63). Thus, a psychopathological diagnosis and explanation is possible, and social conditions may also be a factor: "But whatever the modern explanation might be, and however much psychological or social factors might be involved, it must be stressed that Jesus and his contemporaries (along with people in most cultures) thought that people could be possessed or inhabited by a spirit or spirits from another plane" (64). The same point of view occurs in his discussion of miracles. Borg recognizes "the tendency to see them as 'faith healings,'" which "makes possible a psychosomatic explanation that stretches but does not break the limits of the modern worldview" (66), but he cautions that "within the thought-world of the accounts themselves, Jesus' healings were the result of 'power'" that "flowed through him as a holy man" (66–67).

As noted in chapter 2, Crossan approaches the issue of Jesus' miracles by employing the medical anthropology distinction between "curing a disease" and "healing an illness." In *Jesus: A Revolutionary Biography* (1994), he cites Leon Eisenberg's and Arthur Kleinman's formulations of this difference. Eisenberg writes: "Patients suffer 'illnesses'; physicians diagnose and treat 'diseases'...Illnesses are *experiences* of disvalued changes in states of being and in social function; diseases, in the scientific paradigm of modern medicine, are *abnormalities* in the *structure* and *function* of body organs and systems" (80). Based on Eisenberg's distinction, Crossan considers the difference between curing the disease or healing the illness known as AIDS: "A cure for the disease is absolutely desirable, but in its absence, we can still heal the illness by refusing to ostracize those who have it, by empathizing with their anguish, and by enveloping their sufferings with both respect and love" (81). Or, taking an example from the gospels, he notes that the leper in Mark 1:40–44 had both a *disease* (say, psoriasis) and an *illness*, the personal and social stigma of uncleanness, isolation, and rejection. As long as the disease remained or got worse, the illness would also remain or get worse: "In general, if the disease went, the illness went with it" (82).

On the other hand, "What if the disease could not be cured but the illness could somehow be healed?" This, Crossan contends, is "the central problem of what Jesus was doing in his healing miracles. Was he curing the disease through an intervention in the physical world, or was he healing an illness through an intervention in the social world?" (82). Crossan thinks the latter: "I presume that Jesus, who did not and could not cure that disease or any other one, healed the poor man's illness by refusing to accept the disease's ritual uncleanness and social ostracization. Jesus thereby forced others either to reject him from their community or to accept the leper within it as well" (82). Thus:

> By treating the illness without curing the disease, Jesus acted as an alternative boundary keeper in a way subversive to the established procedures of his society. Such an interpretation may seem to destroy the miracle. But miracles are not changes in the physical world so much as changes in the social world, and it is society that dictates, in any case, how we see, use, and explain the physical world. It would, of course, be nice to have certain miracles available to change the physical world if we could, but it would be much more desirable to make certain changes in the social one, which we can. We ourselves can already make the physical world totally uninhabitable; the question is whether we can make the social world humanly habitable. (82)

As we saw in chapter 2, Borg thinks that Crossan's distinction between "disease" and "illness" contains an "ambiguity," and he asks whether "healing illness" without "curing disease" can make much sense in a peasant society. I share a similar concern with Crossan's formulation of the issue between "disease" and "illness." The problem, however, is not its ambiguity, since it states in quite unambiguous fashion that he believes Jesus cured illness (e.g., the social ostracism to which the leper was subject) but not the disease (e.g., psoriasis). Instead, my concern is that his position tends to minimize the interactive nature of disease and illness. His quotation from Arthur Kleinman helps to make this point. Kleinman writes: "A key axiom in medical anthropology is the dichotomy between two aspects of sickness: disease and illness. *Disease* refers to a malfunctioning of biological and/or psychological processes, while the term *illness* refers to the psychosocial experience and meaning of perceived disease" (Crossan, 1994, 81). Notice that whereas Crossan makes a clear distinction between physical disease and social illness, Kleinman recognizes the ambiguities inherent in the distinction itself when he includes *psychological processes* in his definition of disease and *psychosocial experience* in his definition of illness. In other words, there is a psychological element in both disease and illness. The body of the individual is *psychophysical* and the social world (the body politic) is *psychosocial.*

In *The Duality of Human Existence* (1966), David Bakan illustrates this view of the body as psychophysical. He notes the

> fantastically large literature which seeks a "cause" of cancer…I in no way wish to disparage the research on various aspects of the cancer problem. Certainly, the various discoveries of substances provocative of cancer growth, including the viruses, for example, and the varieties of medical measures associated with the treatment of cancer, are of great value. And yet, one cannot escape the observation that much of this research is premised upon a notion of "otherness" in connection with the "cause" of cancer, that is, the attribution of agency to an outside "agent." (180)

He wants to challenge this notion. He cites George L. Engel's presidential address before the American Psychosomatic Society, in which Engels indicated that even among members of the psychosomatic society "there was 'unconscious resistance' to the study of 'psychogenesis or psychological triggering mechanisms' with respect to cancer" (182). Bakan notes, however, that there is a small literature on the relationship between personality and cancer. He summarizes some of its findings, classifying them under the following headings: (1) sexual maladjustment; (2) inhibition of maternality; (3) lack of social involvement; (4) inhibition of aggression; (5) loss of a significant person; and (6) the relative success of anti-androgenic measures in the treatment of cancer (androgenes, found in both males and females, are produced by the testes, the ovaries, the adrenal glands, and possibly other organs of the body) (179–96).

Bakan uses this empirical evidence in support of his view that there are "two fundamental modalities in the existence of living forms, *agency* for the existence of an organism as an individual, and *communion* for the participation of the individual in some larger organism of which the individual is a part" (15). Agency manifests itself in self-protection, self-assertion, isolation, alienation, and the urge to master, while communion manifests itself in contact, openness, union, noncontractual cooperation, and absence of separations. In his comments on the success of antiandrogenic measures in the treatment of cancers, he acknowledges that

> The nature of the detailed mechanism of the interaction of hormones and personality and the great problems of "cause and effect" in psychosomatic conditions are beyond the scope of this essay. Yet I cannot but be impressed with the fact that "castration" should have been developed as a relatively effective way of controlling cancerous growth. It would appear that certain of the organs of the body are particularly associated with the agentic in human personality and that perhaps the removal of these organs has the effect of reducing the agentic and reducing what may be one of the manifestions of unmitigated agency, the growth of cancerous tissue. (195)

In concluding his discussion, Bakan emphasizes that he is not suggesting that internal and external barriers to social and sexual integration are the only factors associated with the onset of cancer. These factors are, however, certainly relevant (195–96).

My point here is that there is a psychological element in disease. For Freud, this element was most likely that of anxiety. In *Inhibitions, Symptoms and Anxiety* (1926/1959), he defines anxiety as "the reaction to danger" (150) and notes that the perceived danger may be external (a threat from outside) or internal (the desire to act in a manner that is considered dangerous to oneself). Such anxiety is "accompanied by fairly definite physical sensations which can be referred to particular organs of the body," the clearest and most frequent being connected with the respiratory organs and the heart: "They provide evidence that motor innervations…play a part in the general phenomenon of anxiety" (132). If anxieties are generated by a situation of danger, however, "symptoms are created in order to remove the ego from a situation of danger. If the symptoms are prevented from being formed, the danger does in fact materialize…We can also add that the generating of anxiety sets a symptom-formation going and is, indeed, a necessary prerequisite of it" (144). Through symptom formation, then, the ego is "removed from danger" (145). The problem is that the danger–of being overwhelmed by anxiety–is internalized. Thus, in animal phobias, the danger is still felt as an external one, but in obsessional neurosis, the danger is much more internalized (145). For Freud, the symptomology involved in these neuroses is meaningful, in that symptoms replicate, but in highly symbolic ways, the original situation of danger (1916–17/1963, 358–77). As he notes in his essay on

"Obsessive Actions and Religious Practices" (1907/1957), "It is found that the obsessive actions are perfectly significant in every detail, that they serve important interests of the personality and that they give expression to experiences that are still operative and to thoughts that are cathected [i.e., charged] with affect. They do this in two ways, either by direct or by symbolic representation, and they are consequently to be interpreted either historically or symbolically" (120). In citing examples, Freud emphasizes the sexual nature of the dangers involved, typically involving women with marital problems who had contemplated or engaged in acts of infidelity.

In short, Freud is interested in how the organism defends itself from external and internal threat by means of an anxiety reaction. When confronted with external threat, the anxiety reaction is not all that difficult to understand. When the danger is internal, however, the anxiety is less understandable because the threat itself is concealed from view. In general, however, Freud believes that the internal dangers relate to aggressive and sexual impulses that, when not acted upon, nonetheless leave residual symptoms. These symptoms—whether the effect of external or internal threat—need to be taken seriously in their own right, as they generally provide the explanation to the initial danger to which anxiety was a reaction.

At the very least, these views, originally formulated in Freud's work as a neurologist and greatly expanded in his psychoanalytic work, offer a more complex—and necessarily ambiguous—picture of the relationship between disease and illness, and of the role of the psychological in both, than Crossan's distinction between physical disease and social illness allows. To be sure, Crossan notes that "a *disease* is, to put it bluntly, between me, my doctor, and a bug. Something is wrong with my body, and I take it to a doctor to be fixed. What is lacking in that picture *is not just the entire psychological* but, much more important, the entire social dimension of the phenomenon" (1994, 81, my emphasis). The view of disease that I am advocating here, however, considers the psychological to be at least as important as the social. More importantly, the psychological is implicated in both the disease (which is psychophysical) and the illness (which is psychosocial). Both *disease* and *illness* have psychological causes and explanations.

As we turn to Jesus' exorcisms and healings, there is a sense in which the exorcisms are the easiest to explain, as in these cases the complicating element of the disease is not a factor. On the other hand, I think it can be shown, on the basis of our discussion of psychoanalytic theory, that exorcisms and healings are on a continuum and are not as distinct as typologies (i.e., exorcisms, healings, nature miracles) would suggest. The common element in the cases of persons who were either exorcized or healed was anxiety, a reaction to an externally or internally induced sense of danger, manifesting itself in meaningful symptoms. I will also argue, later in the chapter, that certain physiological characteristics of Jews exacerbated these anxieties.

The Exorcisms

In his chapter on Jesus' exorcisms, Meier discusses the following: (1) the demoniac in the synagogue at Capernaum (Mk. 1:23–28; Lk. 4:33–37);

(2) the Gerasene demoniac (Mk. 5:1–20); (3) the possessed boy (Mk. 9:14–29, and parallels in Mt. 17:14–18; Lk. 9:37–43); (4) the mute (and blind?) demoniac (Mt. 12:22–23a; Lk. 11:14); (5) the mute demoniac (Mt. 9:32–37); (6) Mary Magdalene (Lk. 8:2); and (7) the daughter of the Syrophoenician woman (Mk. 7:24–30; Mt. 15:21–28). As for authenticity, Meier concludes that the story of the possessed boy and the reference to Mary Magdalene's exorcism probably go back to historical events in Jesus' ministry, and that the story of the Gerasene demoniac may too, though this is less certain. The others are either early Christian creations or too difficult to judge. For example, the exorcism of a mute (and blind?) demoniac could go back to a historical incident or is a literary creation used to introduce the Beelzebul controversy.

In his discussion of Luke's reference to Mary Magdalene's "seven demons," Meier notes that Luke is not clear as to whether any of the other women besides Mary Magdalene had experienced an exorcism as distinct from the cure of an illness, and adds that the "distinction may not be all that important to Luke, since he narrates some stories of physical healing with exorcistic language (e.g., Simon's mother-in-law and the woman who had been bent over for 18 years)" (658). Also, Jesus is not named as the exorcist in Mary's case, though "Luke obviously presupposes it to be Jesus, since in the context the exorcism explains Magdalene's devotion to and support of Jesus and the Twelve" (658). Given these problems with the exorcism of Mary Magdalene, and the uncertainty surrounding the Gerasene demoniac story, I will focus on the exorcism of the possessed boy in Mark 9:14–29. I will use this story to explore the psychological roots not only of the boy's demon

The Exorcism of the Possessed Boy

[14]When they came to the disciples, they saw a great crowd around them, and some scribes arguing with them. [15]When the whole crowd saw him, they were immediately overcome with awe, and they ran forward to greet him. [16]He asked them, "What are you arguing about with them?" [17]Someone from the crowd answered him, "Teacher, I brought you my son; he has a spirit that makes him unable to speak; [18]and whenever it seizes him, it dashes him down; and he foams and grinds his teeth and becomes rigid; and I asked your disciples to cast it out, but they could not do so." [19]He answered them, "You faithless generation, how much longer must I be among you? How much longer must I put up with you? Bring him to me." [20]And they brought the boy to him. When the spirit saw him, immediately it convulsed the boy and he fell on the ground and rolled about, foaming at the mouth. [21]Jesus asked the father, "How long has this been happening to him?" And he said, "From child-

hood. [22]It has often cast him into the fire and into the water, to destroy him; but if you are able to do anything, have pity on us and help us." [23]Jesus said to him, "If you are able!—All things can be done for the one who believes." [24]Immediately the father of the child cried out, "I believe; help my unbelief!" [25]When Jesus saw that a crowd came running together, he rebuked the unclean spirit, saying to it, "You spirit that keeps this boy from speaking and hearing, I command you, come out of him, and never enter him again!" [26]After crying out and convulsing him terribly, it came out, and the boy was like a corpse, so that most of them said, "He is dead." [27]But Jesus took him by the hand and lifted him up, and he was able to stand. [28]When he had entered the house, his disciples asked him privately, "Why could we not cast it out?" [29]He said to them, "This kind can come out only through prayer."

Mark 9:14–29

possession but also, and more importantly, of Jesus' own identity as exorcist-healer. It therefore serves as the paradigmatic case for my image of Jesus as the village healer.

In addition to the likelihood of its authenticity, there is the further interesting feature, in light of our discussion of the psychological element in disease, that Meier believes the boy suffered from some form of epilepsy. In a footnote reference, he cites Van der Loos's comment that there is "a surprising unanimity" among scholars in this diagnosis, though he notes that Fenner prefers the designation "hysteria," while Wilkinson "claims that some of the symptoms do not correspond to fits of hysteria" (670). Fenner's minority position is important, because it points to the difficulty of determining whether a neurological problem is only physiological or whether it may also have a psychological aspect, an issue quite separate from psychological factors in demon possession. Even more tellingly, the fact that the symptomatology of the possession would even invite a hysteria diagnosis indicates that even if one finally judges it to have been epilepsy—as the vast majority of biblical scholars do—the likelihood of a psychophysiological, as opposed to a purely physiological, disorder presents itself.

Ian Hacking's recent study (1998) of the problem that the "mad traveller" or "fuguer" posed for late-nineteenth-century medical theory bears on this issue. The symptomatology was not (as in the case of the possessed boy) that of falling down and writhing on the ground. Instead, it was a strong impulse to travel, often very long distances, without any conscious awareness of how one got there or how one got home again. Hacking uses these cases to weigh the legitimacy of cultural factors versus physical symptoms in the diagnosis of psychiatric disorders. He argues that psychological symptoms find "stable homes" at a given time and place, in that an illness may prevail for a limited time and then more or less disappear. The significance of his study of fuguers for our purposes is that the psychiatric establishment vigorously debated whether fuguers were epileptics or hysterics. By the late nineteenth century, it was already accepted that epilepsy need not involve classic seizures (*grand mal*). For example, the English physician Hughlings Jackson generalized the concept to include many instances of sudden change in mood or behavior. Thus, "latent epilepsy" was recognized and was applied to patients who did not have seizures but experienced other unusual events, which were described as "epileptic equivalents." Since some epileptics wander in a dazed state after an attack, the question arose whether fugues might be of a purely epileptic origin (34).

Others, however, applied the diagnosis of "hysteria" to fuguers. The French neurologist Jean-Martin Charcot viewed one of the fuguers he studied as a hysteric suffering from "ambulatory automatism." Subsequent studies appeared, arguing that some fuguers may be hysterics, not epileptics, on the grounds that they responded well to hypnosis, while epileptics responded to bromides and not hypnosis. Certain value judgments were present in these debates, as epileptics were viewed as rather lewd and loathsome individuals (who urinated in public, exhibited their genitals, lay naked in the streets) whereas hysterics were considered basically attractive people with a problem

(41). In one sense, viewing these male fuguers as hysterics constituted a less pejorative diagnosis, one previously assigned only to women (thus, the view of hysterics as "more attractive"). Therefore, the reported behavior of the fuguer, even though he had no recollection of it, together with his response to treatment, were major factors in how he was diagnosed. Another factor, introduced by Fulgence Raymond, successor to Charcot, was the "degree of intelligence and coordination of the acts." If they involved complex travel arrangements (even though these were not subsequently remembered), they were different in kind from the "aimless wandering" that sometimes follows an epileptic seizure (47).

Noting the medical establishment's difficulty in determining whether the fuguer phenomenon was epilepsy or hysteria, Hacking identifies two psychosocial factors that have bearing on the phenomenon. One is that fuguers came to prominence during a cultural period of mass tourism. Thus, they engaged in a parody of this highly acclaimed cultural activity, as they learned absolutely nothing from their travels. Yet they were also not vagrants, but fell somewhere between tourists and vagrants. The other factor is that fuguery is "the bodily expression of male powerlessness" (49). Hacking notes that the fuguers who appear in the literature were a gas fitter, a delivery man, a railway clerk, small shopkeepers, carpenters, cobblers, and mirror makers: "They have had some education but usually were sent out to work, at least as apprentices, between the ages of twelve and fifteen. Typically urban, virtually no peasants or farmers. But also not day laborers or factory hands. These were men with a certain amount of, if not autonomy, at least freedom from immediate supervision. Albert [one of the fuguers] is sent on various missions, to buy coke or to install a gas jet in a workshop making women's clothes" (49). As powerless males, fuguers might act unconsciously on the desire to "get away from it all," and they had sufficient autonomy to leave undetected.

Hacking also devotes a chapter to "the wandering Jew," noting that the wandering Jew motif served as a metaphor—usually pejorative—for some students of the mad traveller phenomonen. Charcot himself never connected ambulatory automatisms to Jews. Instead, he viewed Jewish fuguers as neurasthenics because they complained of innumerable illnesses for which they sought treatment. The association, however, suggests that cultural factors were also involved in the diagnosis.

Freud's account in "The 'Uncanny'" (1919/1955) of his disorientation on a walk through the deserted streets of a provincial town in Italy is relevant in this regard. He writes:

I found myself in a quarter of whose character I could not long remain in doubt. Nothing but painted women were to be seen at the windows of the small houses, and I hastened to leave the narrow street at the next turning. But after having wandered about for a time without enquiring my way, I suddenly found myself back in the same street, where my presence was now beginning to excite attention. I hurried away once more, only to arrive by another *détour* at the same place, yet a third time. Now, however, a feeling overcame me which I can only describe as uncanny, and I was glad enough to find myself back at the piazza I had left a short while before, without any further voyages of discovery. (237)

While Freud does not describe this experience as a mild hysterical one, it has the element of "ambulatory automatism" together with the cultural motif of "the wandering Jew." It also, of course, has a sexual dimension, which he elaborates upon later in the essay, when he makes an association with the "unintended recurrence of the same situation" reflected in this episode and the desire of his male patients to return to their maternal home, and, more specifically, to their original home in their mothers' bodies (245).

Hacking's discussion of fuguers suggests that although the question whether the possessed boy in Mark 9:14–29 was an epileptic or a hysteric may be undecidable, in either case a psychological factor is involved in the physiological disturbance. His suggestion that the fuguer be placed in his cultural context, and that gender be taken into account, also introduces relevant psychosocial considerations. His emphasis on male powerlessness is especially germane, but so is the issue of tourism (the first-century Galilean equivalent being the pilgrimage to Jerusalem), and the issue of the wandering Jew, who is ambivalently attracted to and disoriented within strange and unfamiliar—or uncannily familiar—places. The related point that we can make on the basis of Freud's discussion in *Inhibitions, Symptoms, and Anxiety* is that the psychological factor in one or both of the psychophysical and psychosocial dimensions of the possession may be anxiety, and that the symptomatology involved may point to sources or causes of the anxiety (i.e., the symptomatology is meaningful). In addition, we may further hypothesize that the anxiety involved has sexual and/or aggressive connotations.

If the story of the demon-possessed boy has both psychophysical and psychosocial meanings, what might they be? The father reports to Jesus that the boy has suffered since childhood. This, together with the severity of his symptoms, may well have been the reason Jesus (or Mark) considered this an especially difficult case to cure. His childhood symptoms involved falling into fire and water, perhaps suggesting common epileptic symptoms of falling as a consequence of severe dizziness. In addition, this may be viewed as a self-destructive act (the father says that the evil spirit's intent was to "destroy him"). While the unconscious motivation behind such self-destructive acts cannot be explained on the basis of the presented facts, we may surmise (on the basis of Freud's anxiety theory) that these acts internalize a desire to inflict punishments on someone else, quite possibly his mother (who was the primary parent with whom he had relations as a child). Whether he was reacting to severe physical punishment or to severe restrictions on his physical (locomotor) movements is difficult to tell, but the physical pain he experienced—to which his symptomatology had been reactive—must have been very severe to have created such extreme self-destructive reactions (e.g., as falling into fire and water).

If I were to hazard a guess, I would say that the boy's mother beat him unmercifully, as prescribed by Proverbs 23:13, "Do not withhold discipline from your children; if you beat them with a rod, they will not die," and Proverbs 29:15, "The rod and reproof give wisdom, but a mother is disgraced by a neglected child." "Neglect" here means *failing* to reprove and apply the rod. Proverbs 26:3 also indicates that the rod was applied to the "back" of the individual, which, if done with severity, could well have traumatized the boy's central nervous system. In offering this hypothesis, I am challenging Pilch's view (cited by Van Aarde) that childhood was a period of comfort and maternal warmth. While it may have been relatively more benign than puberty, when the father assumed responsibility for treating the boy with severity, I assume that a first-century Galilean boy ("inured to war from his infancy") was subjected to harsh discipline from an early age, unless, of course, he was not considered worth the time and trouble involved (i.e., illegitimate, or a *mamzer*, whose fate was already sealed). Proverbs 29:15 implies that a wayward child will be the disgrace of his mother, implying that it was her responsibility to apply the rod. In other words, the possessed boy's early childhood symptomatology reveals an anxious reaction to severe childhood beatings. Conceivably, they reflect his internalization of rage against his mother, a rage that he dares not act upon (e.g., by hitting her back), but instead acts out in the form of episodes involving falling into fire and water. The "normal" Galilean boy (the social "ideal") would have learned to externalize his rage, not, however, in direct attacks upon his mother, but in aggressive attitudes and behavior against "enemies" (on this point, see Erik H. Erikson's analysis of child-rearing practices among the Dakota Sioux in *Childhood and Society*, 1963, 114–65).

On the other hand, the son is brought to Jesus by his father, suggesting that having reached puberty, he is now under his father's influence and control. The mother is not mentioned. I would like to explore what this aspect of the story may mean for Jesus personally, as well as for Jewish sons at the time this episode occurred, especially with regard to Hacking's theme of the powerlessness of the young male as reflected in epileptic symptomatology. This will enable us to revisit issues raised in the previous chapter in relation to Van Aarde's views on fatherless sons, and to consider their implications for Jesus' understanding of God as Abba and his appropriation of this understanding in his role as exorcist-healer.

In his discussion of the story, Meier notes that "Jesus' interlocutor is not the demon possessing the demoniac, as in the Capernaum and Gerasene stories, but with the distraught father of the boy." Also, "Instead of a supernatural struggle between Jesus and the demon we see a passionate—one might almost say 'pastoral'–struggle. It is a struggle between Jesus, who (only in this exorcism story) demands faith as a condition for the exorcism, and the loving father at his wit's end, who finally cries out, 'I believe, help my unbelief'" (654). Meier also points out that when the father first petitions Jesus for help ("If you can do anything, help us"), "Jesus replies, apparently with some indignation, 'What do you mean, "If you can..."'" (655). The account then relates that when the unclean spirit came out of the boy, he "was like a corpse," prompting some onlookers to declare him dead. But "Jesus took him by the hand and lifted him up, and he was able to stand."

Jesus' "indignant" response to the father, especially in light of his own experience of fathers, seems to imply, "Why do you expect me to succeed where you have failed?" Thus, it may well have communicated a veiled critique of fathers who seem powerless to provide their sons genuine assistance into manhood. As Meier points out, "we have the unusual case of Jesus demanding faith as a condition for the exorcism," as if to suggest that fathers must have faith in their sons; otherwise sons will not have faith in themselves. There is something at stake for Jesus as well. As Meier points out, we have in this story "the possibility–unique within the Four Gospels and indeed the NT–that Jesus speaks of his own faith as the source of his miracles" (655). As I see it, Jesus' own faith–in "Abba"–was being tested. Hence, the story concludes with the disciples asking Jesus why they could not cast out the evil spirit, to which he replies, "This kind can come out only through prayer" (Mk. 9:4). This implies that Jesus had called on "Abba" to defeat the power of the father of unclean spirits, or Beelzebul. Jesus' action of taking the boy by the hand was also a "fatherlike performance," one he appears to have employed in the healing of Jairus' daughter as well. As we have seen (cf. Van Aarde, 460) this is a characteristic of boys who grow up in father-absent households. This behavioral gesture was fatherlike because it mediated the very power of "Abba" to two adolescent sufferers. In turn, the healing of the possessed boy legitimized Jesus' own claim to sonship, that is, as son of Abba. As noted in the preceding chapter, key to his own sense of legitimation was the experience, through John's rite of purification, of being affirmed as a true son of Abraham and son of Abba.

The Psychodynamic Roots of Jesus' Exorcist-Healer Identity

I want to explore what this legitimation meant for his role as exorcist-healer, placing particular emphasis on the psychological and psychosocial dimensions involved. To do so, I will first turn to Crossan's discussion of possession in *The Historical Jesus* (1991), specifically his focus on the healing of the Gerasene demoniac, and then discuss in some detail Freud's essay on a case of demon possession in the seventeenth century. Crossan notes that the Gerasene demoniac account is from the second stratum, having only single attestation, so he employs it "only for general background, not specific foreground. No claim is being made about the historical Jesus" (314). He notes the symbolism in the naming of the demon "Legion," the "fact and sign of Roman power," and that the demon is consigned to swine and cast into the sea, "a brief performancial summary, in other words, of every Jewish revolutionary's dream!" (314). He also cites several anthropological texts on the phenomenon of possession, noting their emphasis on the colonial context in which possession seems to flourish. Then he takes up Paul W. Hollenbach's (1981) interpretation of the story and notes that Hollenbach makes three major points.

The first is that the following situations of social tension are often the causal context of possession: class antagonisms rooted in economic exploitation, conflicts between traditions where revered traditions are eroded, and colonial domination and revolution. Hollenbach cites Franz Fanon's analysis of mental illness during the Algerian revolutionary war against France and quotes Fanon's comment that "the native is an oppressed person whose permanent dream is to become the persecutor." Crossan concludes: "*With such divided minds*, split personalities, and schizoid dreams, it is no wonder 'that the colonial situation of domination and rebellion nourishes mental illness in extraordinary numbers of the population'" (317, my emphasis). Hollenbach's second point is that, in this context, "mental illness can be seen as a socially acceptable form of oblique protest against, or escape from, oppressions," since it constitutes a "fix" for people who see no other way to cope with the horrendous social and political conditions under which they suffer. It does so in a way that does not threaten the social position of the oppressors, whether the state, police, employer, or tax collector. His third point (one that bears directly on the Beelzebul accusation against Jesus) is that there is a "symbolic relationship between possession as protest from the weak to the strong and accused possession as control from the strong to the weak…Hence the illogical logic of the possessed exorcist" (317).

I want to take special note of the term "divided minds," as this invites a psychoanalytic interpretation of the relationship between Jesus' belief in "Abba" and his role as exorcist. Crossan anticipates this interpretation in his discussion of the Beelzebul controversy, the only exorcism that meets his criteria for authenticity. As noted earlier, Meier indicates that it is uncertain whether the story of the mute (and blind?) demoniac (Mt. 12:24; Lk. 11:14–15) is itself historical, or whether it is a literary creation used to introduce the Beelzebul controversy. In his discussion of the Beelzebul controversy itself, he notes that in spite of some recent skepticism there is almost unanimous acceptance of *its* authenticity. The controversy involves the Pharisees claiming that Jesus cast out demons by the power of Beelzebul, "the ruler of the demons," to which Jesus replies, "Every kingdom divided against itself is laid waste, and no city or house divided against itself will stand. If Satan casts out Satan, he is divided against himself; how then will his kingdom stand? If I cast out demons by Beelzebul, by whom do your own exorcists cast them out? Therefore they will be your judges. But if it is by the Spirit of God that I cast out demons, then the kingdom of God has come to you" (Mt. 12:25–29).

Crossan first notes that, in the transmission process, Beelzebul becomes Satan (Mt. 12:26). Unlike the more cosmopolitan Satan, Beelzebul bespeaks a village environment. Second, as with the Gerasene demoniac exorcism, the kingdom language suggests a sociopolitical frame for the story, implying that Satan rules the house of Herod or the kingdom of Rome. Third, "one wonders how Jesus' opponents left themselves open to such a devastating rejoinder. How could one even imagine casting out demons by demon possession?" He notes, however, that this is not as illogical as it may seem. Supporting Hollenbach's point about "the illogical logic of the possessed exorcist," Crossan points to Ioan Lewis' work, which indicates that "establishments strike back somewhat desperately at shamanistic curers of possession by accusing them of witchcraft, that is, of causing what they cured" (319). He also cites George Peter Murdoch's discussion of the deep-seated belief among Mediterranean peoples that a major supernatural cause of illness is "spirit-aggression...the direct, hostile, arbitrary, or punitive action of some malevolent or affronted supernatural being" (319). This belief, together with the deeply rooted belief in "the causation of illness by witchcraft," came together in the Beelzebul incident: "The sick man is possessed, and is therefore a victim of spirit-aggression. Jesus cures him, so how can one denigrate Jesus? He is a witch, himself possessed by or possessive of an evil spirit" (320). As we have seen, John Godfrey chooses not to rebut such argumentation, but turns it to his favor by means of his distinction between Satan (the Evil One) and witches by noting that one may need to entertain the witches in order to hold Satan himself at bay. That is, one may need to consort with the evil spirits in order to exercise power over them. In contrast, Jesus attacks the argument itself by invoking the power of Abba.

There is one additional element in Crossan's discussion of magic that I wish therefore to cite. This concerns tales of Honi, who appears in several Jewish rabbinical writings dating from the third to seventh centuries C.E. Crossan observes that in one tale, Honi "acted toward God like a petulant son," demanding nuts, almonds, and so on, and, in another tale, asks God to send rain. What is noteworthy in both cases is that God is addressed as "Abba." These are the only two cases in the rabbinical literature where he is so addressed, and both cases "are in the context of miracle workers and their imperious, childlike control of the divine power" (147).

With this material as background, I want to take up an argument that Freud develops in his essay on demon possession (1923/1961b). It enables us to augment the essentially sociopolitical interpretation that Crossan provides of the Gerasene demoniac and Beelzebul controversy with a more *psychosocial* analysis, and thus one that probes more deeply into the psychodynamics involved. This analysis has relevance for the illnesses of first-century Jewish males (as revealed in the cases of the possessed boy and the Gerasene demoniac). More importantly, however, this sheds light on Jesus' own role as exorcist-healer. I should note that Miller briefly alludes to Freud's essay on demoniacal possession in his chapter on Jesus' confrontation with Satan, but uses the essay mainly in conjunction with his view that one consequence of the death of Joseph was that Jesus was drawn into the orbit of his mother's influence. He notes, for example, that, in the case Freud discusses, Satan had maternal breasts, and thus serves as "an almost motherly figure...in the midst of the [the young man's] rather excessive dependency needs" (61). Miller's point is not unimportant, but it needs to be placed in a larger context. This context is Freud's view that a fundamental feature of monotheistic religion is that God is subject to image-splitting, with the split-off image becoming Satan. Unlike Miller, who views Jesus' image of God as emotionally congruent

Abba = Joseph
Abba ≠ Joseph (alternative to Joseph)

with his image of Joseph, I view Jesus' image of God–as "Abba"–as an effect of such image-splitting. This has very important implications for Jesus' role as exorcist-healer.

Freud's essay focuses on a seventeenth-century Bavarian painter who made a pact with the devil after the death of his father. Freud's major objective is to show that states of demoniacal possession in earlier centuries are equivalent to neuroses today. Noting that the demonological theory has actually justified itself because of its emphasis on (internal) psychic forces, he points out, however, that "the states of possession correspond to our neuroses of the present day; in explanation of which we once more have recourse to psychical powers. In our eyes, the demons are bad and reprehensible wishes, derivatives of instinctual impulses that have been repudiated and repressed" (72). Thus, psychoanalysis differs from the demonological possession idea in that it explains these phenomena differently: "We merely eliminate the projection of these mental entities into the external world...Instead, we regard them as having arisen in the patient's internal life, where they have their abode" (172). It might be noted, however, that demonological possession theory maintains that the "spirits" are invasive, having taken up residence *inside* the individual. This does not, of course, affect in any material way Freud's distinction between the belief that the symptoms are the "work" or "agency" of another being and his own belief that they are caused by repressed wishes or desires, the repression being due to the perception that these wishes are evil. Thus, one wants to "disown" them.

The painter, Christoph Haitzmann, who had entered into a pact with Satan nine years previously while "in a state of despondency about his art and doubtful whether he could support himself" (74), appeared at Mariazell, a place of pilgrimage. He was convinced that only the grace of the Mother of God at Mariazell could save him by compelling the evil one to disgorge the pact, which had been written in blood. Freud discusses Haitzmann's reasons for the pact, noting that he actually refused the magical powers, money, and pleasures that the devil offered him. If he refused these offerings, what could possibly have been his motive for entering into the pact? To Freud, the answer lies in the painter's acknowledgment that he suffered from a melancholic depression with incapacity for work and a justified anxiety about his future. Further, he had fallen into his melancholic state following his father's death. When he was in the throes of melancholy, the devil appeared before him, inquiring into the cause of his dejection and grief and promising to help him in every way. He signed the pact with the devil–in blood–but the strange thing about the pact was that it required nothing of the devil and only a service that Haitzmann would render the devil, namely, that he would be Satan's "bounden son and in the ninth year belong to him body and soul" (82). Freud interprets this strange pact to mean that the devil bound *himself* for a period of nine years to take the place of the young man's lost father and therefore become a father-substitute. The young man's reasoning seems to have been that "his father's death had made him lose his spirits and his capacity to work; if he could only obtain a father-substitute he might hope to regain what he had lost" (82). Freud expanded on this interpretation in *Inhibitions, Symptoms and Anxiety* (1926/1959), published three years later, where he discusses the danger associated with the loss of an object. One response to such loss is mourning; another response, however, is pain, and still another is anxiety. The latter occurs when the individual feels endangered by the loss of the object (e.g., as leaving him vulnerable and helpless) (169–72). A neurosis may result. This, Freud argues, is precisely what happened in the case of Haitzmann.

But why the devil as a father-substitute? Freud explains it this way: We know that God is a father-substitute comprising the child's earliest image of him as an "exalted father," which is united with the inherited memory-traces of "the primal father" (i.e., prehistoric). We also know that the child's relation to this exalted father was in all probability ambivalent from the outset. Thus, it was composed of two sets of emotions "that were opposed to each other: it contained not only impulses of an affectionate and submissive nature, but also hostile and defiant ones" (85). This ambivalence governs the relations of humankind to its deities. The evil spirit, while regarded as the antithesis of God, is yet akin to God in nature. According to Christian mythology, the evil spirit of the Christian faith, the devil of medieval times, was himself a fallen angel of godlike nature. Thus, it requires no great analytic insight to "guess that God and the Devil were originally identical—were a single figure which was later split into two figures with opposite attributes...The contradictions in the original nature of God are, however, a reflection of the ambivalence which governs the relation of the individual to his personal father" (86).

As Freud acknowledges, for a man to develop melancholic depression and loss of power to work after the death of his father is not unusual. Such depression, however, does not mean that the relationship has been one merely of love: "On the contrary, his mourning over the loss of his father is the more likely to turn into melancholia, the more his attitude to him bore the stamp of ambivalence" (87). (Miller obscures Freud's emphasis on this ambivalence, citing only Freud's statement that "a man who has fallen into melancholia on account of his father's death must have loved that father deeply." Emphasizing only one side of the ambivalence serves his purpose of representing Jesus' relationship to Joseph as unusually positive [40].)

The circumstances behind Haitzmann's "fear and hate" for his father are unavailable, but Freud guesses that his father may have opposed his wish to be a painter. His incapacity to paint following his father's death would then be an expression of "deferred obedience," which rendered him incapable of making a livelihood and increased his longing for his father to stand between him and the cares of life. Thus, by entering into the pact with the devil, he sought to break his father's power to incapacitate him so that he could become productive again. Unfortunately, however, he remained incapacitated, and when his situation became desperate, he sought the help of the fathers at

Mariazell. Through their assistance, he experienced an amazing recovery as the pact with the devil was redeemed through the intercession of the Holy Virgin Mary. Subsequently, however, he experienced a relapse and had several fresh seizures accompanied by visions, convulsions, loss of consciousness, and painful sensations. These visions involved appearances by Christ and the Holy Mother charging him to live up to his resolutions, as well as contrary visions of himself as a well-dressed man accompanied by "a strapping young woman." His punishment for the latter fantasy involved the sensation of scorching heat and foul fumes and scourging by evil spirits with ropes, which, he was told, would continue until he decided to enter the anchorite order. So he returned to Mariazell, in worse shape than before.

Based on his reported fantasies of magnificent halls, high living, silverware, and lovely women, Freud guesses that, as Haitzmann's melancholia lifted, he began to envision himself the recipient of all the enjoyments and temptations the devil had originally offered him, which he had declined. Thus, "after the exorcism, the melancholia seems to have been overcome and all his worldly-minded desires had once more become active" (103). His penurious situation did not change, however, and Freud concludes that he seemed to be of the type "who fails in everything and who is therefore trusted by no one" (103). In the end, he entered a holy order, where his inner conflict as well as his material want came to an end. Freud concludes:

> He wanted all along simply to make his life secure. He tried first to achieve this with the help of the Devil at the cost of his salvation; and when this failed and had to be given up, he tried to achieve it with the help of the clergy at the cost of his freedom and most of the possibilities of life. Perhaps he himself was only a poor devil who simply had no luck; perhaps he was too ineffective or too untalented to make a living, and was one of those types of people who are known as "eternal sucklings"—who cannot tear themselves away from the blissful situation at the mother's breast, and who, all through their lives, persist in a demand to be nourished by someone else. And so it was that in this history of his illness, he followed the path which led from his father, by way of the Devil as a father-substitute, to the pious Fathers of the Church. (104)

This view of Haitzmann's desire for maternal nurturance has basis in the fact that in one of his visions the devil had maternal breasts. Freud attributes the final resolution of his struggles to a desire for self-preservation (299), but at the cost of his independence and his aspirations to become an artist. In his monograph on Leonardo da Vinci (1910/1957), Freud notes that Leonardo, in contrast, triumphed over his father by means of his art, but, even more importantly, in his "astonishing career as a natural scientist" (136).

On the basis of Freud's demon possession essay, I suggest that Jesus' affirmation of "Abba" also required a splitting of the father identification into two distinct images or representations. These were "Abba" (the Father who empowers) and "Beelzebul" (the Father who immobilizes). In demon possession, one projects one's aggression against the human father onto the figure of the devil, thus obscuring its psychodynamic origins and also disowning it as one's own aggression. This explains the deep-seated belief among Mediterranean peoples, noted by Murdock, that a major supernatural cause of illness is "spirit aggression…the direct, hostile, arbitrary, or punitive action of some malevolent or affronted supernatural being" (Crossan, 1991, 319). The disowned aggression, however, is turned inward, against the self, and becomes self-punitive, that is, one "suffers" from the demon possession itself. By affirming God as "Abba," Jesus reversed the process of relinquishing one's aggression to the evil spirit, employing aggression *against* the evil spirit, thus legitimating aggression that was in the service of "Abba." In this way, self-directed aggression is externalized as the evil spirit is "ejected" from one's body. Of course, the origins of the aggression in the father-son relationship itself need never be acknowledged.

The psychodynamic basis of this image-splitting was the father-son relationship. As Crossan's illustration of Honi the magician indicates, the affirmation of God as "Abba" has the effect of rendering or visualizing God in ways that are psychodynamically linked to human fathers. Thus, Honi's grandson, Hanan ha-Nehba, pleaded that "The Holy One, Blessed be He, Master of the Universe, do it [i.e., send rain] for the sake of those who are unable to distinguish between the Father [Abba] who gives rain and the father [abba] who does not" (Crossan, 1991, 147). In other words, when one affirms God as "Abba," one takes the risk of viewing God in ways that are psychodynamically similar to the son's relationship to his human father. This serves the purposes of enabling one to "rework" these father-son psychodynamics, to turn them in a more healthful direction. But it also means that one risks "projecting" one's own father-son relationship onto God, such that the two become indistinguishable. The solution to the latter problem is image-splitting, which also splits the ambivalence normally experienced toward the human father, with God becoming the good or true father, and Satan becoming the evil father, the father of lies and deception.

I suggest that Jesus found such image-splitting unusually convincing because he did not know his natural father and was not adopted by Joseph, and therefore had little if any experience of paternal love. Thus, there was nothing to impede his ascription of all good parental qualities onto "Abba" and all negative paternal qualities onto Beelzebul. For purposes of exorcism, the illegitimate son thus has a certain advantage over those sons who were legitimate, in that his faith in "Abba" could be absolute and uncompromised, while his spirit of aggression against Beelzebul could be no less absolute and uncompromised. Each time he commanded Beelzebul to leave another young man alone, and the command worked, he avenged his own victimization at the hands of human fathers.

In his exorcisms and healings, Jesus' actions were intended to prove the power of "Abba." He did not view himself as employing his own power, but as marshaling Abba's power–the aggressive spirit. This also means, however, that his exorcisms and healings were a "fatherlike performance," that is, the son acting in the father's stead. While our earlier discussion of Van Aarde has already introduced the idea that the secondary identification of fatherless sons leads to behavior, overtly and in fantasy, that produces "fatherlike performance," I would like to expand on this idea of "fatherlike performance," especially the role that image-splitting plays in it, by considering Peter Loewenberg's study of the Nazi cohort group (1971). This study will not only help to shed light on Jesus' "fatherlike performance" as exorcist-healer, but also on the efforts of his disciples to perform similar deeds. The "fatherlike performance" in the case of Jesus' exorcisms and healings is that he acts both in behalf of and in the place of his father "Abba," thus communicating that he is acting as "Abba" acts. Thus, to know the son is to know the father. The son's actions are a visible, tangible, self-evident expression of the invisible father's power. (In light of the recent Holocaust, it may seem inappropriate to use a study of Nazi youth to clarify Jesus' exorcisms and healings as "fatherlike performance." I hope, however, that readers will appreciate that my concern is to provide some analytical concepts for understanding Jesus' and his disciples' roles as healers, and especially to highlight the father-son dynamics involved.)

Loewenberg's article, entitled "The Psychohistorical Origins of the Nazi Youth Cohort," focuses on the concept of the "cohort" group, a term whose Latin etymology refers to a division of a legion in the Roman army. He uses it, though, to apply to an aggregate of individuals within a population who have shared a significant common experience of a personal or historical event at the same time. It is distinguished from the loose term "generation," by which historians usually mean a temporal unit of family kinship structure such as "the founding generation," or, more ambiguously, a broad and often unspecified age span during a particular institutional, political, or cultural epoch, such as the "Baby Boomer generation." An example of a cohort would be college graduates in the year 1929, who completed their educations in prosperity and then in their first years in the labor market experienced the onset of the Great Depression. This cohort is marked by the period-specific stimulus of the economic depression for their entire working years. It is therefore to be distinguished from other cohorts, even thirty years later, by their common experience of having endured significant events simultaneously. According to one demographer: "The concept [of cohort analysis] can be extended to the identification and surveillance of any group in terms of the time it enters any category of exposure to an event or behavior pattern of interest" (Loewenberg, 1466). Loewenberg concludes: "Thus, each cohort is itself unique; its members are different from all those who have preceded it and all who will follow because they have experienced certain traumatic episodes in their collective life at a common time and a specific historical moment" (Lowenberg, 1466).

For his study of the Nazi youth cohort, Loewenberg focuses on young German males who were born during World War I (between 1914 and 1918).

He notes that the emotional constellation of the infancy and early childhood years is decisive for the future psychological health and normality of the adult. If so,

> Modern war conditions, through the long-term breakup of family life, added in some cases to a lack of essential food and shelter, and a national atmosphere highly charged with unmitigated expressions of patriotism, hatred, and violence, must inevitably distort the emotional and mental development of children, for imbalance in the fulfillment of essential psychic and bodily needs in childhood results in lasting psychological malformations. (1480)

In the case of German boys born during World War I, the usual resolution of early childhood conflicts, especially those involving aggression, did not occur. Under normal circumstances, the unmitigated aggressiveness of children is redirected into competence and constructive activity: "The child learns to criticize and overcome in himself his hostile, antisocial wishes, which is to say that he refuses them conscious expression. He accepts that it is bad to hurt, cripple, and kill. He believes that he has no further wish to do any of these violent and destructive things" (1484). This belief, however, can be maintained only if the outer social world is supportive of his struggle by likewise curbing its aggression:

> When a child who is struggling with his aggressive and destructive impulses finds himself in a society at war, the hatred and violence around him in the outer world meet the as yet untamed aggression raging in his inner world. At the very age when education is beginning to deal with the impulses in the inner environment the same wishes receive sanction and validation from a society at war. It is impossible to repress murderous and destructive wishes when fantasied and actual fighting, maiming, and killing are the preoccupation of all the people among whom the child lives. Instead of turning away from the horrors and atrocities of war, he turns toward them with primitive excitement. The very murderous and destructive impulses that he has been trying to bury in himself are now nourished by the official ideology and mass media of a country at war. (1484)

Loewenberg discusses the fact that the child's original object of aggression is the mother. A boy attributes the loss of her love to his own hostility and aggression. Later, his aggression will be directed toward anyone who is the source of frustration, such as a sibling who evokes his jealousy. When frustrated or anxious, he may regress to the period of preindividuation, to a fantasized recovery of emotional merger with his mother. Thus, "The struggle against feminine identification [is] greatly intensified in boys raised without fathers" (1486).

Idealization also plays an important role in early childhood. Such idealization among boys is projected onto the father. The little boys in the Nazi cohort group, however, experienced the extended or total absence of their fathers, who were fighting in the war. Loewenberg cites a study by George R. Bach comparing father-separated from father-at-home elementary school children. Bach found that "father separated children produce an idealistic fantasy picture of the father" that seems "to indicate the existence of strong drives for paternal affection" (1465). Because these drives cannot be met, the father-separated children have "idealistic, wish-fulfilling fantasies" (1465). While the Oedipal theory would suggest that the boys would have strong hostilities toward their fathers, their fathers' absence means that their idealizations are not challenged by countervailing emotions. Thus, normal aggressiveness toward their fathers is not "worked through" but is repressed and displaced: "In wartime the absent father-soldier is idealized. He is glorified and any hostile feelings toward him are projected onto the evil enemy on the other side" (1488). As a result,

> the mentality of a state of war complements the child's most archaic psychic mechanisms for coping with himself and the world, the devices of splitting and projection. Splitting is what a people at war does by dividing the world into "good" and "bad" countries, those on our side who have only virtues and whom we love, and the enemy who is evil and whom we hate. We are thus enabled to get pleasure by gratifying our aggressive feelings. (1487)

For the young child, this splitting is personified, and thus "there are two kinds of men, one 'good' and one 'bad'" (1487–88). Father is unqualifiedly good, and the one who is father's enemy is unqualifiedly evil.

Serious problems develop, however, when the father returns home, especially when his army has suffered a humiliating defeat. Loewenberg cites a clinical study of German university students during World War II that "emphasizes the conflict between the child's perception of the father during the war as a highly idealized fantasy object bearing his ideas of omnipotence and the way in which the father was perceived on his return in defeat" (1492). While he was away, the father was honored and admired, the object of extreme hopes and expectations upon his return. But, once he returned, it quickly became apparent that he was not what had been longed for: "Instead he was a defeated, insecure father breaking into a heretofore fatherless family. Up to this time the mother had represented all aspects of reality. The father, by contrast, was now a demanding rival who left most wishes unfulfilled, who disappointed many hopes, and who set many limits where formerly there had been none" (1492). The fathers were not only unknown men, they were also feared and threatening strangers who claimed rights and control over the lives of their sons. They became "distant but powerful figures who could punish and exact a terrible price for disobedience and transgressions" (1495). This provoked deep resentment in the boy, as the boy, who had displaced his father during his absence, rejected the idea that his father had any legitimate claim to control over him.

Loewenberg's major argument is that this cohort group—young boys who spent their earliest formative years without fathers—were especially attracted to the Nazi movement two decades later. He cites an autobiographical novel by Ernest Glaeser, who relates how he chose to wear a uniform and to iden- tify with the distant and glorified father. Loewenberg explains:

> The identification with the father who went out to war served to erase the memory of the feared and hated strange father who came home in defeat. By being a patriot and submitting to authority, the ambiva- lence of the young boy who gleefully observed his father's humiliat- ing defeat and degradation was denied and expiated. Now he would do obeisance to an idealized but remote leader who was deified and untouchable. (1496)

Thus, members of this cohort turned readily to programs based on facile solutions and to violence when they met new frustrations during the Depres- sion. They reverted to earlier fixations in their child development marked by rage, sadism, and the defensive idealization of their absent fathers: "These elements made the age cohort particularly susceptible to the appeal of a mass movement utilizing the crudest devices of projection and displacement in its ideology. Above all, it prepared the young voters of Germany for submission to a total, charismatic leader" (1501). Tragically, however, "fantasy is always in the end less satisfying than mundane reality…What the youth cohort wanted was a fantasy of warmth, closeness, security, power, and love. What they re- created was a repetition of their own childhoods" (1502).

Loewenberg's study suggests that the image-splitting that I ascribed to Jesus is especially apt to occur among boys who have had experiences of their fathers that severely undermine their idealized images of them. To recover the idealized image, they may comport themselves later in life as the men they imagined their fathers to be, thus engaging in "fatherlike performance." Glaeser describes his cohort's adoption of militaristic uniforms, close-shaven heads, and a menacing appearance, as if to show that they would be the men their idealized fathers ultimately failed to be. I suggest that such image-splitting and fatherlike performance would have special appeal to first-century Pales- tinian young men whose fathers became highly threatening toward them at the onset of puberty (as Pilch shows), thus undermining the more idealized images they held of their fathers during childhood, when their fathers were more distant figures who left the disciplinary role to the boys' mothers. Given this tendency toward image-splitting and fatherlike performance, one would expect that these young men would be unusually susceptible to the influence of leader figures who appear to exemplify the characteristics and behaviors of the idealized father, thus creating an environment in which charismatic lead- ers found a ready-made clientele. Given his focus on the Nazi cohort group, Loewenberg ends his study on a critical note, emphasizing that fantasy is always less satisfying than reality.

What if the idealized father, however, is not a human person, but "Abba"? Such an idealization may then be an empowering one. It offered Jesus a legiti- mate identity. It also enabled him to redirect otherwise self-directed aggres- sion at the very enemy of his idealized father through his fatherlike performance as an exorcist-healer. Moreover, Mark's story of the possessed son indicates that Jesus did not jealously guard this personal empowerment, but invited other father-alienated young men to join with him. He thus recognized them as his cohorts and as having needs and desires–similar to his own–for an idealized father with whom to identify and to engage in similar fatherlike performance. He intervenes only after his disciples fail to cast out the evil spirit. This invitation to other young men, however, required them to relinquish their attachments to their fathers, however ambivalent these were, and to adopt "Abba" as their one and only father. Hence, "Whoever does not hate his father and mother as I do cannot become a disciple to Me." Conversely, "Those here who do the will of My father and My brothers and My mother. It is they who will enter the Kingdom of My Father" (Gos. Thom. 101, 99).

Thus far, I have emphasized Jesus' fatherlike performance in his exorcisms and healings. Underlying this performance, however, was his desire for sonship. His effectiveness as a healer was confirmation of such sonship. This suggests that a key dynamic in his psychological profile was what I have termed "the desire to be another man's son" (Capps, 1995, 112–15). If Loewenberg emphasizes the desire to idealize the father in the case of the Nazi cohort, I would also want to draw attention to their desire to be another man's son, as reflected in their devoted sonship to a fatherlike charismatic leader. Because he was fatherless (i.e., did not live under the protection of his natural father and was not adopted by his mother's husband), Jesus experienced an experiential void as far as his own sonship was concerned. Thus, he had unusually strong motivations for such a desire. Abba filled this very desire.

Freud recognizes the anxiety that such a desire may evoke in a son who *does* have a father, resulting in its repression. In *The Psychopathology of Everyday Life* (1901/1960), he acknowledges his own youthful desire to be the son of another man. In *The Interpretation of Dreams*, he had substituted the name of General Hannibal's brother Hasdrubal for his father's name of Hamilcar (1900/1960, 230). This mistake occurs immediately following his account of an episode in which his father was humiliated by a threatening Christian. Writing about this error in *The Psychopathology of Everyday Life,* he relates his experience of visiting his half-brother in England and discovering that he and his half-brother's oldest son were exactly the same age, suggesting that his half-brother was old enough to be his own father. On recalling this incident in connection with his confusion of the names of Hannibal's father and brother, he became aware of a deeper recollection, the fact that he had wished at the time that he was not the son of his father. He comments on his correction of the original error in subsequent editions of *The Interpretation of Dreams:* "I could have gone on to tell how my relationship with my father was changed by a visit to England…How different things would have been if I had been born the son not of my father but of my brother" (219–20). This illustration suggests that the desire to be another man's son is so anxiety-producing that the son is likely to repress it. In fact, his error in *The Interpretation of Dreams* reveals that "where an error makes its appearance a repression lies behind it" (218). The repressed wish is recovered only many years later when he probes the meaning of his erroneous identification of Hasdrubal as the father of Hannibal. His discussion of such errors in *The Psychopathology of Everyday Life* immediately follows his chapter on the meaningfulness of symptoms, as if to suggest that an error of this kind reveals his anxiety over a desire he could not own.

The desire to be another man's son underlies Jesus' view of God as his personal father, a father who effectively replaces his natural father in his understanding of his own sonship. He would know himself as the son of "Abba"– perhaps playing on the irony that his own father was nameless. Given the threat that fathers posed for their sons on reaching puberty, one may expect that Jesus' male contemporaries had similar, perhaps intensified desires. Because they were not fatherless–as Jesus was–they may have been more conflicted over such desires (experiencing guilt, shame, perhaps fear), especially because Jewish males were under strong religious sanctions to honor their fathers.

Another important factor, however, was that sons who had reached puberty had physical strength they did not possess as small boys. (As we have seen, Puritan New England had strict laws against harming one's father.) If they were enraged by their fathers' harsh treatment, they may have considered fighting back, knowing that they would (in many cases) be able to overpower their fathers. If their rage was great enough, they may have considered not mere self-defense, but harming–even killing–the man who threatened them. But such desires would be highly anxiety-provoking and would need to be repressed. Such repression could then lead to symptomatology precisely as described in the case of the possessed boy in Mark 9:14–29.

Thus, a demon possession that had its onset in puberty would be expected to have symptomatology of muteness, grinding of teeth, and other mouth-related symptoms, as the voice is the organ of verbal aggression (Mk. 9:17–18). In fact, we have noted that name-calling, insults, and slurs were common in Mediterranean societies. We would also expect symptomatology of aggressively flailing arms and feet, a hitting and kicking that does not, however, reach its intended victim (Mk. 9:20). In fact, the very point of the illness is that it does *not* reach its intended victim, for in this way aggression against the father is curtailed and is self-directed instead. Paralysis or immobilization is therefore a related symptomatology.

Young men seem to have been at highest risk for demon possession, and their parents were at a loss as to how to deal with it. *The Life of Apollonius of Tyana*, written about 217 C.E., gives some idea of their dilemma. A mother petitioned Apollonius for help with her sixteen-year-old son, who had been demon possessed for two years. She reported that the demons had driven the boy into deserted places and that he had lost his former voice to another that was deeper and hollow in tone. She said that she had wept and torn her cheeks as well as reprimanded her son, all to no avail, for the boy did not recognize her, having withdrawn, it would appear, into a catatonic state (Twelftree, 1993, 26). The fact that she seems to have vacillated between weeping for her son and reprimanding him illustrates parental frustration over a son's demon possession. They did not know whether to pity or blame their afflicted sons. The son's affliction may therefore have had certain secondary benefits, since it afforded him a certain emotional control over his parents, thus retaliating—though also at his own expense—against harsh parental, especially father-inflicted, treatment.

If Christoph Haitzmann went to a place of pilgrimage for help from the reverend fathers, extended sojourns in desert areas under the care of a holy man appear to have had a similar objective for young men of Galilee. Of course, not all were exhibiting symptoms of demon possession, but no doubt all were troubled in one way or another. Josephus relates that he spent three years in his late teens under the instruction of a desert holy man named Banus (1). John the Baptist may also be viewed in this light. The hallmark of his message, the baptismal rite, was not to be employed "to gain pardon for whatever sins they committed, but as a consecration of the body implying that the soul was already cleansed by right behavior" (Josephus, quoted in Crossan, 1991, 230). This emphasis on an internal cleansing may suggest that John himself was an exorcist and was Jesus' teacher in its methods and techniques.

As Crossan points out, however, there was also a politically explosive aspect to his rite of baptism, for "people cross over into the desert and are baptized in the Jordan as they return to the Promised Land." Thus, like certain millennial prophets between 44 and 62 C.E., John "invoked the desert and the Jordan to imagine a new and transcendental conquest of the Promised Land" (232). This suggests that he helped the young men who came out to the desert to get cured of their father-related neuroses (which, in their more extreme form, would involve "demon possession") by redirecting their internalized fear and rage into the dream of the conquest of the land that was rightfully theirs. Thus, the cure involved two steps. One was to purify themselves of their internalized "evil" by right behavior. The other was to externalize their aggression; not, however, toward the original targets of their rage, but toward more impersonal targets. The aggression toward their fathers (and perhaps other village fathers—elders—in whom the law was vested) could be redirected and projected onto other targets, such as the upper classes, large landowners, foreigners, the House of Herod, the religious establishment, or Rome.

The Gerasene demoniac story (Mk. 5:1–20) reflects this very process of a sociopolitical *redirection* of intergenerational conflict between sons and their fathers. As a second stratum narrative, it takes demon possession out of its original village context and relocates it within a much larger sociopolitical arena. The power of Jesus' religious orientation as focused on "Abba," however, is that it remains close, psychodynamically, to the original conflict between sons and fathers. In this sense, it was closer to village dynamics, to the intergenerational and neighborhood conflicts that we saw in our discussion of witchcraft in Puritan New England. It was certainly possible to draw implications of this conflict for larger sociopolitical grievances, using metaphor to do so (as in the case of the Gerasene demoniac story). In my judgment, however,

Jesus' emphasis on God as "Abba" suggests that his orientation was local, and that it was mainly concerned with intergenerational and village related conflicts. We may judge the story of the possessed boy to be more authentic and the story of the Gerasene demoniac less so precisely because the latter locates the young man's problems in a larger sociopolitical context, thus serving the author's own polemical purposes. To the extent that Crossan focuses more on sociopolitical analyses of demon possession and less on psychological ones (as presented here), he too risks a similar displacement of Jesus' exorcisms from their psychosocial locus in the family and village to the larger sociopolitical context. While the larger sociopolitical context is not unimportant, I believe that we have an adequate explanation for demon possession in Pilch's analysis of the son's passage at puberty into the harsh, authoritarian world of male values, when the son is expected to subject himself "in unquestioning obedience to the severity of the treatment that his father and other males might inflict on him" (Van Aarde, 468). For the son, this is reality. A metaphorical application is well beyond his perceptual field.

Since Jesus also went out to the desert to become a disciple of John the Baptist, we may view him as a young man who had powerful, aggressive emotions—that is, rage—toward his "fathers" (both the one who "begot" him and the one who might have adopted him, but did not). Whether he had the symptoms of "demon possession" noted earlier is impossible to say, but virtually all Jesus scholars view him as having had a strong consciousness of the reality of Beelzebul (or of Satan). Miller contends that Jesus' satanic temptations, following his compelling experience of sonship at his baptism, involved a once-and-for-all decision regarding "which of his conflicting identities that warred within him was really his. Is he his father's beloved son (the child he once was prior to his father's death)? Or is he that grandiose figure that rose up to haunt him at the promptings of 'Satan' (the hyperresponsible and controlling person he was tempted to become in the wake of his father's death)?" Miller suggests that he was able to reject Satan because the "experience of a humbler, more authentic sonship was now too strong within him to be taken captive by such an inflated image of himself" (63). While, for reasons already indicated, I would disagree that Jesus' struggle was between the beloved sonship he experienced prior to and the inauthentic sonship to which he was attracted following Joseph's death, I agree with his view that Jesus may well have experienced such temptations—John the Baptist's "conquest" theme may, in fact, have aroused them—but that his experience of God as "Abba" afforded a different vision of empowerment. I would add, however, that these temptations of worldly honor are precisely those that would cause him to harbor deep resentments in the first place, that is, the fact that owing to his illegitimacy he was unable to experience the prerogatives that came with being a legitimate or even adopted son. In this view, his temptations, fortified by John's "sons of Abraham" rhetoric, are perfectly understandable. Thus, as "son of Abba," he accepted his marginalization, but in so doing became a healer who—through fatherlike performance—exorcized the demons of other endangered young men.

I conclude this discussion of Jesus as exorcist with brief comments on his use of the familiar (and generic) name—"Abba"—for God. In a comparison of the gospel accounts and Greek magical papyri in order to identify differences between them and to justify his disagreement with Morton Smith's and Crossan's view of Jesus as magician, Meier (1994) notes that a typical feature of the spells in the magical papyri is the multiplication of names of various deities and strings of nonsense syllables. Noting that such heaping up of meaningless names and syllables was for the sole purpose of efficacy, Meier suggests that the "the terse, intelligible commands of Jesus, often spoken before an audience, stand out in stark contrast" (550). Meier does not, however, consider that the "Abba" word itself had a quasi-magical quality. Freud helps us see that this was the case, and thus to identify the grounds for its psychological power, hence its efficacy.

In his *Introductory Lectures on Psycho-Analysis* (1916–17/1963), Freud defends his view that talk can cure a person, noting that critics who contend that the patient will be impressed only by "visible and tangible things" are being shortsighted and inconsistent, since they also believe that patients "are 'simply imagining' their symptoms" (17). He adds: "Words were originally magic and to this day words have retained much of their ancient magical power. By words one person can make another blissfully happy or drive him to despair…Words provoke affects [i.e., emotions] and are in general the means of mutual influence among men" (17). When Freud says that words were originally magic, he means this not only phylogenetically, but also developmentally. For the child, the saying of something is synonymous with its occurrence, which is why it is dangerous, for example, to condemn one's parent verbally. The child who exclaims, "I wish you were dead!" has every reason to fear that his parent will die, and that he will have been responsible. Thus, the word "Abba" has magical power, and, when spoken loud enough and often enough for the demons to hear it, it achieves its desired end. As Freud also notes, however, "words call forth emotions," and this fact, I believe, enabled Jesus to exorcize the evil spirit in the possessed boy. In effect, he called forth emotions from the boy's deep and distant past when he spoke the word "Abba." This was the father the boy loved, the father he knew before he also came to know the father (the harsh disciplinarian) whom he hated. Emotions relating to this earlier father, with his association to the (phylogenetic) primal father ("Abba"), were activated in the boy, and these overwhelmed the feelings of aggression toward the father who had, through his harsh severity, made himself a stranger to his son. (The magical papyri, with their repeated nonsense syllables, were instead reminiscent of the babblings of infants, thus, a prelinguistic period of vocal sounds.)

It may also be noted that "Abba" is a distinctive appellation for father in that it is reversible (a palindrome). No doubt this reversibility contributed to the child's sense that the person to whom it applied was himself a magical being. In his short essay "The Antithetical Meaning of Primal Words" (1910/1957), Freud discusses Karl Abel's pamphlet *Über den Gegensinn der Urworte*, published in 1884. Abel noted that a common feature of the Egyptian language is that many words meant both themselves and their opposites, so that the context would need to determine which was meant. Relevant to our discussion of exorcism here is the Hebrew word "bless." As David Bakan points out in his discussion of the book of Job (1968), the word translated "curse" in Job's wife's statement, "Curse God, and die," is actually "bless": "The context is such, however, that the translator is quite correct in interpreting 'bless' as a euphemism for 'curse'. The suggestion is very strong that 'bless' and 'curse' are deeply intertwined, that they are, in some sense, one" (116).

Freud uses Abel's analysis of "antithetical words" to explain why it is difficult to determine whether an element in dream-thoughts is to be taken negatively or positively. He then notes Abel's further comments on the reversal of sound, suggesting that this phenomenon is even deeper than antithetical words. He comments: "We remember in this connection how fond children are of playing at reversing the sound of words and how frequently the dream-work makes use of a reversal of the representational material for various purposes. (Here it is no longer letters but images whose order is reversed.) We should therefore be more inclined to derive the reversal of sound from a factor of deeper origin" (160–61). Thus, "the phenomenon of reversal of sound (metathesis)" may be "even more intimately related to the dream-work than are contradictory meanings (antithesis)" (161). Freud concludes with a note to fellow psychiatrists: "We cannot escape the suspicion that we should be better at understanding and translating the language of dreams if we knew more about the development of language" (161). Applying this analysis of "antithetical words" to Jesus' novel use of "Abba," we recognize that he draws on the most primal emotions of the child in relation to the father. Thus, he seems to have understood the psychological potency of the word itself, attributable to its association with the period in life when words *are* magic due to their uncanny reversibility. (A more elaborate version of such reversal is the "I Am That I Am" of the Moses and the burning bush episode.) I conclude that there was, indeed, an element of magic in Jesus' exorcisms, based on the fact that, for children, words *were* originally magic, especially those that involved reversal of sound. Which is to say that the word and the act are one.

The Healings

As with the exorcisms, I will rely on Meier's work as a basis for determining which of the healings are authentic. My concern here, as well, is to make the case that the physiological (disease) and the social (illness) are mediated by psychological processes. Thus, a prominent psychological element–both psychophysiological and psychosocial–obtains in the healings as well. Meier conveniently divides the healings into these categories: (1) the paralyzed and the crippled; (2) the blind; (3) persons afflicted with "leprosy"; and (4) various healings, of which only one incident is recorded. This latter category includes fever, hemorrhage, dropsy, deaf-muteness, and ear restoration. Meier places the story of the centurion's servant (Mt. 8:5–13; Lk. 7:1–10; Jn. 4:46–47) in a special category, as the illness and its severity are reported differently in Matthew, Luke, and John. He treats the stories about the raising of the dead in a separate chapter.

Regarding the paralyzed and crippled, Meier concludes that there is a historical event from the life of Jesus behind the cures of the man let down through the roof (Mk. 2:1–12) and the man at the pool of Bethesda (Jn. 5:1–9). Cripple stories (withered hand, bent back) are unclear as to authenticity. Among the stories of the blind, he judges the blind Bartimaeus (Mk. 10:46–50 and parallels) and the blind man of Bethsaida (Mk. 8:22–26) to have a historical core. The man blind from birth (Jn. 9:1–41) may be historical, but the fact of his blindness from birth is undecidable. The leprosy healings are complicated because there is uncertainty about what this affliction was. Like Crossan, Meier doubts it was what is now called Hansen's disease. Instead, it concerned a skin condition (such as psoriasis, eczema, or vitiligo). By Jesus' time, it may have included Hansen's disease, a chronic infectious disease that also includes deterioration of body parts. In any case, Meier considers these stories ambiguous as to their authenticity, though the picture of Jesus' cleansing of lepers appears to go back to the life of Jesus himself.

Healings where a single example is cited are not judged inauthentic merely on grounds of their singularity, but the authenticity of fever, hemorrhage, dropsy, and deaf-mute stories is unclear on other grounds, though Meier inclines toward viewing the deaf-mute story (Mk. 7:31–37) as more likely historical. His firmest negative judgment is the ear restoration story (Lk. 22:49–51). As for the cure of the centurion's servant, he thinks Jesus may have been asked to heal the "boy" (whether a slave or son is, however, uncertain) and acceded to the request to heal him at a distance. The rest of the account, however, is the effect of repeated retellings or the creativity of the evangelists. As for the raising the dead stories, Meier believes that a historical event lies behind the raising of the daughter of Jairus (Mk. 5:21–43; Mt. 9:18–26; Lk. 8:40–56). He tends to reject the judgment of some scholars that the story was originally a healing story that was transformed into a raising of the dead story. While he doubts that the historical event itself can be known and does not come down in favor of any particular hypothesis (e.g., that she had lapsed into a coma), he takes seriously the fact she is represented as being near death. Thus, her recovery would have been viewed as extraordinary. The other stories (the son of the widow at Nain and the Lazarus story) were not, in his judgment, created by the early church out of thin air, but the case for the authenticity of the Lazarus story is stronger.

What makes Meier's painstaking work on the healing and raising of the dead stories useful for our purposes here is that, among the healing stories, the best cases for authenticity are those suggesting that Jesus healed the paralyzed and the blind. Regarding the raising of the dead stories, the best case appears to be the raising of Jairus' daughter. As far as gender is concerned, the cases of healings of paralytics and the blind are male, whereas the raising of the dead is female. In the following discussion, I will argue that these gender differences are quite important.

Paralysis Healings

Jesus' Healings of Paralytic Men

[1]When he returned to Capernaum after some days, it was reported that he was at home. [2]So many gathered around that there was no longer room for them, not even in front of the door; and he was speaking the word to them. [3]Then some people came, bringing to him a paralyzed man, carried by four of them. [4]And when they could not bring him to Jesus because of the crowd, they removed the roof above him; and after having dug through it, they let down the mat on which the paralytic lay. [5]When Jesus saw their faith, he said to the paralytic, "Son, your sins are forgiven." [6]Now some of the scribes were sitting there, questioning in their hearts [7]"Why does this fellow speak in this way? It is blasphemy! Who can forgive sins but God alone?" [8]At once Jesus perceived in his spirit that they were discussing these questions among themselves; and he said to them, "Why do you raise such questions in you hearts? [9]Which is easier, to say to the paralytic, 'Your sins are forgiven' or to say, 'Stand up and take your mat and walk'? [10]But so that you may know that the Son of Man has authority on earth to forgive sins"–he said to the paralytic–

[11]"I say to you, stand up, take your mat and go to your home." [12]And he stood up, and immediately took the mat and went out before all of them; so that they were all amazed and glorified God, saying, "We have never seen anything like this!"

Mark 2:1–12

[1]After this there was a festival of the Jews, and Jesus went up to Jerusalem. [2]Now in Jerusalem by the Sheep Gate there is a pool, called in Hebrew "Bethzatha," which has five porticoes. [3]In these lay many invalids–blind, lame, and paralyzed. [5]One man was there who had been ill for thirty-eight years. [6]When Jesus saw him lying there and knew that he had been there a long time, he said to him, "Do you want to be made well?" [7]The sick man answered him, "Sir, I have no one to put me into the pool when the water is stirred up; and while I am making my way, someone else steps down ahead of me." [8]Jesus said to him, "Stand up, take your mat and walk." [9]At once the man was made well, and he took up his mat and began to walk.

John 5:1–9

In the preceding discussion of demon possession, I noted that the possessed boy's immobilization was not a meaningless detail but a meaningful symptom, as it was related to the son's aggression–controlled–against the father. Paralysis is another form of immobilization, and the two healing stories most likely to have roots in the life of Jesus indicate how immobilizing it can be. In the one case (Mk. 2:1–12), the man is brought to Jesus by friends, and he and his mat are let down through the roof of the house. In the other case (Jn. 5:1–9), a man has been lying beside the healing pool for thirty-eight years. Many of the points I have made concerning the possessed boy (Mk. 9:14–29) also apply to these two cases of paralysis.

Even as the symptomatology in a case of possession (grinding of teeth, writhing and kicking on the ground) is meaningful–linked especially to rage against his father–so the symptomatology is meaningful in the case of paralysis. Paralysis is less dramatic than the syptomatology of possession, but it too may be an anxiety reaction either to external or internal threat. In the case of paralyses that are eventually cured, we may suppose that the perceived danger that precipitated the anxiety, leading to paralysis, has in the meantime disappeared, or that the anxiety that was associated with the danger has been replaced by other, positive affects, or some combination of the two. Also possible, however, is that both the perceived danger and anxiety have disappeared, but the paralysis persists for other reasons (e.g., the affected limb or limbs have atrophied from nonuse, the person has become accustomed to certain secondary benefits from being paralyzed, etc.).

While the two cases of paralytic men considered by Meier to have a historical core are not identical, both contain the command, "Stand up, take your mat." The implication is that the paralyzed man *can* get up from his prone position and assume a horizontal one instead. One is struck by the simplicity of the command and by the assumption implied in it that standing up is something the paralytic can do. What seems to be in doubt is whether the paralytic truly believes he can stand up, put his full weight on his legs and feet, and begin walking again. In my view, what Jesus has done here is to confront the anxiety of the paralytic man, commanding him not to be undone by perceived dangers (external or internal), but to have confidence that these dangers, whatever they may be, do not warrant an immobilized existence. The command to the man in Mark 2:1–12 to "go to your home" suggests that the perceived danger is located there, either because he feels threatened at home (e.g., having been treated abusively by his father), or because he is concerned about what he may do to someone at home (e.g., strike his father, take sexual license with a sister). Given the thirty-eight years that the paralyzed man in John 5:1–9 is said to have lain by the pool, we may perhaps assume that the original perceived danger behind his anxiety has long since disappeared, and that his paralysis has become habitual, perhaps having afforded at some point in these many years some secondary benefits. Thus, it is a reasonable question to ask in this case whether he really *does* want to be made well. The obvious ineffectiveness of his plan for healing, yet his persistence in it may suggest a certain ambivalence about getting well. By asking the question, Jesus both expresses his own doubts about the man's desire to get well and elicits the response that the man has tried his best to get into the pool. By thus eliciting the positive side of the man's ambivalence, he has created an opportune moment for the command to "Stand up, take your mat, and walk." In both cases, then, Jesus creates the conditions for an affirmative, energetic response to his command.

Note that I have assumed a psychological element in the paralysis of the two men, using Freud's theory of anxiety to identify its grounds. Thus, paralysis in these two cases involves a somatizing of anxiety. The question this raises is why the somatizing of anxiety would take this precise form (i.e., inability to walk). In a general sense, I have already answered this question by noting that this form of paralysis (in the legs) is immobilizing, and thus precludes feared behavior (by self or others). I would, however, like to give this answer greater specificity by noting some contributing psychosocial factors relating to the fact that these are both Jewish males. This discussion will enable us to locate these healings of paralytic men in their psychosocial context, thus recognizing that paralysis is both a physiological disease and a social illness, with psychological factors pertaining to both.

To address these larger issues, I will draw on Sander L. Gilman's discussion in one of his books on Freud (1993) of "the anthropological constitution of the Jew and the meaning of disease" (11). Gilman explores the outrageous moral judgments about Jews by late nineteenth- and early twentieth-century German authors on the basis of their alleged physiological deficiencies, and, more specifically, their alleged susceptibility to specific disabilities. These pseudo-scientific texts were clearly anti-Semitic and provoked a response from Jewish physicians and medical researchers, who challenged their claims and asserted that, if there was any truth in them, they were due to environmental and not racial causes. In some cases, differences between Eastern European and Western European Jews were used to make this point, invariably to the detriment of Eastern Europeans.

Thus, the Jewish physician Elcan Isaac Wolf rebutted the claims of non-Jewish German authors that Jews were physiologically inferior (i.e., had a weaker constitution than non-Jews) by arguing that if some German Jews were less healthy than their Gentile counterparts, this was not because of any inherent biological difference, but because of the "horrible persecution of heathen tyrants" as well as of "the religious practices of the Jews" (21). By acknowledging religious practices to be a factor, he thus acknowledged that longstanding Jewish customs may have had a negative effect on their physiological development and general health. He expressed his own preference for a secular Jewish culture. On the other hand, he vigorously challenged the claim that constitutional deficiencies were involved, instead attributing any physiological weaknesses to Jews' political subjugation. While he argued against anti-Semitic slurs, Wolf also worked toward the establishment of programs to address the disabilities of Jews. In so doing, he granted that Jews have certain physiological problems that differentiate them from non-Jews.

One such difference is the tendency of Jews toward flatfootedness. Historically, this tendency led to various anti-Semitic slurs, including the text that includes the demon possession account of Christoph Haitzmann, the *Trophaeum Mariano-Cellense* (published in 1677). It drew analogies between Jews and the cloven-footed devil of the Middle Ages (Gilman, 1993, 113). An alleged consequence of their flatfootedness was that Jewish men were less likely to pass the physical test for induction into the German army and were thus more likely to profit from the inflated wartime economy than to suffer on the battlefield. Gilman cites Heinrich Steinthal, the Jewish cofounder of ethnopsychology, who concluded that "the case of [Jewish] physical deformity, especially the deformity of gait," was "the result of the pressures of civilization" (117). He noted that a Jew's body is predetermined to have a "specific gait because of our nature," but this gait has been interfered with—made unnatural—by pressures to conform to the physiological structure of other races (117). Thus, the Jewish "difference" (that of flatfootedness) was not some kind of inherent weakness, an indication that Jews were developmentally less advanced than their Gentile counterparts. Instead, in their efforts to imitate non-Jews in order to become less visible in foreign societies, they had developed certain physiological problems relating to matters of "gait," problems that were the direct result of the attempt to disguise their genetically acquired flatfootedness.

Allegations that Jews were less patriotic, suffer less during war, and so forth, had the effect of producing a countermeasure among Jews, which was advocacy of engagement in sports in order to make a more muscular Jewish male. In a 1908 edition of *Jewish Gymnastic News*, M. Jastrowitz, a Jewish physician, "accepts the basic premise...that the Jewish body is at risk for specific diseases, and attempts to limit and focus this risk. For Jastrowitz the real disease of the Jews, what marks their bodies, is a neurological deficit that has been caused by the impact of civilization. Jastrowitz, like most of the Jewish physicians of the fin de siècle, accepts the general view that Jews are indeed at special risk for specific forms of mental and neurological disease" (Gilman, 1993, 124). He warns, however, that too great reliance on sport as a remedy may actually exacerbate these illnesses because "the attempt to create the 'new muscle Jew' works against the inherent neurological weaknesses of the Jew" (125). Thus, against those who argued that training the body would positively affect the mind, Jastrowitz, "also assuming a relationship" between mind and body, "fears that, given the inherent weakness of the Jewish nervous system, any alteration of the precarious balance would negatively affect the one reservoir of Jewish strength, the Jewish mind" (125). Thus, both advocates and critics of the emphasis on sport agreed on one thing: "The relationship between the healthy body, including the healthy foot and the healthy gait, and the healthy mind, is an absolute one. The only question left is whether the degeneration of the Jewish foot is alterable" (125). On this issue, it was widely recognized that this "is not simply a problem for orthopedists; neurologists, such as Sigmund Freud, also became closely involved in this debate" (125).

They did so in discussions involving the new diagnostic category of "intermittent claudication" (125). This category was created by Jean-Martin Charcot, who described it

> as the chronic recurrence of pain and tension in the lower leg, a growing sense of stiffness, and finally a total inability to move the legs which causes a marked and noticeable inhibition of gait. This occurs between a few minutes and a half hour after beginning an activity such as walking. It spontaneously vanishes, only to be repeated at regular intervals...Charcot determined that this syndrome seemed to result from reduction of blood flow through the arteries of the leg

and led to the virtual disappearance of any pulse from the four arter-
ies that provide the lower extremity with blood. The interruption of
circulation to the feet leads to the initial symptoms and can eventually cause even more severe symptoms such as spontaneous gan-
grene [decay of tissue]. (Gilman, 1993, 125)

It was not long before associations were being made between intermittent
claudication and the preexisting pathology of flat feet (127).

Gilman concludes his discussion of flatfootedness by exploring the theme
of the "degenerate foot" in Freud's work. He notes that *Oedipus* means swollen foot, that Freud's well-known patient Dora suffered from a swollen foot
and limped, and that Freud frequently used limping as a metaphor, as when
he notes in *Beyond the Pleasure Principle* that "we may take comfort, too, for the
slow advances of our scientific knowledge in the words of the poet: 'What we
cannot reach flying we must reach limping...The Book tells us it is no sin to
limp'" (1920/1955, 64). In this discussion Gilman mentions two experiences
relating to Freud's "footwork." The first is Freud's own account (1900/1953)
of the time when he was on a walk as a child with his father when his father
described a previous accident when he was a young man: "I went for a walk
one Saturday in the streets of your birthplace; I was well dressed, and had a
new fur cap on my head. A Christian came up to me and with a single blow
knocked off my cap into the mud and shouted: 'Jew! get off the pavement!'"
When Freud asked his father what he did next, his father quietly replied, "I
went into the roadway and picked up my cap" (197). In contrast, one of Freud's
own sons once gave an account of his father charging, with his stick raised,
into a crowd that had threatened his sons with anti-Semitic remarks (Gilman,
1993, 131). I will return to these father-son stories later, noting their relevance
to Jesus' healings of paralytics.

To augment Gilman's discussion and bring it into closer connection with
the healings of paralytic men attributed to Jesus, I want to take a brief note of
one of Freud's earliest publications, an article on paralysis titled, "Some Points
for a Comparative Study of Organic and Hysterical Motor Paralyses" (1893/
1966). Here, he notes that Charcot, with whom he studied in 1885–86, en-
trusted him with the task of making a comparative study of organic and hysterical motor paralysis. This article, written several years later, reports the
main results of these studies. First, he distinguishes two types of organic paralysis, *peripherospinal paralysis*, which is a paralysis of individual elements,
and *cerebral paralysis*, which is a paralysis en masse. In the former (e.g., the
facial palsy of Bell's syndrome), each muscle or muscle fiber may be paralyzed independently and in isolation, depending on the site and extent of the
nerve lesion, and no definite rule applies to which peripheral element *escapes*
paralysis while another is permanently subject to it. In contrast, cerebral paralysis is a disease that affects a considerable portion of an extremity (e.g., leg,
arm) or a complicated motor apparatus. It never affects one muscle alone.
Also, in cerebral paralyses affecting the extremities, distal segments always

suffer more than proximal ones; the hand or foot, for example, is more paralyzed than the shoulder or thigh.

Moving to hysteria, Freud notes that it simulates "the most various of organic nervous disorders" (162). With hysterical paralysis, however, it always simulates cerebral paralyses, never peripherospinal paralyses. The paralysis is always en masse. On the other hand, hysterical paralysis does not follow the rules of cerebral paralysis. In hysteria, the proximal segment (e.g., shoulder) *may* be more affected than the distal segment (e.g., hand). Thus, what distinguishes hysterical paralysis is that it falls midway between the two forms of organic paralysis. Freud observes that it does not possess all the characteristics of dissociation and isolation found in periphero-spinal paralysis, but neither is it subject to the rules that govern cerebral paralysis. The question is: Why is hysterical paralysis much more dissociated and systematized than cerebral paralysis, the form of organic paralysis that it otherwise most resembles?

Freud suggests that in hysterical paralysis a segment of the anatomy comes under the influence of an "idea" that has such a "precise delimitation" and "excessive intensity" that it cannot enter into association with the other ideas "constituting the ego of which the subject's body forms an important part" (63). The concept "arm," for example, is dissociated from all other concepts and functions independently of them. An illustration is the comic story of a loyal subject who would no longer wash his hand because the king had touched it: "The relation of this hand to the idea of the king seemed so important to the man's psychical life that he refused to let the hand enter into any other relation" (170). Thus, "in every case of hysterical paralysis, we find that the paralyzed organ or the lost function is involved in a subconscious association which is provided with a large quota of affect [i.e., emotion], and it is liberated as soon as this quota is wiped out" (171). In addition, following Charcot's view that a traumatic event lies behind all paralyses, Freud concludes that in hysterical paralysis, the affected body part has an unconscious association with the traumatic event that produced the paralysis. To emphasize the role of the unconscious in the formation of a hysterical paralysis, Freud cites in *The Interpretation of Dreams* (1900/1953) an 1886 report of a dream that resulted in a hysterical paralysis (89). He also cites a study that had drawn attention to certain anxiety dreams that were equivalents of epileptic seizures (89).

As we apply this discussion of Jewish flatfootedness and of hysterical paralysis to Jesus' healings of paralytics, the "new muscle Jew" warrants comment. In noting Jesus' occupation as carpenter, Meier (1991) notes that "while Jesus was in one sense a common Palestinian workman, he plied a trade that involved, for the ancient world, a fair level of technical skill. It also involved no little sweat and muscle power. The airy weakling often presented to us in pious paintings and Hollywood movies would hardly have survived the rigors of being Nazareth's *tekton* from his youth to his early thirties" (281). With this, Meier has entered, however unintentionally, into the discussion that prevailed at the turn of the twentieth century regarding the constitutional weakness of the Jewish male. Those who emphasize that Jesus required a strong constitution in order to live in the out-of-doors have ventured upon the same discussion. As Gilman shows, however, the issue is one of great sensitivity to Jews. I hope that my discussion here reflects my appreciation of its sensitive nature.

Gilman's work leads inevitably to the conclusion that paralysis among Jews is a complex phenomenon, having physiological aspects (especially involving the neurological system) and sociocultural ramifications. In addition, however, a psychophysiological basis to the physiological aspect of paralysis could rarely—if ever—be ruled out, and this, in turn, would add psychosocial implications to its sociocultural meanings. The issue of flatfootedness is especially intriguing in this regard, since it suggests a physical characteristic of Jews that (given Jewish emphasis on maintaining ethnic purity) is very likely to have been present in Jesus' time, and compensatory alterations in gait may well have been common as well. In any event, because men were expected to be more ambulatory than women, one assumes that flatfootedness created special problems for Jewish males. (The literature that Gilman cites focuses exclusively on its effects on males.) In addition to the direct physiological effects of flatfootedness (pain in the lower back and legs), there were many indirect psychosocial effects, including difficulties relating to physical labor, traveling long distances by foot, and so on. A Jewish male suffering from the physiological effects of flatfootedness may be unusually susceptible to the accusation that he was engaging in "footdragging," which heads James Scott's list (cited earlier) of "the ordinary weapons" that comprise the peasant class's everyday expression of resistance. The very fact that Jewish males were afflicted with flatfootedness and its attendant physiological problems would create an ambiguity between "legitimate" and "illegitimate" reasons for an inability to work, to travel, and so forth. Matthew 5:41—"If anyone forces you to go one mile, go also the second mile"—may have bearing on this very issue, since it suggests that one's attitude should be that one will do more, not less, than what is expected of one, thereby—paradoxically—*reducing* the other's control over oneself. That the saying involves walking a certain distance may, in addition, indicate just how wearisome, even painful, such a demand could be.

Charcot's diagnosis of intermittent claudication is also relevant to Jesus' healings of the two paralytic men, as it suggests that neurological factors may have been involved in the paralysis. As Freud's article on hysterical paralysis indicates, however, these neurological factors may have deep psychological roots. Less extreme than the immobilization involved in demon possession, but on a continuum with it, paralysis inhibits movement toward whatever one anticipates at journey's end. It could be a dreaded encounter with a superior, a dull and routine task, a proscribed sexual liason, or an evening of debauchery. The mind perceives dangers, and the legs that would take the body to where the mind perceives danger to exist are unable to function.

Anxiety inhibits the flow of blood to the legs. Thus, anxiety has prevailed, and the perceived danger has been avoided.

But at what cost? In a society in which honor and shame play such an important role in human interaction, one would expect that a disabling paralysis would create a deep sense of shame. As psychophysiologist Arne Öhman points out (1986), fear responses in humans are mediated by the dominance/submission system found in all social organizations. While a human's successful flight from a threatening animal may result in relief, flight from a threatening human also generates feelings of humiliation and defeat, the agony of having "lost face" (124). Thus, one may prefer to stand and fight, even at the risk of one's life, rather than reveal one's fear by fleeing from an opponent. In this case, paralysis may reflect a profound ambivalence, enabling one to avoid flight from a dominant individual or group, but causing shame for failing to stand one's ground. Paralysis in this case suggests that the anxiety behind it relates to aggression and its containment. The two stories about Freud noted earlier are relevant in this connection. While his father did not respond to the insult he had just received, causing Sigmund, his son, to view him as cowardly and to feel shame for him, Freud himself took forceful, vigorous action when his own sons were similarly insulted. While his father was not literally paralyzed, he did not defend himself—either verbally or physically—but controlled his anger and merely stooped down and picked up his cap. Even his account of the episode seems controlled and matter-of-fact. If he was not physically paralyzed, he was emotionally paralyzed, unable to take action.

If, as Josephus says, Galilee had never been "destitute of men of courage, or wanted a numerous set of them" (641), we may assume that Galilean males were under continuing pressure to prove their manhood in face-to-face altercations. Paralysis, then, could well have been an anxious reaction to fear of being put to the test, of being challenged to prove one's courage. If family harmony (as in Puritan New England) and the maintenance of the nuclear family's united front vis-à-vis other families required the displacement of intrafamilial conflict onto the village, we would expect that such encounters (as in Puritan New England) would be commonplace in Galilean village life. Paralysis might then, for example, be construed as the effect of a neighbor's curse when one refuses to respond to the neighbor's request for a scarce commodity because one needed it for oneself or one's own family. As we saw in chapter 4, such conflictual episodes would commonly affect the neurological system, causing stiffening of the spine, immobilization of the limbs, and so forth.

Paralysis due to fear of another person or group, however, relates to external dangers to which there is an anxious reaction. Other precipitators of paralyzing anxiety are internal sources of danger, such as desires that one dare not act upon. In a society in which purity was such an important religious and cultural value, impure desires (e.g., sexual or aggressive ones) would be especially likely to cause an anxious reaction, which may, in certain cases, produce paralysis. In such cases, the fear is not of what someone may do to oneself, but what one may do to another. It is not inconceivable that the discussion about forgiveness of sins in the story of the paralytic man who was let down through the roof by his friends (Mk. 2:6–11) reflects an understanding of the association between impure desires and paralysis. While I will interpret this story later as involving aggression, not sexuality, the New England Puritans' struggle to control fornication among villagers there, and the previous chapter's emphasis on the phenomenon of sexual impurity among Galileans, suggests that paralysis may occur as an anxious reaction to a conflictual situation involving sexual desires, that is, the desire to engage in illicit or proscribed sexual behavior coupled with fear of severe village sanctions if found out. The association of "stumbling" and "sin" in Mark 9:43–47–"If your hand causes you to stumble,…if your foot causes you to stumble,…if your eye causes you to stumble"–may apply to all manner of transgressions, but these would certainly include sexual behavior. As in Freud's illustration of the man whose hand was now associated with the idea of "king," we may assume that in at least some hysterical paralyses in the Galilean context, the "paralyzed organ" or "abolished function" had a subconscious association with a proscribed sexual desire.

While my analysis may seem similar to Crossan's "Jesus healed social illness but did not cure disease" position, it differs in viewing physiological paralysis as having a psychological (largely unconscious) dimension, hence, a more complex understanding of "disease." By the same token, it stresses the *psychosocial* nature of illness, recognizing that a person may experience "illness" not only as a reaction to larger sociopolitical forces, but also–and more routinely–in reaction to everyday conflicts in family and village life. The story of the two sons who are told by their father to go work in the vineyard (Mt. 21:28–32), considered authentic by Crossan, captures such family conflict in the form of father-son relations. These two sons' anxieties over their desire to challenge their father are reflected in their inconsistent behavior, but more anxious sons might instead develop a paralytic condition that makes them physically incapable of working in their father's vineyard. Other potentially conflictual family situations that might produce paralytic symptoms are dangers associated with incestuous desires between brothers and sisters, mothers and sons, or fathers and daughters (see Elizabeth Barnes, 1997), or adulterous relationships involving married persons. As previously noted, several of Freud's illustrations of obsessive acts (1907/1957) were symptoms developed by women contemplating or engaged in extramarital affairs. One of these bordered on a paralysis, as the woman was able to sit on only one chair in the house and could leave it again only with difficulty. Freud discovered that the chair symbolized her husband, to whom she was struggling to remain faithful.

How, then, was Jesus able to heal these paralytics? While it is impossible to know whether the same father-son conflicts that may have been central to the case of the possessed boy were also operative in the healings of the two paralytics, this possibility is suggested in the case of the paralytic in Mark 2:1–12, because it focuses on the young man's sins (hateful feelings toward his father?), on the instruction to return home, and on the fact that the healing involved fatherlike performance, as reflected in Jesus' statement to the paralytic in Mark 2:5, "Son, your sins are forgiven." Such fatherlike performance suggests that the power of Abba was key to the healing, as Abba cast a protective circle around the paralytic, countering his anxiety, which may have been provoked originally by a sense of endangerment at the hands of his father. Admittedly, this is guesswork, but the paralytic's youth (Jesus calls him "son") suggests a possible psychodynamic parallel to the story of the possessed son. The healing of the paralytic in John 5:1–9 is probably less noteworthy for its original conflict situation and more for the long duration of the paralysis (even if thirty-eight years is an exaggeration). It reveals how disabling anxiety can be, especially its capacity to persist long after the original perceived danger is no longer present. On the other hand, given the average life expectancy of Jewish males at this time (about twenty-nine), his advanced age suggests that there were secondary benefits to paralysis, excusing the sufferer from routine work and various tests of male courage that were themselves debilitating and/or life threatening. Perhaps the recognized irony that a paralytic man may enjoy a longer life expectancy was implied in Jesus' question whether he actually wanted to be healed. In any event, we need to recognize that a hysterical paralysis is a compromise—one, however, that is based on fear. By demonstrating the power of Abba through his acts of healing, Jesus communicated his belief that Abba would place his circle of protection around the paralytic who had the courage to stand up and walk away from his place of refuge. Crossan places the "Against Anxieties" complex (comprising Gos. Thom. 36, Lk. 12:22–31, and Mt. 6:25–33) in the first stratum, double independent attestation category, and judges it to be authentic. Luke 12:25–"And which of you by being anxious can add a cubit to his span of life?" (RSV)–may be especially relevant to the paralytic in John 5:1–9, for if getting into the healing pool is itself a competitive matter, he is perhaps no safer there than in the world to which Jesus invites his reentry.

Hypochondria and Conversion Disorder

The complex link between physiological and psychological factors in the case of paralysis leads naturally to a consideration of hypochondria and of its relevance to first-century Galilean diseases. This is a large topic, but I wish to comment on a few salient points. One is that hypochondriacs tend to complain of sexual problems, skin problems, backaches, insomnia, fear of halitosis and body odors, distortions of physical features and of limbs, and mental symptoms (Baur, 1988, 32). Because the great majority of hypochondriacs are suffering from masked depression, therapists today tend to overlook the bodily complaints, viewing them as superficial symptoms. They focus instead on the depression itself, with its classic signs of sadness, hopelessness, feeling of loss, disturbed sleep, fatigue, lack of sexual interest, and unresponsiveness to the outside world. In recent clinical theory, however, hypochondria has increasingly been linked to anxiety disorders. As Susan Baur points out: "Therapists who see this connection point out that anxiety sets a person up for imaginary diseases by heightening his sensitivity to pain and by arousing the autonomic (involuntary) nervous system...Persons who suffer from panic disorder, with that problem's dramatic respiratory and cardiac problems, are especially likely to interpret their sensations as serious illness" (32). Other clinicians, especially those with a strong behaviorist orientation, believe that hypochondria is a learned habit in which one responds to emotional stress with uncomfortable bodily sensations instead of confronting the emotional demands directly. Sociologists and cultural anthropologists emphasize the external stresses–from social and cultural conditions–that make a person susceptible to hypochondria (34).

The *Diagnostic and Statistical Manual of Mental Disorders (DSM-IV)*, published by the American Psychiatric Association, locates hypochondriasis as a subtype of somatoform disorder (formerly hysteria or Briquet's syndrome). This is defined as a "polysymptomatic disorder that begins before age 30 years, extends over a period of years, and is characterized by a combination of pain, gastrointestinal, sexual, and pseudoneurological symptoms" (1994, 445). Hypochondriasis is one of several subtypes of somatoform disorder (others include pain disorder, conversion disorder, body dysmorphic disorder, and undifferentiated somataform disorder). It is the "preoccupation with the fear of having, or the idea that one has, a serious disease based on the person's misinterpretation of bodily symptoms or bodily functions" (445). Common effects are doctor-shopping, the belief that one is not receiving proper medical care, and resisting referral to mental health settings (for depression or anxiety). Complications may result from repeated (and costly) diagnostic procedures that carry their own risks. Social relationships become strained because sufferers are preoccupied with their condition and often expect special considerations. Family life may become disturbed as it centers around the sufferer's physical well-being. Functioning at work may be unaffected if hypochondriacal preoccupation is limited to nonwork time. More often, however, the preoccupation interferes with performance and causes work delinquency. In severe cases, one becomes a complete invalid.

Another somatoform disorder is conversion disorder, whose essential feature

> is the presence of symptoms or deficits affecting involuntary motor or sensory function that suggest a neurological or other general medical condition. Psychological factors are judged to be associated with the symptom or deficit, a judgment based on the observation that the limitation or exacerbation of the symptom or deficit is preceded by conflicts or other stressors. The symptoms are not intentionally produced or feigned, as in Factitious Disorder or Malingering. (452)

The *DSM-IV* provides the following illustration of a conversion disorder:

A "paralysis" may involve inability to perform a particular movement or to move an entire body part, rather than a deficit corresponding to patterns of motor innervation. Conversion symptoms
are often inconsistent. A "paralyzed" extremity will be moved inadvertently while dressing or when attention is directed elsewhere. If
placed above the head and released, a "paralyzed" arm will briefly
retain its position, then fall to the side, rather than striking the head.
Unacknowledged strength in antagonistic muscles, normal muscle
tone, and intact reflexes may be demonstrated. (453)

Conversion disorder (Freud called it "conversion-hysteria") gets its name from
"the hypothesis that the individual's somatic symptom represents a symbolic
resolution of an unconscious psychological conflict, reducing anxiety and serving to keep the conflict out of awareness ('primary gain')" (453). The individual may also derive "secondary gains" from the conversion symptom, "that
is, external benefits are obtained or noxious duties or responsibilities are
evaded" (453). While the hypothesis of a symbolic meaning to the symptom
is unnecessary, "a close temporal relationship between a conflict or stressor
and the inhibition or exacerbation of a symptom may be helpful" in making
the diagnosis (453–54). Conversion symptoms in children under ten years of
age are usually limited to gait problems or seizures. In men, an association
with antisocial personality disorder is sometimes evident and is often seen in
the context of industrial accidents or the military. Age of onset is usually from
late childhood to early adulthood, rarely before age ten or after age thirty-
five. Symptoms are usually of short duration, but recurrence is common. Symptoms of paralysis, aphasia [loss of voice], and blindness are associated with a
good prognosis, whereas tremor and seizures are not.

While conversion disorder seems an especially accurate diagnosis for many
healings attributed to Jesus in the gospels, the hypochondria literature helps
to identify other relevant psychosocial factors besides specific symptomatology. Hypochondriasis was known in antiquity as a disease of the digestive
organs. It was associated with and distinguished from hysteria, which was
considered a woman's disease (owing to a wandering uterus). Hypochondriasis was viewed as a male disease (Kellner, 1986, 1–2). In the beginning, it was
an anatomical term referring to a specific location in the body (under the
ribs), with the right hypochondrium comprising the liver and gall bladder
and the left involving the spleen. In the second century B.C.E. it acquired its
more popular meaning as a temperamental type (linked to melancholia), and
over the next four hundred years other attributes besides digestive disorders
were added, including preoccupation with disease, inexplicable periods of
anxiety, nightmares, and so forth.

Of particular interest is that hypochondria is most common among Mediterranean peoples, and that Greeks, Italians, North Africans, and Jews tend to
somatize their problems (Baur, 162; also Kellner, 75–78). A recent study of
mentally distressed individuals showed that 32 percent of Jewish immigrants

from Iraq, North Africa, and the Middle East had hypochondriacal symptoms, whereas only 9 percent of Jews from Europe, the Balkans, and Rumania complained of undiagnosed illness (Baur, 163). Baur concludes that the highest levels of hypochondria are found among Jews, followed by Italians (165). In her view, this reflects a deeply held Jewish belief that if subordinates are rash enough to be happy, the powerful will ask more of them. Thus, "Hypochondria, with its continual succession of headaches, fatigue, and upsets, was both the self-inflicted misery that protected many weak persons from what they imagined would be a harsher punishment at the hands of the powerful and the excuse necessary to justify a temporary respite from endless work" (164).

Carla Cantor (1996) cites research by medical anthropologist Mark Zborowski, who found in a study of Jews, Italians, Irish, and "old" Americans that Jews and Italians had a lower tolerance for pain, but whereas Italians were concerned with relieving their immediate pain, Jews "tended to focus on the implications of their symptoms and what they meant for future health and welfare—their own and their families" (178). She also cites the view of a French-Jewish psychiatrist who treated Holocaust survivors in 1947–48: "The general inclination of the Jew toward hypochondria...must be allowed for," for "it is another manifestation of the insecurity which tortures the Jewish spirit," and is expressed "most often in the anxious preoccupation shown in the case of illness" (176). In Cantor's view, what sets Jews apart "could be a longstanding pattern of describing disease in detail as well as a more positive attitude toward seeking help" (179). She compares this Jewish trait to the British habit of waiting patiently in long lines and talking incessantly about the weather.

Another noteworthy study is cited by Kellner (1986) in his hypochondria literature review. It focused on the skin lesions produced by hypochondriacal patients in attempts to remove parasites with pins, tweezers, scissors, and scalpels (154). This study may have significance for the healings attributed to Jesus of individuals suffering from "leprosy," which, as Meier and Crossan note, was not Hansen's disease but various skin conditions.

The fact that hypochondriasis was originally viewed as a disorder related to the digestive organs raises a final issue that I can only touch upon here. It concerns Jesus' statement that it is not what goes into the mouth but what comes out of the mouth that defiles a person (Gos. Thom. 14:3; Mk. 7:14–15; Mt. 15:10–11; as a first stratum, multiple attestation complex, Crossan considers it authentic). Mark's version reads thus: "Do you not see that whatever goes into a person from outside cannot defile, since it enters, not the heart but the stomach, and goes out into the sewer?" Here, the implication is that the locus of human intentions—good or evil—is the heart, and that the digestive system is therefore declared to be morally neutral. As far as Matthew is concerned, this view appears to differentiate Jesus from his teacher, John the Baptist (cf. Mt. 3:4 and 11:18–19). As Gilman points out, however, a common explanation for Jews' diseases throughout the centuries has been that they have poor diets. This view was in fact held by the Jewish physician Elcan Isaac Wolf (identified earlier), who believed that it was not only their limited activity, but also their poor diet that contributed to their illnesses (1993, 21). In her discussion of hypochondria found in children, Susan Baur notes that "among children the stomachache seems to be the most common of all un-founded complaints," and frequently this complaint marks the beginning of a lifelong tendency toward hypochondria (50). Baur quotes the British psychiatrist Michael Balint, who notes: "It is impossible not to notice the high emotional importance of eating in all gastric…diseases [and] of the digestive functions in intestinal disorders, particularly in chronic constipation" (56). While the matter of poor diet is most certainly influenced by many sociocultural factors (especially economic and class related), the tendency of Jews to somatize their emotional problems suggests that intestinal disorders in Jesus' day were likely to have an emotional basis, perhaps attributable to controlled or internalized rage. Jesus' views about eating and drinking are not normally considered integral to his role as healer, but perhaps they should be considered in this way. His dissociation of digestive matters from the moral domain may have been an effort to view their attendant disorders as having little if anything to do with issues of moral purity. In this sense, his healer role–focused as it was on the emotions that underlie overt behaviors–extends to dietary matters as well.

Blindness

Jesus' Healings of Two Blind Men

[22]They came to Bethsaida. Some people brought a blind man to him and begged him to touch him. [23]He took the blind man by the hand and led him out of the village; and when he had put saliva on his eyes and laid his hands on him, he asked him, "Can you see anything?" [24]And the man looked up and said, "I can see people, but they look like trees walking." [25]Then Jesus laid his hands on his eyes again; and he looked intently and his sight was restored, and he saw everything clearly. [26]Then he sent him away to his home, saying, "Do not even go into the village."

Mark 8:22–26

[46]They came to Jericho. As he and his disciples and a large crowd were leaving Jericho, Bartimaeus son of Timaeus, a blind beggar, was sitting by the roadside. [47]When he heard that it was Jesus of Nazareth, he began to shout out and say, "Jesus, Son of David, have mercy on me!" [48]Many sternly ordered him to be quiet, but he cried out even more loudly, "Son of David, have mercy on me!" [49]Jesus stood still and said, "Call him here." And they called the blind man, saying to him, "Take heart; get up, he is calling you." [50]So throwing off his cloak, he sprang up and came to Jesus. [51]Then Jesus said to him, "What do you want me to do for you?" The blind man said to him, "My teacher, let me see again." [52]Jesus said to him, "Go; your faith has made you well." Immediately he regained his sight and followed him on the way.

Mark 10:46–52

Meier believes that the story of Jesus' healing of the blind beggar Bartimaeus (Mk. 10:46–50) points to "a primitive tradition." He bases this judgment on the fact that Bartimaeus is named and that he calls Jesus "Son of David," which is "most probably not a product of Christian theology but a relic of how some Palestinian Jews with infirmities actually looked on Jesus," as "a miraculous healer a la Solomon" (1994, 690). The story in Mark 8:22–26 of the blind man of Bethsaida also has a strong claim to authenticity because of its strangeness, including its account of Jesus' spitting into the man's eyes, placing his hands on him, and asking, "Do you see anything?" The man indicates that he has regained partial vision because he can see men in the distance, but they look like trees walking around. Jesus again places his hands on the man's eyes, and now he sees perfectly, with no blurred vision.

Meier notes that this story was omitted by Matthew and Luke, suggesting that it apparently sounded strange to them as well. On the basis of criteria of embarrassment and dissimilarity (i.e., from other miracle stories in the New Testament), Meier judges it to have a historical core. Especially striking is the question that Jesus puts to the man–"Do you see anything?"–implying less "the words of healing" and more a "physician-like inquiry" (694). In fact, asking questions seems characteristic of his healing method. As in my discussion of Jesus' healings of paralyzed men, I will focus on the psychological elements associated with physiological afflictions and on psychosocial considerations raised by cultural and gender factors (as with the paralytics, both blind persons are male).

In *The Historical Jesus*, Crossan cites David Gilmore's statement that in Mediterranean societies "the evil-eye belief is widespread" and is "probably one of the few true Mediterranean universals. It is also one of the oldest continuous religious constructs in the Mediterranean area" (7). Gilman's study of Freud (1993) includes a section on "The Gaze of the Jew." He notes the work of Francis Galton, the English psychological researcher at the turn of the century, who tried to capture the uniqueness of Jewish physiognomy through composite photos of boys in the Jewish Free School in London. Galton observed that "there was no sign of diffidence in any of their looks, nor of surprise of the unwanted intrusion. I felt, rightly or wrongly, that every one of them was coolly appraising me at market value, without the slightest interest of any other kind" (Gilman, 1993, 44). Galton's phrase–"coolly appraising me at market value"–reveals his own anti-Semitic view of Jews as inordinately consumed with greed and avarice. Gilman, however, is especially interested in what Galton's comments reveal concerning non-Jews' attitudes toward "the Jewish gaze." According to S. Seligman, many Germans believed that the Jews possessed the evil eye (44). Freud commented on Seligman's work in "The 'Uncanny'" (1919/1955) and identified dread of the evil eye as attributed envy:

> Whoever possesses something that is at once valuable and fragile is afraid of other people's envy, in so far as he projects on to them the envy he would have felt in their place. A feeling like this betrays itself

by a look even though it is not put into words; and when a man is prominent owing to noticeable, and particularly owing to unattractive, attributes, other people are ready to believe that his envy is rising to a more than usual degree of intensity and that this intensity will convert it into effective action. What is feared is thus a secret intention of doing harm, and certain signs are taken to mean that that intention has the necessary power at its command. (240)

By "unattractive attributes," Freud has in mind the Jewish gait and the Jewish nose (his sensitivity to the latter is discussed in Gilman, 1998, 84–91). Of particular note here, however, is Freud's view that the "evil eye" was projected onto the Jew and attributed to envy, an envy so strong that the Jew was suspected of the intention to harm the envied one. One explanation of why Galton perceived the Jewish boys in his study to have "a coolly appraising" look may be found in an essay by the nineteenth-century Jewish social scientist Joseph Jacobs in the *Jewish Encyclopedia*. He made the observation that while "the eyes themselves are generally brilliant, [the] eyelids are heavy and bulging, and it seems to be the main characteristic of the Jewish eye that the upper lid covers a larger proportion of the pupil than among the other persons. This may serve to give a furtive look to the eyes, which, when the pupils are small and set close together with semi-strabismus, gives keenness to some Jewish eyes" (in Gilman, 1993, 49). His observation that the closeness of the eyes may contribute to the perception of a special "keenness" is supported by an essay on "The Face and the Mind Behind It" by Rudolf Arnheim (1996). Arnheim cites the work of Carl Gustav Carus, the nineteenth-century physiognomist, physician, and painter, who used a rudimentary drawing of a face with two dots for the eyes, a vertical line for the nose, and a horizontal one for the mouth to show that "by simply moving the distance between the eye dots, the rudimentary face can be made to intensify the glance, piercing the viewer" (142). Gilman cites the view of Moses Julius Gutmann, a nineteenth-century Jewish physician, that the depth that heavy eyelids give to the eyes behind them contributes to another impression, that of a "melancholy, pained expression" (49). In "The 'Uncanny'", Freud also comments on "the fear of damaging or losing one's eyes" as "a terrible one in children. Many adults retain their apprehensiveness in this respect, and no physical injury is so much dreaded by them as an injury to the eye" (231). He discusses E. T. A. Hoffman's story of "The Sand-Man" who tears out children's eyes.

As our earlier citation from the *DSM-IV* indicates, double-vision and blindness are among the more common symptoms of conversion disorder. Gilman's evil eye discussion, however, enables us to place this particular conversion disorder in the context of first-century Galilean life. While the literature that Gilman cites focuses on the ascription of the evil eye to Jews by non-Jews, in first-century Galilee this ascription would also have been applied by Jews to other Jews, especially those who were lower in social status. They would be considered envious and as having intentions to do harm. As our discussion of New England communities indicates, an individual's hostile look or stare could generate anxiety and fear in the neighbor; physical symptoms might also occur, providing "evidence" that the envious had invoked Satan in their own behalf. The uncanniness of a stare may be a more effective "curse" than a verbal one.

In a culture where belief in the evil eye was pervasive, the anxious defense of blindness should not surprise us. It is as though the blind person reasons: "If I cannot see the evil eye of others, I protect myself from their evil intentions." Thus, if the blindness reduces anxiety by keeping the conflict out of awareness ("primary gain"), one derives a "secondary gain" from the fact that the evil intentions of the other are rendered ineffective. Also, a blind person would be considered incapable of visiting evil on another individual, and may, therefore, become the object of genuine sympathy (a "tertiary gain" resulting from blindness).

The *DSM-IV* conversion disorder discussion indicates that blindness may come, go, and then recur. This may also have been the case with first-century Galileans. Moreover, it may be noted that average life expectancy was much shorter. Crossan cites Thomas Carney's estimate that 75 percent would die by age twenty-six and 90 percent by forty-six (1991, 4). Burial inscriptions indicate twenty-nine years was the average life expectancy of Jewish males. While this does not prove they were not afflicted with degenerative eye disease, the fact that they fell within the normal age for conversion disorder (between ten and thirty-five) supports the idea that, even if physiological factors were involved, psychological ones were likely to have accompanied them. Ralph Waldo Emerson's biographer, Robert D. Richardson, Jr. (1995), notes that the eye disease that struck Emerson at age twenty-three and lasted nine months was almost certainly ureitis, or rheumatic inflammation of the eye, whose underlying cause was probably tuberculosis. Richardson also notes, however, that stress probably helped to bring on the episode, as Emerson's eyes failed him in the middle of an essay he was writing about the centerpiece of Unitarian theology, an essay called "The Unity of God" (63). Also, as Richard A. Hutch points out (1983), Emerson wrote of a certain student, Martin Gay, in his notebook, "Why do you look after me? I cannot help looking out as you pass" (Hutch, 83). Both Hutch and Richardson suggest that Gay may have been arousing homoerotic feelings in Emerson, which indicates that his blindness was an anxiety reaction due to perceived external and internal dangers.

This raises the issue of the role of sexual conflict in eye disorders. In his study of the influence of defective vision on art and character, Patrick Trevor-Roper (1988), an English ophthalmologist, discusses the age-old belief that intrusive young men have been blinded because they observed naked women (153–54). Freud notes that Oedipus blinded himself when he realized he had committed incest with his mother. A discussion of scopophilia (gazing impulse) immediately precedes his analysis of the Oedipus myth in his *Introductory Lectures on Psycho-Analysis* (1916–17/1963, 327–28). Trevor-Roper also cites an 1882 article in *Archives of Ophthalmology* entitled "Eye Diseases and Masturbation" (155). While any alleged causal connection between masturbation and eye disease is spurious, blindness as a conversion disorder may, in some instances, be precipitated by sexual-related anxiety.

Galilean households undoubtedly required considerable gaze aversion by adolescent males vis-à-vis their mothers and sisters (on gaze aversion and its relation to shame, see Darwin [1872/1998, 327; also Tomkins, 1963]). We should also recall David Gilmore's point (in Crossan, 1991, 10) that Mediterranean honor is a "libidinized social reputation," and "it is this eroticized aspect of honor—albeit unconscious or implicit—that seems to make the Mediterranean variant distinctive" (10). Freud notes in "The 'Uncanny'" that "the study of dreams, fantasies and myths has taught us that a morbid anxiety connected with the eyes and with going blind is often enough a substitute for the dread of castration." He contends for "the substitutive relation between the eye and the male member" (137). Providing support for Freud's argument, Trevor-Roper notes that "schizophrenics, burdened with sex-guilt, have on many occasions removed either their testicles or their eyes, as vehicles for their shameful needs" (156). Relevant here was the very low social placement for eunuchs "who had been unmanned since birth" (Van Aarde, 463), and a specific reference to the offending eye in Mark 9:47: "And if your eye causes you to stumble, tear it out; it is better for you to enter the kingdom of God with one eye than to have two eyes and to be thrown into hell."

What, then, may we conclude regarding the two episodes where Jesus cured blind men? As with the paralytics, I suggest that Jesus was dealing here with physiological disturbances precipitated by psychological anxieties, which related either to matters of aggression (their own or someone else's), sexuality, or both. Our evil eye discussion suggests a counteraggressive component to loss of eyesight. In a society where an individual "sees himself always through the eyes of others" (P. Bourdieu, quoted in Crossan, 1991, 9) and where the ultimate dishonor is to be rendered invisible, a nonentity (Crossan, 1994, 126–27), much aggression—and counteraggression—centered around the experience of seeing and being seen.

Our discussion of the sexual element in gazing, however, adds a libidinal connotation to male blindness, especially in cases where (as the Bartimaeus story suggests) a degenerative disease was not involved. Also, and relatedly, male powerlessness was the larger frame within which blindness functioned. Owing to his blindness, Bartimaeus was reduced to begging—the expendable class—and was therefore dependent on the sympathy of passersby. This also meant, however, that he made himself vulnerable to their contempt as well. According to Frederick Denny (1987), ancient Greek magical practices call for one to spit into the eye of a close relative to prove the absence of evil-eye intentions (463). Whether Matthew and Luke found this behavior of Jesus "embarrassing" because it was crude or because it implied Jesus' adoption of Hellenistic magic, Meier does not say. In any case, it may well have been an example of paradoxical intention (Frankl, 1975), as it effectively "cleansed" the man's eyes of whatever evil they had witnessed or envisioned, enabling him to trust in them again.

The Raising of Jairus' Daughter

[21]When Jesus had crossed again in the boat to the other side, a great crowd gathered around him; and he was by the sea. [22]Then one of the leaders of the synagogue named Jairus came and, when he saw him, fell at his feet [23]and begged him repeatedly, "My little daughter is at the point of death. Come and lay your hands on her, so that she may be made well, and live." [24]So he went with him...

[35]While he was still speaking, some people came from the leader's house to say, "Your daughter is dead. Why trouble the teacher any further?" [36]But overhearing what they said, Jesus said to the leader of the synagogue, "Do not fear, only believe." [37]He allowed no one to follow him except Peter, James, and John, the brother of James. [38]When they came to the house of the leader of the synagogue, he saw a commotion, people weeping and wailing loudly. [39]When he had entered, he said to them, "Why do you make a commotion and weep? The child is not dead but sleeping." [40]And they laughed at him. Then he put them all outside, and took the child's father and mother and those who were with him, and went in where the child was. [41]He took her by the hand and said to her, "Talitha cum," which means, "Little girl, get up!" [42]And immediately the girl got up and began to walk about (she was twelve years of age). At this they were overcome with amazement. [43]He strictly ordered them that no one should know this, and told them to give her something to eat.

Mark 5:21–24, 35–43

[18]While he was saying these things to them, suddenly a leader of the synagogue came in and knelt before him, saying, "My daughter has just died; but come and lay your hand on her, and she will live." [19]And Jesus got up and followed him, with his disciples. [20]Then suddenly a woman who had been suffering from hemorrhages for twelve years came up behind him and touched the fringe of his cloak, [21]for she said to herself, "If I only touch his cloak, I will be made well." [22]Jesus turned, and seeing her he said, "Take heart, daughter; your faith has made you well." And instantly the woman was made well. [23]When Jesus came to the leader's house and saw the flute players and the crowd making a commotion, [24]he said, "Go away; for the girl is not dead but sleeping." And they laughed at him. [25]But when the crowd had been put outside, he went in and took her by the hand, and the girl got up. [26]And the report of this spread throughout that district.

Matthew 9:18–26

[40]Now when Jesus returned, the crowd welcomed him, for they were all waiting for him. [41]Just then there came a man named Jairus, a leader of the synagogue. He fell at Jesus' feet and begged him to come to his house, [42]for he had an only daughter, about twelve years old, who was dying...

[49]While he was still speaking, someone came from the leader's house to say, "Your daughter is dead; do not trouble the teacher any longer." [50]When Jesus heard this, he replied, "Do not fear. Only believe, and she will be saved." [51]When he came to the house, he did not allow anyone to enter with him, except Peter, John, and James, and the child's father and mother. [52]They were all weeping and wailing for her; but he said, "Do not weep; for she is not dead but sleeping." [53]And they laughed at him, knowing that she was dead. [54]But he took her by the hand and called out, "Child, get up!" [55]Her spirit returned, and she got up at once. Then he directed them to give her something to eat. [56]Her parents were astounded; but he ordered them to tell no one what had happened.

Luke 8:40–42, 49–56

The Raising of Jairus' Daughter

In the late nineteenth century, Jairus' daughter's illness would almost certainly have been viewed by the psychiatric community as an instance of hysteria. Owing to its prejudicial and misogynist history as a diagnostic category, hysteria is no longer identified as a disorder in the *DSM-IV*.

While Mark S. Micale notes (1995) that the historical research on hysteria has been increasing even as hysteria itself has almost disappeared, the new diagnostic category, "the borderline personality," may be its successor, especially since the *DSM-IV* indicates that this disorder is diagnosed predominantly (about 75 percent) in women (652). Since Freud used the term "conversion hysteria," conversion disorder retains features of "hysteria," as does "histrionic personality disorder" (655). Both are found in the *DSM-IV*, with conversion disorder reported to be more common in rural populations, individuals at lower socioeconomic status, and individuals less knowledgeable about medical and psychological concepts, and histrionic personality disorder only marginally, if at all, more common among women. Histrionic personality disorder has particular relevance to the story of the raising of Jairus' daughter, as one of its features is that if histrionics "are not the center of attention, they may do something dramatic (e.g., make up stories, create a scene) to draw the focus of attention on themselves" (655). Also, "without being aware of it, they often act out a role (e.g., 'victim' or 'princess') in their relationships to others" (656).

In her psychoanalytic interpretation of "the hysterical woman" in late nineteenth-century America, Carroll Smith-Rosenberg (1981) emphasizes the influence of inflexible role socialization for women in a time of enormous social change. Those most affected were between fifteen and forty years of age, and it was more common among the urban middle and upper middle classes. The most characteristic and dramatic symptom was the hysterical "fit," which mimicked an epileptic seizure, usually brought on by

> a sudden or deeply felt emotion—fear, shock, or sudden death, marital disappointment—or by physical trauma. It began with pain and tension, most frequently in the "uterine area." The sufferer alternately sobbed and laughed violently, complained of palpitations of the heart, clawed her throat as if strangling, and, at times, abruptly lost the power of hearing and speech. A death-like trance might follow, lasting hours, even days. (210)

Elisabeth Bronfen points out (1992) that Alice James, the sister of William and Henry James, considered herself a hysteric. She described her nervous illness as developing from her courtship with death, which served as a defense against living in "this deadness called life." Commenting on Alice's invalidism, Bronfen notes that

> the particular twist Alice James gives to the disease of the hysteric is that she makes literal what the histrionic self-display figurally signifies.

For she not only chooses to turn her life into a theatrical scene, enacting her absence or lack of social place by taking on other roles. Rather what she simulates is the scene of perpetual dying. Repeatedly she speaks of death as her one dramatic moment, her one significant gesture, for which she must prepare and which she must contemplate in advance. Always adding self-irony to the imaginative staging of this somber moment, she suggests, "I might pose to myself before the footlights of my last obscure little scene, as a delectably pathetic figure." (389)

Her brother William telegraphed their brother Henry in response to Henry's cable confirming her death, cautioning him "to make sure the death was not only apparent, because her neurotic temperament and chronically reduced vitality are just the field for trance-tricks to play themselves upon" (391). Henry, however, describes his dead sister as appearing "most beautiful and noble—with all of the august expression you can imagine" (391–92).

Since Mark identifies Jairus' daughter as twelve years old (just having reached marriage age), her age would support the diagnosis of conversion hysteria. As Micale shows, "hysteria" has a very long history, dating back to an Egyptian medical papyrus from about 1900 B.C.E. The Egyptians recognized that there were "a battery of bizarre physical and mental symptoms" associated with it (20). They reasoned that it was caused by the restless movement of the uterus, a movement owing to prolonged barrenness after puberty. Ancient Greek therapies, based on the views of Hippocrates' school (fifth century B.C.E.) recommended immediate marriage in such cases. As Jairus' daughter was twelve years old (thus marriageable), she may have been diagnosed by her own contemporaries as afflicted with hysteria. Thus, the suggestion that we view the affliction as mainly psychological may have been shared by many contemporaries of Jesus. The statement attributed to him—"the girl is not dead but sleeping"—and its evocation of laughter may reveal contemporary controversy over deathlike trances: Is the sufferer actually or apparently dead? As with Alice James, it may be hard to tell. This also means that the distinction drawn by Jesus scholars between the "ancient" and "modern" mind when discussing attitudes toward healing may be vastly overdrawn. The fact that the three accounts do not identify the cause of "death" lends further credence to the likelihood of an awareness that the girl's affliction may have been "hysteria."

Jesus' success in healing her may have been due, in part, to the fact that the purpose of her "death" was to bring attention to herself. Such attention *was* achieved when her father succeeded in bringing a holy man, his entourage, and village onlookers into the house—a histrionic's dream come true. In addition, his own gestures may have contributed to the dramatic staging of this somber scene. Mark 5:41 indicates that he took her by the hand and said, "Little girl, get up!" thus engaging in fatherlike performance. What is also noteworthy is the likelihood that Jairus' daughter was about the same age as Mary when she conceived Jesus. Thus, his act of raising her from the "dead" may have evoked in him associations of a deeply emotional kind between Jairus' daughter and his own mother as a young girl. By saving Jairus' daughter, he was doing for her what he could not do for his own mother; her fate was already determined. In the following chapter, however, I will argue that his disruption in the temple was an action intended, in part, to be reparative in this very regard and was therefore integral to his role as exorcist-healer.

The Healing of the Hemorrhaging Woman

²⁴And a large crowd followed him and pressed in on him. ²⁵Now there was a woman who had been suffering from hemorrhages for twelve years. ²⁶She had endured much under many physicians, and had spent all that she had; and she was no better, but rather grew worse. ²⁷She had heard about Jesus, and came up behind him in the crowd and touched his cloak, ²⁸for she said, "If I but touch his clothes, I will be made well." ²⁹Immediately her hemorrhage stopped; and she felt in her body that she was healed of her disease. ³⁰Immediately aware that power had gone forth from him, Jesus turned about in the crowd and said, "Who touched my clothes?" ³¹And his disciples said to him, "You see the crowd pressing in on you; how can you say, 'Who touched me?'" ³²He looked all around to see who had done it. ³³But the woman, knowing what had happened to her, came in fear and trembling, fell down before him, and told him the whole truth. ³⁴He said to her, "Daughter, your faith has made you well; go in peace, and be healed of your disease."

Mark 5:24–34

²⁰Then suddenly a woman who had been suffering from hemorrhages for twelve years came up behind him and touched the fringe of his cloak, ²¹for she said to herself, "If I only touch his cloak, I will be made well." ²²Jesus turned, and seeing her he said, "Take heart, daughter; your faith has made you well." And instantly the woman was made well.

Matthew 9:20–22

⁴²As he went, the crowds pressed in on him. ⁴³Now there was a woman who had been suffering from hemorrhages for twelve years; and though she had spent all she had on physicians, no one could cure her. ⁴⁴She came up behind him and touched the fringe of his clothes, and immediately her hemorrhage stopped. ⁴⁵Then Jesus asked, "Who touched me?" When all denied it, Peter said, "Master, the crowds surround you and press in on you." ⁴⁶But Jesus said, "Someone touched me; for I noticed that power had gone out from me." ⁴⁷When the woman saw that she could not remain hidden, she came trembling; and falling down before him, she declared in the presence of all the people why she had touched him, and how she had been immediately healed. ⁴⁸He said to her, "Daughter, your faith has made you well; go in peace."

Luke 8:42b–48

Transferring Energy

My argument for a large, even predominant psychological factor in Jesus' healings may prompt the rejoinder that I have thereby minimized his healing power. I would note, however, that psychological afflictions are no less difficult to cure than purely physiological ones, and psychophysiological (or

psychosomatic) afflictions are among the most difficult to treat due to difficulty in determining "how much" is physiological and "how much" is psychological. I do not think it demeans our image of Jesus to view him as a sort of
community psychiatrist, dealing with problems that did not lend themselves
to remedies designed for purely physiological maladies, if indeed there were
such. As we gain only glimpses of his therapeutic methods in the stories handed
down to us, how Jesus healed these individuals, and whether or not those who
were healed experienced relapses are difficult questions to answer. This should
not, however, dissuade us from offering hypotheses for how he effected these
cures. To this end, I will conclude this discussion on Jesus as healer with a
hypothesis put forward by Erik Erikson, in a discussion of the healing of a
hemorrhaging woman.

In two separate places, Erikson discusses the healing of the woman with
the hemorrhage, which all three gospels insert within the story of the healing
of Jairus' daughter (Mk. 5:24–34; Mt. 9:20–22; Lk. 8:43–48). The first is in
Dimensions of a New Identity (1974), where he takes Thomas Jefferson to task
for eliminating the healing stories from his abridged version of the gospels: "I
cannot forgive him for omitting the story which we need dearly so as to remain oriented in the history of healing concepts which…change with any
new identity" (48). Calling this "the decisive therapeutic event in the Gospels," he notes:

> This story conveys themes which renew their urging presence in each
> age: There is the assumption of certain quantities lost and regained
> and with them a quantity of virtue has passed from him to her–and
> this as she touched him, and not (according to the age-old technique)
> as his hand touched her. He felt her touch even in the general press
> that surrounded him, and this solely because her faith thus magneti-
> cally attracted some of his strength before he quite knew it. There
> could be no doubt, then, that it was her faith in his mission that had
> made her whole. (49)

Erikson views this story as "an exalted illustration of that dynamic element"
that has always fascinated members of the healing professions, including Freud,
who "assumed the misplacement of quantities of love and hate to be intrinsic
to emotional disturbance, and transference essential for their cure" (49). He
concludes that historical transformations in the sense of identity bring with
them new approaches to sickness and madness, and that historically, these
have been characterized by a "greater internalization of the cause as well as
the cure of the sickness" (49).

The statement, "Your faith has made you well," however, suggests an
early recognition that "faith" itself is a "therapeutic agent of wholeness." This
is because it initiates the "transference" between patient and healer, enabling
the patient to draw upon the healer's own strength (which may, in turn, result
in his own sense of depletion). Thus, in his essay on the Galilean sayings of

Jesus (1981), published seven years later, Erikson returned to this healing story, and again suggested a parallel to Freud's concept of transference, noting that Jesus felt the woman's touch "as an acute loss of a powerful quantity of something vital." This "is comparable to and, indeed, is a parabolic representation of a certain interplay or mutual 'transfer' of energy (Freud called it libido, that is, love-energy) which is assumed to take place and must be understood—as 'transference'—in any therapeutic situation" (342). Jesus' awareness of the crucial role of "transference" in healing is confirmed by his acknowledgment of "the woman's aptitude for trust and her determination to reach him as an essential counterpart to his capacity to help her" (342). Erikson concludes that Norman Perrin, the biblical scholar on whom he mostly relies, while not prepared to argue for the total authenticity of these healing narratives, does claim that "the emphasis upon the faith of the patient, or his friends, in that tradition is authentic" (343).

To what, then, is Jesus' healing power to be attributed? Erikson believes it was his recognition that he could not heal without a true attitude of trust by those who were beneficiaries of the healing. I suspect that scholars (e.g., Meier) who take Crossan and Smith to task for viewing Jesus as a magician are, in effect, contending that the magical view of healing omits this element of trust. Smith and Crossan, however, seem to lay themselves open to this contention when they focus essentially on a sociological view of the magician (i.e., as operating outside established religious institutions) and fail to develop a corresponding psychological understanding of Jesus' magical efficacy. Erikson's introduction of Freud's views on transference offers such an understanding, especially in his view that a "mutual 'transfer' of energy" occurs in Jesus' healings. While there are other means of mutual transfer of energy—such as touch and gaze—words have a special efficacy because, to cite Freud again, "Words and magic were in the beginning one and the same thing, and even today words retain much of their magical power. By words one of us can give to another the greatest happiness or bring about utter despair...Words call forth emotions and are universally the means by which we influence our fellow-creatures" (1920/1955, 21–22). Where Jesus differed from the magicians of the Greek magical papyri (Meier, 1994, 550) is that he used no special, artificially constructed words, but instead employed words that were well known to the afflicted, but had not been addressed to them. Foremost among these magical words was the simple word "Abba," which was very familiar but long forgotten. Abba was the father—the phylogenetic or "prehistorical" father—whose presence the son had felt long before his "real" father came into clear focus. This secondary father proved, inevitably, to be a man who could not be in all respects the father his son needed him to be. His words did not always issue in deeds, but instead suffered a thousand intervening qualifications. In contrast, Abba's words and deeds are thoroughly consistent—I Am Who I Say I Am—and he is therefore the very personification of magic, and altogether worthy of trust.

8

Utopian-Melancholic Personality: The Temple Disturbance

> *"Jesus said, 'Whoever does not hate his father and his mother as I do cannot become a disciple to Me. And whoever does not love his father and his mother as I do cannot become a disciple to Me. For my mother gave me falsehood, but my true mother gave me life.'"*
>
> GOSPEL OF THOMAS 101

In *Young Man Luther*, Erik H. Erikson suggests that the biographer's plight is akin to that of the viewer of a large portrait. The biographer who sets out to "describe the whole man" has a limited range of choices. One can step so far back that the subject's contours appear complete but hazy, or one can step closer and closer, gradually concentrating on a few aspects of the life, seeing one part as revealing of the whole. If neither approach works, there is always polemics (1958, 36).

In the two preceding chapters, our perspective has been relatively close up. I have focused on Jesus' early years and on his public role as exorcist-healer. In this chapter, I will take a few steps back, positioning myself at roughly the same distance that portrait artists establish between themselves and their live subjects. This position, some eight to fifteen feet removed, enables the portraitist to generalize from the subject's specific features and capture his "personal identity" (Brilliant, 1991, 9). Thus, the present chapter is an attempt to "describe the whole man." I am mindful, however, of Kathleen Nicholson's observation that "if unstable meanings surface in the portraits it is because the contradictions are within the cultural matrix" (1997, 58). Given two millennia of viewing Jesus as the most perfect human being who ever lived, one is tempted to portray him as having reconciled, in both his internal dynamics and social role, the contradictions not only of his own culture but of human experience itself. This temptation was a major impulse toward the transformation of the historical Jesus into the Christ of Christianity. Such transformation is not the focus of this book. Rather, my concern is to portray Jesus as a man who was on the road toward solving some of these contradictions—within himself and in his responses to the world around him—when his life was tragically ended. Considering Crossan's observation that his life ended at roughly the same age that many of his Jewish male cohort's lives ended, I assume that their journeys were also—if not always as violently—cut short in this regard. This does not mean, however, that those blessed with longer lives necessarily achieve such solutions. It only means that they are given more time to do so.

My emphasis here is Jesus as a "utopian-melancholic personality." While neither term is ordinarily applied to him, I consider this a point in their favor. Every portraitist should attempt to see in the subject something essential that others have overlooked or have failed to register as significant. This view of Jesus also bridges the usual gap in Jesus studies between the "man" and his "mission," or the "private" and the "public" Jesus. As Erikson makes clear, personal identity has two foci, a subjective sense of "I-ness" and a sense that one is connected to something that transcends oneself. For the former, he cites William James's comment in a letter to his wife: "A man's character is discernible in the mental or moral attitude in which, when it came upon him, he felt himself most deeply and intensely active and alive. At such moments there is a voice inside which speaks and says, '*This* is the real me!'" (1968, 19). For the latter, he cites this passage from Freud's address to the Society of B'nai B'rith in Vienna in 1926:

> What bound me to Jewry was (I am ashamed to admit) neither faith nor national pride, for I have always been an unbeliever and was brought up without any religion though not without a respect for what are called the "ethical" standards of human civilization...But plenty of other things remained over to make the attraction of Jewry and Jews irresistible—many obscure emotional forces, which were all the more powerful the less they could be expressed in words, as well as a clear consciousness of inner identity, the safe privacy of a common mental construction. And beyond this was a perception that it was to my Jewish nature alone that I owed two characteristics that had become indispensable to me in the difficult course of my life. Because I was a Jew I found myself free from many prejudices which restricted others in the use of their intellect; and as a Jew I was prepared to join the Opposition, and to do without agreement with the "compact majority." (Erikson, 1968, 20–21)

Erikson notes that these two fundamental statements occurred in special communications, not theoretical works: "A letter to his wife from a man who married late, an address to his 'brothers' by an original observer long isolated in his profession. But in all their poetic spontaneity they are the products of trained minds and therefore exemplify the main dimensions of a positive sense of identity" (21). In what follows, I will be proposing that these two dimensions of Jesus' identity are captured, more or less, in the phrase "utopian-melancholic personality." I will first take up the "utopian" aspect.

Jesus as Utopianist

In chapters 1 and 2, we saw that contemporary Jesus scholars disagree about the traditional eschatological view of Jesus. In Sanders' view, Jesus announced an imminent divine destruction of the temple. This suggests that he believed God was going to replace the old temple with a new one, thus ushering in a new age, a new kingdom either on earth or in heaven. In Crossan's view, Jesus spoke of the kingdom of God not as an apocalyptic event in the imminent future, but as an ethical, nonviolent way of life. For him, Jesus' vision of "shared egalitarianism" had central importance. Therefore, Jesus was a social and political reformer whose open sharing of healing and food—open commensality—was a strategy for building or rebuilding peasant community on radically different principles than those of honor and shame, patronage and clientage.

I will invoke here the concept of utopia in order to offer a different view of how Jesus thought about these matters. While I agree with Sanders that Jesus had apocalyptic thoughts and with Crossan that he had certain egalitarian views, the question is whether either of these—or both together—were the central factors in his understanding of his vocation or mission in life. To prefigure my argument, I believe that these two views—apocalypticist and sociopolitical reformer—present Jesus as acting more rationally (Sanders) and strategically (Crossan) than he was actually disposed to act. While it may be too extreme to say, with Burton Mack, that "Jesus had no sense of mission or purpose; in an important sense, he was aimless" (Borg, 1994a, 23), my argument here will suggest that Mack is closer to the truth than either Sanders or Crossan, and those who share their respective views. One does not need, however, to turn to Cynicism to find a basis for this view of Jesus. A more natural locus for it exists in Jewish peasant life.

In presenting Jesus as having a utopian life-orientation, I also take exception to Bryan Wilson's characterization of utopians in his classification of religious movements (cited by Crossan, 1991). Wilson proposes "a seven-fold typology based on the diverse ways in which people *respond to the world* when salvation from evil is no longer found adequately within the standard religious resources of their tradition" (Crossan, 72). These include the conversionist, manipulationist, thaumaturgist, revolutionist, introversionist, reformist, and utopian types. According to Wilson, if reformists believe that "God calls us to amend" the world, utopians believe that "God calls us to reconstruct" the world: "This presumes 'some divinely given principles' of reconstruction, is much more radical than the reformist alternative, but, unlike the revolutionist option, insists much more on the role human beings must take in the process" (73). Contemporary utopian theorists, however, raise serious questions about the accuracy of this description of the utopian impulse. It not only fails to take account of the diversity within utopianism, but also places too great emphasis on world reconstruction and the role of human agency in such reconstruction. In addition, it takes insufficient account of the role of psychological factors in utopianism.

James Scott's views on utopia (quoted in Crossan, 1991) also need certain corrections. Writing about peasant cultures, he notes: "The popular religion and culture of peasants in a complex society are not only a syncretized, domesticated, and localized variant of larger systems of thought and doctrine. They contain almost inevitably the seeds of an alternative symbolic universe– a universe which in turn makes the social world in which peasants live less than completely inevitable" (263). He suggests that "this symbolic opposition represents the closest thing to class consciousness in preindustrial agrarian societies," as "those who find themselves at the bottom of the social heap develop cultural forms which promise them dignity, respect, and economic comfort which they lack in the world as it is" (263). Like Wilson, however, Scott seems to believe that these alternative symbolic constructions become the basis for actual social reform. Thus, this reflexive symbolism

> nearly always implies a society of brotherhood in which there will be no rich and poor, in which no distinctions of rank and status (save those between believers and non-believers) will exist. Where religious institutions are experienced as justifying inequities, the abolition of rank and status may well include the elimination of religious hierarchy in favor of communities of equal believers. Property is typically, though not always, to be held in common and shared. All unjust claims to taxes, rents, and tribute are to be nullified. The envisioned utopia may also include a self-yielding and abundant nature as well as a radically transformed human nature in which greed, envy, and hatred will disappear. While the earthly utopia is thus an anticipation of the future, it often harks back to a mythic Eden from which mankind has fallen away. (264)

To the extent that Scott views peasant visions of an alternative reality as anticipations of a realizable future, he misses, in my view, the deep fatalism that inspires peasant-style utopian thinking. As Krishan Kumar (1991) notes, there are many varieties of the ideal society or the ideal condition of humanity. Identification of these enables us to see what is distinctive about peasant-style utopianism. Four types of ideal human conditions, or societies, may be identified, including (1) the golden age, arcadia, or paradise; (2) the land of Cockaygne; (3) the millennium; and (4) the ideal city. Kumar emphasizes the class differences involved in the first two. The golden age and its various derivatives are considered the original state of humanity and are the visions of the literate elite (poets and priests), with their devotion to simplicity and spirituality. The mythical Eden is such a vision. In contrast, the medieval land of Cockaygne is the "poor man's heaven" and is a kind of extravagance, exuberance, and excess: "Everything is free and available for the asking. Cooked larks fly straight into one's mouth; the rivers run with wine; the more one sleeps, the more one earns; sexual promiscuity is the norm; there is a fountain of youth that keeps everyone young and active" (5). This is "a popular fantasy of pure hedonism: a cockney paradise" (6). Therefore, it is a peasant-class utopia, as reflected in Amos 7:13: "The mountains shall drip sweet wine, and all the hills shall flow with it."

The third form, the millennium, connects with the golden age, linking the primitive paradise and the promised land: "Both the beliefs and the movements associated with them oscillate constantly between the two poles, lending to millenarianism equally the characteristics of extreme conservativism and extreme radicalism" (6–7). It is also, however, "in its forward-looking character that the millennium most clearly distinguishes itself from the Golden Age and Paradise...The millennium faces the future more than it harks back to the past...Of ideal society concepts, it is the millennium which most forcibly introduces the elements of time, process and history" (7). In Western thought, Christian millenarianism continues Jewish messianism. The fourth type, the ideal city, is the contribution of the ancient Near East (e.g., Egypt) and Hellenism. This is the philosophers' contribution to ideas of the ideal society. If poets and priests pictured the golden age, peasants yearned for the land of extravagance and excess, and devotees anticipated the millennium, then philosophers "invented the ideal city as the early embodiment of the cosmic order which they deduced from first principles. The ideal city was the microcosmic reflection of the divinely regulated macrocosmic order" (12).

To be sure, these four types have not remained entirely distinct, but have drawn upon one another, and the "religious connotations of many of these terms also point to their interconnection with overarching religious cosmologies" (17). While utopia is more than an amalgam of these conceptions, each makes an "elemental" contribution to it. Cockaygne contributes the element of *desire,* paradise adds that of *harmony,* the millennium introduces *hope,* and the ideal city provides the element of *design.* These four elements go into the making of utopia, but "utopia does not simply recombine these elements. It has its own inventiveness. Once established, it provides a map of quite different possibilities for speculating on the human condition" (19).

In Kumar's view, utopia distinguishes itself from other forms of the ideal society and from other forms of social and political theory by being "in the first place a piece of fiction." When we encounter utopia, "the first thing we encounter in most cases is a story" (20). Its basic narrative pattern is one where a visitor from another place or time encounters a superior civilization. This device creates room for comic misunderstanding, thwarted intrigue, and romance. It also involves satire, "the holding up of an unflattering mirror to one's own society" (26). This satirical strand led to the formulation of a separate subgenre, the dystopia or antiutopia, where the narrator depicts a hellish society whose similarity to the author's own is all too apparent.

In contrast to abstract schemes of conventional social and political theory, through which "we are *told* that the good society will follow from the application of the relevant general principles," in utopia "we are *shown* the good society in operation, supposedly as a result of certain general principles of social organization" (31). Because Christianity is so closely identified with millenarianism, this is a major reason why utopia has developed in the West and nowhere else. On the other hand, the millennium is not utopia because "its ideal order is predetermined. It is brought in by divine intervention. Human agency remains questionably relevant" (36). In contrast to millenarianism, utopia—even for devoutly Christian thinkers—is "an order belonging unambiguously to this world, to be achieved with its materials and by the free agency of its human inhabitants. To Christian thinkers utopia might not be the summit and end of man's destiny; that must be for another world. But so far as this world was concerned it represented the best order that could be achieved by unaided human purpose and design" (36). Thus, Christian formulations of utopia tend to integrate the millennium and the ideal city, and to elevate the elements of hope and design. No doubt this is the model of utopia that informs Wilson's description of utopianists in his typology of religious movements and is also implied in Scott's depiction of the earthly utopia despite the fact that he is discussing peasant classes. This, however, is only one form of utopia and is quite dissimilar to the utopia envisioned by peasant classes (as reflected, for example, in the medieval vision of the land of Cockaygne).

Finally, Kumar argues that the element of *desire*—which he identifies with the land of Cockaygne—is utopia's primary contribution to visions of an ideal society or ideal condition of humanity: "Utopia opposes as well as proposes. Its pictures of a fulfilled and happy humanity are premised on the rejection of some social impulses and the elevation of others. It is through this wilful suppression, by not showing certain things from our own world, that it negates their persistence into the future. Things need not continue as they are. Out of this defiance, set in a context that proposes an alternative, comes the desire for change" (107). Because *desire* is fundamental to utopianism, the peasant classes provide the fundamental stimulus for utopian visions. This is the social class among whom utopian visions originate.

Ruth Levitas (1990) discusses the two elements of hope and desire in utopian thinking and, like Kumar, concludes that desire is the more fundamental. She bases this conclusion on the fact that the idea of utopia as a "possible world" is too limiting, for

> an imagined world may carry out any of the functions of compensation, criticism or change without being possible…To function as criticism or compensation, utopia does not even need to be believed to be possible. Thus while the questions of whether alternative worlds are theoretically or practically possible, and whether they are believed to be so by those who produce, peruse or pursue them, are important questions to ask, again, they cannot be definitional ones.(190)

Thus, the problem with restricting utopia to the "possible world" is "that it conflates the categories of hope and desire, and limits utopia to the question 'what may I hope?' and refuses the question 'what may I dream?' It implies also that the function of utopia is necessarily that of change" (190).

Examination of "the land of Cockaygne" shows that the question of possibility seems quite beside the point:

> There are rivers of oil, milk, honey and wine, as well as healing springs and springs of wine. The garlic-dressed geese that fly roasted on the spit and the cinnamon-flavored larks flying into the mouth do indeed, in [David] Riesman's terms, "violate what we know of nature." So too does the much later song, "The Big Rock Candy Mountains," with its little streams of alcohol, its lakes of stew and whiskey, where "The jails are made of tin, And you can bust right out again, As soon as they put you in." Not only are these fantasies both theoretically and practically impossible–in other words, they are not possible worlds–but we have every reason to suppose that audiences knew this to be the case. Medieval peasants did not believe that larks could fly when cooked. American hobos did not believe in alcoholic lakes or totally ineffective jails. Yet both these examples are expressions of desire–desire for the effortless gratification of need and the absence of restrictive sanctions; they are not expressions of hope. (190)

Also, "if utopia is hoped for, then it must indeed be set in the future." Instead, utopia "is really the expression of desire." It may also include criticism of existing conditions, but this too is not absolutely necessary (190). Thus, Levitas notes that early utopias–including Sir Thomas More's–were more commonly located elsewhere in space than in some future time. The problem was not that they were temporally distant, but hard to get to. Reflecting this spatial, not temporal priority, Oscar Wilde quipped, "A map of the world that does not include Utopia is not worth glancing at" (quoted in Kumar, 95). Levitas concludes that

> utopia expresses and explores what is desired; under certain conditions it also contains the hope that these desires may be met in reality, rather than merely in fantasy. The essential element in utopia, however, is not hope, but desire–the desire for a better way of being. It involves the imagining of a state of being in which the problems which actually confront us are removed or resolved, often, but not necessarily, through the imagining of a state of the world in which the scarcity gap is closed or the "collective problem" solved. (191)

This definition goes beyond that of an alternative world, possible or otherwise, for these two reasons: "First, the pursuit of a better way of being does not always involve the alteration of external conditions, but may mean the pursuance of spiritual or psychological states" (191–92). These *could* mean a withdrawal of utopia from the social to the personal or private. Second, the definition is intended to be analytic rather than descriptive and thus to include the utopian aspects of a wide range of cultural forms and behaviors. In other words, "the subject-matter is not defined in terms of form, but neither is utopia limited to a specific function" (192). Thus, the fact that the Cockaygne myth is an expression of desire and not a view of a possible future liberates its content from the constraint of plausibility and its function from that of stimulus to social change. Instead, its functions are to provide a compensatory vision and, secondarily, to criticize the powers that be (which could well include the Creator himself) for the existing world.

A third theorist of utopia who has relevance for peasant-style utopianism is E. M. Cioran (1987). In "Mechanisms of Utopia," he notes that whenever he happens to be in a city of any size, he marvels that riots do not break out every day: "How can so many human beings coexist in a space so confined without destroying each other, without hurting each other *to death*? As a matter of fact, they do hate each other, but they are not equal to their hatred. And it is this mediocrity, this impotence, that saves society, that assures its continuance, its stability" (80). Occasionally, of course, riots *do* break out, but when they do, "afterward men go on looking each other in the face as if nothing had happened, cohabiting without too obviously tearing each other to shreds. Order is restored, a ferocious calm as dreadful, ultimately, as the frenzy that had interrupted it" (80).

While he marvels that there are not more such riots, Cioran confesses to even greater wonderment that some individuals have ventured to conceive a different society: "What can be the cause of so much naivete, or of so much inanity?" To find out, he decided to spend several months steeping himself in utopian literature. From this, he arrived at several conclusions. One is that utopian systems are "dear to the disinherited" and that "poverty is in fact the utopianists' great auxiliary, it is the matter he works in, the substance on which he feeds his thoughts, the providence of his obsessions. Without poverty he would be empty; but poverty occupies him, allures or embarrasses him, depending on whether he is poor or rich" (81–82). Thus, if you question why another individual would engage in endless meditation, even obsessional thinking about another earth, this is because "you have not tasted utter indigence. Do so and you will see that the more destitute you are, the more time and energy you will spend in reforming everything, in thinking—in other words, in vain" (82). By "reforming everything," Cioran means

> not only institutions, human creations; those of course you will condemn straight off and without appeal; but objects, all objects, however insignificant. Unable to accept them as they are, you will want to impose your laws and your whims upon them, to function at their expense as legislator or as tyrant; you will even want to intervene in the life of the elements in order to modify their physiognomy, their structure. Air annoys you: let it be transformed! And stone as well. And the same for the vegetal world, the same for man. Down past the foundations of being, down to the strata of chaos, descend, install

yourself there! When you haven't a penny in your pocket, you strive, you dream, how extravagantly you labor to possess All, and as long as the frenzy lasts, you do possess that All, you equal God, though no one realizes it, not even God, not even you. The delirium of the poor is the generator of events, the source of history: a throng of hysterics who want another world, here and now. It is they who inspire utopias, it is for them that utopias are written. But *utopia*, let us remember, means *nowhere*. (82)

Note Cioran's suggestion here that true utopian thinkers are hysterics, and his earlier comment that they are given to obsessional thinking. Obviously, he does not view the true utopianist as a "rationalist" in his orientation to life, nor does he think that the utopianist is much disposed to "listen to reason."

Cioran notes that conceiving a true *utopia,* sketching with conviction the structure of an ideal society, requires "a certain dose of ingenuousness, even of stupidity, which, being too evident, ultimately exasperates the reader" (83). Consequently, the only readable utopias are the false ones, ones written in a spirit of entertainment or misanthropy, like *Gulliver's Travels,* which is a utopia without hope: "By his sarcasms, Swift undeceived a genre to the point of destroying it" (83). Also, if utopia is nowhere, it is as likely to be "internal" as "external." In fact, "When [Jesus] promised that the 'kingdom of God' was neither 'here' nor 'there,' but within us, he doomed in advance the utopian constructions for which any 'kingdom' is necessarily *exterior,* with no relation to our inmost self or our individual salvation" (91). And yet, Christianity has sought to exteriorize it, locating the kingdom in the unfolding of history: "Unable to find 'the kingdom of God' within themselves, or rather too cunning to want to seek it there, Christians placed it in the course of events—in becoming: they perverted a teaching in order to ensure its success" (91). Jesus, however, sustained the ambiguity himself. On the one hand, "answering the insinuations of the Pharisees, he recommended an interior kingdom, remote from time; and on the other he signified to his disciples that, salvation being imminent, they and the 'present generation' would witness the consummation of all things. Having understood that human beings accept martyrdom for a chimera but not for a truth, he came to terms with their weakness. Had he acted otherwise, he would have compromised his work" (91–92).

It should be noted that Cioran has taken for granted a much-debated thesis, that is, whether the historical Jesus did or did not envision the imminent consummation of all things. As noted earlier, E. P. Sanders' affirmation of this view has been challenged by other scholars. The viewpoint I am arguing for here is that Jesus was not, as Cioran claims, the source of this "ambiguity"—for he belonged to the peasant class—but that the "externalization" of the kingdom of God was the work of early Christians, who envisioned a future kingdom, thus adding the element of hope to a utopia originally based on desire only.

While the question of the meaning of the "kingdom of God" sayings in the gospels is far too complex for us to explore here, I suggest that sayings such as Luke 17:20–21, "The kingdom of God is not coming with things that can be observed; nor will they say, 'Look, here it is!' or 'There it is!' for, in fact, the kingdom of God is among you"–indicates a peasant-style utopian image precisely because Jesus does not speak of its location in space or realization in time. Neither, however, does he suggest that it is more "internal" ("within you") than "external" (in the "social world"). Its imaginary power is in the fact that it is "nowhere," that is, not among any "possible worlds." Utopia means nowhere (*outopia*) and also somewhere good (*eutopia*), thus playing on a paradox (Kumar, 1991, 1). Had he represented it as an already present or realizable future, peasant classes would not have found it believable. As Jesus portrayed it, the kingdom *was* a chimera, and therein lay its inspirational (imaginative) power. It was never intended to be "true" or "realizable." In this sense, the "already/not yet" formulation that has been so attractive to mainstream biblical scholarship on the kingdom of God misses the point, as it futurizes a utopian image based on pure–unrealizable–desire. As Kumar points out, however, what distinguishes utopia from social and political theories of the ideal society or the human condition is that it tells a story. Unlike utopias that offer a detailed account of an ideal society, leading to the exasperation of the reader who finds the author's inanity almost beyond belief, a parable about the kingdom has brevity, allusiveness, and imprecision. Therefore, it is not as likely to task the listener's patience, insult one's native intelligence, or provoke a sarcastic response. Thus, a parable works more like the fanciful story of the land of Cockaygne or the unbelievable lyrics of "The Big Rock Candy Mountains." It changes nothing, but it offers its own compensations and invites those who are so disposed to use it to criticize the status quo. I will consider Jesus' parables later.

To conclude this discussion of utopia theorists, I wish to return to my earlier comments regarding Sanders' view of Jesus' anticipation of an apocalyptic event that would usher in a new kingdom on earth or in heaven, and Crossan's view of Jesus as a social and political reformer who sought to create a new social order based on radically egalitarian principles. While their views of Jesus' eschatological vision are at virtually opposite poles, they agree on one thing: That Jesus was either mistaken, failed, or both. For Sanders, his expectation that the end was imminent was mistaken. For Crossan, the Jesus movement became anything but the ideal society that he envisioned: "As one ponders that progress from open commensality with Jesus to episcopal banquet with Constantine, is it unfair to regret a progress that happened so fast and moved so swiftly, that was accepted so readily and criticized so lightly?" (1994, 201).

If we view Jesus as fundamentally a peasant-style utopianist, however, we need not conclude that he was mistaken or failed. The utopianist who has not wedded the element of desire with that of hope–that is, linked the land of

Cockaygne with millennial expectations–does not really believe that things will change. Such a utopianist is into something far more elemental than a new social order, whether this is conceived as one involving direct divine intervention or one envisioning a new society based on social egalitarianism. As Cioran suggests, the pure utopianist concentrates on such elementals as air and stone. With Amos, he imagines the mountains literally flowing with wine. Or, with Cockaygne adherents, he envisions birds flying straight into the hungry mouth, thus "violating what we know of nature." Against these impossible visions, social egalitarianism, and even a millennial reign of God, are rather tame stuff. They are the work of poets, priests, philosophers, and social activists, and are rather far removed from the dreams–perhaps aided by alcohol or intoxicating herbs–of penurious peasants. For them, such dreams occurred in the "no-where" between thwarted desire and enervating boredom. Noting that the idea of utopia goes back to "the oldest cultural stratum of Mesopotamia" (Cioran, 35), Frank E. and Fritzie P. Manuel conclude their massive history of utopian thought in the Western world with this observation: "Experimenters tell us that as we sleep the eyeballs persist in going through their rapid movements four or five times a night, bearing witness to dreamwork. Western civilization may not be able to survive long without utopian fantasies any more than individuals can exist without dreaming" (1979, 814).

The Psychological Origins of Desire

For all their clarifications of what utopianism does and does not mean, an issue that receives inadequate attention by the theorists thus far cited concerns the psychological origins of desire. It might, for example, be argued that the desire behind utopia has its psychological basis in envy. As we have seen, Freud attributes the evil eye theory to the belief of those better off that others envy their possessions and are planning to take them away by dishonest or surreptitious means. Psychoanalyst Melanie Klein (1956/1986) has argued persuasively for the origins of envy in early infancy, thus giving weight to its role in the evocation of fundamental desire. That the utopian desire centers on the unattainable, however, suggests that its psychological roots are even more fundamental than an expression of envy. Envy of the "haves" by the "have-nots" may play some role in utopianism, but it is more of a stimulus or catalyst for the reformist type. True utopianists have desires that, psychologically speaking, are deeper and more pervasive.

Ernst Bloch's views on utopia enable us to identify what these deeper psychological roots of utopian desire may be. In a conversation with Theodor W. Adorno on "the contradictions of utopian longing," Bloch (1988) suggested that the decisive incentive toward "utopia" is captured in Berthold Brecht's short sentence, "Something's missing." This something is perhaps best portrayed in a "picture," such as the picture "found in the old peasant saying, there is no dance before the meal. People must first fill their stomachs, then they can dance" (15). Thus, Bloch uses a peasant saying about eating to illustrate the experience of "something's missing" and the desire, therefore, to address this sense of lack. The image of food, however, is part of a larger theme in Bloch's utopian theory, that of the desire to be at home in the world. As he puts it, the utopianist imagines something coming "into being in the world that shines into everyone's childhood and where no one has yet been–home" (quoted in Relf, 1993, 128). In her discussion of Bloch, Levitas quotes this passage, rendering the word "home" as "homeland" (95). Either way, the desire is not for the home that one once had but has since lost, but for the home for which one has always longed, always feeling its absence in this world. According to Levitas, Bloch envisions "the overcoming of [the] antagonism between humanity and the world," so that one may have a sense of "feeling at home in the world" and no longer feeling "humiliated, enslaved, forsaken, scorned, estranged, annihilated, and deprived of identity" (95). It is the polar opposite of life as a daily crucifixion (see Crossan, 1994, 124–27).

Erik Erikson helps us to see the relevance of this desire to Jesus and to his own form of utopianism. The theme of "home," and its association with the "maternal matrix," occurs in three places in Erikson's essay (1981) on the Galilean sayings of Jesus. First, in explaining his focus on only the Galilean aspect of Jesus' life, forgoing the events in Jerusalem, he notes Mark's report (14:28) "that Jesus and the disciples, right after the last supper, went out to the Mount of Olives, where he added to all his sad predictions of the disciples' impending betrayal a most touchingly intimate remark: 'But after I am raised up I will go before you into Galilee.'" Erikson comments: "His reported reference to the resurrection may not be authentic; but this statement suggests on his part or on that of the witnesses what may well have been a feeling shared with them by the earthly Jesus, namely, that Galilee was home" (1981, 328).

Second, in discussing the role of family life in the survival of Judaism, he quotes Joseph Klausner's *Jesus of Nazareth,* which speaks of "a unifying tendency which broke down the dividing wall between religion and daily life, making daily life an essential part of religion and religion an essential part of daily life. That which was holy was not thereby profaned but was brought down to earth, while the secular life was transformed into the sacredness of a religious duty." Erikson adds:

> But not even Klausner, at this point, mentions a "phenomenon" in Jewish daily life which both confirmed and compensated for the creedal emphasis on a dominating masculinity of Being. How the *Jewish mother,* in daily and weekly life, in Palestine and throughout the Diaspora, continued to play the role of a most down-to-earth goddess of the hearth–that would call for an intimate cultural history which is grounded in some special chapters of the Old Testament and yet also represents one of the most consistent trends in Jewish history. (340)

Third, he comments on the *missing mother* in the parable of the prodigal son: "And the Abba was steadfast in loving both these sons–so different in familial status and in personality. Almost like a mother, some readers may be tempted to say, and, indeed, as one reviews this parable's theme of the healing of the generational process, one cannot help asking: was there, in this earthly vision of the comparison, no mother, either dead or alive? And if alive, was she not called to say hello, too?" (355). He seems tempted to conclude that this "missing mother" theme (356) reveals something about Jesus himself–his own son-mother relationship–but exercises restraint, noting that "a parable is not a case history or even history." Also, if there is an implied comparison in the story of the father with God Himself, "it must be remembered that in all the masculinity dictated by the patriarchal 'system' and the rules of language, the dominating quality of the deity was that of a pervasive spirit, out of bounds for any personal characterization: 'I am that I am'" (355–56). In other words, the parable's focus on father and not mother must be understood within the context of a religious tradition that did not assign ultimate significance to any personal characterization of God, masculine *or* feminine. Desire itself, however, is most deeply expressed in longing for the "missing mother."

The Problem of Boredom

As I *am* engaged in a kind of "case history" of Jesus, the issue of being "at home in the world," and the related themes of "the goddess of the hearth" and the "missing mother," invite further exploration. As I will indicate, they are central not only to Jesus' utopian desires but also to his melancholia. To begin to establish the connection between peasant-style utopian desire and melancholia, however, I wish to comment briefly on the problem of boredom in peasant society. Crossan (1991) cites an eloquent description of peasant life as "vegetating in the teeth of time" (125). In *Boredom* (1995), Patricia Meyer Spacks notes that "Boredom provides a provocative literary subject partly because the internal experience of paralyzing monotony often impels its victims to dramatic action in an attempt to evade what they feel. Strange that boredom, in itself so staid and solid, should have such power to set in motion, Kierkegaard remarks. Calling boredom's influence magical, he points out that it is 'not the influence of attraction, but of repudiation'" (166). In this view, boredom "becomes the opposite of desire, but like desire a principle of action...Boredom provides a negative stimulus for action, thus an impetus for narrative" (166). A person who has "limited opportunities for action" may also make others his or her "surrogates for excitement" (168). The various personages in one's village may become the "nucleus for a nonexistent plot," and this "figment of her imagination" may represent "the most she can hope for, a vision of action and of possibility that does not materialize" (168). Thus, boredom may be a catalyst for the creation of an illusory world where interesting things happen. It may even give rise to dramatic actions of one's own, perhaps in a desperate attempt to evade what one feels.

In reviewing literature on boredom, Spacks cites psychoanalyst Otto Fenichel's 1934 essay "The Psychology of Boredom." He defines boredom as "an unpleasurable experience of a lack of impulse" and cites its connection with depression, loneliness, and restlessness. He emphasizes that the bored person does not experience the "lack of impulse" as a pleasurable condition. This is because boredom also includes a "need for intense mental activity." In the bored person, this need cannot find gratification by generating its own impulse, but instead seeks "incitements" from the outside world. Boredom is also a state of internal tension in which instinctual aims are repressed. One turns to the external world for help in the struggle against the tension that results from such repression. Fenichel distinguishes between "pathological" and "normal" boredom. Common to both states is that "something expected does not occur." Their differences are that in pathological boredom this expected event fails to occur because one "represses his instinctual action out of anxiety," whereas in normal boredom it fails to occur because the external world does not give what "we have a right to expect" (Spacks, 5). Thus, in pathological boredom, the inadequacy lies within, while in normal boredom, the inadequacies are external.

What happens to an individual who does not experience sufficient "incitements" from the external world? For Fenichel, depression, loneliness, and restlessness are among the consequences of such inadequate stimulation. The depression associated with boredom is especially noteworthy in connection with utopianism, because, as Seymour Fisher and Rhoda L. Fisher (1993) note, depressed persons are *less* likely than nondepressed persons to have and maintain illusions about themselves and their lives. They cite S. E. Taylor's conclusion, from his study of persons experiencing a traumatic threat, that "successful adjustment depends, in a large part, on the ability to sustain and modify illusions that buffer not only against present threats but also against possible future setbacks" (9). Taylor adds: "As the literature on depression and the self make clear, normal cognitive processing and behavior may depend on a substantial degree of illusion, whereas the ability to see things clearly can be associated with depression and inactivity. Thus, far from impeding adjustment, illusion may be essential for adequate coping" (10). To avoid depression and its various side effects, utopian illusions may be essential for those who experience the external world as inadequately stimulating. Such illusions may counter pathological boredom resulting from repression of desires. Additionally, they may reduce the anxiety resulting from perceived dangers involved in acting on these desires.

In short, when the external world does not give what "we have a right to expect" (normal boredom) one is also vulnerable to pathological boredom, the boredom that results from the repression of instinctual aims due to the fact that they create anxieties. Conversely, one who is already prone to pathological boredom owing to an inability to act on desires—which would otherwise reduce or eliminate his boredom—because they are anxiety provoking may be unable to respond to the external pleasures that *do* present themselves. The susceptibility of monastics to *acedie* (a rough equivalent to the English word "boredom") suggests that the absence of stimulants from the external world may exacerbate the boredom already present due to the repression of sexual and aggressive desires. The lassitude and locomotor restlessness common to *acedie* may therefore have both internal and external causes, the one exacerbating the other. Utopian illusions may provide compensations for the absence of that which "we have a right to expect," thus addressing both forms of boredom simultaneously. Therefore, the utopian visions' value is not their ability to stimulate persons to action, inspiring social reformist initiatives. Rather, they dissuade persons from acting on the basis of their boredom, which, as Spacks points out, is "a negative stimulus for action." Thus, utopian visions may deter individuals from acting in self-destructive ways. More importantly, however, utopian visions allow for the *expression* of desires that have been repressed, but in a manner that would only be dangerous if one actually believed they were realizable. If a utopian community were formed on the basis of the myth of Cockaygne, it would most likely be a worse hell than existing peasant life. Utopian experiments typically founder on how to handle matters of aggression and sexuality within the community. The virtue of Jesus' "kingdom of God" is that it expresses real desires, yet has no location and occurs without social reformist activities and blueprints. As Luke 17:20–21 says, it is neither "here" nor "there." Conversely, it encourages the pathologically bored to look for evidence of the desired in the external world, evidence that one's anxiety has prevented one from recognizing.

The Melancholic Condition

The perception of a relationship between melancholia and the utopian imagination is one of very long standing. It occurs, for example, in Robert Burton's *The Anatomy of Melancholy* (1979), the first edition of which was published in 1621, nearly a century after Sir Thomas More's *Utopia*. Burton introduces himself in the guise of Democritus, Jr., heir of the Greek philosopher who had searched for the cause of melancholy by cutting up several beasts. In his opening remarks to the reader, Democritus, Jr., contends that the disease of melancholy is especially apparent in societies where there are "many discontents, common grievances, complaints, poverty, barbarism, begging," and so on. Such a society "must needs be discontent, melancholy, hath a sick body, and had need to be reformed" (23). His own country, England, is melancholic and its reformation would require skills surpassing those of Hercules himself. Nonetheless, "to satisfy and please myself," he has chosen to "make an Utopia of my own, a new Atlantis, a poetical Commonwealth of mine own, in which I will freely domineer, build cities, make laws, statutes, as I list myself" (25). He follows this declaration with a description of his own Utopia, and then observes, "All the world is melancholy" (28). This being so, his own "purpose and intent" is "to anatomize this humor of melancholy" and "to shew the causes, symptoms, and several cures of it, that it may be better avoided" (29). He concludes: "Being then it is a disease so grievous, so common, I know not wherein to do a more general service, and spend my time better, than to prescribe means how to prevent and cure so universal a malady, an epidemical disease, that so often, so much, crucifies the body and mind" (29).

While Burton's text provides a very detailed picture of melancholia, Freud's essay "Mourning and Melancholia" (1917/1957) explores its psychological causes. It begins by identifying similarities and differences between the normal grieving process ("mourning") and the pathology of "melancholia." The major similarity is that both are reactions to the loss of someone or something deeply loved. In the case of mourning, one adjusts to the loss in the normal course of time, whereas melancholia is a pathological condition that may require medical treatment. How to account for these divergent outcomes?

In Freud's view, what characterizes melancholia are a profoundly painful dejection, diminished interest in the outside world, loss of the capacity to love, inhibition of all activity, and a lowering of one's self-regarding feelings to such a degree that one engages in self-reproach and self-revilings, often culminating in a delusional expectation of punishment. Many of the same traits are found in grief: The same feelings of pain, the loss of interest in the outside world, an incapacity to adopt any new object or objects of love, and a turning away from active effort that is not connected with thoughts of the dead person. In mourning, however, there is little of the self-reproach that is always present in melancholia, and no anticipation of impending punishment. In mourning, the loss is deeply painful, yet it is experienced not as punishment but as a normal part of life.

Why this loss of self-esteem, this self-abasement, in melancholia? Why this "delusional belittling" of self, and expectation of chastisement? Some of this self-criticism is no doubt justified. After all, the patient is as lacking in interest and incapable of love and achievements as he says he is. Moreover, in his self-criticisms he has a keener eye for truth than nonmelancholiacs, for others cling to views of themselves and human nature that are much too positive. For Freud, however, the issue is not whether such distressing self-abasement is justified in others' opinions, but whether one is correctly describing his experience of himself and its underlying reasons. If he has lost his self-respect, is there good reason for this, as he seems to believe? For Freud, the more he protests having lost his self-respect for unassailable reasons, the more hollow these protests seem. Given his loss of self-esteem, melancholia seems the very antithesis of grief, for grief involves loss of an object in the external world while melancholia involves the loss of self. This difference, however, is only apparent, and further probing reveals why. Like the griever, the melancholiac has experienced the painful loss of a loved object. While the griever mourns the loss of the loved object, however, the melancholiac experiences its loss with great ambivalence since he feels that his loss is the objects's own fault, that he is the victim of abandonment. This sense of abandonment is not one he can openly acknowledge because it is even more painful than bereavement, where the loved one has been "taken away" against her will. So his reproachful feelings toward the lost object are turned against himself. The lost object is not relinquished and released, as in grief, but internalized, becoming an aspect of the ego, so that the ego itself becomes the focus of reproach and delusions of future punishment. Thus, reproaches against the external object are redirected against the self. As a result, "in the clinical picture of melancholia, dissatisfaction with the ego on moral grounds is far the most outstanding feature; the patient's self-evaluation concerns itself much less frequently with bodily infirmity, ugliness or weakness, or with social inferiority" (247–48).

When the melancholiac's self-reproachings are viewed as reproach of the lost object turned against the self, another puzzling feature of melancholia becomes more comprehensible. This is that the melancholiac exhibits little if any "feelings of shame in front of other people" (247). We would expect that one who genuinely feels himself to be worthless would shrink from the gaze of others. This is not, however, the case with melancholiacs: "On the contrary, they make the greatest nuisance of themselves, and always seem as though they feel slighted and had been treated with great injustice. All this is possible only because the reactions expressed in their behavior still proceed from a mental constellation of revolt" (248). This means, in effect, that he has vengeful feelings toward the lost object, and his revenge is the pathology itself, for by this means he torments the one who has forsaken him. Such tormenting is possible because—unlike the lost object in mourning—the "person who has occasioned the injury to the patient's feelings, and on whom his illness is centered, is usually to be found in his immediate environment" (251). Thus, his relationship to the lost object takes two forms: internalization of the object, with resulting self-reproach, and punishment of the object via the pathology itself.

Is melancholia curable? Freud notes that it is more complicated than mourning because the lost object evokes deeply ambivalent feelings. In melancholia, "countless struggles are carried on over the object, in which hate and love contend with each other" (256). Also, whereas in mourning the object is finally relinquished, its release in melancholia is greatly complicated because one is unconscious of the causes of his pathology. As grieving enables the ego eventually to relinquish the object, however, so in melancholia each single conflict of ambivalence, by disparaging and denigrating the object, loosens the fixation to it. Thus, the process in the unconscious may come to an end, either because the fury has spent itself or the object is abandoned. Which of the two possibilities will bring melancholia to a merciful end is impossible to determine. It concludes, however, when the sufferer experiences "the satisfaction of knowing itself as the better of the two, as superior to the object" (257).

Freud emphasizes that the object is the internalized other, which only partially resembles the real-life other. The struggle is an internalized one in which the ego wrestles ambivalently—loving and hating—with the internalized other. Its internalization helps explain why the melancholiac may experience symptoms of both mania and depletion. Mania usually accompanies the sense of triumph over the internalized other, while depletion reveals that the ego is weak, unable to hold its own against the superior power of the internalized other. When the ego feels strong, it has the ability to "slay" the object, bringing the melancholia to an end. Therapeutically, the goal is to strengthen the ego so that it may neutralize the internalized object, thus achieving through insight what may otherwise be acted out in manic reprisals against the internalized object.

The essay concludes with a discussion of suicide and mania. Suicide occurs when the ego is too weak to defend itself against the desire to destroy the internalized hated object, and mania occurs when the ego "masters" the "complex" to which it has succumbed in melancholia. Freud admits that he finds mania difficult to account for, but suggests that it occurs as a consequence of the "long-sustained condition of great mental expenditure" involved in melancholia, during which time great psychic energy has been stored up, and is finally–in the manic period–discharged. He compares it to the experience of "some poor wretch" winning a large sum of money, who is "suddenly relieved from chronic worry about his daily bread" and "finds himself in a position to throw off at a single blow some oppressive compulsion, some false position he has long had to keep up" (254). Thus, the popular conception of someone in a manic state delighting in his movements and actions "because he is so 'cheerful'" is incorrect: "This false connection must of course be put right. The fact is that the economic condition in the subject's mind referred to above has been fulfilled"–that is, one is suddenly in a position to throw off at one blow some heavy burden–"and this is the reason why he is in such high spirits on the one hand and is so uninhibited in action on the other" (175).

In *Group Psychology and the Analysis of the Ego* (1921/1955), published four years after "Mourning and Melancholia," Freud notes that "a change into mania is not an indispensable feature of the symptomatology of melancholia depression. There are simple melancholias, some in single and some in recurrent attacks, which never show this development" (132). On the other hand, in melancholias that "occur after the loss of a loved object," such a "psychogenic melancholia" may end in mania, and this cycle can be repeated several times. Psychodynamically, this change into mania may be understood as a "periodic rebellion" of the ego against the ego ideal (which is more fully conscious), and which, in normal times, "relentlessly exhibits its condemnation of the ego in delusions of inferiority and in self-deprecation" (132). Thus, in mania, there is a "temporary suspension" of the ego ideal, a hiatus in which the ego throws off the self-critical blandishments of the ego ideal. Freud concludes: "In the psychogenic kind [of melancholia] the ego would be incited to rebellion by ill-treatment on the part of its ideal–an ill-treatment which it encounters when there has been identification with a rejected object" (133).

While Freud does not identify the "lost object" in his discussion of melancholia–this depends on the individual patient–he notes that this person is usually to be "found in his immediate environment" and is considered by the patient to have "abandoned" him. It makes sense, therefore, to presume that the "lost object" is often a parent or parental figure. Also, while Freud attributes Christoph Haitzmann's melancholia to a *dead* "lost object," the more likely case is that the "lost object" is still alive, thus enabling the melancholiac to "punish" this individual by means of the pathology itself. (Haitzmann's pact with the devil, however, *might* be viewed as a means of punishing his dead father in his new locus in the spiritual world.)

To suggest that the melancholic's mother is the even more likely "lost object," another essay by Freud has particular relevance. This is "The 'Uncanny'" (1919/1955), to which I have previously alluded, published two years after "Mourning and Melancholia." It addresses the phenomenon that was the focus of Freud's earlier essay, "The Antithetical Meaning of Primal Words" (1910/1957), the fact that the German word *heimlich* (homelike) "is a word the meaning of which develops in the direction of ambivalence, until it finally coincides with its opposite, *unheimlich*" (226). He consults Grimm's dictionary and finds the notation that "from the idea of 'homelike,' 'belonging to the house,' the further idea is developed of something withdrawn from the eyes of strangers, something concealed, secret" (255). Examples of its use are:

> "I feel *heimlich*, well, free from fear"; *Heimlich*, in the sense of a place free from ghostly influences, familiar, friendly, intimate; *Heimlich* places of the human body, pudenda, as in "the men that died not were smitten on their *heimlich* parts" (1 Sam. 5:12); *Heimlich*, as used of knowledge, mystic, allegorical; *Heimlich*, as withdrawn from knowledge, unconscious; *Heimlich*, as that which is obscure, inaccessible to knowledge, as in "Do you not see? They do not trust me; they fear the *heimlich* face of the Duke of Friedland"; *Heimlich*, as the notion of something hidden and dangerous, as in "At times I feel like a man who walks in the night and believes in ghosts; every corner is *heimlich* and full of terrors for him." (225–26)

In several of the above examples, Freud notes that the word *unheimlich* would have been as appropriate as *heimlich*.

In *Sigmund Freud and the Jewish Mystical Tradition* (1958), David Bakan notes that Freud used the word *heimlichkeit* in his address to the B'nai B'rith Society in Vienna (in the section from which Erikson quoted): "But there remained enough other things to make the attraction of Judaism and Jews irresistible—many dark emotional forces, all the more potent for being so hard to group in words, as well as the clear consciousness of our inner identity, the intimacy that comes from the same psychic structure (*die Heimlichkeit der gleichen seelischen Konstruktion*)" (305). Thus, while *heimlichkeit* (translated "intimacy") has associations of the familiar, friendly, and intimate, it also has "many dark emotional forces," ones that shade over into the *unheimlich*. Similarly, Freud notes in "The 'Uncanny'" that whether we trace the meanings attached to the word *unheimlich* or focus on the properties of persons, things, sensations, experiences, and situations that arouse the feeling of the *unheimlich* in us, we come to the same conclusion, that "the 'Uncanny' is that class of the frightening which leads back to what is known of old and long familiar" (220). One point of the essay, therefore, is to show how "the familiar can become uncanny and frightening" (220). As noted in chapter 6, Freud suggests that one way this occurs is where "that which ought to have remained hidden and secret" is made visible. In such cases, either word–*heimlich* or *unheimlich*– would be appropriate.

In the explicitly psychoanalytic section of the essay, Freud contends that the experience of the "return of the repressed" accounts for the anxiety that accompanies the uncanny. The uncanny is "something familiar and old-established in the mind that has been estranged only by the process of repression." An example of the return of the repressed "taken from psycho-analytical experience" is when

> neurotic men declare that they feel there is something uncanny about the female genital organs. This *unheimlich* place, however, is the entrance to the former *Heim* [home] of all human beings, to the place where each one of us lived once upon a time and in the beginning. There is a joking saying that "Love is home-sickness"; and whenever a man dreams of a place or a country and says to himself, while he is still dreaming, "this place is familiar to me, I've been here before," we may interpret the place as being his mother's genitals or her body. In this case too, then, the *unheimlich* is what was once *heimlich*, familiar; the prefix ["un"] is the token of repression. (245)

Thus, a man's mother is linked to the very ambivalence reflected in the shading of the *heimlich* into the *unheimlich*. Her body–especially aspects with which he was most intimately familiar–has become estranged, defamiliarized, no longer the place where he was once at home. This de-familiarization, with all its anxieties, is implicated in every subsequent experience of the uncanny. Freud's own uncanny experience of his involuntary return to the street where the painted women were plainly visible at the windows of their small houses is a case in point. So, too, were the experiences of bewitchment by young males in Puritan New England. Only John Godfrey perceived that the witches– mothers in their threatening guise–could be disempowered, won over, by treating them to beer and victuals.

This invites the conclusion that the "lost object" of "Mourning and Melancholia" may be the mother who, having become *unheimlich,* now arouses anxiety in her son. This sense of uncanniness is greater for the male than for the female child because his physical difference from his mother is precisely where the *heimlich/unheimlich* ambivalence is so emotionally powerful. While he makes no direct connection between the uncanny and melancholia, Freud's analysis of the uncanny suggests their relationship. Unlike mourning, melancholia is a state of anxiety where one is truly ambivalent, lamenting the loss of the familiar object, yet fearing her return. Even nighttime dreams of her return occasion an anxious reaction. Thus, if the familiar object is given up and relinquished in mourning, in melancholia there is no final relinquishing of the object. Its return in a new guise for the purpose of hurting or terrorizing its victim is an enduring threat. If Freud's analysis of melancholia alerts us to the loss of the loved object and the emotions this loss occasions—including feelings both of love and hate for the one who abandoned him—"The 'Uncanny'" directs us to the emotions aroused by the threat of its return in a new, unloving guise. The two essays together enable us to identify the anxieties underlying the melancholic condition and to recognize that they are two sides of the same coin, for the object would not return to haunt him unless she had discovered his hateful feelings toward her, unless his awful secret had been revealed to the very one from whom he most wanted to conceal it.

I realize that some readers will view Freud's emphasis on male anxiety concerning the mother's genitals as typical psychoanalytic excess. It is useful to keep in mind, however, that he is drawing on the free associations (or unrepressed thoughts) of patients in therapy. Under normal conditions, these thoughts remain hidden, unavailable to consciousness. On the other hand, awareness of the "uncanny" aspects of the mother's body may have been more vivid—thus anxiety provoking—in Jesus' time because of prevailing cultic rules and regulations concerning the purification of the body, especially those involved in conception and childbearing (see Booth, 1986). Thus, Freud's analysis of melancholia, when expanded in light of his reflections on the uncanny, suggest a psychosexual element in melancholia. In addition, his use of the word "*heimlichkeit,*" Bloch's association of utopia with longing for a home never experienced, and Erikson's reference to the Jewish mother as "a most down-to-earth goddess of the hearth," invite us to locate the melancholic condition in the wider psychological context of estrangement from the *home* over which the mother is something of a presiding deity. At this psychosocial level of analysis, male melancholia may be compared with agoraphobia among women. The *DSM-IV* defines agoraphobia as fears that "include being outside the home alone," leading to avoidance of travel. It notes that panic disorder with agoraphobia is diagnosed three times as often in women (397–99), thus establishing agoraphobia as a woman's affliction. The corresponding male affliction—melancholia—involves a deep-seated anxiety about home, including the perception that it is actually a more dangerous place than the external world. This sense of home's inherent dangers has its roots in early childhood and is specifically associated with the boy's anxieties over his relationship to his mother.

An especially relevant discussion of such anxieties is Norman Bryson's (1990) analysis of the male still-life artist, which expands on Freud's essay on the uncanny to include male attitudes toward the place called "home." Citing Joshua Reynolds' view that "high focus and minute transcription are *the* dominant characteristics of the genre" of still life (170), Bryson notes:

It is as if the world of the table and domestic space must be patrolled by an eye whose vigilance misses nothing. And in trying to understand this emphasis on gripping every last detail of that visual field through high-tension focus, the factors of gender asymmetry and male exclusion cannot be considered accidental. The male artist is peering into a zone that does not concern him directly. In a sense its values are alien to the masculine agenda. And spatially, it cannot be known from the inside. The result is often the production of the uncanny: although everything looks familiar, the scene conveys a certain estrangement and alienation. (170)

For Bryson, this estrangement and alienation is due to the fact that the home is the mother's milieu, and that

the persistence of [the boy's] desire to remain within the maternal orbit represents a menace to the very center of his being, a possibility of engulfment and immersion that threatens his entire development and viability as a subject...The seductiveness of the mother's body, together with her milieu and its mystique, become dangers he must escape; and he can do so by no other means than by claiming as his another kind of space, [one] that is definitely and assuredly *outside*. (172)

Thus: "Still life bears all the marks of this double-edged exclusion and nostalgia, this irresolvable ambivalence which gives to feminine space a power of attraction intense enough to motor the entire development of still life as a genre, yet at the same time apprehends feminine space as alien, as a space which also menaces the masculine subject to the core of his identity as male" (172–73).

To be sure, still life painting in modern Europe is very distant in time and place from first-century Galilee. Its preoccupations, however, are close to those of Jewish peasant life, even as they are integral to the New England communities that John Demos portrays in *A Little Commonwealth* (with its chapters on furnishings and clothing). Crossan, for example, has placed high priority on Jesus' practice of "open commensality" as emblematic of his social egalitarianism. Bryson, along similar lines, notes that food and the table are central to still life. Yet here again, he emphasizes that these subjects occupy a space that is "alien to the male painter, incapable of being occupied from the inside, and at the same time as a place of fascination and obsessive looking," thus pointing "to an ambivalence which the discourse of psychoanalysis does much to clarify. Still life of food, in particular, seems to require extremes of rationalization and displacement" (173–74). In addition:

The table is marked by complex signs of hesitation, bordering on refusal and the re-assertion of masculine identity. In the still life of luxury, the space is rebuilt in terms of male wealth and ownership. In all these cases one finds the same pattern of rejection of the space of the table *per se:* to be acceptable it must present itself as some other thing—art, morality, prestige, production—through which male superiority may be re-affirmed. Above all, the space must be controlled: subjected to a relentless and strenuous focus...a tremendous *exertion* of masculine resources operating upon the scene from outside. (174)

In a similar vein, Edward Snow (1994) comments on Vermeer's "Soldier and Young Girl Smiling," in which "the woman and the space she occupies appear to recede from the soldier, while he in turn becomes a dark, looming presence, alien and ominous in his place [at the table] opposite her...There is, from where we look, a cramped, defensive uneasiness about his posture, and an indrawn, evasive quality about his gaze" (82, 84).

At a more macrolevel, a similar male ambivalence toward the mother is reflected in the restless desire to leave home and to relocate elsewhere (recall Joseph Ryder's decision to leave Plymouth Colony being sabotaged by his mother's threat to go with him); or to travel to kingdom come (recall Hacking's male "mad travelers"). There is also the seductive allure of "mother nature" (her beauty, her charms) versus the desire to control, domesticate, and conquer "mother earth" so as to claim sovereignty over a piece of her ("homeland"). Relf (1993) cites Dorothy Dinnerstein's account of male and female relationships to nature. Women "have largely remained outside of the 'nature-assaulting parts of history' because their reparative feelings extend to nature as well as to women; whereas men's reparative feelings have a 'predominantly self-interested character'" (119). Thus:

Men's exploitation of Mother Nature has so far been kept in check largely by their conception of the practical risk they themselves ran in antagonizing, depleting, spoiling her...As technology has advanced, and they have felt more powerful [this fear] has abated. A euphoric sense of conquest has replaced it: the son has set his foot on the mother's chest, he has harnessed her firmly to his uses, he has opened her body once and for all and may now help himself at will to its riches. (119)

This is Freud's melancholia-into-mania writ large, on the very face of the earth herself.

Male Melancholia in Lower Galilee

Does this discussion of "the melancholic condition" apply to Jesus? I believe it does. But how? To lay the groundwork for my answer, I need first to establish that he lived within a male subculture in which melancholia (as characterized by Freud) was a prevailing psychosocial reality. For this, I will focus on three issues that receive a great deal of attention in the gospels (which, as Crossan points out, reflect the male scribal tradition). These are: (1) food and table; (2) stories and sayings; and (3) visions of the kingdom. My consideration of each of these cannot be exhaustive; a few indicators will have to suffice.

Food and Table

Crossan notes (1994, 54–74) that, for Jesus, the table was "a miniature model" of the kingdom. He links kingdom, parable, and open commensality in discussing the parable in the Q tradition (Mt. 22:1–13; Lk. 14:15–24) and the Gospel of Thomas (64) about the man whose invitations to dine at his house were turned down with "quite valid and very politely expressed excuse" (67), prompting him to send his servant out into the streets to invite whomever he found. As Crossan notes, such a random search would result in classes, sexes, and ranks all mixed up together: "Anyone could be reclining next to anyone else, female next to male, free next to slave, socially high next to socially low, and ritually pure next to ritually impure" (68). Assuming that Jesus

> lived out his parable, the almost predictable counter-accusation to such open commensality would be immediate: Jesus is a glutton, a drunkard, and a friend of tax collectors and sinners. He makes, in other words, no appropriate distinctions and discriminations. And since women were present, especially unmarried women, the accusation would be that Jesus eats with whores, the standard epithet of denigration for any female outside appropriate male control. (69)

Roger P. Booth (1986) discusses a similar tendency of Jesus to ignore distinctions and discriminations relating to food. He notes that the statement "Nothing going into a man from outside can defile him as much as the things that come out from a man" (Mk. 7:15) reflects Jesus' view that "cultic impurity *in toto* does not harm a man as much as moral impurity" (219). The generality of this response also suggests that Jesus "may have been unversed in some aspects of purity law" (207). As Booth notes, this created problems for the early church, especially in disputes over the application of dietary and other cultic laws to Gentile Christians. He attributes Jesus' unfamiliarity with the finer legal points of cultic law to the likelihood that, as Geza Vermes contends, he was a charismatic *hasid* and a Galilean one at that (207). Because his brother James was sufficiently versed in cultic law to debate Paul over these issues, we might also attribute Jesus' unfamiliarity with the fine points of cultic law to Joseph's failure to instruct him in these matters, owing to his marginal status in the family. In any case, the important fact is that disputes centered around food matters: what, when, and with whom one is permitted to eat.

There is also the issue of the table and the question whether the table is an exclusively male domain. If the mother is "goddess of the hearth," our still life discussion indicates that males were determined to be the kings and rulers of the table. In *Private Women, Public Meals* (1993), Kathleen E. Corley cites social anthropological studies showing that meal customs are resistant to change. Because they are, "fluctuations in those customs indicate an ongoing social renovation at a basic level of society" (181). Meal customs *were* changing during the Greco-Roman period, "so that women were beginning to attend public meals with men, a behavior previously associated with prostitutes and slaves" (181). Among the synoptic gospels, Mark is the least concerned for the impropriety of the scenes involving women in his narrative, yet women, "although present, are never explicitly depicted as reclining with men for meals" (183). A typical feature of Mark is to focus on other issues than male-female relationships per se, such as Jewish-Gentile relationships. Thus, in the story of the woman who anoints Jesus with oil, the issue is the ointment's cost, not the impropriety of her presence at the meal. In fact, "she neither reclines with Jesus nor is pictured as actually lying at the table with him" (105). Luke upholds the traditional submissive role for women, and "consistently avoids depicting women as reclining with men for meals" (183). While generally considered "the most androcentric of all the Synoptics," Matthew is the only gospel that portrays women reclining with men for meals: "Only in Matthew are women offered an equal place at the table. Women and children join the men for the miraculous feedings, meals Matthew characterizes as Eucharistic family feasts. Thus, Matthew portrays an egalitarian community which awaits the messianic banquet, a family affair for which even unmarried women prepare" (183).

Corley's study indicates a concern within early Christianity with an early tradition portraying Jesus as having disregarded sexual propriety matters in relation to the eating of meals. Mark shifts the emphasis to other issues, Luke affirms the traditional Greco-Roman practice, and Matthew locates the new practice within a familial setting. Each, in his own way, reflects deeply rooted male sensitivities concerning control of the table. If Jesus was prepared to relinquish such control—perhaps because he had never personally benefited from it—these male scribes were concerned about the loss of male prerogatives implied in the opening of the table to women. On the other hand, male ambivalence is reflected in their desire for women's company at meal times, and the fact that reclining together was involved gave the event a decidedly erotic quality.

What does this discussion of food and meals have to do with melancholia? The connecting link is the mother, who is associated with food—and feeding—from early infancy. Another meaning of "commensality" besides the one Crossan emphasizes (i.e., eating at the same table) is "an animal or plant that lives on, in, or with another, sharing its food but neither parasitic on it nor injured by it" (*Webster's New World Dictionary*, 1966). This describes the fetus/mother relationship, and even the first few months of feeding. At some point, however, this sense of commensality is threatened, even lost, and is replaced with anxieties due to awareness that such a dependent relationship has dangers for both parties. From such anxieties, estrangement follows. By linking both meanings of commensality—sharing the table and living on the life of another without harming the other—we can begin to see how disputes involving the table—what to eat and drink, whom to eat and drink it with—reflected male melancholia. The emotional investment in these disputes about the table was overdetermined (i.e., not wholly attributable to purity laws per se), suggesting that the table was the locus of a profound male ambivalence with melancholic features. A discussion by Erik Erikson explains how and why this was.

In *Young Man Luther* (1958), Erikson uses the word "melancholy" to capture the emotional tone of the disruption of the "open commensality" that previously marked the feeding ritual between mother and infant. He quotes a long passage from William James's *The Varieties of Religious Experience* in which James compares examples of "insane melancholy" among humans with the fights for life that occur among the animals and reptiles. James invites his readers to consider the museum specimens that seem so benign: "Yet there is no tooth in any one of those museum-skulls that did not daily through long years of the foretime hold fast to the body struggling in despair of some fated living victim" (120). Erikson notes that "the tenor of this mood is immediately convincing. It is the mood of severe melancholy, intensified tristitia, one would almost say tristitia with teeth in it." He adds: "James is clinically and genetically correct, when he connects the horror of the *devouring* will to live with the content and the disposition of melancholia. For in melancholia, it is the human being's horror of his own avaricious and sadistic orality which he tires of, withdraws from, wishes often to end even by putting an end to himself" (121). This is not the orality of the first—the toothless and dependent—stage but of "the tooth-stage and all that develops within it, especially the prestages of what later becomes 'biting' human conscience" (121). Erikson relates this loss of "open commensality" with the mother, and the anxiety that inevitably follows from it (i.e., the knowledge that one is capable of dangerous actions when one feels desperate), to the loss of paradise:

> The image of a paradise of innocence is part of the individual's past as much as the race's. Paradise was lost when man, not satisfied with an arrangement in which he could pluck from the trees all he needed for upkeep, wanted more, wanted to have and to know the forbidden—and bit into it. Thus he came to know good and evil. It is said that after that he worked in the sweat of his brow. But it must be added that he also began to invent tools in order to wrest from nature what it would not just give. (121)

Thus, the issue whether to allow women to join the men at table was psychodynamically rooted in male melancholia, itself originating in the struggle with and against the mother for life itself. If mother is the melancholiac's "lost object," food and meals are the context in which his ambivalences toward her continue to play themselves out. While Erikson emphasizes aggression toward the mother (which has its adult corollary in the determination to exclude women from the table), there is also the fact that the feeding ritual involving mother and infant is deeply erotic, the infant's first sexual experience (the second, as we saw earlier, is being beaten by her). Thus, debates over the matter of allowing women to recline at table with the men were not only about adult sexuality, but also—on a more primitive level—about male longings for maternal nurturance versus fears of maternal engulfment, hence, ambivalence.

Stories and Sayings

Our exploration of male melancholia in first-century Galilee continues with consideration of the parable of the prodigal son (Lk. 15:11–32) and the issue of the "missing mother." This parable is widely considered authentic, at least in its essential form (cf. Crossan, 1973, 73–75; 1991, 449). Naming it "A Man Had Two Sons," Bernard Brandon Scott points out: "Case law reminds us that our parable construes the family in a very narrow vein. The family consists of a father and younger and elder sons; missing are the mother and daughters. Since the claim of daughters and mothers for maintenance from the property precedes the sons' right of inheritance, their omission from the story indicates how limited the focus is" (111). Scott footnotes the mishnaic instruction that "if a man died and left sons and daughters, and the property was great, the sons inherit and the daughters receive maintenance; but if the property was small the daughters receive maintenance and the sons go a-begging."

The chapter in which Scott discusses this parable is titled "I Remember Mama" (recalling the popular 1950s TV show involving a Swedish immigrant family). He identifies several implicit maternal themes in the story. The first occurs when the prodigal son's situation reaches its lowest ebb. He is hungry, but also passive: "He does not eat the pigs' food—the carob beans—because no one would give them to him. He has will and desire but is without action" (114–15). Why is his poverty described in terms of food, when there are many other possibilities for describing his poverty? Because "nourishment is associated with female, maternal metaphors, and the family-system repertoire has cast the family in the especially male terms of property, inheritance, and the legal code. The mother, the unspoken binary of the father, is here implied in the son's starvation" (115). Another maternal theme occurs when the father welcomes his son. This welcome has "the quality of burlesque. The father goes overboard, and his behavior is out of character for an eastern master/patron, for it violates his honor…Embracing and kissing are signs of forgiveness, but to kiss affectionately hints at the maternal theme…The father's initial response indicates that he will not follow legal or paternal roles; he will play the nourishing role" (117). A third instance of a maternal theme is when the father addresses the elder son as "dear child," and assures him that "you are always with me, and everything that is mine is yours." Thus, he plays the maternal role toward the elder son as well. Scott concludes:

> A subterranean movement in the story has associated nourishment with a maternal theme. That theme resurfaces in the final address, for the father dismisses the legal title and deals with his sons as children. The kissing and embracing of the younger son signals the same

function as addressing the elder as child. The father combines in himself the maternal and paternal roles. As a father he is a failure, but as a mother he is a success. It is his forgiving, nourishing character that has entranced generations of hearers and readers. (122)

Richard Q. Ford (1997), however, finds his behavior somewhat less than "entrancing." In his view, the father's apparent nurturing of his sons preempts "the risks each child must take to become adults." Thus, "the father may be seducing each to remain a child" (95). (Note his seduction language.) He quotes Peter Blos, reputed for his psychoanalytic work with adolescents, who points out: "We must remember that every boy once–fleetingly or more lastingly–identified with the role of the envied and admired procreative woman: the mother. I have observed how these trends in the small boy become pathologically aggravated when his father, disillusioned in his conjugal life, shifts his need for emotional fulfillment from his wife to his son" (97). Thus, both sons, "in order to nourish their father–and, perhaps, to retain the securities such regressive strategies supply–may be tempted to betray their own becoming; both may fear their success will subject their father to failure" (97). The younger son "engineers a separation that by unconscious design leads to a resourceless dependency," while the elder son "flees in the opposite direction, into compliance. Yet he too, like his wayward brother, seems determined to discover himself resourceless. By his gift-giving in the absence of confident limit-setting, the father may be depriving his growing sons of a father who deprives" (97). By assuring the elder son that he can provide everything his son needs, the father fails to meet his son's need for "a father who will provide more than provision, who will develop into other than the mother of an infant, who will express a confident anticipation of his son's own, separate achievements, and who will thereby become truly excited about his son's autonomous functioning" (114). Unfortunately, the son does not yet grasp "that his father cannot fulfill this longing," but "instead he persists in attributing his father's unresponsiveness to a lack, not within the father, but within himself. Unable either to connect or to separate, the two circle each other relentlessly. The son is sure there is still something missing; the father sees nothing missing at all" (114).

Here, Ford comments on the elder son's immobility, thus recalling our earlier discussion of the boy who was possessed and whose liberation depended upon his father's belief that his son's fate could be changed. Also, the son's recognition that his father cannot fulfill his longing–that in spite of his father's best efforts there is still "something missing"–points to the utopian desire for what one knows one never had, as well as to the melancholiac's conviction that the longing is mother, not father, related. Thus, Ford challenges Scott's more sanguine conclusion, suggesting that this–and other stories that Jesus told–are inherently ironic (124). Where readers have been encouraged to view the father as a "figure for God," Jesus may instead be presenting him as a negative example who "fails to suspect that his undisciplined generosity may be destroying his children's ability to discipline themselves" (126). Scott implies that Jesus may have gone beyond irony, venturing into the melodramatic with his "burlesque" portrayal of the father acting like a mother would act. They could both be right. In any case, both emphasize that there is "something missing" in the story—and this "missing something" points in the mother's direction. As we have seen, Erikson puts the question of her absence in the parable in this way: Was there no mother, either dead or alive? And if alive, was she not called to say hello too? To which we might add: Did her husband play her role because she was disinclined to be the nurturing parent herself? Did she contribute to her younger son's determination to leave home, perhaps because she favored his elder brother? And how does the legal code that the story ignores fit into all this? Are sons resentful when their sisters are given the property and they are forced to "go a-begging"? These are some of the questions that the story is likely to have provoked in the male melancholiacs of Jesus' own time.

Besides stories, there are sayings deemed authentic to Jesus that have a similar melancholic aspect. These include his dismissal of his mother and brothers (Mk. 3:31–34) and his stinging response (Lk. 11:27–28; Gos. Thom. 79:1–2) to the woman who called out to him: "Blessed is the womb that bore you and the breasts that nursed you": "Blessed rather are those who hear the word of God and obey it!" As Crossan indicates, this interchange dates to the first stratum and has multiple attestation. There is also the enigmatic statement in the Gospel of Thomas 101: "For my mother gave me falsehood, but my true mother gave me life," and the conversation between Jesus and Simon Peter that concludes the Gospel of Thomas: "Simon Peter said to them, 'Let Mary [Magdalene?] leave us, for women are not worthy of Life.' Jesus said, 'I myself shall lead her in order to make her male, so that she too may become a living spirit resembling you males. For every woman who will make herself male will enter the Kingdom of Heaven.'" The first saying implies image-splitting—the false mother and the true mother—suggesting a deep ambivalence toward the mother. The second indicates male resistance to the admission of women into an exclusively male brotherhood (compare the secret societies in late-nineteenth-century America, which excluded women and threatened severe punishment for informing one's wife of "the concerns of the order" [Carnes, 1989, 79]). Other relevant sayings are Jesus' references to his homelessness (Lk. 9:58; Mt. 8:19–20; Gos. Thom. 86). He could have noted the self-sufficiency implicit in his homelessness, but instead emphasized his lack of a place "to lay his head."

In short, the stories and sayings attributable to Jesus reveal themes of male melancholia: the missing mother, the humorous (caustic?) portrayal of the father trying to assume her role, the withering comment to the woman who credited his mother with making him the man he had become, the uncertainty among his male friends as to women's place in the kingdom, and his own sense of being without a home, condemned to itinerancy. Various characteristics of melancholia are evident here: estrangement, reproach, irony, self-protectiveness, restlessness, loneliness. Through stories and sayings, Jesus addressed the melancholy men (men of sad and penetrating eyes) who were strangers in the very villages where they had grown up, and who were struggling to find some sense of being at home in their literal or psychic wildernesses.

The Kingdom of God

We may view eating and table issues as concerning the most primordial–psychophysiological–aspects of the male's relations with his mother (feeding upon her body) while the story and sayings expand on these to include, as well, the psychosocial dynamics of interpersonal and familial relations. The kingdom of God motif adds a macrolevel dimension having sociopolitical, but also transcendental, implications. We have already seen its relation to utopianism and have made a general association of this motif to melancholia in noting Burton's utopia/melancholia connection. But how is it specifically related to the underlying theme of mother-son relationships in melancholia? A comparison of John the Baptist's utopian vision and Jesus' kingdom of God motif will help in this regard. As previously noted, John's baptism ritual was politically explosive because it involved undergoing the rite of purification on recrossing the Jordan and returning to the promised land; with this ritual, John came "dangerously close to certain millennial prophets" who "invoked the desert and the Jordan to imagine a new and transcendental conquest of the Promised Land" (Crossan, 1991, 231–32). This symbolic "conquest" would hold special interest for disinherited and otherwise propertyless males. Jesus, however, viewed male "homelessness" rather differently. He did not focus on the desire to "take control" of the land–the more aggressive side of male ambivalence–but on the desire to overcome the separation and estrangement between mother and son. I have already implied this more deeply emotional tone to his kingdom of God image by associating it with deep-seated desires and with an indeterminate physico-geographical location. Such longing for reparation between mother and son is the psychological import of the enigmatic saying in the Gospel of Thomas: "For my mother gave me falsehood, but my true mother gave me life." The life-giving mother is the object of his desire. This is the side of male ambivalence that he longs to recover. This does not mean that he did not have an aggressive side, nor does it imply that John the Baptist was necessarily lacking in human feeling. There is, however, a strategic difference between them reflected in the fact that Jesus returned to village life with the intention of performing reparative deeds there. I suggest that the roots of these reparative acts go back, ultimately, to the early estrangement between mother and son.

In "The Theme of the Three Caskets" (1913/1958) Freud notes that a man has three inevitable relations with a woman, including the one with the mother who bears him, the woman who is his mate, and the woman who destroys him; or that they are the three forms taken by the figure of the mother in the course of a man's life: the mother herself, the beloved one who is chosen after her pattern, and lastly the Mother Earth who receives him once more. But it is in vain that an old man yearns for the love of woman as he had it first from his mother; the third of the Fates alone, the silent goddess of Death, will take him into her arms. (301)

This essay on the three forms in which the mother relates to her son was preceded—and influenced—by a dream he reports in *The Interpretation of Dreams* (1900/1953) titled "The Three Fates." The central woman in his dream, an inn-hostess who tells him he must wait for his food, prompting him to leave feeling injured, signifies "the mother who gives life, and furthermore (as in my own case) gives the living creature its first nourishment" (204). Commenting on Freud's dream, Erikson (1964) notes that it "reaches back into problems of the *oral* stage" of development (178). It expresses "oral desire" with "immediate needfulness" and appeals to "the Alma Mater, the Mother of Wisdom who gives you more than perishable gifts, and provides you with the means to make something of yourself, to *change your fate*" (183, his emphasis).

By linking this image of the mother who gives more than perishable gifts and provides her son with the means to change his fate with the "true mother" of the Gospel of Thomas logion, we can see that the maternal theme is central to Jesus' vision of the kingdom of God. Key to this vision is a man's ability *to make something of himself, to change his fate.* The mother, not the father, provides the means for this. *This* mother is not the mother of falsehood and death, but the true mother of life. *She* is the "something missing" from the life of the melancholic male, and he suffers because she has not yet materialized. Nor will she materialize until the false mother has been routed. Exorcism of the false mother is, in my view, what Jesus' disruption in the temple was most profoundly about.

Before turning to the temple disturbance, however, I want to recapitulate the main points I have made regarding the utopian-melancholic personality as reflected in Jesus and his male cohorts. Concerning the utopian dimension, I have argued that his social location—peasant class—would suggest that his was a pure utopianism, that is, fueled by desire, but with little expectation of the realization of these desires through human initiatives (e.g., strategies toward social and political reform). On the other hand, there is minimal apocalypticism in his utopianism (i.e., expectation of the imminent destruction of the known world). Rather, his "kingdom of God" motif encouraged individuals to perceive signs of Abba's power in their daily affairs, signs that their anxieties, on the one hand, and overwhelming boredom, on the other, precluded their noticing. His exorcisms and healings testified to such powers. Thus, I view his utopianism as far more oriented to psychological—or psychosocial—concerns at the family and village level than sociopolitical and historical, and as based on a longing for what one has always felt one lacked, but may imagine having had at the very beginning of one's life, in a time of which there is no longer any recollection. Thus, utopia for Jesus and his cohorts has maternal associations and centers around fundamental desires for food, drink, and sexual pleasure. These desires cluster around the theme of home–or at-homeness–a mythical place where one is safe, secure, and well nourished, where there is no reason to be anxious.

Melancholia is the other side of the coin, the condition that gives rise to utopian desires. It expresses one's sense of estrangement and loss–hence, the element of sadness in melancholy–but, in addition, it has a deeper element of reproach and rage. I view Jesus as especially susceptible to this element of reproach and rage, owing to his illegitimacy and (as I have argued) his non-adoption by his mother's husband. His reproach is most deeply felt toward his mother, because she is the parent who is the most available target of his anger. (She is also most likely to have been the one who disciplined him in the early years of his life.) In melancholia, however, such reproaches are internalized, becoming self-directed. Thus, Jesus took upon himself the blame and punishment for what his mother (and natural father) did to him. It was not until his baptism, when he was cleansed of the sexual pollution in which he had been conceived, that he could begin to overcome this self-reproach. The affirmation of him as the beloved son of Abba at his baptism (Mk. 1:11; Mt. 3:17; Lk. 3:22), whether authentic or not, is psychologically astute, as it transfers his identity as son of a nameless father to that of son of Abba. Baptism is a ritual in which a rebirth and a renaming is symbolized. Thus, he was now legitimated.

On the other hand, the primary and continuing object of his reproach was the internalized mother. As Freud indicates, there would need to be some "triumph" over this internalized mother for there to be a lasting cure of his melancholia. Only then would his effort to change his fate (from illegitimate and thus marginalized in every respect) be complete. The event that marked the culmination of the process begun with his baptism was the temple disturbance. Thus, these two symbolic events–baptism and temple disturbance–were psychologically linked. They needed, of course, to be symbolic, for Jesus' whole adult life was dedicated to the symbolic realization of that which he had been denied in the "real world." This, however, is also why I view him as a pure utopianist, for he turned to the symbolic world–the world from which he could not be arbitrarily excluded–for the empowerment he needed in order to change his fate. As Cioran argues, the true utopian is concerned with the most elemental matters, ones that go well beyond concern for reform of human institutions. For Jesus, these centered in his desire to have an identity–something others merely took for granted. Utopia for him meant being able to say "I am." In this respect, he was *homo religiosus*, because existential concerns–of being and nonbeing–were the very core of his search for identity, or what Erikson calls "a sense of 'I'" (1981).

The Disruption in the Temple

¹²Then Jesus entered the temple and drove out all who were selling and buying in the temple, and he overturned the tables of the money changers and the seats of those who sold doves. ¹³He said to them, "It is written,

'My house shall be called a house of prayer';

but you are making it a den of robbers."

¹⁴The blind and the lame came to him in the temple, and he cured them. ¹⁵But when the chief priests and the scribes saw the amazing things that he did, and heard the children crying out in the temple, "Hosanna to the Son of David," they became angry ¹⁶and said to him, "Do you hear what these are saying?" Jesus said to them, "Yes; have you never read,

'Out of the mouths of infants and nursing babies

you have prepared praise for yourself'?"

¹⁷He left them, went out of the city to Bethany, and spent the night there.

Matthew 21:12–17

⁴⁵Then he entered the temple and began to drive out those who were selling things there; ⁴⁶and he said, "It is written,

'My house shall be a house of prayer';

but you have made it a den of robbers."

⁴⁷Every day he was teaching in the temple. The chief priests, the scribes, and the leaders of the people kept looking for a way to kill him; ⁴⁸but they did not find anything they could do, for all the people were spellbound by what they heard.

Luke 19:45–48

⁷¹Jesus said, "I shall destroy this house, and no one will be able to rebuild it."

Gospel of Thomas 71

¹⁵Then they came to Jerusalem. And he entered the temple and began to drive out those who were selling and those who were buying in the temple, and he overturned the tables of the money changers and the seats of those who sold doves; ¹⁶and he would not allow anyone to carry anything through the temple. ¹⁷He was teaching and saying, "Is it not written,

'My house shall be called a house of prayer for all the nations'?

But you have made it a den of robbers."

¹⁸And when the chief priests and the scribes heard it, they kept looking for a way to kill him; for they were afraid of him, because the whole crowd was spellbound by his teaching. ¹⁹And when evening came, Jesus and his disciples went out of the city.

Mark 11:15–19

¹³The Passover of the Jews was near, and Jesus went up to Jerusalem. ¹⁴In the temple he found people selling cattle, sheep, and doves, and the money changers seated at their tables. ¹⁵Making a whip of cords, he drove all of them out of the temple, both the sheep and the cattle. He also poured out the coins of the money changers and overturned their tables. ¹⁶He told those who were selling the doves, "Take these things out of here! Stop making my Father's house a marketplace!" ¹⁷His disciples remembered that it was written, "Zeal for your house will consume me." ¹⁸The Jews then said to him, "What sign can you show us for doing this?" ¹⁹Jesus answered them, "Destroy this temple, and in three days I will raise it up." ²⁰The Jews then said, "This temple has been under construction for forty-six years, and will you raise it up in three days?" ²¹But he was speaking of the temple of his body. ²²After he was raised from the dead, his disciples remembered that he had said this; and they believed the scripture and the word that Jesus had spoken.

John 2:13–22

The Disruption in the Temple

I suggest that Jesus' disruption in the temple was an extension–and the culmination–of Jesus' role as exorcist-healer. In this act, he experienced a personal triumph and made a decisive step toward the healing of his–and other men's–melancholia. While Freud's term, *mania*, may give an unintentionally pejorative connotation to such triumph, his point is that this is the triumph of the "ego" over the internalized self-disparagement to which the melancholiac is even more routinely subject. When applied to Jesus' reparative achievements in the temple disturbance, *mania* also has a uniquely positive meaning, because it directly challenges another possible interpretation of the temple disturbance, that is, that it was intentionally suicidal. As Freud's "Mourning and Melancholia" shows, suicide occurs when the ego finds it cannot maintain itself against the derogations of the internalized other. In "mania," the opposite occurs, as the ego "triumphs" over the internalized object and its message of self-recrimination.

In the following discussion of the temple disruption, I will view this action in light of my conclusion (in chapter 6) that he was Mary's illegitimate son and therefore "fated" to be a "nobody," bereft of any social identity whatsoever. Thus, the temple disturbance was the culminating event in his effort to "change his fate," which began with his own purification through the ritual cleansing in the river Jordan and continued in his exorcist-healer role, which drew upon the power of "Abba." Thus, the disruption in the temple occurred in a more volatile context than his exorcisms and healings, but was on a continuum with them.

Before exploring this episode's meaning for Jesus' melancholia, I want to return to an issue raised in my discussion of E. P. Sanders' view of the disruption (chapter 1). I agreed with Powell's point that "no scholar" would suggest that Jesus' actions were "simply a spontaneous tantrum on his part," but I also contended that this does not preclude Jesus' acting under the influence of "strong expressions of feeling" or "the flux of emotions." Before I explore the deeper emotions involved, I want to comment on the more immediate emotions that may have triggered the action at this particular time. In other words, I wish to make a case for the spontaneity of the action, perhaps as resulting from the carnival atmosphere created by the large number of pilgrims in Jerusalem at the time, aided perhaps by the euphoria of the entry into Jerusalem event, which Sanders considers one of the "five main scenes that compose the drama of Jesus' last week" (1993, 252).

Impulsive Action

To consider Jesus' immediate emotional state, we may usefully draw on psychological theories and research concerning *impulsive action*. In light of evidence that he probably acted alone, that this was not part of an orchestrated takeover of the temple, and that he was apparently the only person arrested for the disruption, we may reasonably conclude that the temple disruption was, to some degree at least, an impulsive action, not one that he and his companions had planned in advance. Because it had an element of impulsivity, the action may be all the more meaningful–symbolically speaking–for being so. Dreams are not premeditated or preplanned, yet, as psychoanalysis has shown, they are meaningful for this very reason. The same may be said for some impulsive actions.

Psychoanalyst Melvin R. Lansky (1992) suggests: "Impulsive action can be understood as a dramatization of life themes that are 'acted out' instead of remembered" (94). He adds:

> Impulsive action is often a part of a larger picture that can be understood as an attempt to recreate and master situations that were traumatic in the past. The problem of repetition, whether or not one uses the term compulsion to repeat, is a difficult one for psychoanalytic theory. Repetition of major life themes cannot be ignored, however, in the explanation of human action. Repetition aims, however unsuccessfully, to solve something troubling the patient. (95)

Lansky notes that patients give explanations for their impulsive actions, offering them as "rationalizations" of the act. While such interpretations may be correct as far as they go, they are likely to miss more covert aspects of the process being interpreted. In this sense, they are inexact. Furthermore, "impulsive behavior often occurs after a change in a relationship with a significant person, both as a reaction to the narcissistic injury resulting from the change and as an attempt to control it" (97–98).

S. J. Dickman (1990) differentiates two types of impulsivity: *dysfunctional* impulsivity, or the tendency to act with absence of forethought when this behavior can create problems; and *functional* impulsivity, or the tendency to act without forethought when this behavior is beneficial. Also, Eysenck and others (cited in Parker and Bagby, 1997) have assessed two broad impulsivity dimensions, which they name "impulsiveness," or behaving without thinking and without reckoning the risk involved in the behavior, and "venturesomeness," which they define as "being conscious of the risk of the behavior but acting anyway" (144). Jesus' disruption in the temple may have been more akin to "functional impulsivity" or "venturesomeness" than to "dysfunctional impulsivity," especially given the fact that he seems not to have placed the lives of others at risk. It could still, however, have been stimulated by strong feelings of anger or rage. In studies of impulsivity, rage is among the most common emotions identified, and Donald G. Dutton (1997) cites an experiment he conducted showing that "greater rage was associated with low [social] status" (39). On the other hand, Robert Menzies (1997) notes that impulsivity is "as much a cultural and moral ascription as it is a clinical commodity," and we therefore need to exercise caution when judging an action to be impulsive. We especially need to

> explore the construct's political connotations. Surely, for example, the very behaviors that one might deplore as impulsive in some contexts can be highly adaptive, and even imperative, elsewhere. In the

terrain of human conflict, our victors are recurrently lauded and li-
onized for their assertiveness, decisiveness, spontaneity, fast thinking, and quick action, whereas the defeated, deviant, and deficient
are deplored for their impetuousness, rashness, recklessness, irratio-
nality, nonutilitarianism, lack of control—in short, their impulsivity.
(57–58)

He asks whether it is possible to decide if behaviors are adaptive or maladap-
tive, decisive or rash, rational or pathological, without taking appropriate account of "the structural, cultural, linguistic, and just plain human circumstances
with which these people are playing out their lives?" (58).

In my view, Jesus' temple disturbance, however impulsive, makes sense
because his life would have continued to be a casualty of the temple religion
had he not taken steps to "change his fate." As we have seen, the power of
temple religion to assign social status along hierarchical lines relegated "fatherless" sons to a permanent exclusion from "the structures of honor" (Van
Aarde, 1997, 463). The attraction of John the Baptist for him was that John's
purification rite stood over against the temple, ascribing "honor" to young
men like Jesus who could not acquire it through the official temple religion.
As I now want to show, however, John's baptism was only the first part of a
two-part reparative project. In this sense, Lansky's view that "impulsive action is often a part of a larger picture that can be understood as an attempt to
recreate and master situations that were traumatic in the past" applies to the
temple disturbance. It now remains for us to establish these connections.

The Temple Disturbance as Reparative Act

In his chapter titled "History and Psychoanalysis: The Explanation of
Motive" (1964), the historian H. Stuart Hughes argues that historians and
psychoanalysts share in common the quest for human motives. Also, for "the
historian as for the psychoanalyst, an interpretation ranks as satisfactory not
by passing some formal scientific test but by conveying an inner conviction.
For both, plural explanations are second nature. The former speaks of 'multiple causation'; the latter finds a psychic event 'over determined'...Both deal
in complex configurations, searching for a thread of inner logic that will tie
together an apparent chaos of random words and actions" (47).

Hughes notes that a particularly vexing problem for historians is "how to
deal with contradictions," as when an obvious discrepancy between word
and deed occurs, or between a statement's content and the emotional tone in
which it is said, or when an apparently careless phrase or gesture betrays an
unrecognized intention. These discrepancies and unintentional revelations
have often left historians at a loss. In such cases, the psychoanalytic concept
of unconscious motivation proves invaluable. In its support, he cites the case
of the "strenuous pacifist" whose "longing for harmony" and "passionate
advocacy of peace" emerges "from the sublimation of deep-seated aggression" (51). Thus, the historian who "comes to recognize that an unconscious
or half-conscious motive can alone bring into a clear pattern the pieces of a

hopelessly jumbled puzzle" has "reached the threshold of a psychoanalytic interpretation" (51–52).

This means that, with Jesus' temple disruption, one would want to look for both conscious and unconscious motivations, and for the discrepancies between them that afford "unintentional revelations." One would also want to consider Hughes's observation that in history, as in psychoanalysis, "the explanation of motives runs from the single human being to others comparable to him" (64). That is, one would presume that he was not acting for himself alone, but was expressing the motives of others who were themselves unable or unwilling to act. The political authorities' awareness of such motives in others was surely a compelling reason for his arrest and execution.

As we have seen, biblical scholars tend to agree on these two points: that the temple incident happened (there are three independent sources for the incident [Mk. 11:15–19, and parallels in Mt. 21:12–16 and Lk. 19:45–48; Gos. Thom. 71; Jn. 2:14–17]); and that it led to Jesus' arrest and execution. There is much less agreement regarding accounts of legal maneuverings and trials between the incident and execution. Crossan suggests that Jesus was arrested and summarily executed without benefit of a trial (1994, 140–41), while Sanders (1993) believes that he shared a last meal with his disciples, was taken before the high priest and his council, then sent to Pilate, who interrogated him and then ordered his crucifixion (252–53). Its symbolic nature is also widely accepted, with two competing theories about its symbolic meaning. Traditionally, it has been referred to as "the cleansing of the temple," the supposition being that he was objecting to fraudulent behavior in the buying, selling, and money changing operations conducted in the outer courts of the temple. Following Sanders, however, the majority of scholars now view his action as a "symbolic destruction" of the temple. Here, the supposition is that he was not "cleansing" but "destroying" the temple by temporarily impeding its fiscal, sacrificial, and liturgical operations (Crossan, 1994, 130–33). In Sanders' view (1993), the temple cleansing interpretation resulted from gospel authors' desire to separate Jesus' threatening predictions of the temple's destruction from his own temple disruption (258), thereby countering accusations that he meant to destroy it himself. Thus, as the gospel writers portray it, "on one occasion he cleansed the Temple, on another he predicted its destruction" (258).

I agree with the prevailing view that the temple disruption is to be understood as a "symbolic destruction," and with Sanders' explanation for why the "temple cleansing" interpretation found its way into the tradition. A symbolic action—because it is "over determined"—is likely, however, to have multiple meanings. From a psychoanalytic perspective, it will have consciously intended meanings (of which the actor is fully aware) and less conscious meanings (of which the actor may not be aware, or which have been forced to the periphery of his awareness because the action is so highly and forcefully intentional). In his "social drama" study of the fateful interaction between Thomas Becket and Henry II leading to Becket's murder, Victor Turner (1976) suggests that Becket came under the influence of a "root-paradigm," which is not a stereotyped guideline for ethical, esthetic, or conventional action, but rather goes beyond the cognitive and moral to the existential domain, and in so doing becomes "clothed with allusiveness, implicitness, and metaphor—for in the stress of vital action, firm definitional outlines [become] blurred by the encounter of emotionally charged wills" (156). Such root-paradigms "reach down to irreducible life stances of individuals, passing beneath conscious prehension to a fiduciary hold on what they sense to be axiomatic values, matters literally of life and death" (156). In my view, the deeper layer of Jesus' action *does* fall under the terms "cleansing of the temple," though not in its traditional meaning, that is, as Jesus' objection to fraudulent buying, selling, and money changing operations. The "cleansing" was much deeper than that, and was therefore on a continuum with Jesus' role as exorcist-healer. This "cleansing" concerned his illegitimacy, and his mother's role in it. Because of this, it went to the very existential core of his personal identity conflicts.

Sanders and others have emphasized that the "symbolic destruction" related to Jesus' understanding that the temple is the house, or abode, of God the Father. Belief that the temple is where God lives was a longstanding Jewish tradition. It was originally built so that God would have a permanent home. Since Jesus experienced God as "Abba," the temple may be viewed as the Father's house. The Luke 2:41–51 story of twelve-year-old Jesus in the temple, while of doubtful authenticity, reflects this fundamental understanding: "Did you not know that I must be in my Father's house?" Thus, the symbolic destruction of the temple relates to his understanding that while it belonged to his Father, it had become uninhabitable. The Father whom he knows, whose power he has experienced, would never inhabit a house such as this. Crossan (1994) puts it this way: "I am not sure that poor Galilean peasants went up and down regularly to the Temple feasts. I think it is quite possible that Jesus went to Jerusalem only once and that the spiritual and economic egalitarianism he preached in Galilee exploded in indignation at the Temple as the seat and symbol of all that was nonegalitarian, patronal, and even oppressive on both the religious and the political level" (133). Thus, his symbolic destruction of the temple expressed "what he had already said in his teachings, effected in his healings, and realized in his mission of open commensality" (133). He was so offended by what the temple had come to represent that he "exploded in indignation" and "symbolically destroyed" it. Crossan cites the Gospel of Thomas 71: "Jesus said, 'I shall destroy this house, and no one will be able to build it.'" He also cites these verses from the Jewish *Sibylline Oracles* 4:8–11 (100 C.E.): "For the great God does not have a house, a stone set up as a temple, dumb and toothless, a bane which brings many woes to man, but one which it is not possible to see from earth nor to measure with mortal eyes, since it was not fashioned by mortal hands." For Jesus, "God's house or Temple is not on earth but in heaven" (130–31). Thus, like Jesus himself, God is without a home in the world.

By claiming that this symbolic destruction was consistent with what Jesus had already been teaching, Crossan implies that this was the conscious intention for his action. If Jesus "exploded in indignation," this was because the temple represented everything that he opposed in his teaching and other actions. While "exploded" suggests an emotional reaction, the language of "indignation" adds the qualification that his emotional response was nevertheless considered and controlled. (According to *Webster's New World Dictionary*, indignation means "anger or scorn resulting from injustice, ingratitude, or meanness; righteous anger.") Thus, we are to infer that Jesus' action–as "symbolic destruction"–was deliberate and intentional.

In my view, however, the temple disruption was also influenced by a deeper, less conscious or intentional desire, one having more to do with Jesus' melancholia. On this level, his emotions reflected a deeper sense of rage and–as he carried out the action–a considerable degree of "manic" self-triumph. The more traditional insight that he was engaging in an act of "cleansing" or "purification" of the temple, while technically in error, points to this other meaning. Crossan claims that "the *Temple Cleansing*" is "a most unfortunate term for what was actually a symbolic destruction of the Temple," as it implies that Jesus was merely attacking the buying, selling, or money-changing operations conducted in the outer courts of the temple (130). If "cleansing" were the only meaning ascribed to Jesus' action, and such "cleansing" were merely viewed in relation to allegedly fraudulent business practices in the temple courtyard, I would wholeheartedly agree. "Symbolic cleansing," however, points to the deeper motivation for Jesus' action. In psychoanalytic terms, his rage signaled the "return of the repressed," for this deeper, more or less unconscious response was occasioned by the fact that the temple is symbolic of the mother's body. Thus, ironically, the temple cleansing tradition, while without historical basis, unintentionally offers a psychoanalytic interpretation of Jesus' action. Besides the tradition that the temple is God's abode on earth, a parallel tradition affirmed that it symbolizes the mother. If the temple belongs to God, the temple itself is maternal. It symbolizes her body. Thus, it may have all the implications of male ambivalence toward it that were brought out in our discussion of Freud's "The 'Uncanny.'" Symbolically understood, the temple integrated within itself the various levels of male melancholia described earlier: the psychosexual, the psychosocial, and the political-transcendental.

A psychoanalytic text that bears directly on this suggestion that the temple cleansing was related to Jesus' association of the temple with the maternal themes previously explored is David J. Halperin's *Seeking Ezekiel: Text and Psychology* (1993). Rabbinical commentators considered Ezekiel's writings dangerous to read and inappropriate for public reading in the synagogue, lest they confuse or even corrupt the spiritually immature reader. Their sexual connotations were especially problematic. Halperin argues that "Ezekiel unconsciously perceived the Temple as a woman, whose 'hidden place' is to be penetrated by alien males" (152). The "abominations" that he attributed to the temple were not factual (i.e., alleged crimes by temple priests were not actually committed), so Ezekiel was projecting "abominations" that were deeply rooted in his own personal history. Halperin surmises that these concerned

illicit sexual liaisons involving his mother and various men, and, more specifically, his mother's practice of offering up her son, Ezekiel, for her male
lovers' sexual pleasure. Thus, Ezekiel's charges of "child sacrifice" in the temple
relate to the sexual abuse that he suffered as a child.

In Halperin's view, fantasies of the temple's destruction have deep roots
in Ezekiel's "relationship with his mother" and an "even more deeply buried
rage, directed against the male figure who is likely to have been the worst of
his abusers" (208). This male figure becomes associated with God, but Ezekiel
cannot bring himself to address his rage against an all-powerful deity, so he
finds it "safer to turn most of his wrath against the female" (208). Even the
female, however, "in her original form, was an unacceptably dangerous target," for "Ezekiel's religious culture taught him that his rage against his mother
must be ferociously repressed" (208). As Exodus 21:17 warns, "He who curses
his father or his mother shall surely be put to death." By placing vile, violent
words against the temple in God's mouth, Ezekiel could not be held responsible for them, nor could it be claimed that he directed them against his mother.
By condemning the temple, he found an outlet for "symbolic disguises and
displacements of his rage" (209).

Ezekiel also conceived of a "fantasy city and Temple." Halperin suggests
that this fantasized city and temple is the "good mother" who contrasts with
the "bad mother," or the actual Jerusalem and the real temple, "which he
hates with fanatic intensity" (211). The passage that depicts "the ideal Temple
[who] will open her 'gates' only to Yahweh and to the 'prince'–surely the
infant Ezekiel–who sits nourishing himself within (44:1–3) has been viewed
by traditional Christian expositors as a prophecy of the Blessed Virgin" (211).
Also, "In the Gospels, Jesus regularly refers to himself as 'son of man,' an
exceedingly mysterious usage that is perhaps rooted in Ezekiel, or Daniel, or
both" (219).

If Halperin argues that Ezekiel's rage was not provoked by the temple
priests' own actions, Crossan makes a similar point regarding Jesus: "There
was absolutely nothing wrong with any of the buying, selling, or money-
changing operations conducted in the outer courts of the Temple. Nobody
was stealing or defrauding or contaminating the sacred precincts. These activities were the absolutely necessary concomitants of the fiscal basis and sacrificial purpose of the Temple" (131). Crossan makes this point in order to
argue against the "cleansing" or "purification" interpretation of the temple
incident; that is, Jesus' intention was not to "clean up" but to "destroy" the
temple and all that it represented. When this point is juxtaposed to Halperin's
argument that Ezekiel's revulsion toward the temple and its abominations
were rooted in his personal history, however, it supports my view that the
temple disruption was similarly rooted in *Jesus'* personal history. What needed
cleansing was his mother's body, which was polluted by her illicit sexual act,
by means of which Jesus was conceived. (Assuming that Mary was twelve
years old when this fateful episode occurred, the account in Luke's gospel of

twelve-year-old Jesus' precocious demonstration of wisdom stands in marked contrast.) There is, however, a fundamental difference between Jesus and Ezekiel. While both felt deep rage for what had been done to them, and in both cases the wrong committed against them involved sexual misconduct, Jesus' action had a reparative intention. Through this act, he symbolically "cleansed" the mother's body of its impurity—restoring her to her virginal innocence—and completed his own transformation from the son of a nameless seducer (a mere "begetter") to son of "Abba." Thus, the temple incident was a symbolic rebirth, one through which he triumphed over the "false mother" whom he had internalized and who was the object of his melancholic self-approach.

In short, Jesus' temple disturbance was symbolic on two levels. As the majority of Jesus scholars now maintain, it *was* a symbolic destruction of the temple, an attack on the religious system that had made Jesus himself an outsider. It was also, however, a symbolic cleansing—an exorcism, if you will—in which the evil that had been perpetrated against him, causing him to be conceived in sin, was "cast out," even as the money changers were routed, so that he could experience "rebirth" as the son of "Abba" and of the "true mother who gives life." In a vengeful act appropriate to the depths of his grievance against his natural parents, he returned to that primal scene and reenacted it, changing the fate to which this impure action had condemned him. As T. S. Eliot notes in "Little Gidding" from *Four Quartets* (1980, 145):

> We shall not cease from exploration
> And the end of all our exploring
> Will be to arrive where we started
> And know the place for the first time.

In concluding my analysis of the temple disturbance, I want to anticipate two possible objections. First, my attribution of "more-or-less unconscious" motives to Jesus runs the risk of imputing motives that Jesus himself may not have had, or would not have recognized or acknowledged had my analysis been pointed out to him. I defend my argument, however, on the grounds that he intended his temple action to be "symbolic" (i.e., he was not attempting a literal destruction of the temple, though, as Sanders notes, he may well have been trying to influence God to do so). This being the case, more meanings were attached to it than even he may have been aware. On the other hand, his personal view of "Abba" suggests that his symbolic universe was closely linked to the psychodynamics of his personal life and not abstracted from them. Thus, that he actually thought along the very lines that I have suggested here is entirely possible. Whether the meaning I have assigned to his temple action is in fact assignable to it is impossible to prove. It does, however, cohere with the meanings that others have assigned to the action. That is, it supports rather than contradicts the "symbolic destruction" thesis and is congruent with the portrait of Jesus developed in the two preceding chapters. In effect, it brings the "illegitimate and unadopted" image of Jesus together with the "exorcist-healer" image in the fateful action in the temple.

Second, some readers may prefer to apply "symbolic destruction" language to the deeper motivational level as well, doing so on grounds that Jesus was not attempting to "cleanse" but to destroy and obliterate the "primal scene" of his conception. My objection to this alternative view is that it fails to take into account that Jesus' action in the temple may be viewed as a "fatherlike performance" in behalf of his mother Mary. "Cleansing" implies that *her* fate could be changed as well, that she could be "reborn" as the true mother he– as a child–believed her to be before discovering the truth about his conception. In his attack on the money changers, he may well have identified them with his natural father, who destroyed the life of the twelve year old girl– about the same age as Jairus' daughter–who was to become his mother. Unlike the language of destruction, cleansing language has reparative connotations that, in my view, are central to the meaning of the temple action and account for the fundamental difference between Ezekiel and Jesus. In this sense, the temple disturbance was also expressive of Jesus' utopian desires. In this symbolic act, he created a picture in which nothing is missing, where father, mother, and son are one, and the son is restored to full legitimacy. The son is no longer looking from the outside on the spiritual home from which he had been excluded, but is now a certified insider (precisely as Lk. 2:41–51 portrays him). If there was a note of manic triumph in this seemingly impulsive act, it was the consequence (as Freud describes mania in "Mourning and Melancholia") of the long-sustained condition of great mental expenditure involved in melancholia, during which time great psychic energy had been stored up and was finally discharged. Jesus found himself in a position "to throw off at a single blow" the "false position" he had long endured. That it cost him his life does not in the least detract from this symbolic realization of his deepest utopian desires. He had taken possession of his Father's house and routed those who had no business there. The dispossessed son had come home, and had done so with a vengeance.

Jesus as *Homo Religiosus*

I have argued in this chapter that Jesus was a melancholic male who turned to an alternative religious formulation–based on belief in Abba–to address and overcome his melancholia. The very fact that he was a religious man supports this view of him as melancholic. The epigraph to Geza Vermes' chapter "The Religious Man" in *The Religion of Jesus the Jew* (1993) is this quotation from T. M. Manson: "We are so accustomed…to make Jesus the object of religion that we become apt to forget that in our earliest records he is portrayed not as the object of religion, but as a religious man" (184). As I have argued elsewhere (Capps, 1997), there is a strong relationship between male melancholia and the development of a religious disposition to life. I will not repeat that argument here, though elements of it have been incorporated into the preceding discussion. I wish, however, to conclude my discussion of Jesus as a utopian-melancholic personality with a brief consideration of its implications for the view that Jesus was an exemplary *homo religiosus* (a claim that Marcus Borg has been most concerned among our portraitists to advance).

I find it noteworthy that Erik Erikson, who also expressed interest in *homo religiosus* (cf. Erikson, 1958, 261; 1969, 395–410), uses a similar symbolically resonant event in Mohandas Gandhi's life both to make his case for Gandhi's status as *homo religiosus* and to explore what can only be called Gandhi's melancholia. That is, Erikson comes closest in his psychobiographical studies to the themes of melancholia identified here (in discussion of Jesus' temple disturbance) in his consideration of Gandhi's first court appearance as a lawyer after returning to his native India from studying law in England. He discusses this event under the heading, "Arjuna in the Court of Small Claims" (1969, 153–64), thus associating Gandhi with the mythical figure, Arjuna, during his first day in battle. While this experience occurred earlier in Gandhi's career as *homo religiosus* than did the temple disturbance in Jesus', it had a similar symbolic dimension and, at the same time, was deeply rooted in his melancholia, related to his ambivalent emotions toward his mother.

On returning to Bombay, Gandhi learned that his mother had recently died, having lived "just long enough to hear, with tears, of his graduation." While he confessed that his grief was "even greater than over my father's death," he also said that he immediately "took to life as though nothing had happened" (154). This comment prompts Erikson to surmise that Gandhi's mourning was lessened in the case of his mother "because he knew she was in him and was at the core of the best in him" (155). This incorporation of his mother was reflected in his preoccupation with food, which was obsessive and faddish, and "much of his deep ambivalence toward the 'good' and the 'bad' mother survived in his dietary scruples" (154). His dietary struggle was

> a fundamental solution to an existential problem. At the beginning when the mother is truly the matrix of survival, we can learn to trust the world and to develop the basic ingredient of all vitality: hope. Having tasted our mother's body with mouth and senses, we remain a part of it and yet also become strong enough to part from it. Our first firmament is the mother's face, shining above the goodness of nourishment; and only the study of universal mythology and of the deepest mental pathology can give us an inkling of the sinister rages and the confused imagery which that early trust must help us to contain before we can emerge from the maternal matrix. (154)

These "moods" of sinister rage and the confused imagery accompanying them "must often be lived through again in adolescence—and this especially in passionate youths beset with a sense of sin—when the original trauma of separation from the mother's body is repeated in the necessity to leave 'home'—which…may include motherland, mother tongue, mother religion" (154–55).

Erikson notes that "every child feels abandoned and betrayed by his mother, though often in a proverbial and later unconscious way," but "Gandhi gives indications of a more extraordinary conflict." If his father was "given to carnal pleasure," then "his young mother was either the father's more or less willing conspirator or his victim; and the implication is that little Moniya is himself the living issue of what, perhaps, might better not have been" (155). On the other hand, Gandhi "came to regard a real death (that is, relief from rebirth) as a cure from life," and, therefore, the "relationship to the internalized mother is highly complex," for here,

> the very hope for life as nourished in the infant by his mother must become faith in the possibility of *not* being reborn, of overcoming the necessity for rebirth through a love which is nondestructive because it transcends bodily existence with its sexual differentiation. In this Gandhi seems to have felt supported by the memory of his highly religious mother. Had she not after his birth ceased to have children? He himself, then, had been the cause of her determination to let procreation come to an end—and lovingly so. (156)

His abstemious behavior in relation to food, and, years later, in relation to sex, however pathological it seems to the Western observer, may instead be viewed as "a secret agreement with his mother which united them both as it emancipated both: where the mother who gives and the mother who denies thus becomes one benevolent agency, a rare energy of loving self-denial and self-denying love may well be a lasting emotional treasure" (156).

Thus, Erikson envisions a scenario in which son and mother are united and emancipated (from the father?) through "a rare energy" derived from their mutual participation in loving self-denial and self-denying love. The "secret agreement" between them, based on voluntary abstinence, was grounds for hope, leading to "faith in the possibility of *not* being reborn," that is, of *not* being condemned to repeat the process that produced the child in the first place. In other words, this is faith in the possibility that one's fate may be changed—in Gandhi's case, of future rebirth. Faith in a fundamental change in one's fate: This is faith that religion alone can give and is its most important contribution to the lives of individuals and groups. This is the fundamental meaning of the temple disruption. Through it, Jesus completed the reparation of the fate of his illegitimate birth and the failure of Joseph to adopt him as his own. Had more of Jesus' own followers understood the significance this event had for him—and for others like him—they might have made it the center of the religion established in his name. Other interests, however, prevented this, including the need for women to lament his death, and the need for men to glorify it. Perhaps we may yet recognize, however, its transforming power.

Our portrait of Jesus thus concludes on the theme of faith, hardly a novel conclusion. Faith that one's fate is changeable, however, *is* truly utopian, and occasionally, utopia happens. In his discussion of "the well-springs of Jesus' religion," Vermes (1993) notes that faith was its central component. In Jesus' view, faith meant taking risks. Thus, according to Vermes, the opposite of faith is anxiety, which he describes as "careful forethought, precaution, planned provision for the future," but which we, following Freud, have viewed as a symptomatic reaction to the avoidance of perceived external or internal danger. If I were a portrait painter, the greatest challenge that Jesus would pose for my artistic skills would be to capture his "sense of 'I'" immediately following the temple disturbance. Absent this, there is Mark's story about the stilling of the storm:

> A great windstorm arose, and the waves beat into the boat, so that the boat was already being swamped. But he was in the stern, asleep on the cushion; and they woke him up and said to him, "Teacher, do you not care that we are perishing?" He woke up and rebuked the wind, and said to the sea, "Peace! Be still!" Then the wind ceased, and there was a dead calm. He said to them, "Why are you afraid? Have you still no faith?" (4:37–40)

Is this, as Erikson (1968) asks, "the kind of storm which Shakespeare in *King Lear*, according to dramatic laws of representation, projects on nature and yet clearly marks as an inner storm"? If so, Mark's parallel between the "dead calm" following Jesus' rebuke of the sea and that which followed his rebuke of the evil spirit in the story of the possessed boy (Mk. 9:14–29) is a brilliant artistic stroke. More deeply still, it captures the "inner calm" of the man who had at last triumphed over reproachings without and within through this culminating act of healing. It is the inner calm that followed the release of rage in an act of self-exorcism. Dare one imagine that as he stood in the temple court, awaiting arrest, he raised his face to the heavens and said, "It is finished"?

The "Appearances" of Jesus

To conclude this chapter, I want to comment briefly on the "events" that followed in the wake of Jesus' death, focusing on tales of his appearances among those who had been close to him. This is a large topic, one with which I can deal only cursorily here, but my comments will reflect the themes of this chapter—melancholia and utopia.

There are several ways that the psychologist could broach the subject of these appearances. For example, Brooke Hopkins (1993) offers an explanation for the effectiveness of the resurrection myth based on D.W. Winnicott's theory of "object use," that is, the infant's need for the other—ordinarily the mother—not only to survive one's attempt to "destroy" her but also to refuse to retaliate, thus proving the reliability of her love. In his view, this theory accounts for why the resurrection story "would have such (relatively) lasting appeal," for "if Jesus, as an analogue of the mother or of the loved object, is 'always being destroyed,' he is also *always surviving*, always *not retaliating* against those who, in their 'sinfulness,' destroy him" (256).

Another way to broach the subject, however, is to avail ourselves of the phenomenon—to which biblical texts themselves refer—of dreams. I would suggest either that the stories of Jesus' appearances originated in dreams—

where he appeared to the dreamer—or that the creation of such stories was comparable to the involuntary production of dreams (and not, therefore, driven by ideological purposes of conscious political strategy). In *Seeing in the Dark* (1997), Bert O. States cites Ernest Hartmann's view that dreaming may serve a "quasi-therapeutic role in the sense of integration and healing in resolving trauma, in adaptation to stress, and in dealing with painful or difficult new material" (27). Noting his own interest in the narrative or serial quality of dreams (States, 1993), he indicates that Hartmann does not deal much with dream narratives, but would probably argue that they "are not so much interested in going someplace as in smelling out the roses of resemblances along the way, all in the interest, in his (and Macbeth's) image, of 'knit[ting] up the ravell'd sleave of care'" (27).

States' own view of dream narratives is that they

> are simply extensions of empirical life, with respect to their organizational logic: some things are planned (I want to go to the hardware store today), some partly planned (I may stop at the pharmacy), some unplanned—all of these sets continually impinging on each other and changing the direction of the day's narrative. Certainly day experience doesn't really mean anything (in the sense of intending to project a theme); but then it is not chaotic either. (158)

For States, the logic or shape of daily life may be thought of as a continual tension—or reciprocity—between motive ("Today I must go to the hardware store") and contingency ("Suddenly, who walks up to me but John!"). Dream narratives follow a similar logic, and the appearance in a dream of someone who has died is almost always experienced as on the side of contingency. On waking, this person's appearance in the dream has the force of utter surprise: "Suddenly, who appeared in my dream but John!" I suggest that this is precisely how an appearance by Jesus in a dream would have been experienced by those who knew him. This would enforce the sense that he initiated these appearances, that they were not motivated by the dreamer's need to see him (though such need was undoubtedly present as well).

Erik Erikson makes a further contribution to this consideration of the role of dreams in the appearances of Jesus in "The Dream Specimen of Psychoanalysis" (1987). He notes that when Freud was involved in making a case for the use of dreams in therapeutic treatment, he became almost obsessed with the idea that a dream (including his own) must yield to his efforts to discover its hidden meanings. Otherwise, his theory about dreams might not be empirically supported. In Erikson's view, Freud came to view the "Dream Problem" (i.e., how to penetrate the "one point at which it becomes unfathomable") as compared to a woman. As Erikson puts it: "The Dream, then, is just another haughty woman, wrapped in too many mystifying covers and 'putting on airs' like a Victorian lady. Freud's letter to [Wilhelm] Fliess spoke of an 'unveiling' of the mystery of the dream, which was accomplished when he subjected the Irma dream to an 'exhaustive analysis.' In the last analysis, then, the dream itself may be a mother image; she is the one, as the Bible would say, to be 'known'" (270). Erikson adds that "it is clear that the first dream analyst [i.e., Freud] stands in a unique relationship to the Dream as 'Promised Land'" (271).

Thus, for those close to Jesus, dreams may well have had a quasi-therapeutic role in the sense of integration and healing in resolving the trauma of Jesus' sudden death by crucifixion. In addition, he may have appeared to them in dreams, and such appearances would have been experienced as contingent, unmotivated by the dreamer, and thus as initiated by Jesus himself. In these two ways, dreams would have enabled the bereaved to mourn their loss, but also to affirm that he had not abandoned them (but had "gone before them into Galilee"). In these two ways, dreams would help them come to terms with their own melancholia, which may well have included not only profound sadness, but also some degree of rage that he had gotten himself into a situation where he was vulnerable to the religious and political authorities. In addition, however, the dream has bearing on the theme of utopia. If the temple was the body of the false mother, the dream could be the body of the true mother, and thus the locus of the true utopia—the "promised land," which is neither "here" (in the empirical world) nor "there" (in a world to come), but in the "no-place" where one dies to the world in order to rise again in the morning.

Epilogue

In the preface, I noted that many of the unsolved problems in Jesus studies center around the question of Jesus' identity. This question proved irresolvable on theological grounds, and thus figured significantly in the turn to the social sciences. I noted, however, that this is not an issue that can be settled on sociological grounds alone (i.e., viewing Jesus' identity solely in terms of socioreligious types), as it also has a psychological dimension. This study represents my exploration of the identity question from the perspective of psychology.

Crossan's chronological stratification of the Jesus Tradition shows that the question of Jesus' identity goes back to the earliest strata of Christian writings, as it is posed in the Gospel of Thomas (30–60 C.E.) and reappears in the gospel of Mark (60–80 C.E.) in the well-known account of Jesus and his disciples' dialogue on the way to Caesarea Philippi (Mk. 8:27–30). Jesus asks: "Who do people say that I am?" and they answer him, "John the Baptist; and others, Elijah; and still others, one of the prophets." He then asks them, "But who do you say that I am?" and Peter answers, "You are the Messiah." Jesus then orders them not to tell anyone about him. In Matthew (16:13–20) and Luke (9:18–21) the same questions are asked, with essentially the same responses given (Matthew: "You are the Messiah, the Son of the living God; Luke: "The Messiah of God"). These dialogues in the canonical gospels are far less enigmatic than the earlier Gospel of Thomas version, which has the following dialogue (log. 13):

> Jesus said to his disciples, "Compare me to someone and tell me whom I am like." Simon Peter said to him, "You are like a righteous angel." Matthew said to him, "You are like a wise philosopher." Thomas said to him, "Master, my mouth is wholly incapable of saying whom you are like." Jesus said to him, "I am not your master. Because you have drunk, you have become intoxicated from the bubbling spring which I have measured out." (Barnstone, 1984, 301)

Whereupon, Jesus takes Thomas aside, tells him three things (which are not identified), and when Thomas returns, the other disciples ask him what Jesus said to him. His response: "If I tell you one of the things which he told me, you will pick up stones and throw them at me; a fire will come out of the stones and burn you up" (301).

While these various responses to questions regarding Jesus' identity would seem to have little in common—except for the synoptic tradition of Messiah—the one thing they agree upon is that his identity is fundamentally other than his *attributed identity* (i.e., the statuses assigned to him by his society). Even if "the people" (in the canonical gospels' version) get it wrong; they, no less than Jesus' insiders, ascribe to him identities that derive from a different order.

He is John the Baptist, Elijah, Jeremiah, or some other prophet come back from the grave. The Gospel of Thomas presses this point even further, in that it has Jesus asking to whom he might be compared, and then saying to Thomas that he is not who Thomas thinks he is. The question of his identity is shrouded in mystery.

While these dialogues about Jesus' true identity may be cause for despair, they have instead been one of the main stimuli behind Jesus studies, and the portraits presented in chapters 1 and 2 are indicative of the fact that scholars in the field have not given up the effort to identify Jesus. In these concluding remarks, I want to make a final suggestion for how psychology may contribute to this admittedly complex and potentially perilous effort. I preface this suggestion with a reference to John William Ward's "Who Was Benjamin Franklin?" (1963). This essay, in a sense, normalizes the question of identity by indicating that the question arises with any subject of biographical interest. As Ward notes, the question typically arises when one is confronted with a subject who seems to have contained "various opposites with complete serenity" within his own personality. He identifies several of these opposing qualities in Franklin:

> He was an eminently reasonable man who maintained a deep scepticism about the power of reason. He was a model of industriousness who, preaching the gospel of hard work, kept his shop only until it kept him and retired at forty-two. He was a cautious and prudent man who was a revolutionist. And, to name only one more seeming contradiction, he was one who had a keen eye for his own advantage and personal advancement who spent nearly all his adult life in the service of others. (541)

Ward notes that the usual approach of biographers to such oppositeness is either to lift out a primary feature of the subject's personality (perhaps on the basis of the biographers' own personal preferences), or to find some way to show that all of these opposites reflect some higher consistency or transcendent unity. Instead, Ward decides that the better approach to Franklin is to accept that he was many "different characters," and that this may be "the single most important thing about him" (542).

With Jesus, we might ask the same question: What is the single most important thing about him? Unlike Franklin, it is not that he was many different characters (as *could* be implied in the fact that so many identities were evidently attributed to him). Rather, the single most important thing about him—as far as the identity issue is concerned—was that his identity was, as noted, other than his socially attributed identity. The dialogues noted above treat his identity as something that cannot be decided on ordinary social terms. The dialogue in Mark 15:2 (with parallels in Mt. 27:11 and Lk. 23:3) between Pilate and Jesus reinforces this sense that his identity is not his attributed identity but derives from another world. The oft-quoted conclusion by Albert Schweitzer in *The Quest of the Historical Jesus* (1906), "He comes to us as one unknown…" expresses this in a wonderfully poetic way.

Perhaps the psychologist should let the matter rest precisely here and leave the determination of his other worldly identity to the biblical scholars and theologians. I think, however, that the psychologist may have something to contribute even to this discussion. It may not help to decide who Jesus "really" was, but it may help to explain why Jesus would have become the object of this question among his own contemporaries. A theory that sheds some light on the issue is that of "the fictive personality." Jay Martin (1988) explores the phenomenon of the fictive personality in the writings of psychoanalytic thinkers from Alfred Adler to Heinz Kohut, and cites the cases of several of his patients who lived fictive lives. One patient, Melissa, had the idea that understanding the world required three keys:

> Her theory was that the world had three shapes, corresponding to her three favorite books–*Little Women, Gone with the Wind,* and *The Wizard of Oz.* One had only to select the appropriate book and passage to interpret whatever aspect of the world a problem brought to hand, and the way of dealing with it would become evident. Never mind if the way of dealing didn't work: the "key" remained right, though the world might be wrong. (74)

She confessed to Martin that "I tend to live in a fantasy world," and Martin comments that her poems "seemed more truly herself than the unfamiliar self that managed a household or went to school. But mostly she used fictions to keep reality false" (75). Undergoing psychoanalysis helped her in this sense. If, prior to psychoanalysis, she "had treated the world *as if* it were real; now, in psychoanalysis, she began to come from behind the veil and live in the world's reality" (76). A major breakthrough occurred when she made "a crucial distinction between fantasies that supplant reality and fantasies of power that helpfully release anxiety" (76). I believe it can be said that Jesus reflected the latter–"fantasies of power that helpfully release anxiety"–whereas Ezekiel (as presented by Halperin) reflected more the former.

An especially fine example of "the fictive personality" is Erik Erikson's account (1959) of his work with a high-school girl of middle European descent who secretly kept company with Scottish immigrants, carefully studying and easily assimilating their dialect and their social habits:

> With the help of history books and travel guides she reconstructed for herself a childhood in a given milieu in an actual township in Scotland, apparently convincing enough to some descendants of that country. Prevailed upon to discuss her future with me, she spoke of her (American-born) parents as "the people who brought me over here," and told me of her childhood "over there" in impressive detail. I went along with the story, implying that it had more inner truth than reality to it. (141)

When he finally asked her how she managed to marshal all the details of life in Scotland, this was her response: "'Bless you, sir,' she said in pleading Scottish brogue, 'I needed a past'" (141). Erikson could have added that his tendency to "go along with the story" because it had a certain "inner truth" may have been due, in part, to the fact that he was illegitimate (did not know his natural father) and lived the first three years of his life with his mother. After having been adopted by his stepfather, Theodor Homburger, at age three, and feeling himself an outsider in his parents' home, he took refuge "in fantasies of how I, the son of much better parents, had been altogether a foundling" (1975, 27). His adoption of a new surname may be explained, to a degree, as typical of American immigrants, but the choice of "Erikson" has a fictive quality to it, implying that he is his own father. To imagine oneself as one's father is also a fantasy of power that helpfully releases anxiety.

As I have presented Jesus in this study, his fictive personality was that of "son of Abba." To the blessing he is said to have received at his baptism: "You are my beloved son," he could well have responded, "Bless you, for I needed a future." And what a future it has proven to be! He continues to support fantasies of power that helpfully release anxiety, and one who has found such support from him will have no inclination to disparage such fantasies if this is, indeed, their effect. As the title to a poem by William Stafford suggests, they are "A Story That Could Be True" (1977:4). Stafford imagines a scenario in which the reader was exchanged in the cradle and his mother died without ever telling the story, while "your father is lost" and "can never find how true you are." Supposing you began to ask yourself, "Who am I, really?" The only answer in a dark, cold world could be, "Maybe I'm a king."

The portrait that I have offered here is not exactly surprising, as it has focused on Jesus as a son (doing fatherlike things): son of Mary and son of Abba. If son of Abba figures most prominently—as figure—in this portrait, it should be emphasized, by way of conclusion, that every man's portrait is grounded in his experience of mother. As Richard Brilliant (1991) points out:

> The dynamic nature of portraits and the "occasionality" that anchors their imagery in life seem ultimately to depend on the primary experience of the infant in arms. That child, gazing up at its mother, imprints her vitally important image so firmly on its mind that soon enough she can be recognized almost instantaneously and without conscious thought...A little later a name, "Mama" or some other, will be attached to the now familiar face and body, soon followed by a more conscious acknowledgment of her role vis-a-vis the infant as "mother" or "provider"...Eventually the infant will acquire a sense of its own independent existence, of itself as a sentient being, responding to others, and possessing, as well, its own given name. (9)

He adds that in this encounter between infant and mother are

> the essential constituents of a person's identity: a recognized or recognizable appearance; a given name that refers to no one else; a social, interactive function that can be defined; in context, a pertinent characterization; and a consciousness of the distinction between one's own person and another's, and of the possible

relationship between them. Only physical appearance is naturally
visible, and even that is unstable. The rest is conceptual and must be
expressed symbolically. (9)

This presents a tremendous challenge for the "artistic ingenuity and empathetic
insight" of the portrait painter.

Throughout the centuries, painters have, in fact, risen to the challenge of
representing this original utopia of the infant Jesus with his loving mother.
Erikson, however, thinks that Luther found a different way to experience this
utopia of basic desire. He writes in *Young Man Luther* (1958): "I think that in
the Bible Luther at last found a mother whom he could acknowledge: he
could attribute to the Bible a generosity to which he could open himself, and
which he could pass on to others, at last a mother's son" (208). What Erikson
does not say—perhaps because it goes without saying—is that Luther thus read
the Bible not as an adult but as an abandoned child. In his early essay,
"Children's Picture Books" (1931/1987), Erikson points to certain medieval
depictions of the Mother of God or the Holy Family, noting that "we see,
among the mature, tender human faces, that the countenance of the little
Savior or other children are strangely distorted: ill; somewhat embryolike;
somewhat senile" (32). While it may seem as though this merely reflects the
artist's intention to depict the Christ Child as an "old infant," mature at birth
and childlike in death, Erikson suggests that it is actually symptomatic of the
artist's unconscious need to distort childhood itself, "refusing to recognize a
child as he really is" (32).

One also wonders, however, if these painters were seeing the distortion
that is inherent to childhood, and were observing that Jesus was not spared
this fate. What, then, could be more reflective of the Bible as gracious mother
than her preservation of the words her son says in his own—and other children's
behalf—"Take care that you do not despise one of these little ones; for I tell
you, in heaven their angels continually see the face of my Father in heaven"
(Mt. 18:10)? Perhaps the most stunning fatherlike performance of all is to
proclaim all children the sons and daughters of the heavenly Father. His refusal to see himself as unique in this regard may be the very nucleus of his
identity.

If so, I can imagine that this fatherlike performance is the "general idea"
that directed the brushstrokes of the artist who painted the portrait of Jesus
that graces the dust jacket of this book. The sad, heavy-lidded eyes, the tear-
stained cheek, the mouth with tongue exposed, convey a profound sorrow;
not, however, for himself, for he knows the Father to whom he belongs, but
for those who will view his death as confirmation that we, however begotten,
are helpless to change our fate. Against this, I can also imagine that the artist,
in portraying his eyes turned heavenward, has captured Jesus in another reparative act, crying out, "Father, forgive them, for they do not know what
they are doing" (Lk. 23:34), thus signifying, at the last, that his exorcist-healer
role knew no limits, while also depriving his executioners—and the father
who had forsaken him at birth— of the power to seal his fate. Because it is of
doubtful authenticity, yet consistent with the character of Jesus as revealed in

his acts of healing, this appeal to his Father marks that moment when the historical Jesus began to recede from view, replaced by the Jesus of human inspiration. The picture of the former that I would like to leave with the reader is that of a man whose spirit was immune to scourgings more dehumanizing than parental beatings and torments more vicious than demon possessions because he had already finished his life's work.

References

American Psychiatric Association (1994). *Diagnostic and Statistical Manual of Mental Disorders (DSM-IV)*, fourth edition. Washington, D.C.

Arnheim, Rudolf (1996). The Face and the Mind Behind It. In *The Split and the Structure*. Berkeley: The University of California Press, pp. 139–43.

Bainton, Roland (1959). Luther: A Psychiatric Portrait. *Yale Review* 48: 405–10.

—— (1971). Psychiatry and History: An Examination of Erikson's "Young Man Luther." *Religion in Life* 40: 451–78.

Bakan, David (1958). *Sigmund Freud and the Jewish Mystical Tradition*. New York: Schocken Books.

—— (1966). *The Duality of Human Existence: An Essay on Psychology and Religion*. Chicago: Rand McNally.

—— (1967). A Reconsideration of the Problem of Introspection. In *On Method: Toward a Reconstruction of Psychological Investigation*. San Francisco: Jossey-Bass, pp. 94–112.

—— (1968). *Disease, Pain, and Sacrifice: Toward a Psychology of Suffering*. Chicago: The University of Chicago Press.

Barbu, Zevedei (1960). *Problems of Historical Psychology*. New York: Grove Press.

Barlow, Paul (1997). Facing the Past and Present: The National Portrait Gallery and the Search for "Authentic" Portraiture. In Joanna Woodall (Ed.). *Portraiture: Facing the Subject*. Manchester: Manchester University Press, pp. 219–38.

Barnes, Elizabeth (1997). *States of Sympathy: Seduction and Democracy in the American Novel*. New York: Columbia University Press.

Barnstone, Willis, Ed. (1984). *The Other Bible*. San Francisco: Harper-San Francisco.

Barzun, Jacques (1974). *Clio and the Doctors: Psycho-History, Quanto-History and History*. Chicago: University of Chicago Press.

Baur, Susan (1988). *Hypochondria: Woeful Imaginings*. Berkeley: University of California Press.

Bloch, Ernst (1988). Something's Missing: A Discussion Between Ernst Bloch and Theodor W. Adorno on the Contradictions of Utopian Longing. In Ernst Bloch, *The Utopian Function of Art and Literature: Selected Essays*. Jack Zipes and Frank Mecklenburg (Trans.). Cambridge: The MIT Press, pp. 1–17.

Booth, Roger P. (1986). *Jesus and the Laws of Purity: Tradition History and Legal History in Mark 7*. Sheffield, England: Department of Biblical Studies of the University of Sheffield.

Borg, Marcus J. (1984). *Conflict, Holiness, and Politics in the Teachings of Jesus*. Lewiston, N.Y.: Edwin Mellen Press. San Francisco: HarperSanFrancisco.

————— (1987). *Jesus: A New Vision.* San Francisco: HarperSanFrancisco.

————— (1994a). *Jesus in Contemporary Scholarship.* Valley Forge, Pennsylvania: Trinity Press International.

————— (1994b). *Meeting Jesus Again for the First Time: The Historical Jesus and the Heart of Contemporary Faith.* San Francisco: HarperSanFrancisco.

Brilliant, Richard (1991). *Portraiture.* Cambridge: Harvard University Press.

Bronfen, Elisabeth (1992). *Over Her Dead Body: Death, Feminity and the Aesthetic.* New York: Routledge.

Bryson, Norman (1990). *Looking at the Overlooked: Four Essays on Still Life Painting.* Cambridge: Harvard University Press.

Burton, Robert (1979). *The Anatomy of Melancholy.* Joan K. Peters (Ed.). New York: Frederick Ungar.

Burton, R. V., and J. W. M. Whiting (1961). The Absent Father and Cross-Sex Identity. *Merrill-Palmer Quarterly* 7: 85–95.

Bushman, Richard L. (1966). On the Uses of Psychology: Conflict and Conciliation in Benjamin Franklin. *History and Theory* 5: 225–40.

Cantor, Carla (1996). *Phantom Illness: Recognizing, Understanding, and Overcoming Hypochondria.* Boston: Houghton Mifflin Company.

Capps, Donald (1995). *The Child's Song: The Religious Abuse of Children.* Louisville: Westminster John Knox Press.

————— (1997). *Men, Religion, and Melancholia.* New Haven: Yale University Press.

Carnes, Mark C. (1989). *Secret Ritual and Manhood in Victorian America.* New Haven: Yale University Press.

Cioran, E. M. (1987). *History and Utopia.* Richard Howard (Trans.). Chicago: The University of Chicago Press.

Collins, Bradley I. (1997). *Leonardo, Psychoanalysis and Art History: A Critical Study of Psychobiographical Approaches to Leonardo da Vinci.* Evanston, Illinois: Northwestern University Press.

Corley, Kathleen E. (1993). *Private Women, Public Meals: Social Conflict in the Synoptic Tradition.* Peabody, Massachusetts: Hendrickson Publishers.

Crossan, John Dominic (1973). *In Parables: The Challenge of the Historical Jesus.* New York: Harper & Row.

————— (1980). *Cliffs of Fall: Paradox and Polyvalence in the Parables of Jesus.* New York: The Seabury Press.

————— (1983). *In Fragments: The Aphorisms of Jesus.* San Francisco: Harper & Row.

————— (1991). *The Historical Jesus: The Life of a Mediterranean Jewish Peasant.* San Francisco: HarperSanFranciso.

————— (1994). *Jesus: A Revolutionary Biography.* SanFrancisco:HarperSan Franciso.

————— (1998) *The Birth of Christianity: Discovering What Happened in the Years Immediately After the Execution of Jesus.* San Francisco: HarperSan Francisco.

Darwin, Charles (1872/1998). *The Expression of the Emotions in Man and Animals*, third edition. Paul Ekman (Ed.). New York: Oxford University Press.

Demos, John (1970). *A Little Commonwealth: Family Life in Plymouth Colony.* New York: Oxford University Press.

—— (1972). *Remarkable Providences 1600–1760.* New York: George Braziller.

—— (1982). *Entertaining Satan: Witchcraft and the Culture of Early New England.* New York: Oxford University Press.

Denny, Frederick M. (1987). Postures and Gestures. In Mircea Eliade (Ed.). *The Encyclopedia of Religion*, Vol. 11. New York: Macmillan Publishing Company, pp. 461–64.

Dickman, S. J. (1990). Functional and Dysfunctional Impulsivity: Personality and Cognitive Correlates. *Journal of Personality and Social Psychology* 58: 95–02.

Dutton, Donald G. (1997). A Social Psychological Perspective on Impulsivity/Intimate Violence. In Christopher D. Webster and Margaret A. Jackson (Eds.). *Impulsivity: Theory, Assessment, and Treatment.* New York: The Guilford Press, pp. 32–41.

Edwards, Douglas (1992). The Socio-Economic and Cultural Ethos of the Lower Galilee in the First Century: Implications for the Nascent Jesus Movement. In Lee I. Levine (Ed.). *The Galilee in Late Antiquity.* New York: The Jewish Theological Seminary of America, pp. 53–73.

Eliot, T. S. (1980). *The Complete Poems and Plays 1909–1950.* New York: Harcourt, Brace and Company, 1980.

Erikson, Erik H. (1958). *Young Man Luther: A Study in Psychoanalysis and History.* New York: W. W. Norton.

—— (1959). *Identity and the Life Cycle.* New York: International Universities Press.

—— (1963). *Childhood and Society*, rev. ed. New York: W. W. Norton.

—— (1964). Psychological Reality and Historical Actuality. *Insight and Responsibility: Lectures on the Ethical Implications of Psychoanalytic Insight.* New York: W.W. Norton, pp. 161–215.

—— (1968). *Identity: Youth and Crisis.* New York: W. W. Norton.

—— (1969). *Gandhi's Truth: On the Origins of Militant Nonviolence.* New York: W. W. Norton.

—— (1974). *Dimensions of a New Identity: The 1973 Jefferson Lectures in the Humanities.* New York: W. W. Norton.

—— (1975). "Identity Crisis" in Autobiographic Perspective. In *Life History and the Historical Moment.* New York: W. W. Norton, pp. 17–47.

—— (1981). The Galilean Sayings and the Sense of "I." *The Yale Review* 70: 321–62.

———— (1987). *A Way of Looking at Things: Selected Papers from 1930 to 1980.* Stephen Schlein (Ed.). New York: W. W. Norton.

Fisher, Seymour, and Rhoda L. Fisher (1993). *The Psychology of Adaptation to Absurdity: Tactics of Make-Believe.* Hillsdale, N. J.: Lawrence Erlbaum.

Ford, Richard Q. (1997). *The Parables of Jesus: Recovering the Art of Listening.* Minneapolis: Fortress Press.

Frankl, Viktor E. (1975). Paradoxical Intention and Dereflection. *Psychotherapy: Theory, Research and Practice* 12: 226–37.

Freud, Sigmund (1893/1966). Some Points for a Comparative Study of Organic and Hysterical Motor Paralyses. In James Strachey (Ed. and Trans.). *The Standard Edition of the Complete Psychological Works of Sigmund Freud* [hereafter *The Standard Edition*], Vol. 1. London: The Hogarth Press, pp. 157–72.

———— (1900/1953). *The Interpretation of Dreams.* In James Strachey (Ed. and Trans.). *The Standard Edition,* Vols. 4 and 5. London: The Hogarth Press.

———— (1901/1960). *The Psychopathology of Everyday Life.* In James Strachey (Ed. and Trans.). *The Standard Edition,* Vol. 6. London: The Hogarth Press.

———— (1907/1957). Obsessive Actions and Religious Practices. In James Strachey (Ed. and Trans.). *The Standard Edition,* Vol. 9. London: The Hogarth Press, pp. 115–27.

———— (1910/1957). *Leonardo da Vinci and a Memory of His Childhood.* In James Strachey (Ed. and Trans.). *The Standard Edition,* Vol. 11. London: The Hogarth Press, pp. 59–137.

———— (1910/1957). The Antithetical Meaning of Primal Words. In James Strachey (Ed. and Trans.). *The Standard Edition,* Vol. 11. London: The Hogarth Press, pp. 153–61.

———— (1913/1958). The Theme of the Three Caskets. In James Strachey (Ed. and Trans.). *The Standard Edition,* Vol. 12. London: The Hogarth Press, pp. 289–309.

———— (1916–17/1963). *Introductory Lectures on Psycho-Analysis.* In James Strachey (Ed. and Trans.), *The Standard Edition,* Vols. 15 and 16. London: The Hogarth Press.

———— (1917/1957). Mourning and Melancholia. In James Strachey (Ed. and Trans.). *The Standard Edition,* Vol. 14. London: The Hogarth Press, pp. 239–58.

———— (1919/1955). "The Uncanny." In James Strachey (Ed. and Trans.). *The Standard Edition,* Vol. 17. London: The Hogarth Press, pp. 218–56.

———— (1920/1955). *Beyond the Pleasure Principle.* In James Strachey (Ed. and Trans.). *The Standard Edition,* Vol. 18. London: The Hogarth Press, pp. 3–64.

———— (1921/1955). *Group Psychology and the Analysis of the Ego.* In James Strachey (Ed. and Trans.). *The Standard Edition*, Vol. 18. London: The Hogarth Press, pp. 67–143.

———— (1923/1961a). *The Ego and the Id.* James Strachey (Ed. and Trans.). *The Standard Edition*, Vol. 19. London: The Hogarth Press, pp. 3–66.

———— (1923/1961b). A Seventeenth Century Demonological Neurosis. In James Strachey (Ed. and Trans.). *The Standard Edition*, Vol. 19. London: The Hogarth Press, pp. 69–105.

———— (1926/1959). *Inhibitions, Symptoms and Anxiety.* In James Strachey (Ed. and Trans.). *The Standard Edition*, Vol. 20. London: The Hogarth Press, pp. 77–175.

———— (1930/1961). *Civilization and Its Discontents.* In James Strachey (Ed. and Trans.). *The Standard Edition*, Vol. 21. London: The Hogarth Press, pp. 59–145.

———— (1939/1964). *Moses and Monotheism: Three Essays.* In James Strachey (Ed. and Trans.). *The Standard Edition*, Vol. 23. London: The Hogarth Press, pp. 3–137.

Freyne, Sean (1992). Urban-Rural Relations in First-Century Galilee: Some Suggestions from the Literary Sources. In Lee I. Levine (Ed.). *The Galilee in Late Antiquity.* New York: The Jewish Theological Seminary of America, pp. 75–91.

Friedman, Lawrence J. (1999). *Identity's Architect: A Biography of Erik H. Erikson.* New York: Charles Scribner's Sons.

Funk, Robert W. et al. (1998). *The Acts of Jesus: The Search for the Authentic Deeds of Jesus.* San Francisco: HarperSanFrancisco.

Gaventa, Beverly Roberts (1995). *Mary, Glimpses of the Mother of Jesus.* Columbia: The University of South Carolina Press.

George, Alexander L., and Juliette L. George (1964). *Woodrow Wilson and Colonel House: A Personality Study.* New York: Dover Books.

Gilman, Sander L. (1993). *The Case of Sigmund Freud: Medicine and Identity at the Fin De Siecle.* Baltimore: The Johns Hopkins University Press.

———— (1998). *Creating Beauty to Cure the Soul: Race and Psychology in the Shaping of Aesthetic Surgery.* Durham: Duke University Press.

Hacking, Ian (1998). *Mad Travellers: Reflections on the Reality of Transient Mental Illnesses.* Charlottesville: The University of Virginia Press.

Halperin, David J. (1993). *Seeking Ezekiel: Text and Psychology.* University Park: Pennsylvania State University Press.

Hanson, K. C., and Douglas E. Oakman (1998). *Palestine in the Time of Jesus: Social Structures and Social Conflicts.* Minneapolis: Fortress Press.

Hollenbach, Paul W. (1981). Jesus, Demoniacs, and Public Authorities: A Socio-Historical Study. *Journal of the American Academy of Religion* 49 (4): 567–88.

Hopkins, Brooke (1993). Jesus and Object-Use: A Winnicottian Account of the Resurrection Myth. In Peter L. Rudnytsky (Ed.). *Transitional Objects and Potential Spaces: Literary Uses of D.W. Winnicott.* New York: Columbia University Press, pp. 249–60.

Horsley, Richard A. (1987). *Jesus and the Spiral of Violence: Popular Jewish Resistance in Roman Palestine.* San Francisco: Harper & Row.

——— (1989). *Sociology and the Jesus Movement.* New York: Crossroad.

Hughes, H. Stuart (1964). *History as Art and as Science: Twin Vistas on the Past.* New York: Harper & Row.

Hutch, Richard A. (1983). *Emerson's Optics: Biographical Process and the Dawn of Religious Leadership.* Washington, D.C.: The University Press of America.

Jacobs-Malina, Diane (1993). *Beyond Patriarchy: The Images of Family in Jesus.* New York: Paulist Press.

James, William (1982). *Essays in Morality and Religion.* Frederick H. Burkhardt, (Ed.). Cambridge, Mass.: Harvard University Press.

Jeremias, Joachim (1969). *Jerusalem in the Time of Jesus: An Investigation into Economic and Social Conditions During the New Testament Period.* Philadelphia: Fortress Press.

Josephus, Flavius (1987). *The Works of Josephus: Complete and Unabridged.* William Whiston (Trans.). Peabody, Massachusetts: Hendrickson.

Kee, Howard Clark (1992). Early Christianity in the Galilee: Reassessing the Evidence from the Gospels. In Lee I. Levine (Ed.). *The Galilee in Late Antiquity.* New York: The Jewish Theological Seminary of America, pp. 3–22.

Kellner, Robert (1986). *Somatization and Hypochondriasis.* New York: Praeger.

Kibbey, Ann (1986). *The Interpretation of Material Shapes in Puritanism: A Study of Rhetoric, Prejudice and Violence.* Cambridge: Cambridge University Press.

Klein, Melanie (1956/1986). A Study of Envy and Gratitude. In Juliet Mitchell (Ed.). *The Selected Melanie Klein.* London: Penguin Books, pp. 211–29.

Kumar, Krishan (1991). *Utopianism.* Minneapolis: The University of Minnesota Press.

Lansky, Melvin R. (1992). *Fathers Who Fail: Shame and Psychopathology in the Family System.* Hillsdale, N. J.: The Analytic Press.

Levenson, Jon D. (1993). *The Death and the Resurrection of the Beloved Son: The Transformation of Child Sacrifice in Judaism and Christianity.* New Haven: Yale University Press.

Levinson, Daniel J. et al. (1978). *The Season's of a Man's Life.* New York: Alfred A. Knopf.

Levitas, Ruth (1990). *The Concept of Utopia.* Syracuse: Syracuse University Press.

Loewenberg, Peter (1971). The Psychohistorical Origins of the Nazi Youth Cohort. *American Historical Review* 76: 1457–502.

Lüdemann, Gerd (1998). *Virgin Birth? The Real Story of Mary and Her Son Jesus.* Harrisburg, Pennsylvania: Trinity Press International.

Malina, Bruce (1986). Religion in the World of Paul. *The Bible Today* 16: 92–101.

——— (1993). *The New Testament World: Insights from Cultural Anthropology.* Louisville: Westminster/John Knox Press.

——— and Jerome H. Neyrey (1996). *Portraits of Paul: An Archeology of Ancient Personality.* Louisville: Westminster John Knox Press.

Manuel, Frank E., and Fritzie P. Manuel (1979). *Utopian Thought in the Western World.* Cambridge, Massachusetts: Harvard University Press.

Martin, Jay (1988). *Who Am I This Time: Uncovering the Fictive Personality.* New York: W. W. Norton.

Mazlish, Bruce (1971). What is Psycho-history? *Transactions of the Royal Historical Society of London* 21: 79–99.

Meier, John P. (1991, 1994). *A Marginal Jew: Rethinking the Historical Jesus,* Vols. 1 and 2. New York: Doubleday Books.

Menzies, Robert (1997). A Sociological Perspective on Impulsivity: Some Cautionary Comments on the Genesis of a Clinical Construct. In Christopher D. Webster and Margaret A. Jackson (Eds.). *Impulsivity: Theory, Assessment, and Treatment.* New York: The Guilford Press, pp. 42–62.

Micale, Mark S. (1995). *Approaching Hysteria: Disease and Its Interpretations.* Princeton: Princeton University Press.

Miller, John W. (1997). *Jesus at Thirty: A Psychological and Historical Portrait.* Minneapolis: Fortress Press.

Nicholson, Kathleen (1997). The Ideology of Feminine "Virtue": The Vestal Virgin in French Eighteenth-Century Allegorical Portraiture. In Joanna Woodall (Ed.). *Portraiture: Facing the Subject.* Manchester: Manchester University Press, pp. 52–72.

Öhman, Arne (1986). Face the Beast and Fear the Face: Animal and Social Fears as Prototypes for Evolutionary Analyses of Emotions. *Psychophysiology* 23: 123–45.

Parker, James D. A., and R. Michael Bagby (1997). Impulsivity in Adults: A Critical Review of Measurement Approaches. In Christopher D. Webster and Margaret A. Jackson (Eds.). *Impulsivity: Theory, Assessment, and Treatment.* New York: The Guilford Press, pp. 142–57.

Pilch, John J. (1991). "Beat His Ribs While He is Young" (Sir. 30: 12): Cultural Insights on the Suffering of Jesus. Unpublished paper presented at the Context Group Meeting in March, 1992, Portland, Oregon.

Powell, Mark Allan (1998). *Jesus as a Figure in History: How Modern Historians View the Man from Galilee.* Louisville: Westminster John Knox Press.

Rapaport, Uriel (1992). How Anti-Roman Was the Galilee? In Lee I. Levine (Ed.). *The Galilee in Late Antiquity.* New York: The Jewish Theological Seminary of America, pp. 95–105.

Relf, Jan (1993). Utopia the Good Breast: Coming Home to Mother. In Krishan Kumar and Stephen Bann (Eds.). *Utopias and the Millennium.* London: Reaktion Books, pp. 107–28.

Runyan, William McKinley (1984). *Life Histories and Psychobiography: Explorations in Theory and Method.* New York: Oxford University Press.

—— Ed. (1988). *Psychology and Historical Interpretation.* New York: Oxford University Press.

Safrai, Zeev (1992). The Roman Army in the Galilee. In Lee I. Levine (Ed.). *The Galilee in Late Antiquity.* New York: The Jewish Theological Seminary of America, pp. 103–14.

Saldarini, Anthony J. (1992). The Gospel of Matthew and Jewish-Christian Conflict in the Gailee. In Lee I. Levine (Ed.). *The Galilee in Late Antiquity.* New York: The Jewish Theological Seminary of America, pp. 23–38.

Sanders, E. P. (1985). *Jesus and Judaism.* Philadelphia: Fortress Press.

—— (1993). *The Historical Figure of Jesus.* London and New York: Penguin Books.

Schaberg, Jane (1987). *The Illegitimacy of Jesus: A Feminist Theological Interpretation of the Infancy Narratives.* San Francisco: Harper and Row.

Schiffman, Lawrence H. (1992). Was There a Galilean Halakhah? In Lee I. Levine (Ed.). *The Galilee in Late Antiquity.* New York: The Jewish Theological Seminary of America, pp. 143–56.

Schoeps, Hans (1968). *The Religions of Mankind.* Richard and Clara Winston (Trans.). Garden City, N. J.: Doubleday.

Schüssler Fiorenza, Elisabeth (1983). In *Memory of Her: A Feminist Theological Reconstruction of Christian Origins.* New York: Crossroad.

Schweitzer, Albert (1906/1968). *The Quest of the Historical Jesus: A Critical Study of the Progress from Reimarus to Wrede.* New York: Macmillan.

Scott, Bernard Brandon (1989). *Hear Then the Parable: A Commentary on the Parables of Jesus.* Minneapolis: Fortress Press.

Shorter, Edward (1971). Illegitimacy, Sexual Revolution, and Social Change in Modern Europe. In Theodore K. Rabb and Robert I. Rotberg (Eds.). *The Family in History: Interdisciplinary Essays.* New York: Harper and Row, pp. 48–84.

Smith-Rosenberg, Carroll (1981). The Hysterical Woman: Sex Roles and Role Conflict in Nineteenth-Century America. In Robert J. Brugger (Ed.). *Our Selves/Our Past: Psychological Approaches to American History.* Baltimore: The Johns Hopkins University Press.

Snow, Edward (1994). *A Study of Vermeer,* rev. ed. Berkeley: University of California Press.

Spacks, Patricia Meyer (1995). *Boredom: The Literary History of a State of Mind.* Chicago: The University of Chicago Press.

Stafford, William (1977). *Stories That Could Be True: New and Collected Poems.* San Francisco: HarperSanFrancisco; New York: Harper and Row.

Stannard, David E. (1980). *Shrinking History: On Freud and the Failure of Psychohistory.* New York: Oxford University Press.

States, Bert O. (1993). *Dreaming and Storytelling.* Ithaca: Cornell University Press.

────── (1997). *Seeing in the Dark: Reflections on Dreams and Dreaming.* New Haven: Yale University Press.

Stearns, Peter N. (1989). *Jealousy: The Evolution of an Emotion in American History.* New York: New York University Press.

────── and Carol Z. Stearns (1987). Emotionology: Clarifying the History of Emotions and Emotional Standards. In Geoffrey Cocks and Travis L. Crosby (Eds.). *Psycho/History: Readings in The Method of Psychology, Psychoanalysis, and History.* New Haven: Yale University Press, pp. 284–309.

Sulloway, Frank J. (1996). *Born to Rebel: Birth Order, Family Dynamics, and Creative Lives.* New York: Random House.

Theissen, Gerd (1978). *Sociology of Early Palestinian Christianity.* John Bowden (Trans.). Philadelphia: Fortress Press.

────── and Annette Merz (1996). *The Historical Jesus: A Comprehensive Guide.* John Bowden (Trans.). Minneapolis: Fortress Press.

Todd, Emmanuel (1985). *The Explanation of Ideology, Family Structures and Social Systems.* D. Garrioch (Trans.). Oxford: Blackwell.

Tomkins, Sylvan S. (1963). *Affect, Imagery, Consciousness: The Negative Affects.* New York: Springer.

Trevor-Roper, Patrick (1988). *The World Through Blunted Sight: An Inquiry into the Influence of Defective Vision on Art and Character,* rev. ed. London: The Penguin Press.

Turner, Victor (1976). Religious Paradigms and Political Action: "The Murder in the Cathedral" of Thomas Becket. In Frank E. Reynolds and Donald Capps (Eds.). *The Biographical Process: Studies in the History and Psychology of Religion.* The Hague: Mouton Press, pp. 153–86.

Twelftree, Graham H. (1993). *Jesus the Exorcist: A Contribution to the Study of the Historical Jesus.* Peabody, Mass.: Hendrickson Publishers.

Van Aarde, Andries G. (1997). Social Identity, Status Envy and Jesus' *Abba. Pastoral Psychology* 45: 451–72.

Vermes, Geza (1973). *Jesus the Jew.* New York: Macmillan.

────── (1993). *The Religion of Jesus the Jew.* Minneapolis: Fortress Press.

Wach, Joachim (1944). *Sociology of Religion.* Chicago: The University of Chicago Press.

Ward, John William (1963). "Who Was Benjamin Franklin?" *American Scholar* 32: 541–53.

Weber, Max (1963). *The Sociology of Religion.* Ephraim Fischoff (Trans.). Boston: Beacon Press.

Weintraub, Karl Joachim (1978). *The Value of the Individual: Self and Circumstance in Autobiography.* Chicago: The University of Chicago Press.

Wendorf, Richard (1990). *The Elements of Life: Biography and Portrait-Painting in Stuart and Georgian England.* Oxford: Clarendon Press.

Witherington, Ben III (1994). *Jesus the Sage: the Pilgrimage of Wisdom.* Minneapolis: Fortress Press.

The World Publishing Company (1966). *Webster's New World Dictionary of the American Language.* Cleveland and New York.

Wright, N. T. (1996). *The Original Jesus: The Life and Vision of a Revolutionary.* Grand Rapids, Mich.: Eerdmans.

Scripture Index

Subject Index

Abba, and empowerment, 190–91; and father-image splitting, 181–82; and father-son conflict, 189–90; as Jesus' adoptive Father, 152, 159–60, 188; as Jesus' personal address to God, 16, 42, 132–33; and Jesus' personal psychodynamics, 259; and Jesus' role as healer, 176, 182–83, 190–91, 203; and kingdom of God, 249; and magic, 178, 191–92, 217; and patriarchal values, 150.

adoption of Jesus, by Joseph, 139; questions concerning, 144–47, 153–59.

ambulatory automatism, 172–74. See also healings of paralytics.

anxiety, compared to fear, 93–94; Freud's theory of, 169–70; and group panic, 93–94; in persons Jesus healed, 174, 195–96, 200–3, 209–11; in Plymouth Colony, 92–93.

attributional identity, 152–53, 267–68.

baptism of Jesus, as conversion experience, 136; as experience of God as Father, 133–34, 250; and fatherlessness, 148; and holiness, 42; and his identity, 38; as purification rite, 154, 159, 250.

Beelzebul, as father of unclean spirits, 176; as immobilizing father, 182; Jesus' consciousness of, 190; as ruler of demons, 177; and village conflict, 177–78.

Bible, as mother, 271.

biography, 3–4, 31, 219. See also psychobiography.

birth-order theory, 156.

boredom, in peasant society, 35; psychology of, 231–33; and utopian visions, 233.

brokerage system, 27.

brokerless kingdom, 27–29.

celibacy, attributed to Jesus, 12, 14, 16, 19, 130–32.

childhood aggression, 184–85; absence of, 153.

childhood beatings, 175.

childrearing practices, in first-century Palestine, 159–60; in Plymouth Colony, 72–75.

cities, heterogenetic and orthogenetic, 112–13.

cohort groups, 183–86.

commensality, Jesus' form of, 24–25; and infant-mother relationship, 243–45; and magic, 34.

conversion disorder, 204–5, 213. See also healings of the blind.

conversion experience, attributed to Jesus, 21, 134–35. See also baptism.

cursing, and social conflict, 84–86; and staring, 210; and verbal ambiguity, 192.

Cynic philosophers, 26–27.

demon possession, and baptism, 189; and colonial power, 28; exorcism of, 171–76; Freud's essay on, 178–81; and parent-child relations, 175–76, 188–89, 246; psychophysical meanings of, 174–76; symptomatology of, 174–76, 194–95.

destruction of the temple, 113–14. See also disruption in the temple.

devil, as father substitute, 180. See also Beelzebul.

diffused identity, of Jesus, 153, 160.

285

Karry Beiloo
212 838 4000